SCANDINAVIAN CINEMA

SCANDINAVIAN CINEMA

A survey of the films and film-makers of Denmark, Finland, Iceland, Norway and Sweden

by Peter Cowie

in collaboration with
Françoise Buquet, Risto-Mikael Pitkänen
and Godfried Talboom

Produced by The Tantivy Press (London) on behalf of
'Scandinavian Films' – Nordic Cinema/Cinéma Nordique

Distributed in the United States by
Samuel French Trade, Hollywood

This book was originally published in French in the series 'Cinéma/pluriel', directed by Jean-Loup Passek, Film Adviser at the Centre Georges Pompidou in Paris. The publication coincided with a season of Nordic films presented at the Centre Pompidou during 1990.

The author wishes to thank the following organisations and individuals for their help in the creation of this book:

Eila Anttila
Susanne Båge
Lissy Bellaiche
Gudmundur Karl Björnsson
Kirsten Bryhni
Bengt Forslund
Gudbrandur Gisláson
Knutur Hallsson
Jan Erik Holst
Anna Maria Karlsdóttir
Torsten Kälvemark
Aleksander Kwiatkowski
Satu Laaksonen
Ib Monty
Pekka Päivärinta
Tito Pannaggi
Risto-Mikael Pitkänen
Ove Svensson
Godfried Talboom
Karı Uusitalo
Vidar Víkingsson
Bertil Wredlund

Grateful thanks are also due to the Nordic Cultural Fund (Copenhagen), and the Holger and Thyra Lauritzen Foundation for promotion and research into film history (Stockholm).

Original layout: Françoise Lion
Original editing and co-ordination: Isabelle Ribadeau Dumas
Production: Bernadette Borel-Lorie
Original publication © Editions du Centre Pompidou, Paris – 1990

English language version
© 1992 Peter Cowie (text) and 'Scandinavian Films'

ISBN 0-573-69911-9

Cover photo: Greta Garbo in *The Atonement of Gösta Berling*, directed by Mauritz Stiller (1924).

Typeset in Great Britain by Avonset, Midsomer Norton, Bath
Printed and bound in Great Britain by Dotesios Ltd, Trowbridge

Contents

Ingmar Bergman during the shooting of *Fanny and Alexander* (1982)

Introduction

The five Nordic countries are linked by more than mere geographical location. Throughout the centuries, political and economic ties have prevailed. Sweden held sway over Finland from around 1155 to 1809. The Union of Kalmar in 1397 rendered Norway in effect a possession of Denmark, and for four centuries the Norwegians had to speak Danish in all official matters and travel to Copenhagen if they wanted higher education. A deal between the Danish and Swedish governments in 1814 meant that Norway would spend the entire 19th century under rule from Stockholm. Iceland developed as a colony of Denmark from the late 13th century until the island finally grasped independence in 1944.

Yet this violently shifting pattern of Nordic history has bred several common features and since the establishment of the Nordic Council in 1952 the five nations (three kingdoms, two republics) have dealt with their affairs in a harmonious atmosphere not yet achieved by the European Community or the Organisation for African Unity. Nordic citizens can move freely within the region, without so much as a passport; they can work at will in any of the other Nordic countries; and there is a host of Nordic committees that offer cultural succour to pan-Nordic ventures within and beyond the borders of what the rest of the world calls 'Scandinavia' although the correct term is 'Norden' (comprising Denmark, Finland, Iceland, Norway, Sweden, and the three quasi-independent territories of Greenland, the Faroes, and the Åland Islands).

The current that flow between the Nordic countries may be readily detected in their art forms. The three greatest composers from the region, Jean Sibelius (Finland), Edvard Grieg (Norway), and Carl Nielsen (Denmark), all responded to the sounds of the natural landscape enveloping them. Their music evinces a spaciousness and a rigour in the writing that reflect the rhythm of life in Norden. Writers like Finland's F.E. Sillanpää, Iceland's Halldór Laxness, and Norway's Sigrid Undset accent the role of Nature in human destiny, to a degree bordering on pantheism.

The tendency of Nordic painters to dwell on pastoral and maritime imagery during the late 19th century has strengthened the outside world's conviction that Norden must be a region bereft of human conglomerations and the problems attendant on them. But Denmark is a thickly populated nation, in stark contrast to Finland, where for every fifty inhabitants there is a lake or an island. The anguish of the Norwegian Edvard Munch's paintings and woodcuts spring from an emotional claustrophobia familiar to the city-dweller in any country, and many of the most provocative Nordic films have brought a harsh judgement to bear on life in modern Copenhagen, Stockholm, Oslo, or Helsinki.

There are paradoxes, too. Nordic architecture, cars, furniture, tools, and kitchen implements adhere to strictly functional designs, while abstraction governs modern art in the region to a greater extent than elsewhere in Europe.

Film, as the youngest of the accepted arts, inspired some of the most enterprising and inventive figures in the early years of the century: Ole Olsen, founder of Nordisk Films Kompagni in Denmark; Charles Magnusson, the guiding light of Svenska Bio; Victor Sjöström and Mauritz Stiller; Benjamin Christensen and Georg af Klercker. Etymologists often point out that the Scandivanian languages are inextricably bound up with German. Certainly, in the pioneering days of silent cinema, the fate of Denmark and Sweden depended in large measure on what was happening south of the Baltic, and vice versa. In modern times, this connection has withered away; but the fact remains that during the second decade of the century the German film industry would have collapsed had it not been for an injection of successful movies and talent from Denmark.

In terms of form, the Nordic cinema has never embraced avant-garde tendencies. The great directors discussed in this book react to their circumstances and their material with expediency and opportunistic flair. They revert to common themes, which thread their way through the films of all five nations. The most familiar of these topics run the risk of being dismissed as clichés by the cynical foreign observer. The fierce ecstasy of summer love, for example, confronted with the inexorable onset of autumn. The long, dark winters that drive strong men to a dependence on liquor, and to the tormented discussions associated with Ibsen and Strindberg as much as with Bergman and Dreyer. The contrast between an unspoilt wilderness environment and the ugly, inhuman face of the city (viz the Kaurismäkis). The emotional repression that breeds outbreaks of unexpected violence followed by an ineradicable sense of guilt. The social conscience that has provoked the Nordic nations (and especially Sweden) to suppress non-conformism as home and to champion the cause of the developing nations abroad.

All of these themes may be laid, like templates, over the films described in this book. They do not always fit, however, and the individualism of the Nordic director helps him to elude easy classification. Film-makers in

Denmark, Finland, Iceland, Norway, and Sweden enjoy many of the advantages of a capitalist system of production but also rely on a system of subsidies more often associated with Eastern Europe. The constraints of language and population have imposed a severe handicap on the Nordic cinema. Few films, with the exception of national epics or mass-appeal comedies, can recoup their costs on the domestic market. Festival awards do not pay the bills, and even Ingmar Bergman could never have built such a remarkable career without an international audience.

So the Nordic governments have lent their support to the film industry in each of the five nations, in ever-increasing ways since the end of the Second World War, and in particular since the foundation of the Swedish Film Institute in 1963. Now, after years of discussion and negotiation, the Nordic Council of Ministers has established a Nordic Film Fund. During its first five years, the Fund is receiving $30 million for its activities, provided by the governments, the national TV stations, and the film institutes and foundations of Denmark, Finland, Iceland, Norway, and Sweden. Most of the money will go to co-productions, involving at least two of the five nations.

It should be noted, however, that the various countries have arranged co-productions among themselves with some degree of success. Henning Carlsen's *Hunger* involved Norway, Sweden, and Denmark; *Hip Hip Hurrah!* did likewise; and *Pelle the Conqueror* was a co-production between Denmark and Sweden. Directors of one Nordic nation have found a welcome in the others: Benjamin Christensen, who made *Witchcraft through the Ages* for a Swedish company; Carl Theodor Dreyer, who shot *The Bride of Glomdal* in Norway; and Max von Sydow, who had to go to Denmark to find a producer for *Katinka*.

The Nordic film powers-that-be have also welcomed foreign talent. Not just Andrei Tarkovsky, whose Swedish production, *The Sacrifice*, deserved the Palme d'Or in Cannes in 1986, but directors as disparate as Agnès Varda (*Les Créatures*), Susan Sontag (*Duet for Cannibals*), Peter Watkins (*The Gladiators*), and Gianni Lepre (*Henry's Back Room*).

In an age when the winds of Reaganism and Thatcherism have swept across Europe, this benevolent government support for the cinema in Norden should be cherished. In Poland, where the rigid structures of state control have been dissolved to make way for private enterprise, many film-makers have expressed grave doubts as to the future. Krzysztof Zanussi recently warned that the new 'freedom' might replace political censorship with a form of 'capitalist censorship', whereby commercial success became the sole synonym for quality. Nordic films are fighting desperately to retain their identity in the face of tightening government budgets and an all-conquering American cinema. Between July and September 1989, for example, Danish films accounted for only 4% of box-office takings at movie theatres in Denmark.

Despite these problems, Nordic cinema survives to tell its tale. Quite apart from the colossal figures of Bergman, Dreyer, Sjöström, and Stiller, the region has produced films distinguished by excellent acting (due in large measure to the strength of theatre in Norden) and scintillating technique. The Nordic cinema also accommodates a wealth of documentaries, animated shorts, and films for young people that cannot, for reasons of space, be accorded due recognition within these pages.

Witchcraft through the Ages (1922), directed by Benjamin Christensen

Poster for *The Skyship* (1918), directed by Forest Holger-Madsen

Chronology (1896-1991)

Françoise Buquet

	Political and Cultural Events	The Cinema
1896	August Strindberg returns to Sweden.	The Lumière brothers organise the first screenings in Helsinki (Finland), Malmö (Sweden), and in Denmark. First cinematographic presentations in Oslo (Norway) by the Skladanowsky brothers.
1897	The Swedish engineer, S.A. Andrée, tries in vain to reach the North Pole by balloon. Strindberg's *Inferno* appears. Tsar Nicholas II of Russia gives dictatorial powers to Bobrikov, governor-general of Finland.	The Swedish Royal Court photographer, Ernest Oliver Florman, makes his country's first fiction film, a farce, *The Village Barber*.
1898	Universal (male) suffrage in Norway. The Norwegian writer Knut Hamsun publishes *Victoria*.	
1899	Appearance of *Finlandia* and *Symphony No. 1* by the Finnish composer Sibelius. The Finns protest against Russian domination after the 'February Manifesto' is signed.	
1900		
1901	First Nobel Prizes awarded. A leftwing coalition succeeds the Conservative government in Denmark.	First cinema opens in Helsinki.
1902	Finnish is recognised as an official language alongside Russian.	
1903	The Norwegian writer Björnstjerne Björnson wins the Nobel Prize for Literature.	First film showing in Iceland. Peter Elfelt, the Danish Court photographer, makes the first Danish fiction film, *Capital Punishment (Henrettelsen)*
1904	Assassination of Bobrikov, governor-general of Finland.	First movie theatre opens in Christiania (Oslo).
1905	End of the Swedish-Norwegian Union, with Prince Charles of Denmark taking the crown of Norway and becoming King Haakon VII. General strike in Finland.	The Swede, Charles Magnusson, films the arrival of Haakon VII in Christiania. Opening of the first movie theatre in Sweden by N.H. Nylander. Opening of the Biograph Teater cinema in Copenhagen. K.E. Ståhlberg opens the Apollo studios in Finland.
1906	Death of the Norwegian writer, Henrik Ibsen. In Denmark, Frederik VIII succeeds King Christian IX. Universal suffrage for both men and women in Finland.	Ole Olsen founds Nordisk Films Kompagni A/S in Denmark. Bioscope, the first production firm, is set up in Iceland. First movie theatre opens in Reykjavík. Ole Olsen films the arrival of King Frederik VIII in Denmark.
1907	Gustav II succeeds King Oscar II in Sweden.	The Swedes Wiberg and Nylander establish Svenska Bio. First fiction film in Finland, *The Moonshiners (Salaviinanpolttajat)*, by Louis Sparre and Teuvo Puro.
1908	Edvard Munch returns to Norway for good.	Ole Olsen establishes Nordisk Film Studio in Denmark. First fiction film in Norway, *The Dangers of a Fisherman's Life — An Ocean Drama (Fiskerlivets Farer . . .)*, made by the Swedish cameraman Julius Jaenzon and Hugo Hermansen. In Denmark, *The Lion Hunt (Løvejakten)*, directed by Viggo Larsen.
1909	The Swedish writer Selma Lagerlöf becomes the first woman to receive the Nobel Prize for Literature. Universal male suffrage in Sweden.	Charles Magnusson joins Svenska Bio as head of production.

Political and Cultural Events	The Cinema
1910 Martin Andersen Nexø, the Danish writer, publishes *Pelle the Conqueror.*	*The White Slave Trade (Den hvide slavehandel)* by August Blom, and *The Abyss (Afgrunden)* by Urban Gad, with the actress Asta Nielsen, mark a turning point in Danish cinema. Establishment of 'Kinografen' in Denmark.
1911 Death of the Danish author, Herman Bang.	Svenska Bio moves to Stockholm; Ole Olsen opens a studio in Lidingö. International success for the Danish film, *The Flying Devils (De fire djævle)* by Robert Dinesen and Alfred Lind. Carl Th. Dreyer joins Nordisk in Denmark. Urban Gad and Asta Nielsen leave Denmark for Germany.
1912 Death of the Swedish author, August Strindberg. Knut Rasmussen and Peter G. Freuchen set up a base at Thule in Greenland, the departure point for Polar expeditions until 1933. In Denmark, Christian X succeeds Frederik VIII.	
1913 Universal female suffrage in Norway. A liberal administration takes power in Norway.	*Ingeborg Holm*, by the Swedish director Victor Sjöström. *Vampire (Vampyren)* by Mauritz Stiller. First cinema law in Norway gives the state the right of censorship and allows local communities to exert effective control over movie theatres.
1914 Gustav V declares Sweden's neutrality in the First World War. Denmark also neutral.	
1915 New constitutional law guarantees universal suffrage in Denmark and Iceland.	*The Night of Revenge (Hævnens nat)*, directed by Benjamin Christensen in Denmark.
1916	*The Wings (Vingarne)*, by Stiller. Sjöström directs *Terje Vigen*.
1917 Finland declares independence from the Russian Empire. The Norwegian novelist Knut Hamsun publishes *The Fruits of the Earth.*	In Norway, the municipal cinemas form a national association: *Kommunale kinematografers landsforbund.*
1918 Civil War rages in Finland from January to May. Iceland becomes independent from Denmark but remains loyal to the King. With the help of the Germans, General Mannerheim disarms the pro-Soviet Red Guards in Finland. Iceland governed by the regent Sveinn Björnsson.	*The Skyship (Himmelskibet)*, by the Dane, Holger-Madsen.
1919 Republic established in Finland. Finland intervenes in eastern Karelia.	The Association of Municipal Cinemas in Norway sets up its own distribution circuit. Erkki Karu founds Suomi-Filmi Oy in Finland. Stiller directs *Sir Arne's Treasure (Herr Arnes pengar)* in Sweden, with the actress Mary Johnson. Attendances break all records in Sweden with 8 million tickets sold. Svenska Bio expands to become AB Svensk Filmindustri.
1920 Nobel Prize for Literature awarded to the Norwegian Knut Hamsun. The Treaty of Tartu brings about peace between Finland and the U.S.S.R.	The Norwegian municipal cinemas become involved in production. Rasmus Breistein shoots the first feature-length film in Norway, *Anna, the Gypsy-Girl (Fante-Anne)*. Lau Lauritzen establishes Palladium in Denmark. Stiller makes *Erotikon*. Dreyer's first film as director, *The President (Præsidenten)*.
1921 Universal suffrage granted to women in Sweden.	Benjamin Christensen directs *Witchcraft through the Ages (Häxan)* in Sweden; Victor Sjöström makes *Thy Soul Shall Bear Witness (Körkarlen)*.
1922	Law introduced in Denmark that regulates the screening and projection of films in cinemas.

	Political and Cultural Events	The Cinema
1923		Abel Adams founds the Finnish Film Chamber. Sjöström leaves for Hollywood. First Icelandic film: *Hadda padda*, by Gudmundur Kamban and Gunnar Robert Hansen. Erkki Karu makes *When Father Has Toothache (Kun isällä on hammassärky)* in Finland.
1924	First Social-Democrat government in Denmark, headed by Thorwald Stauning.	Greta Garbo appears in Stiller's *The Atonement of Gösta Berling (Gösta Berlings saga)*.
1925	Norway declares sovereignty over the archipelago of Spitzberg.	Benjamin Christensen leaves for Hollywood, as so Mauritz Stiller and Greta Garbo. *Master of the House (Du skal ære din hustru)*, by Dreyer. *Ingmar's Inheritance (Ingmarsarvet)* by Molander.
1926		Dreyer goes to Paris to shoot *The Passion of Joan of Arc (La passion de Jeanne d'Arc)*.
1928		Death of Mauritz Stiller. Charles Magnusson resigns from Svensk Filmindustri.
1929		Alf Sjöberg (Sweden) makes his debut with *The Strongest (Den starkaste)*.
1930	The Conservatives triumph in the Finnish elections.	George Schnéevoigt makes the first Danish sound film, *Eskimo*.
1931	Widespread strikes in Sweden as a result of the 1929 crash. The Finn F.E. Sillanpää publishes his novel *Silja, Fallen Asleep When Young)*.	*The Vicar of Vejlby (Præsten i Vejlby)*, by George Schnéevoigt. Tancred Ibsen makes the first Norwegian talkie, *The Big Baptism (Den store barnedåben)*.
1932	Karen Blixen, the author, returns to Denmark from Kenya. P.A. Hansson leads the Social Democrats to power in Sweden. The Swedish magnate, Ivar Kreuger, majority shareholder in Svensk Filmindustri, commits suicide during the economic crisis. Attempted coup d'état by the extreme Right in Finland. Helsinki and Moscow sign a non-aggression pact.	Norsk Film A/S established in Norway. Dreyer makes his first sound film, *Vampyr*, in France.
1933	The Norwegian Quisling sets up the National Socialist party.	The 1922 cinema law in Denmark is revised, encouraging among other things the production of shorts and documentaries.
1934		*Palo's Wedding (Palos brudefærd)* by Friedrich Dalsheim, the first fiction film shot in Greenland, and produced by the Danish company, Palladium. *Synnöve Solbakken*, by Tancred Ibsen (Norway).
1935	The Socialists win power in Norway.	
1936		Ingrid Bergman plays the leads in Gustaf Molander's *Intermezzo*.
1937		The Swede, Anders Sandrew, creates his distribution outfit, AB Sandrews Biograferna. Success for Norsk Film A/S with *Two Living, One Dead (To levende og en død)* and *Fant*, by Tancred Ibsen.
1938	The basics of 'Swedish model' socialism are laid down in the Saltsjöbaden agreement.	Sandrew begins producing films. *Stolen Death (Varestettu kuolema)*, by the Finn, Nyrkki Tapiovaara.
1939	Finland resists Russia's invasion of the disputed region of Karelia. F.E. Sillanpää wins the Nobel Prize for Literature.	Establishment of Statens Filmcentral in Denmark (government body for non-commercial production and distribution of shorts and documentaries). Tancred Ibsen makes *Gjest Baardsen*.

Heinz Edelmann's poster for Ingmar Bergman's *A Lesson in Love*, designed for Atlas Film in Germany

F. and D. Fischer-Nosbisch's poster design for the Atlas Film release of Bergman's *The Silence*

Political and Cultural Events	The Cinema
1940 The Germans occupy Denmark and Norway after a two-month campaign of resistance. Sweden neutral during the War. Swedish writer Selma Lagerlöf dies.	Germans take control of film industry in Norway. Nyrkki Tapiovaara disappears while on patrol in Finland's 'Winter War' with the U.S.S.R. Alf Sjöberg's *They Staked Their Lives (Med livet som insats)* evokes the Baltic Republics' struggle for freedom.
1941 Finland allies with Germany against the Soviet Union. Allied forces arrive in Iceland. Sweden allows Nazi troops (the Engelbrecht division) to pass across its borders.	A fire at the Lidingö Studios destroys a majority of the films by Stiller and Sjöström.
1942 The head of the Norwegian pro-Nazi party, Quisling, forms a government of collaboration.	Carl Anders Dymling becomes managing director of Svensk Filmindustri. *The Road to Heaven (Himlaspelet)*, by Alf Sjöberg.
1943 Heavy water programme successfully sabotaged at Rjukan in Norway.	Ingmar Bergman starts work in the screen-writing department of Svensk Filmindustri. *Day of Wrath (Vredens dag)*, by Dreyer. Gustaf Molander describes Norway under the Occupation in *There Burned a Flame (Det brinner en eld)*.
1944 Death of the Norwegian painter, Edvard Munch. Iceland declares independence from the Danish crown and sets up a republic with S. Björnsson as President. Socialists gain majority in Norwegian elections. Death of the Danish writer Kaj Munk, author of *The Word*. Nobel Prize for Literature goes to the Dane, Johannes V. Jensen. Finland signs an armistice with the Soviet Union and declares war on Germany. Mannerheim is recalled to be President of the Finnish Republic.	*Frenzy/Torment (Hets)*, Bergman's first screenplay, is directed by Alf Sjöberg.
1945 Establishment of the Swedish Institute in order to promote Swedish culture abroad. Astrid Lindgren (Sweden) publishes her first children's book, *Pippi Longstocking*.	Bergman directs his first film, *Crisis (Kris)*.
1947 Tage Erlander succeeds P.A. Hansson as leader of the Social Democrat government in Sweden.	The Norwegian parliament establishes various initiatives to support the film industry, among them Statens Filmsentral.
1948 Finland and the Soviet Union sign mutual aid treaty. The Faroe Islands obtain independence from Denmark.	Loftur Gudmundsson makes the first Icelandic sound film, in colour, *Between the Mountains and the Sea (Milli fjalls og fjöru)*. Titus Vibe-Müller (Norway) and Jean Dréville (France) make *The Battle for Heavy Water (Kampen om tungtvannet)*.
1949 Denmark, Norway and Iceland join NATO. The Swede, Vilhelm Moberg, publishes his novel, *The Emigrants*.	Arne Skouen (Norway) makes his debut with *Street Urchins (Gategutter)*.
1950 Gustav VI becomes King of Sweden.	
1951	Death of the Swedish director, Georg af Klercker. *Miss Julie (Fröken Julie)* shares the Palme d'Or at Cannes for Sweden and director Alf Sjöberg.
1952 Establishment of the Nordic Council, organising the legal, social, economic, cultural, and communications activities of the five nations. Ásgeir Ásgeirsson becomes President of Iceland.	Erik Blomberg's *The White Reindeer (Valkoinen peura)* wins a prize at Cannes for Finland. Bergman joins the Municipal Theatre in Malmö, with immediate success.
1953 Reform of the 1849 constitution in Denmark.	Sven Nykvist makes the first of his twenty feature films with Bergman: *Sawdust and Tinsel (Gycklarnas afton)*.
1954 The five Nordic nations agree to allow a free labour market from one country to another within the Nordic region. First TV transmission in Denmark.	*New Role (Nytt hlutverk)*, by Óskar Gislason (Iceland). Edda Film set up in Iceland. Carl Th. Dreyer makes *The Word (Ordet)*. Matti Kassila (Finland) films *Blue Week (Sininen viikko)*.

	Political and Cultural Events	The Cinema
1955	The Icelandic author Halldór Laxness wins the Nobel Prize for Literature.	The Norwegian government decides to give direct subsidies up to 55% of a film's production costs. Norwegian Film Institute opens in Oslo. Edvin Laine enjoys immense popular success with his screen version of Väinö Linna's *The Unknown Soldier (Tuntematon sotilas)*. *Smiles of a Summer Night (Sommarnattens leende)* wins a Jury Prize at Cannes for Bergman.
1956	King Olav V ascends the Norwegian throne. Urho Kekkonen elected President of the Finnish Republic. First TV transmission in Sweden.	
1957	First TV transmission in Finland.	Aito Mäkinen and Jörn Donner found the Finnish Film Archive. Edvin Laine makes *Black Love (Musta rakkaus)*. Ingmar Bergman's *The Seventh Seal (Det sjunde inseglet)* opens in Sweden.
1958		Bergman's *Wild Strawberries (Smultronstället)* wins the Golden Bear at the Berlin Festival.
1959		Death of Benjamin Christensen.
1960		Death of Victor Sjöström.
1961		*The Virgin Spring (Jungfrukällan)* wins an Oscar as Best Foreign Film for Bergman. Max von Sydow is invited to Hollywood to play Christ in *The Greatest Story Ever Told*.
1962	Nordic Literature Prize established. The main aims of Nordic co-operation and the function of various institutions are inscribed in the Treaty of Helsinki.	Risto Jarva and Jaakko Pakkasvirta make *Night and Day (Yö vai päivä)* in Finland. Bergman wins his second successive Academy Award, this time for *Through a Glass Darkly (Såsom i en spegel)*.
1963		The Swedish Film Institute is established, thanks to the pioneering energy of Harry Schein. Bo Widerberg makes his first feature, *The Pram/The Baby Carriage (Barnevagnen)*.
1964		A new law secures the creation of the Danish Film Foundation, aimed at encouraging the production of quality feature films. Mai Zetterling returns to Sweden from the U.K. to direct her first feature, *Loving Couples (Älskande par)*. Dreyer's final film, *Gertrud*, has its world première in Paris.
1965	In Norway, Per Borten forms a government made up of Conservatives and Liberals.	
1966	First TV transmissions in Iceland.	*Persona*, directed by Ingmar Bergman. Jan Troell (Sweden) makes a stunning début with *Here Is Your Life (Här har du ditt liv)*. *Once There Was a War (Der var engang en krig)*, by Palle Kjærulff-Schmidt (Denmark). Per Oscarsson wins the Best Actor award at the Cannes Festival, for his performance in *Hunger (Sult)*.
1967		Pia Degermark wins the Best Actress award at Cannes for *Elvira Madigan*, directed by Bo Widerberg (Sweden).
1968	Kristján Eldjárn is elected President of Iceland.	Death of Carl Theodor Dreyer. A new distribution circuit, FilmCentrum, is established in Sweden to help unusual and socially-committed films.
1969	Olof Palme succeeds Tage Erlander as Prime Minister of Sweden.	Adult film censorship is abandoned in Denmark.

	Political and Cultural Events	The Cinema
1970		The Finnish Film Foundation opens its doors. The Norwegian state becomes majority shareholder in Norsk Film A/S. Launch of a Norwegian cinema fund (Norsk Kino og Filmfond).
1971	A Socialist government succeeds the Conservatives in Norway. The Nordic Council becomes the Nordic Council of Ministers (see 1962). Signing of a cultural agreement between the five nations in order to pool resources for research, education, etc.	*The Emigrants (Utvandrarna)*, by Jan Troell (Sweden). Opening of the 'Film House' in Sweden, a new home for the Swedish Film Institute and related organisations, as well as for some new film studios.
1972	Norwegians reject the idea of joining the European Common Market. Queen Margarethe II ascends the throne in Denmark. A Social Democratic government is formed in Denmark by Anker Jørgensen.	The Danish Film Foundation becomes the Danish Film Institute after a change in the film law. Bergman makes *Cries and Whispers (Viskningar och rop)*.
1973	Denmark joins the Common Market. Charles XVI Gustaf becomes King of Sweden. The Swedish Prime Minister Olof Palme is obliged to come to terms with the conservative parties in Sweden.	The Finn Rauni Mollberg makes his début with *Earth Is Our Sinful Song (Maa on syntinen laulu)*. The Finnish Film Archive gets funds to preserve films made prior to 1953.
1974	Changes to the Swedish constitution leaves the King with only ceremonial functions, and gives the Prime Minister responsibility before Parliament. The Swedish writer Eyvind Johnson shares the Nobel Prize for Literature.	*Wives (Hustruer)*, directed by Anja Breien (Norway).
1975	Establishment of the Nordic Investment Bank. Helsinki Accord on European security is signed.	The film and TV industries agree to set up a common Fund to aid production. *Strike! (Streik!)*, by Oddvar Bull Tuhus recreates the dispute at the Sauda plant in Norway during the 1970's.
1976	The Moderates (previously known as the Conservatives) take over from the Social Democrats in Sweden, under the leadership of Thorbjörn Fälldin.	Ingmar Bergman goes into voluntary exile in Germany after a tax dispute. *A Sunday in Hell (En forårsdag i helvede)* by Jørgen Leth (Denmark).
1977		Death of the Finnish director Risto Jarva in a car accident. Reynir Oddson makes *Murder Story (Mordsaga)* in Iceland.
1978		*Winter Born (Vinterbørn)* by Astrid Henning-Jensen (Denmark).
1979	Greenland becomes an autonomous province of Denmark.	Icelandic Film Fund set up. Jörn Donner presides over changes in the functioning of the Finnish Film Foundation.
1980	Vigdís Finnbogadóttir elected to be the first female President of Iceland. Sweden disturbed by serious disputes over collective bargaining procedures.	*Land and Sons (Land og synir)*, by Ágúst Gudmundsson, is the first film produced with the help of the Icelandic Film Fund. Death of Alf Sjöberg in Stockholm.
1981	Election of a Conservative government in Norway. Urho Kekkonen forced to resign the Finnish Presidency due to ailing health.	Nils Malmros (Denmark) makes *The Tree of Knowledge (Kundskabens træ)*.
1982	A Conservative government takes over from the Social Democrats in Denmark. Maunu Koivisto elected President of Finland. The Social Democrats retrieve control in Sweden.	Jan Troell makes his film of the ill-fated polar expedition of 1897: *The Flight of the Eagle (Ingenjör Andrées luftfärd)*. A tax is levied on all video-cassettes, with the proceeds going to the Swedish Film Institute. The 1972 film law in Denmark is reformed. Bergman makes his final cinema film, *Fanny and Alexander (Fanny och Alexander)*.

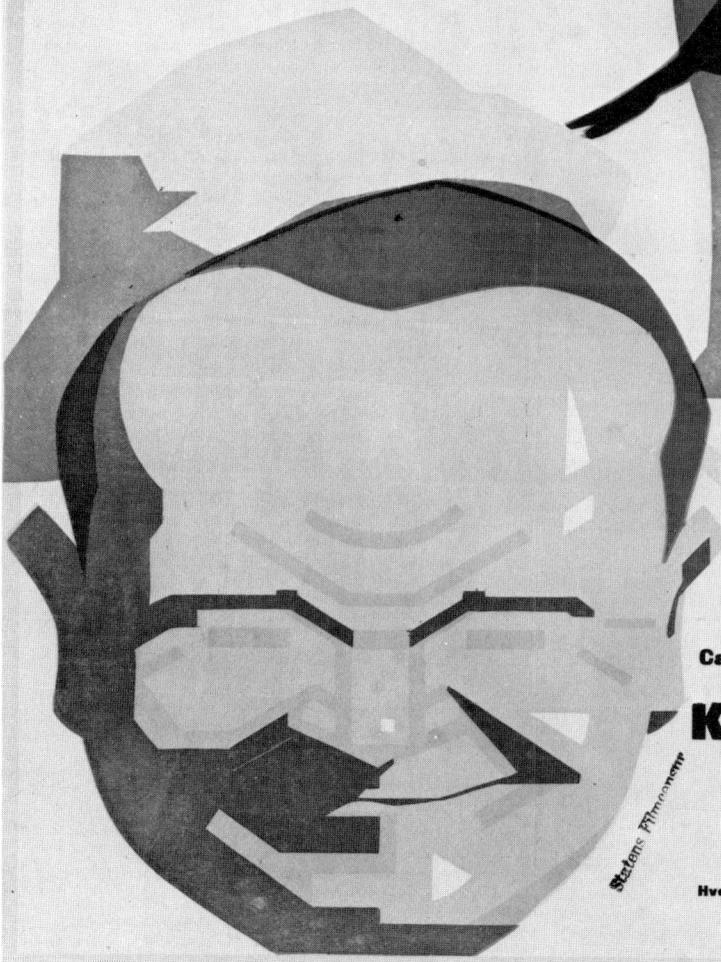

WORLD
CINEMA
CIRKUS
VARIÉTÈ

Mandag d. 27. Marts Kl. **8** pr. Premiere

Landligger -
Idyl - Vandgang

Palladium-Lystspil i 2 Akter - Iscenesat af Lau Lauritzen

I Hovedrollerne
**Ruth Heiman - Gerda Madsen
Hugo Brun - Budtz Egede Møller
Carl Schenstrøm - Miehe-Madsen**
„Fyrtaarnet" og „Bivognen"

Kvindehjerter

Skuespil i 6 Akter
efter **Robert W. Chambers** Roman
„The fighting Chance"
Aft.-Telefon
Notering **2192**
Forhøjet Salg hver Dag fra Kl. II 3½.
Ordinært Salg fra Kl. 4.
Hver Søndag Efterm. Kl. 4: Folkeforestilling
Smaa Priser.
Eftm.-Telefon
Notering **4443**

Poster for *Long and Short*, designed in 1922

Political and Cultural Events	The Cinema
1983	Co-production agreement signed between Finland and France. Finnish Film Foundation restructured. Carl Th. Dreyer's original version of *The Passion of Joan of Arc* is restored.
1984 Economic crisis in Iceland.	*Fanny and Alexander* wins four Academy Awards in Hollywood. The Icelandic parliament votes to reform the film law of 1979, but financial pressures prevent its immediate application.
1985	Rauni Mollberg releases his remake of *The Unknown Soldier (Tuntematon sotilas)*.
1986 Olof Palme, Prime Minister of Sweden, is assassinated.	Andrei Tarkovsky makes *The Sacrifice (Offret)* in Sweden. The Icelandic Film Law of 1984 comes into effect.
1987 Social Democrats and Conservatives are obliged to form a coalition government in Finland.	Norway reforms its film legislation, and imposes a tax on video-cassettes. An amendment to the Danish Film Law enables private producers to obtain up to 50% subsidy for their projects from the Danish Film Institute. *My Life as a Dog (Mitt liv som hund)*, directed by Lasse Hallström (Sweden), earns some $7 million at the U.S. box-office.
1988	*Babette's Feast (Babettes gæstebud)* marks a comeback for veteran director Gabriel Axel, and wins the Academy Award for Best Foreign Film in Hollywood. *Pathfinder (Ofeläs/Veiviseren)*, directed by the young Norwegian, Nils Gaup, is nominated for an Academy Award. Bille August's *Pelle the Conqueror (Pelle Frobreren)* is awarded the Palme d'Or at the Cannes Festival.
1989	*Pelle the Conqueror* goes on to win the Oscar for Best Foreign Film. The Nordic Council of Ministers sets up the Nordic Film & TV Fund to finance co-productions between the five nations. Katrin Ottarsdóttir makes the first film in the Faroe Islands.
1990	Death of Greta Garbo, in New York. Death of Mikko Niskanen, in Helsinki. Aki Kaurismäki completes trilogy of films about modern Finland, with *The Match Factory Girl (Tulitikkutehtaan tyttö)*. Kaspar Rostrup's *Waltzing Regitze (Dansen med Regitze)* earns Denmark its third Academy Award nomination in three years.
1991 Death of King Olav of Norway. Social Democrats lose power to the centre and conservative parties in Sweden. Sweden decides to apply for membership of the European Community in 1997.	Two screenplays by Ingmar Bergman go into production: *The Best Intentions (Den goda viljan)*, directed by Bille August, and *Sunday Children (Söndagsbarn)*, directed by Daniel Bergman.

Herman (1990) by Erik Gustavson

The Evangelist (1914), by Forest Holger-Madsen

Denmark

Geography, demographics, and temperament have conditioned the Danish cinema from its inception. It is tempting to take the Danes as they appear at first glance — relaxed and cheerful as regards beer, sex and climate, and far and away the most liberated of the Nordic nations. Danish films, it may be argued, do not suffer from the *Angst* and spiritual guilt that permeate their Swedish counterparts, and at the same time they do not evince the anarchic desperation of the Finnish directors. But how to account for the sobriety and spiritual intensity of Carl Th. Dreyer's greatest work?

Perhaps Dreyer, like Bergman in Sweden, transcends national boundaries. But recent re-viewing of his early work suggests that even Dreyer possessed a mischievous sense of humour, and that a subcutaneous erotic language may be heard in his most formal relationships. His Danish productions refer eloquently to the topography of his native country, to the open fields and neat cottages of an agricultural community that has existed for centuries on what amounts to a series of promontories, peninsulas, and islands on Europe's northern fringe. Denmark contains no mountains, no tracts of virgin forest like her Nordic neighbours. The high density of population (5.1 million in just 43,000 sq. km, compared with Sweden's 8.5 million in 450,000 sq. km) makes silence a rare and precious commodity. It also means that the Danes dwell within the confines of cities and towns with more ease than those Swedes, Finns, or Norwegians who have migrated for economic reasons from their rural origins. Not surprisingly, certain genres have appealed to Danish film-makers more than they have to other Scandinavians — the melodrama, or the drawing-room comedy, for example.

The contrast between Denmark and its two offshore possessions, Greenland and the Faroe Islands, could not be more pronounced. On their rare visits to these remote regions, Danes are confronted with the icy peaks, barren shorelines, and untamed wilderness to which most Nordic peoples are accustomed. How ironic, then, that the very first 'film' made in Denmark is nothing more nor less than a fake enactment of Greenland huskies dragging a sledge through the 'snow'! Only 17 metres in length, *Greenland Dogs Pulling a Sledge (Kørsel med grønlandske hunde)* was the first of almost 200 'documentaries' made by Peter Elfelt between 1897 and 1914. According to Martin Drouzy, 'from 1902 onwards he began experimenting in another direction and filmed short ballets in his photography studio. It is to him too that we owe the first fiction film ever made in Denmark, *Capital Punishment*, showing a mother condemned to death for having killed her ten children and who walks towards the scaffold. Despite the success of these early shorts, Elfelt regarded ''animated pictures'' as a mere secondary occupation. He was and remained first and foremost a photographer.'[1] Ron Mottram has pointed out that *Capital Punishment (Henrettelsen*, 1903) 'shows a sophisticated use of space', with characters gesturing to people beyond the edge of the frame. 'In addition to these gestures and glances, the film contains a number of exits and entrances of the characters that, combined with the camera's immobility in relation to the given space, also create a strong sense of a world existing beyond the frame.'[2]

Just as Sweden was fortunate in having Charles Magnusson to seize the opportunities afforded by the new medium, Denmark owed its escape from the backwaters of film production to the enterprising showman, Ole Olsen. He had started as a penniless farm labourer, became a fairground operator, and subsequently a cinema owner. In November 1906, he established Nordisk Films Kompagni. The firm's rise to power was extraordinary even by the standards of the age. Within six years Nordisk had acquired a staff of 1,700 people, and enjoyed a dominant place in the European market, second only to Pathé. As Drouzy has noted, 'If Ole Olsen knew how to give such a rapid stimulus to his company, it was not due just to his sense of occasion and his gifts as a financier and organiser. It was also because his temperament led him to emphasise two factors which have not been sufficiently noted: the quality of the films themselves, and the tastes of his audience.'[3]

Under his leadership, Nordisk became known throughout the world under its trademark — a polar bear atop the globe. All filming was done in the open air, with a hand-cranked camera and only a few actors (Olsen paid a derisory wage) posing in front of fragile sets painted to look like interiors. Olsen's early successes included two 'documentaries', *Hunting a Bear in Russia (Bjørnen løs*, 1906) and *The Lion Hunt (Løvejagten*, 1908), the sales of which reached 91 and 259 copies respectively, although Olsen's slaughter of two imported lions for the sake of realism incurred the wrath of the Minister of Justice, who promptly withdrew Olsen's licence as exploitant. *The Lion Hunt* obviously takes place in a parkland exterior, posing as a jungle. The close-ups of the animals were shot in a zoo and then intercut with images of the hunters being led by their black guide to a camp where they have a smoke and settle down for the night. Next morning, they are awoken by the appearance of a lion. They shoot the beast in a nearby 'lake', examine its mouth and paws in great excitement, and then proceed to skin it (offscreen!). 'Because of its montage,' claims Mottram, 'the film anticipated the experiments of Lev Kuleshov over a decade later, although the montage ideas in *The Lion Hunt* were arrived at pragmatically rather than theoretically and [. . .] were never followed up by [. . .] any other Danish director.'[4]

Nordisk reached far and wide for its subject matter. The studio churned out comedies, costume dramas, primitive thrillers, and even the odd western. Between 1907 and 1910 more than 560 films emerged from Olsen's factory. Celebrated stage actors were introduced to the screen, among them Bodil Ipsen, Clara Pontoppidan, Olaf Fønss, Poul Reimert, and the legendary Asta Nielsen. The most popular of the Nordisk formula pictures was the 'white slave' drama. The first, *The White Slave (Den hvide slavinde*, 1906) was directed by the prolific Viggo Larsen and heralded a stream of films dealing with social issues — a genre still attractive to Danish directors today.

The sequel, *The White Slave Trade II* (*Den hvide slavehandels sidste offer*, 1911), tackles its subject with the same unashamed, melodramatic verve as Louis Feuillade was doing in France. In the opening sequence, a girl responds to an advertisement in a Danish newspaper. August Blom uses a split-screen − on either side we see the girl calling and a man replying, while in the central panel two women are chatting on a balcony, overlooking the busy traffic of central Copenhagen (and the background is in perfect focus!). Trapped in London (conveniently indicated by a photograph of Big Ben imposed over a window), the girl manages to write to her parents. Her father sells his furniture to pay for the fare to England, and joins with local detectives in defeating the white slavers and recovering his daughter. The chase sequences differ from their Hollywood counterparts in their sinister, ruthless quality. Like the struggles in the films of Benjamin Christensen (see below) and Georg af Klercker (see SWEDEN), they attest to a savage confrontation between the forces of good and evil.

While the early Swedish and Finnish films took their cue from Lumière, the Danish pioneers followed the winding path of Méliès. A delightful short such as *The Witch and the Cyclist* (*Heksen og cyklisten*, 1909) provides the excuse for some trick effects that would have delighted the Frenchman. A witch torments a blasé cyclist by placing his machine high up in a tree, and then by making him ride backwards at great speed. When he mounts a penny-farthing, it changes instantly into a minute toy bicycle − and so on. At length the unfortunate young man realises that he has been dreaming − a habit common to many individuals in the early Danish cinema. Life looms as a waking dream, a source of endless imaginative adventures, yet without the sombre, moral overtones that Nordic directors like Sjöström and Bergman impart to their nightmares.

The profusion of high-quality releases from the Danish studios between 1910 and 1913 confirm the visual inventiveness of their directors, and of the special-effects artistes of the period. *The Flying Devils* (*De fire djævle*, 1911) burgeons with visual *legerdemain* in its depiction of a circus milieu. In a bizarre opening sequence, a scruffy old man trains youngsters for the circus, forcing them to caper and dance in the sawdust ring. The directors, Robert Dinesen and Alfred Lind, create a vivid sense of life being played out in small, drab rooms. These circus performers exist in an intimacy apparently beyond the ken of the upper classes. The women radiate an aggressive eroticism unimpeded by social etiquette. The film turns on an act of sexual betrayal, and when Aimée, one of the four 'Flying Devils', discovers that the man she loves has spent the night with another woman, she lets him plunge to his death in the ring. She then leaps into the void herself. The trapeze stunts are described in convincing detail for the period. Ebbe Neergaard has termed *The Four Devils*, 'the first film told in reasonably modern film language',[5] and Ron Mottram, in his recent book on silent Danish cinema, points out that it 'utilizes a variety of camera distances and angles (unlike Nordisk films), a panning camera to follow the action in several scenes, careful matching of the action from one shot to another and, in one sequence, cross-cutting between Fritz

as he tries to decide whether to keep his appointment with the countess, and Aimée as she worries about Fritz's strange behaviour.'[6]

In most reference books the year 1910 is mentioned as heralding the birth of the Danish cinema, by virtue of one film, *The Abyss* (*Afgrunden*). Its director, **Urban Gad**, had attended art school in Paris and written various plays before making his début with his protégée, Asta Nielsen, in the leading role. But today the film looks less impressive than some of the other productions of those first vital years in Danish cinema history. The narrative progresses in fits and starts, and the lack of intertitles becomes a handicap rather than a bold innovation. Nothing matches the summer light and promise of the opening scenes, as young Magda (Asta Nielsen) is approached by an eager admirer, Knud. When he takes her to visit his father, a minister, in the countryside, he loses her to the handsome Rudolph, a 'cowboy' in an itinerant circus troupe. Once immersed in the sweaty intimacy of the travelling entertainers, Magda's repressed feelings brim to the surface. She performs with relish one of the silent cinema's most lurid and celebrated stage acts: a dance with Rudolph that climaxes with her lassooing him to a pole and sinuously rubbing her body against his. The inexorable tempo of the act is reminiscent of Ravel's 'Bolero', and its unequivocal perversity (the male rendered helpless and devoured by a predatory female) quickly established for *The Abyss* the notoriety of a pornographic film. Gad has the courage to pursue his theme even after this erotic highpoint. He shows Magda fighting with another dancer who dares to flirt with Rudolph. She is almost recovered by the ardent, clean-living Knud, but when Rudolph confronts her in fury, she stabs him to death, and is led away to prison.

In terms of mise-en-scène, *The Abyss* does not break new ground. Its significance lies in its fatalistic content, in its adumbration of the theme of the Nordic woman revealing her true nature only when liberated from an orthodox existence, and above all in the screen personality of Asta Nielsen. Sloe-eyed, lithe, and clad forever in clothes as raven-black as her long hair, she commands respect as the cinema's first 'vamp', some years in advance of Theda Bara, whose makeup and body language owe much to the Danish actress. Indeed, the early Danish cinema contains several examples of the aggressive female, smoking cigars, wielding a whip, taunting arrogant young men into performing dangerous feats (e.g. Edward Schnedler-Sørensen's *Life in the Circus* [*Mellem storbyens artister*] and *Conquered* [*Den stærkeste*], both released in 1912).

Asta Nielsen made two further films in a similar idiom in Denmark, *The Black Dream* (*Den sorte drøm*) and *The Dancer* (*Balletdanserinden*) before accepting an offer to go to Germany. Marrying Urban Gad in 1912, she widened her range of expression to embrace comedy as well as vampish roles. She returned briefly to her native country in 1918 to shoot *Towards the Light* (*Mod lyset*) for Holger-Madsen, but again settled in Germany until the rise of Nazism spurred her to come home for good. Compared at the outset of her career to stage goddesses like Eleanora Duse and Sarah Bernhardt, she was in many ways ahead of her epoch.

The cult surrounding her name is rivalled only by that of Louise Brooks.

The masculine equivalent of the Danish 'vamp' may be found not only in the villainous characters populating the work of Benjamin Christensen (see below), but also in the series of short films charting the infamous exploits of 'Dr. Gar El Hama.' This demon among criminals, a forerunner both of Fantômas in France and Dr. Mabuse in Germany, makes his debut in *The Illusion of Death (Bedraget i døden,* 1911). Acted by Aage Hertel, under the direction of Schnedler-Sørensen, this Oriental doctor has a bewildering selection of disguises to hand, and succeeds in outwitting the authorities at every turn. In *Dr. Gar El Hama II* (1912), he escapes dressed as a tramp and, once in his hideout, dons the uniform of 'President of the Anti-Criminals League'. His antagonist, the worthy but hapless Dr. Watson (presumably a reference to Conan Doyle), soon falls foul of Gar El Hama's dastardly schemes. Most exciting is a sequence in which Watson finds himself trapped in a chamber filled with rapidly rising water, and manages to swim out into the harbour at the last moment. Like some malevolent Houdini, Gar El Hama slits the cloth coachwork at the back of the car taking him to prison. When, at the very end, he is flung into convict's clothes, he has the impudence to turn his malevolent gaze towards the camera, in a gesture prefiguring by long decades the accusing regard of Harriet Andersson in *Summer with Monika* and Jean-Pierre Léaud in *The 400 Blows*.

August Blom had replaced Viggo Larsen as the leading director at Nordisk Film in 1911, and displayed his technical skills in *The Dancer*, starring Asta Nielsen. Prior to this, he had essayed numerous genres, including horror *(The Necklace of the Dead [Den dødes halsbaand]),* social drama *(The Storm of Life [Livets storm]),* and literary adaptation *(Robinson Crusoe, Hamlet,* and *Dr. Jekyll and Mr. Hyde).* Some of his output suffers from haste and clumsy execution. *The Shop Girl (Exspeditricen,* 1911), for example, develops an interesting theme — pert little shop assistant charmed by a wealthy customer — but is badly acted and confusingly edited. The palpable guilt of the foppish young aristocrat after the girl has died in child-labour at least proves that the Danish cinema was tackling such issues before Sjöström began his career at Svenska Bio.

Ron Mottram has evaluated many films made by Blom during his most productive period, 1910-1914. In *Revenge (Hævnet,* 1911) and *The Three Comrades (De tre kammerater,* 1911), he notes the significance of the military man who, 'whether as husband or lover, is a familiar figure in Danish films. Along with the dissolute son of a wealthy family, the circus performer, the landowner, the count, and others, he is one of the stock characters of the social melodrama.'[7] Mottram also emphasises the audacity of Blom's approach to his subject matter. In *The Bride of Death (Dødens brud,* 1911) he charts the physical passion that devours two lovers (one committing adultery already during her wedding reception), and in *The Mormon's Victim (Mormonens offer,* 1911) he paints a lurid picture of the perils awaiting those who succumb to the blandishments of

'The Church of Jesus Christ of Latter Day Saints'.

Valdemar Psilander, relatively unknown prior to joining Nordisk Film, acted in many of these Blom featurettes. Within a few years he was a household name throughout Europe, but at the age of 33 he succumbed to heart attack; some claimed that he had committed suicide, buckling under the strain of his celebrity. He did not appear, however, in the most prestigious of August Blom's 'literary' films: *Atlantis* (1913). Massive in form (eight reels), and ponderous in execution, *Atlantis* remains faithful to the novel by Gerhart Haupmann about an intense and somewhat libidinous biologist (played by Olaf Fønss) and his journey to America aboard an ocean liner. *Atlantis* boasts some stirring scenes, such as the attack on the sleeping doctor by his deranged wife, wielding a pair of scissors; and the sinking of the transatlantic steamship.

The End of the World (Verdens undergang, 1916) prefigures the German cinema of the 1920's and although handicapped by Blom's tendency to formalise his compositions, and to point a moral whenever the opportunity arises, survives as his most impressive achievement. Recklessly blending science fiction, social melodrama, and suspense, *The End of the World* reverberates with overtones from the Great War being waged in Flanders and northern France. Olaf Fønss creates an ambiguous anti-hero in Stoll, the company director who persuades the country girl, Dina West (Ebba Thomsen) to elope with him, quitting her native mining community for the opulent bustle of Copenhagen. Johan Ankerstjerne, one of the finest cinematographers at Nordisk, captures the contrast between the factory chimneys and grimy streets of Dina's home and the vivid activity around the Stock Exchange where Stoll is in his element. When his scientist cousin predicts that a comet will crash into the Earth, Stoll capitalises on the situation, buying up shares while others are selling in panic. Blom observes this dignified ballet of anxiety from a single, static camera setup, so that the top-hatted individuals buying and selling their paper money appear like nothing so much as a swarm of ants.

Stoll's folly reaches its limit in a lavish dinner held on the day when the comet is due to collide with Earth. Dancing girls gyrate before the guests even as fragments from the nucleus set fire to the district. The irony is that Stoll has chosen a secret passage in the mining region in which to hide. When the enraged mineworkers learn of this, and of Stoll's perfidy in stealing Dina from her sailor fiancé, they storm his mansion.

This revolt by the proletariat against the tyranny of capitalism is cast in a lurid, apocalyptic light during the final mêlée, which Blom orchestrates with aplomb. Cows flee the smoke and incandescence, Dina's lover succumbs to gas in the mine, and houses are inundated with the floods provoked by the comet's impact. Morality gains the upper hand when a wandering preacher manages to rescue Dina's sister Edith from the floods. As the sun rises over the ravaged landscape, Edith staggers into a remote church, and tolls the bell. By some miracle her fiancé, having lurched ashore from the boat on which he serves as a Ship's Officer, hears the tolling and hastens towards his love. . . .

Down with Weapons! (1915) by Forest Holger-Madsen

While *The End of the World* cannot match the fervid imagination of Gance's *J'accuse*, made only two years later, or even of Holger-Madsen's *Down with Weapons!* (1915), is assured command of physical and mental turmoil proves that the Danish cinema possessed an entirely independent flavour of its own.

The Idealism of Holger-Madsen

In this climate, with Nordisk Films Kompagni producing a torrent of pictures (143 releases in 1915), Blom found himself challenged by **Holger-Madsen**, a director who refused to abandon his own strong commitment in favour of the eclectic diet upon which most directors at Nordisk thrived. Ib Monty has noted his predilection for *The Evangelist (Evangeliemandens liv,* 1914), 'in which Valdemar Psilander plays the leading part of a dissolute

young man of good family who suddenly realises how empty and pointless his life is'. Holger-Madsen, says Monty, was attracted to 'extraordinary, often bizarre images and picturesque surroundings. With his cameraman, Marius Clausen, he emphasised the visual look of his films. His use of side light, inventive camera angles and close-ups, combined with unusual sets, made him an original artist.'[8] Most of the film takes the form of a flashback, as the stern-faced wharfside preacher (not unlike Karl Malden in *On the Waterfront*) tells his story to a young lad. Holger-Madsen depicts the wages of sin with masterly relish − from the melodramatic shooting of a vampish prostitute that sends the future preacher unjustly to jail, to the claustrophobic prison environment. The prisoners, clad in neutral grey, listen to the Word of God in a chapel so fiendishly designed that each man's head is concealed from the others'. Psilander's hero is reduced to a pathetic, prematurely-aged man by the experience. As in the Asta Nielsen films a few

26

The Skyship (1918) by Forest Holger-Madsen

years earlier, women are perceived as engineering the downfall of decent men. Holger-Madsen shows them loitering with long, unkempt hair, smoking cigarettes, waiting to devour their prey.

Down with Weapons! (Ned med vaapnene, 1915), made a few months earlier, is free of this misogynistic trait, and features a courageous heroine caught up in an apocalyptic war. Part of the credit must be ascribed to the screenplay, by Carl Dreyer, who had been engaged as as scriptwriter at Nordisk since 1912. Martha (Augusta Blad) embodies the divided loyalties and instincts of many women whose lives were changed by the Great War. Her husband is killed at the front, she remarries, this time an officer with pacifist sentiments. Holger-Madsen underscores the terrible emptiness of the heart of war in scenes like the one where Martha, searching for her husband among the field hospitals, enters a huge shed filled with nurses and wounded men, all immobilised into absolute stillness.[9] Georges

Sadoul notes that when *Down with Weapons!* was screened in Berlin in February 1917: 'The local critics admired the richness of the *mise-en-scène,* the director's mastery, the magnificent crowd movements, and declared it to be a sublime work.'[10] The deep-focus photography of Marius Clausen in the battle scenes, and the constant emphasis on *crowded* trains, *crowded* hospitals, *crowded* battlefields, intensify the anti-war spirit of the film.

The Skyship (Himmelskibet, 1918) crowns the career of Holger-Madsen. It focuses on its central theme − the conflict between scientific reason and the impossibility of the romantic dream − with a persistence worthy of Fritz Lang. When a spaceship from Earth arrives on Mars, the astronauts discover to their surprise that the Martians are far from the monsters they have anticipated. Dignified in white and dark silk robes, these extraterrestrials look uncomfortably like human beings, as they exchange food and drink with the crew of the spaceship. This illustrates

Holger-Madsen's argument, namely that all creatures are the same beneath the skin and that aggression is born of ignorance and prejudice. Mars appears to these voyagers from Earth as a kind of Paradise, untainted by greed. As the astronauts summon up memories of an Earth convulsed by war, it becomes clear that the difference between the two planets is not so much of topography as of *values*. When the spaceship returns home in triumph, bearing on board the daughter of the Martian leader as a goodwill visitor, vast crowds surround it in jubilation. The scornful old Professor who had predicted a catastrophic outcome for the voyage is now in disgrace, and falls to his death from a lofty crag. Idealism waxes triumphant, as yet another Danish film passes comment on the First World War and its impact. None of the other Nordic countries can claim to have done as much, and not even Stiller or Sjöström dared to address the issue.

The Mysterious World of Benjamin Christensen

Like his spiritual counterpart in Sweden, Georg af Klercker, **Benjamin Christensen** made his best films for a small company. By training an actor and opera singer, he joined Dansk Biografkompagni in 1911, and soon succeeded Carl Rosenbaum as president of that organisation. Christensen's background gives some clue to the eclectic, fastidious quality of his screen *œuvre*. He studied the Romance languages at school in Viborg, and dabbled in the importation of French wines before seeking employment at Dansk Biografkompagni. He is the first Danish director whose profile, as well as his personality, emerges from his surviving films. He acts as a rather agreeable Devil in *Witchcraft through the Ages* (see SWEDEN), and he appears himself at the start of *The Night of Revenge*. His leading role, however, is in his first film, *The Mysterious X (Det hemmelighedsfulde X,* 1914). A story of espionage and blackmail, *The Mysterious X* transcends the stilted acting of Christensen as a compromised naval lieutenant, and reveals the rich promise of the director and his cameraman, Emil Dinesen. Perhaps for the first time in the history of the cinema, nocturnal locations come alive on the screen. Two riders approach a windmill in the windswept darkness. . . . Lights are switched on and off, communicating the fundamental theme of all Christensen's work, the conflict between light and shadow. The villainous Count Spinelli is trapped in the mill during a later scene. He descends into the cellar, and the wind pushes a door in the mill into position above the trapdoor. . . . As the Count struggles in vain to push the trapdoor upwards, one thinks of the death of the Doctor in Dreyer's *Vampyr* eighteen years later. Despite the desperate situations described in *The Mysterious X*, Christensen never loses his tongue-in-cheek sense of humour, a quality he shares with Tod Browning, his only peer in the early horror film. For instance, the lieutenant's wife has a dream that enables her to prove her husband's innocence, and it takes the form of a message scrolling out along a telephone cable, with the compromising letter superimposed over an image of the sleeping woman, who

Benjamin Christensen's *The Mysterious X* (1914)

realises that the solution to the terrible mystery must lie in the abandoned windmill.

The Night of Revenge (Hævnens natt, 1915) signifies a considerable advance not only in the career of Christensen himself, but of Nordic cinema as such. Once again he plays the principal role, that of a convict on the run who snatches a baby from the Poor House and foists himself upon a young bourgeois woman, Ann, begging milk for his 'son', before he is recaptured and consigned to jail. Christensen wanted the ending of the film to accentuate the theme of social injustice (the 'convict' John is in fact innocent), but Dansk Biografkompagni felt that a sentimental tableau was vital for a contemporary audience, and so *The Night of Revenge* closes abruptly on an absurd shot of John on his deathbed, attended by his young son and the doting Ann. This does not detract from the overwhelming sense of agitation, yearning, and finally poignancy, which permeate this masterpiece. Christensen starts the film on the same note of danger and suspense as *The Mysterious X*, as John, pursued by officers with rifles, reaches the manor on New Year's Eve. Ann, in panic, tries to secure the door against the intruder; while she does so, Johan Ankerstjerne's camera pulls back *through a window*, signalling to the spectator both her vulnerability and the fact that John will enter the room via the window. As the drama unfolds, and John's background as a strongman at a Danish circus emerges, another Christensen theme growls like a coarse bass-line just below the surface of the melody. The upper classes live in fear of the wild and the physical, represented not just by 'Strong John' but by the threats to Ann ('I'll tie a rope around her neck!') and the bizarre appearance of three Chinese fakirs at the circus. For Christensen, as for Tod Browning (and for Sjöström in *He Who Gets Slapped*), the circus serves as a refuge for the outcasts of society, their physical deformity symbolising the perverse 'threat' they pose to a conformist bourgeoisie. Many critics have commented on the audacity of Christensen's visual skill in *The Night of Revenge*. 'Most startling of all,' John Gillett has written, 'is the camera style, with its stressing of detail in close-ups and gradual revelation of what the characters are doing, as in the scene where one is shown by a subtly panning camera exactly how the boy, locked in a closet, reaches out with a pole to help his trapped stepfather reach a telephone. The story, in fact, is seen through the camera and not merely recorded by it, not least in the climax with its veritable flurry of cross-cutting as the avenging convict stalks the mistress of the house [Ann] from room to room.'[11]

Carl Dreyer described Christensen as 'a man who knew exactly what he wanted and who pursued his goal with uncompromising stubbornness.' Curiously, he did not direct a film for seven years after *The Night of Revenge*, and then only in Sweden (see *Witchcraft through the Ages*, page 128). Between 1926 and 1934 he worked in Hollywood, where in films like *The Devil's Circus*, *Mockery*, and *Seven Footprints to Satan* he created a gallery of weird, diabolical characters (none better than Creighton Hale in *Seven Footprints to Satan*, suavely shooting out candles as a form of 'target practice'). At once ahead of his epoch, and yet standing in its margins, Christensen may be regarded as one of the authentic pioneers in Nordic cinema, his intensity of purpose ultimately flawed only by an affection for the frivolous and the melodramatic.

Masters of Farce and Literary Adaptation

Increased competition on the international market, and rising production costs at home, meant that Nordisk Films Kompagni began losing its momentum during the 'teens. Ole Olsen lacked the team manager's skill that enabled Charles Magnusson to flourish for so long at the head of Svenska Bio. He was, in the words of Marguerite Engberg, 'a great man of business, but unfortunately he lacked the sense of assembling the best talents in his company. He let Asta Nielsen go, did not persuade Alfred Lind and Benjamin Christensen to work for him, just to mention some of the gravest errors he made.'[12] By the middle of the decade, the brain-drain from Nordisk was alarming: the

actress Clara Pontoppidan, actors Carlo Wieth and Valdemar Psilander, cameramen Axel Sørensen and Johan Ankerstjerne, and directors Robert Dinesen, Edward Schnedler-Sørensen, soon to be followed by Lau Lauritzen and Holger-Madsen. By 1920, the annual output of films from Nordisk had shrunk to a mere *eight*. In the words of Henri Langlois, 'The War and the Russian Revolution had already cast a shadow over the international sparkle of the Danish cinema, while the Swedish cinema's star was rising in Scandinavia.'[13]

Certain gifted individuals remained, however, to sustain the Danish cinema. **Anders Wilhelm Sandberg** had helped Christensen on the production of *The Mysterious X* at Dansk Biografkompagni, and in 1914 he joined Nordisk. He soon became one of the most prolific directors at the studio, turning out as many as 14 films in a single year. In 1917 he scored a hit with *The Clown (Klovnen)*, which was set, like so many Danish films of the early period, in a circus milieu. Sandberg's fondness for emotional drama led him to the novels of Charles Dickens. He made no fewer than four adaptations from the English writer's œuvre, of which the best-known are *David Copperfield* (1922) and *Little Dorrit (Little Dorrit,* 1924). Nordisk hoped that it could recapture the overseas marketplace with these films, but to Olsen's great disappointment the Dickens' pictures did not shine at the box-office in the United States or Britain. John Gillett has commented apropos of Sandberg's *Great Expectations (Store forventninger,* 1921): 'Although certain of [Dickens's] eccentricities have been toned down, Sandberg took tremendous trouble to achieve the atmosphere and look of Dickens's world, working on carefully selected locations and designing detailed interior sets.'[14] Sandberg could not aspire to the technical inventiveness of a Christensen or a Holger-Madsen, but his devotion to his material gives a warmth to even the most laborious of his scenes.

While the Swedes preferred sophisticated, drawing-room comedy, and the Finns produced rustic farce, the Danes were captivated by a pair of comedians who may be regarded in many ways as the forerunners of Laurel and Hardy. 'Long and Short' were played by Carl Schenstrøm and Harald Madsen. Schenstrøm had appeared in comedies at Nordisk Films Kompagni since 1913, but Madsen had to be lured from the circus as late as 1921, when Lau Lauritzen teamed him and Schenstrøm in the first of 46 films together (of which 30 were directed by Lauritzen for Palladium). Lauritzen's natural flair for comedy timing may be gauged in the 1915 court-métrage, *Moving Day Troubles (Flyttedagsskvaler),* in which Oscar Stribolt, in the manner of John Bunny or Fatty Arbuckle, plays a stout, middle-aged man who gets drunk on the day of his moving house, and returns to his former residence at night, to the great confusion of the new residents.

'Long', slender, gangling, and ennobled with a wispy moustache, forms the ideal contrast to his inseparable companion 'Short', who is stout, sturdy, and rather ponderous. In *Long and Short, Heroes of the Cinema (FY og BI filmens helte,* 1921), they grasp at anything to keep themselves in food and lodging, including employment as actors in a Western – with disastrous results! In *Dødsbokseren* (1925),

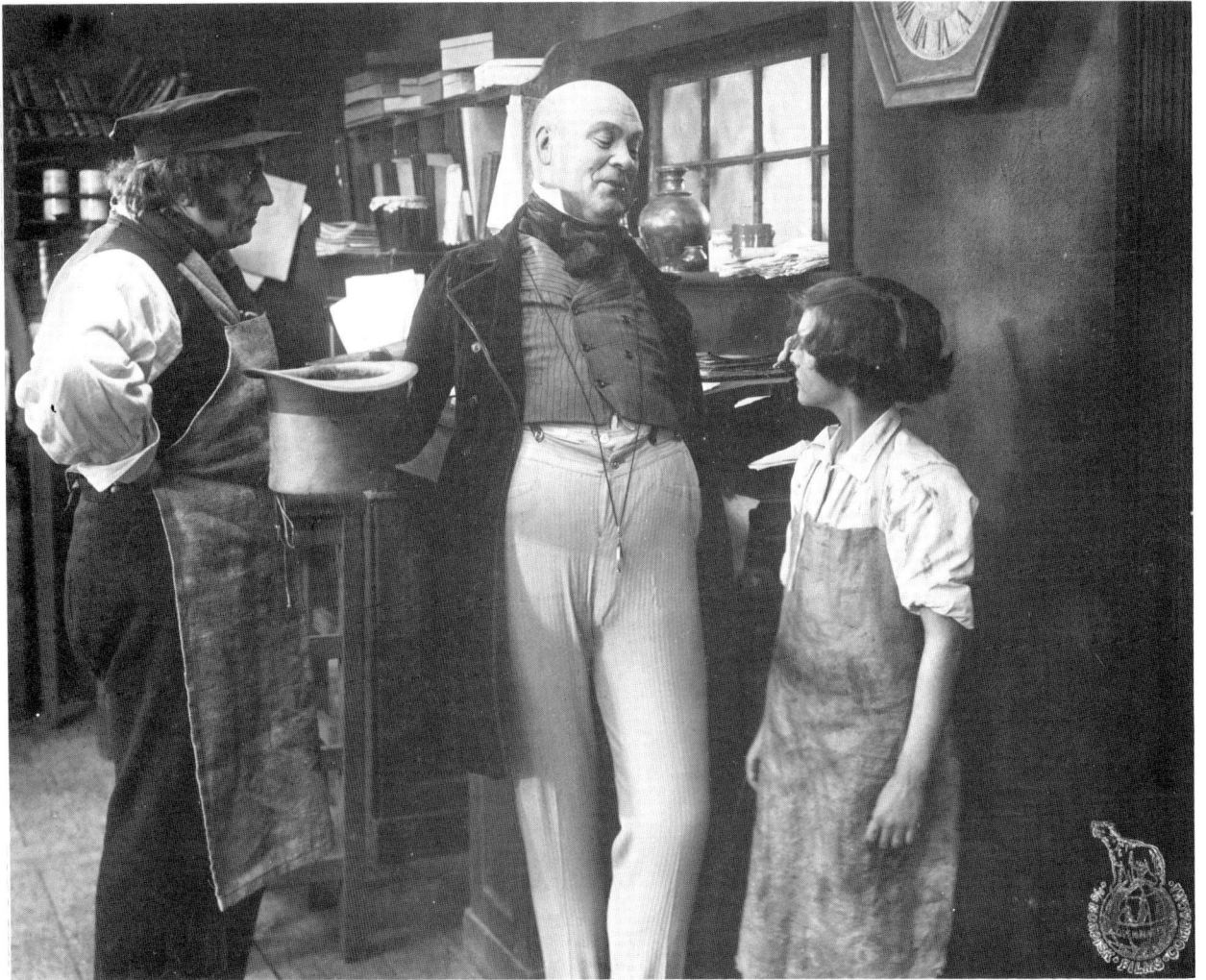

Anders Wilhelm Sandberg's *David Copperfield* (1922)

'Long and Short', the comedy pair in a series of films made by Lau Lauritzen

they survive with difficulty the rigours of shipboard life, and Short finds belated glory as a boxer in Le Havre. Probably their most inspired and hilarious achievement was *Don Quixote* (1926), for their figures and personalities were ideally suited to Sancho Panza and his vainglorious Master. The immense popularity of Chaplin must have influenced Lauritzen's treatment of his two comedians, and especially their garb (Long's jacket held around his midriff with a piece of string, and Short's fastened with a prominent safety-pin). Their impoverished appearance reflected the proletarian reality of the 1920's, much as Edvard Persson's would mirror the Swedish bucolic conservatism of the 1930's.

The Luminous Magic of Carl Th. Dreyer

Ole Olsen may have resigned in 1924, but he could scarcely have realised that despite the declining fortunes of Nordisk Films Kompagni at least one of his recruits would survive to take an imperishable place in the Pantheon of world cinéastes. Ironically, Denmark did not embrace the talents of its greatest film visionary; Dreyer was obliged to seek financing for his work outside the country, and some of his finest films *(La Passion de Jeanne d'Arc, Vampyr)* were made for French or German corporations.

Dreyer began his film career in 1912, at the age of 23, when he provided the screenplay for *The Brewer's Daughter (Bryggerens datter,* directed by Rasmus Ottensen), and for the next five years he laboured in the so-called 'Poets' Caravan' at Nordisk, where, like Ingmar Bergman in the early 1940's, his duties included the revision of scripts by other authors as well as the development of or original ones for certain directors and actors. In 1918 he was at last given the opportunity to direct, although not a subject of his own. *The President (Præsidenten,* released only in 1920) comes from a sentimental novel by Karl-Emil Franzos about a judge torn between duty and blood ties when his illegitimate daughter appears before his tribunal, accused of infanticide. Despite a poignant explanation of her youthful problems, the woman is condemned to death. The judge makes his decision. By night, he smuggles her out of detention, marries her off, and then leaps to his own death from the walls of Fødcby Castle. Within the framework of this tear-jerking melodrama may be located both the distinctive characteristics of Dreyer's mise-en-scène and the thematic links with Nordic cinema as a whole. Victorine, the accused women, bears a strong resemblance to Helga in Sjöström's *The Girl from the Marsh Croft,* while her mother calls her to mind the unfortunate Ingeborg Holm. The class prejudice displayed by the judge's father on his deathbed echoes sentiments readily found in the Swedish and Finnish cinema of the 1910's and 1920's. Dreyer's puckish sense of humour, which deserted him in later years, mitigates the solemnity of the story. At Victorine's wedding, he incorporates shots of the quaint old servants, a cheerful blind organist, and three chirpy dogs, who race in from outside and listen to the ceremony. Most idiomatic of all are the eloquent close-ups – not just of craggy faces but also of hands clasping and

unclasping in consternation behind a person's back. Dreyer's fondness for the interplay of light and darkness is illustrated in scenes of local folk, bearing torches and approaching from either side of the screen out of the blackness, and in the silhouette of a nightwatchman guzzling beer.

Dreyer's second film, *Leaves from Satan's Book (Blade af Satans bog,* 1921) falls, like Griffith's *Intolerance,* into four segments, charting the Devil's tempting of mankind throughout the ages: the trial of Christ, the Spanish Inquisition, the French Revolution, and – most intriguing from a Nordic standpoint – the impact of Bolshevism on Finland in the wake of the Russian Revolution. Conservative and staid by comparison with the wit and wisdom of Christensen's *Witchcraft through the Ages,* the film acknowledges a debt more to Sjöström and Stiller than to Griffith. 'Stiller, and especially Sjöström,' said Dreyer in an interview later, 'really invented the poetic effect in cinema. That meant a great deal at that period. [. . .] It was there that I achieved a close-up of the leading actress for the first time.'[15]

During the ensuing four years, Dreyer would make films in Sweden, Germany, Norway and Denmark. Yet wherever he worked, he imposed his instantly recognisable signature on his material. *The Parson's Widow (Prästänkan,* 1920) is rich in its social observation, unmasking the hypocrisy of 17th-century Norwegian community life as an ambitious young man cynically marries the pastor's widow in order to assume the office himself. Dreyer's choice of camera angle permits him to distort, and mock, the faces of his characters; he watches them from all sides as they speak with a gripping intensity. George Schnéevoigt, one of Dreyer's favourite cameramen, responds brilliantly to this challenge, and also endows the country landscape with a sunstruck brightness. Dreyer's fascination with close-ups extends to some memorable experiments, such as the 'split-screen' effect when the 'widow' listens to her 'husband' climbing furtively up some steps to visit his secret fiancée.

The Bride of Glomdal (Glomdalsbruden, 1925) takes place in the same environment (rural Norway) but lacks the hard-edged quality of *The Parson's Widow.* Once again, however, the tensions involved in a marriage between people of different social classes are of concern to Dreyer. As Armond White has noted, its 'exuberant nature celebration steadily sheds its bucolic heartiness until Dreyer's couple become figures of primeval destiny'.[16] Altogether more successful, and as bright as a new penny when viewed today, is *Master of the House (Du skal ære din hustru,* 1925), shot a few months earlier in the studios of Palladium and opening on October 5, 1925 to considerable box-office success. While his contemporaries in Germany concentrated on expressionistic effects, Dreyer preferred a naturalistic approach to domestic matters. Audiences could readily relate to the Copenhagen household portrayed in *Master of the House.* Although most of the action takes place inside the family apartment (the film was based on a play), Dreyer intersperses shots of an almost documentary realism, showing the husband walking through the nearby streets, with factory chimneys in the background. To enhance the sense of merciless scrutiny, Dreyer and Schnéevoigt frequently use a 'spotlight' effect, leaving the edges of the frame dark so that the eye focuses exclusively on the character being observed. And what characters! Johannes Meyer gives a rounded portrait of Viktor, the supercilious young prig of a husband who is by degrees outwitted and restored to human decency by the wiles of the old family nanny. The battle between these two tough characters produces a steady flow of amusing incidents. Viktor passes sardonic judgement on every aspect of his wife's household management, and bears down on his son with a martinet's rigour. But perhaps the single most common misconception concerning Dreyer's work is that his men and women are cast in stone rather than being creatures of flesh and blood. The nanny in *Master of the House* certainly *looks* formidable: hair drawn back strictly over her skull, steel-rimmed glasses giving her an inquisitorial aspect, and pursed lips suggesting a bitter temper. But by the close of the film both she and the husband have sloughed off this rancorous integument, as it were, and emerge as soulmates. The nanny undermines Viktor's humourless approach to his family with a shrewd, relaxed determination (note the amusing scene when she makes sandwiches, not for the 'Master of the House', but for herself!) To the end, however, the nanny belongs among Dreyer's most ambiguous female personalities, exuding a baleful, even witch-like intensity as she peers through a crack in the doorway, one eye watching like a hawk as Viktor gradually becomes more placid and domesticated. Despite the presence of wife, son, and daughter, *Master of the House* remains unequivocally a spiritual struggle between Viktor and the old nanny. The spectral force of this conflict presages to an uncanny degree the theme of later Dreyer masterpieces like *Vampyr, Day of Wrath* and even *Gertrud*.

Although *Michael (Mikaël,* 1924) possesses a grave, stifling beauty, its latent homosexuality is better explored in Stiller's version of the same novel by Herman Bang (see *The Wings*, page 118). In Dreyer's words, 'The action takes place in a spirited and excessive period, when feelings were readily exaggerated; a time of very false styles — which may be seen in the decor, with its overloaded interiors.'[17] Filmed almost entirely in sombre interiors, *Michael* again manifests Dreyer's fondness for compelling the spectator to look only at certain areas of the frame, by masking his camera lens so that one has the impression of staring through a telescope or a pair of binoculars.

The offer which Dreyer received from Société Générale de Films in Paris, to make a film in France, may be attributed to the popular appeal of *Master of the House*. Dreyer's acceptance, however, must have been influenced at least in part by the lamentable standards of Danish film production in the late 1920's. Like Sweden, Denmark lost its momentum as the silent era drew to a close. Innocuous comedies, alongside some ponderous literary adaptations, formed the staple diet of domestic studios.

Made only a few months after Sjöström's *The Wind* had been released in the United States, *The Passion of Joan of Arc* stands alongside it as the greatest silent achievement by a Nordic director. Rejecting the fashionable 'organic' montage of Eisenstein, Dreyer's film relies on an extraordinary intimacy of expression (the action outruns the projection times by only a tiny amount). Dreyer scrutinises his heroine from every angle and distance; figuratively speaking, he lays bare her soul. Only when a soul is confronted by death, Dreyer seems to be saying, does it reveal its true richness and nobility. Everything in the film is subordinate to the burning question of *faith* that runs like an artery through each sequence. Every gesture, every slow-running tear, is minutely examined. The camera *sympathises* with Joan while at the same time sucking the life from her. Falconetti clearly sacrifices herself utterly to the part (like Bresson's leading players, Dreyer's rarely appear in a major role again).

The final segment of the film, as Joan is burnt at the stake, accelerates in pace and demonstrates that Dreyer could perform technical pyrotechnics when he so desired. His ascetic approach to the prolonged interrogation scenes bears witness to the unflinching discipline of his film language. These sequences may be theatrical in appearance, but not in tone. The gigantic close-ups become symbolic in a way that could never be achieved on a stage. According to André Bazin, 'Dreyer banned all make-up, the monks' heads were shaved and, with the whole crew in tears, the executioner really did cut Falconetti's hair before leading her to the stake. But it wasn't really a case of tyranny. We owe him this indisputable sense of the soul's expression. The warts on Silvain (Cauchon), the blotched skin of Jean d'Yd, the wrinkled features of Maurice Schutz are consubstantial to their soul, and signify more than their acting.'[18]

The Passion of Joan of Arc, although made in France and concerning a French historical figure, shares the austerity of many of the most enduring Nordic films, from *The Phantom Carriage* to *Winter Light*. In effect, Dreyer imposes a Lutheran severity on a 15th-century situation, while also abhorring the intolerance that brands Joan as a heretic (just as Anne Pedersdotter is condemned in *Day of Wrath*).

Dreyer's visual style, which in *The Passion of Joan of Arc* has been compared to such painters as Van der Weyden, Giotto, and Vermeer, undergoes a peculiar change in *Vampyr* (1932). While viewing the early rushes, Dreyer and his cameraman, Rudolph Maté, discovered that the image was suffused with a grey luminescence. A light had been erroneously reflected by the camera lens. Spontaneously, Dreyer and Maté decided to adopt this glaucous look for the rest of the film, and did so by projecting a light through a veil and thence on to the lens. This 'milky' tone endows the bizarre story of David Gray with a dream-like mystery and intensity. To a large extent the sinister reverie Dreyer seeks to achieve is dissipated by the clumsy performance of the Baron Nicolas de Gunzberg as Gray — but as he had engineered the financial package that enabled *Vampyr* to be made at Tobis-Klangfilm, Dreyer could not complain. Despite this handicap, the film belongs with Murnau's *Nosferatu* and Browning's *Dracula* among the greatest of vampire movies. The scene in which David Gray sees himself trapped in a coffin makes superb use of the subjective camera, and has been imitated often in the intervening decades, most notably by Bergman in the opening nightmare of *Wild Strawberries*. The death of the villainous doctor, suffocated in a rising tide of flour, functions both on the level of horror but also as a visual extension of the 'white' look so assiduously sought by Dreyer and Rudolph Maté. As Gray wanders distractedly through the park surrounding Courtempierre, the images throb with an hallucinatory life of their own. Nordic film-makers, like the fin-de-siècle painters of the Skagen school, share an ability to site their human characters in emphatic relationship to the space and texture of the natural landscape. In the cinema, this creates both a physical and a spiritual stereoscopy, drawing the audience into the drama and allowing them to stand at a distance from the characters even as they may be compelled to share their dreams and nightmares. Tarkovsky's *The Sacrifice* (1986), shot on Gotland and concluding with a small boy's dream of a better future, has a psychological affinity with Dreyer's *Vampyr*, not least in the somnambulistic movements of its actors.

As a consequence of the commercial and critical failure of *Vampyr*, Dreyer returned to the profession of journalist that he had abandoned twenty years earlier. Not until 1943, in the midst of the Nazi occupation of Denmark, could he muster the wherewithal for another feature film. *Day of Wrath (Vredens dag,* 1943) is based on a play by the Norwegian dramatist Hans Wiers-Jenssen, which Dreyer had first seen performed in 1925. In a detailed comparison of play and film, the American critic Miles Coiner concludes that 'it is a tribute to Dreyer's genius that he was able to transform this cheap, reactionary tale of passion into a tribute to an anarchic humanism which sees all attempts to reduce men and women to slaves of conventional morality as being linked to the forces of death emanating from authoritarian families, from religion, or from the state.'[19]

After Dreyer's disastrous encounter with the magic of sound technique in *Vampyr* (the dialogue being dubbed into English, French, and German versions), the subtlety of the soundtrack in *Day of Wrath* adds a new dimension to his art. The tranquillity of Marte Herlof's house is disturbed by the sounds of an approaching crowd and the frantic tolling of a church bell. Sensing danger, she makes her escape through the pigsty at the back of the house. Once caught, after trying to hide in the parsonage inhabited by the elderly pastor and his young wife Anne, she alludes to the film's central conflict by pleading for *life* instead of her soul's salvation. 'I don't fear heaven or hell,' she snarls. 'I fear dying.'

Day of Wrath, long underestimated even by Bazin, looms more and more clearly as Dreyer's masterpiece, the only film in which his complex metaphysical arguments are presented in supple, controlled cinematic terms. It may be regarded, like Carné and Prévert's *Les Visiteurs du soir*, as a veiled comment on the horrors of the Nazi mentality and especially the dread of betrayal by informers. But the film deals also with the conflict between love and death. When the pastor's son Martin, who has become infatuated with Anne, tells her that he wants to die alongside her 'to atone for our sin', she replies ardently: 'Is it a sin to love? As the apple tree among the trees of the wood, so is my beloved among the sons [a quotation from *The Song of Solomon*].'

This spiritual conflict acquires a visual metaphor in the struggle between darkness and light. Dreyer's characters pass from the shadows into the sunlight, thus achieving transcendence. The parsonage resembles a prison, with its spartan rooms and its barred windows. By comparison, the countryside beyond is lush with meadows, streams, and glistening birch groves. When, at towards the end of the film, the passion of Anne and Martin evaporates, Dreyer provides a visual sign for this process, in the form of morning mist cloaking the superabundant nature enveloping the parsonage. Another effective metaphor involves the dress code so obligatory to a Denmark gripped by Lutheran fervour. Like the characters in *Les Visiteurs du soir*, another oblique comment on the perils of fascism, Anne, Absalon, and his mother are clad in stern, high-necked robes, close-fitting caps, and pure-white ruffs. When Anne removes her cap for Martin, her hair appears as seductive as a modern woman's bare legs.

The moral ambiguity of *Day of Wrath* adds to its complexity. Anne may declare to Martin that 'My only crime is that I love you,' but her admission to the elders that she used the power of the 'Evil One' both to kill her husband Absalon, and to lure his son into her affections may not be so inaccurate or unjust as it sounds. Dreyer cuts eloquently, for example, between shots of Anne in the parsonage saying she imagines her husband were dead, and images of the doomed Absalon staggering in the grip of a storm and muttering to the man alongside him, 'It's as though Death had brushed my sleeve.' This sinister undercurrent is all the more chilling when felt in the context of a film that describes the burning of Marte Herlof in such unadorned detail (the horror compounded by a children's choir singing 'Dies Irae' while the flames flare up, and by the 'official record' saying that Marte was burned 'on a fine day, happily').

If Anne's gleaming white garb in the final sequence may show her in a positive light by contrast with the black-robed figures surrounding her, then Dreyer affords no such approval to Absalon's mother Merete, who denounces those closest to her with a bitter self-righteous satisfaction. Her hypocrisy, which is shared to a less cruel degree by her son, interests Dreyer more than the social patterns or injustices of the period. The ultimate force of *Day of Wrath* stems from Dreyer's comprehension of the role of the supernatural in the lives of *both* religious fanatics and those less wedded to the faith.

No other Dreyer film marches forward from start to finish with such unequivocal conviction. The stern logic of the montage is in alignment with the inflexible attitudes of a society that acknowledges the Church as dictating the course of political and family existence in a country whose monarch, Christian IV, had 'Piety Strengthens the Kingdom' as his motto. For Edvin Kau,[20] Dreyer's concern with the human right to love, happiness, and self-determination confirms that this auteur stands firmly in the midst of the 20th century even as he filters his historical subject-matter from the standpoint of a critico-sceptical Danish tradition.

In his own words: 'We want the cinema to open a door for us into the unexplainable. We want to undergo a tension that

Day of Wrath (1943) by Carl Dreyer

is the result less of an external action than of a struggle within the soul. There are many such conflicts in *Day of Wrath*.'[21]

Like his closest cinematic heir, Robert Bresson, Dreyer allowed each of his films a longer and longer time in which to grow and mature in his mind before committing them to production. *The Word (Ordet,* 1955) earned for Dreyer the only real festival recognition of his career — the Lion d'Or at Venice. Taken from Kaj Munk's play of 1932, this luminous homage to faith is set in a small Danish village, torn by the differences between the pharisaical 'death-seeking' sect and its 'life-affirming' counterpart. For enhanced verisimilitude, the exteriors were filmed in Munk's own parish of Veders. Dreyer's screen version breathes a more ethereal atmosphere than Gusfaf Molander's 1943 film of the same play, and the natural environment participates in the drama even more pervasively than in *Day of Wrath*. The wind racing through

the high grasses of the Jutland meadows carries the same sense of extraterrestrial influence as does the vegetation agitated by the arrival of the 'mother ship' in *Close Encounters of the Third Kind*. The broad skies above the farm are like an opening into the Infinite. The interiors acquire a similar weight and significance. The rooms of the homestead resemble a clean, well-lit church, their walls adorned only by portraits of sober forebears and a clock that might have strayed from a local vestry. *The Word*, along with *Gertrud*, contains Dreyer's most sophisticated and carefully-executed camera movements, circling, advancing, and retreating within the confined space of each room. The minutiae of domestic life are observed with the same loving gaze as Dreyer brought to *Master of the House*. This naturalism heightens even the climactic 'miracle' scene, when Inger returns from the dead to the sound not just of Johannes' incantatory 'word' but also to the accompaniment of a horse whinneying in the yard outside.

Carl Th. Dreyer's *The Word* (1955)

The film is activated by a central collision of faiths –
between the Christianity of Morten Borgen, the farmer, and
the Free Church fundamentalism of Peter the Tailor. Dreyer
does not take sides, but adheres to the spirit of the Munk
play in letting the crisis of Inger's parturition serve as a
solvent for the doctrinal dispute between the two village
families. The expectations of the film rise and fall and rise
again, as Inger's pregnancy promises a new life, and then
the infant is born dead, only for Inger herself to revive at the
miraculous close.

Dreyer has often been compared to Bergman, by virtue of
both his Nordic austerity and his obsession with issues
touching on religion. While Bergman's characters are with
few exceptions (Tomas in *Winter Light*) reluctant adherents
to the faith, Dreyer's move like Bresson's within a field of
grace: from the kindliest to the most malicious among them,
they never seek to evade their responsibilities as part of a
preordained universe. If Dreyer is closer in this respect to
Bresson than he is to Bergman, he shares with the Swedish
director a belief in the power of corporeal love. There is the
bond between Anne and Martin in *Day of Wrath*, the
physical allure that Gertrud radiates towards all the men in
her life, and Mikkel's attraction to his wife in *The Word*. As
Dreyer said apropos of this latter film: 'For Kaj Munk, love
amounted not just to the lovely, good thoughts that can link
a man and a woman, but also a very profound bond. And for
him, there was no difference between sacred and profane
love. Take *The Word*. The father says, "She is dead. . . .
She is no longer here. She is in heaven. . . ." And the son
replies: "Yes, but I also loved her body." ' [22]

Gertrud (1964), Dreyer's swansong, deserves the epithet
Kammerspiele more than any other of his works. Based on
a play by Hjalmar Söderberg (and ostensibly a portrait of his
own mistress), *Gertrud* is typical of Nordic film and theatre
in its analytical discussion of emotional circumstances. In a
physical sense, Gertrud's horizons diminish as she drifts
through life and into old age. A social prisoner within the
confines of her marriage (treated like a servant by her
mother-in-law), she cannot establish a secure relationship
with any of her three admirers, Gabriel, Axel, or the
younger Erland. In a spiritual sense, however, Gertrud
manages to control her feelings and to believe to the end in
a dialectic between love on the one hand and solitude and
freedom on the other. 'Amor omnia' (Love is Everything) is

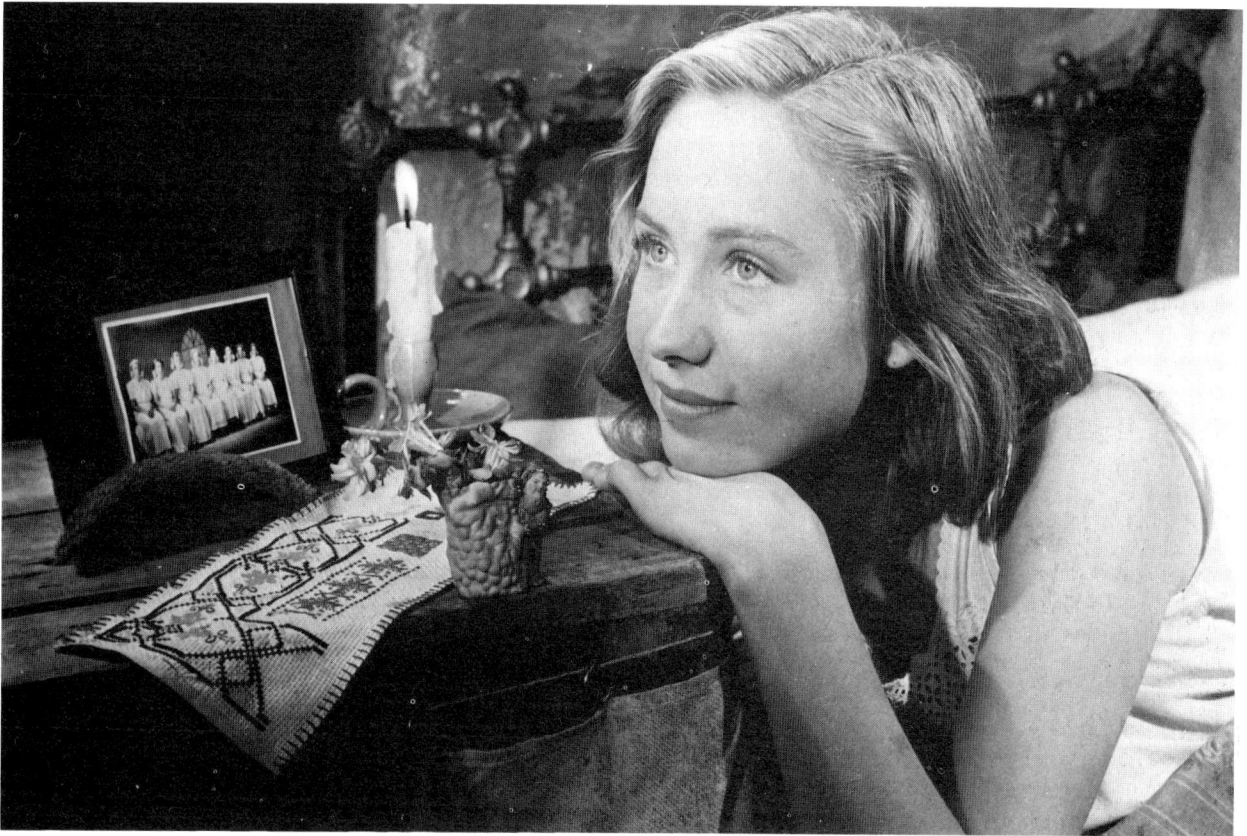

Ditte, Child of Man (1946), directed by Astrid and Bjarne Henning-Jensen

the epitaph she has ordered for her gravestone, she tells Axel in the closing sequence.

The delicate texture of this film has deceived many critics, who have condemned its solemn pace and restrained expression. Closer scrutiny reveals a host of images that vibrate with sentiment. When Gertrud first visits her young lover Erland, the sun pours through the windows like a blessing, and Henning Bendtsen's camera conveys the underlying passion of the scene by means of soft focus. Certain gestures, such as the touching of foreheads, or the exchange of a lighted cigarette, carry a palpable erotic charge within the context of the formal clothes and décor of the film. Gabriel Lidman, on the surface a staid middle-aged bourgeois, has reached young people through his poems enunciating the theme of love as a true union of hearts and minds, and through his rejection of the earlier generation's disavowal of erotic love. Söderberg may have seen himself in all four of the men in Gertrud's life, and the famous line from Gabriel's verse sums up his philosophy: 'I believe in the pleasures of the flesh and the incurable loneliness of the soul.' Dreyer also emphasises a sub-text, suggesting that fame and power cause men to dismiss love from their lives as messy and irrelevant. The prosperous circumstances of Kanning, her husband, and also of Gabriel, may be regarded in Dreyer's eyes as rigidifying, even mortifying, his life, rendering the man indifferent to the desires of his partner – a theme often explored by Ingmar Bergman and typified in the personality played in film after film by Erland Josephson.

Gertrud, like a profound string quartet, is suffused with the meditative melancholy of an artist seeking to reduce his experience of life to the sparest of forms. Gertrud sifts through the embers of her existence, and blows out the candles that stand on either side of the mirror originally given her by Gabriel. Grave and sensual, the film's texture approximates to Gertrud's definition of life as 'a long, long row of dreams overlapping one another.'

*   *   *

Like Sjöberg, Dreyer spent many years as *persona non grata* in the studios. Late in life he was granted a licence to run the Dagmar Cinema in central Copenhagen, but the vilification heaped upon him both at home and abroad when

37

Gertrud received its world première in Paris in 1964 is inexcusable. The brutal fact is that for almost four decades Danish film had languished in the doldrums. The 1920's produced a fair share of comedies, but even the most distinguished of Danish film historians, Ib Monty, can point only to a single documentary (*Danmark*, by the architect and cultural critic Poul Henningsen) as being worthy of mention during the 1930's.[23] This served as the forerunner of a substantial number of documentaries made by Danish directors. Today, the tradition continues through the outstanding work of the Statens Filmcentral, for whom film-makers like Jørgen Leth (see below) and Hans-Henrik Jørgensen have produced excellent studies of people and places. An admirer of the British documentary movement and of John Grierson in particular, **Theodor Christensen** quickly established himself as the most progressive and influential of Danish documentarists during the 1940's. It was a period dominated by the Nazi Occupation, and disposed increasingly to a realistic view of the everyday world. Benjamin Christensen returned to Denmark from the United States, but none of the four final features he made there can be compared to his silent masterpieces. Dreyer, like Bergman in Sweden a generation later, ploughed his solitary furrow and cannot be considered characteristic of Danish cinema in the 1940's and 1950's. The total ban on films from Britain and the United States during the war gave some incentive to Danish producers, and the output of feature films rose from 9 in the 1939-40 season to 18 in 1941-42 and 19 the following year. The Danish government was among the first in the western world to support domestic film production, and even before the establishment of the Danish Film Foundation in 1965 modest sums had been granted to independent producers. The American entertainment newspaper, *Variety*, described this subsidy system as a potential threat to U.S. studios! 'In Denmark, theatre owners have to pay heavily from their profits to the state film fund to provide rewards to the Danish producers. Almost every maker of serious films gets a ''reward'' from the government. And cartoon studios that make films which do not resemble those of Walt Disney too closely get an extra subsidy.'

The truth was of course very different. The swelling flood of motion pictures from Hollywood, many of them bolstered with their own form of 'subsidy' thanks to the Marshall Plan, rendered it difficult for a small country's movie industry to survive without some degree of state support.

Two new faces entered the scene at the start of the war. **Astrid** and **Bjarne Henning-Jensen** had married in 1938 and soon enrolled at Nordisk Films Kompagni where they directed or co-directed a sequence of documentaries that met with much acclaim. In 1943 Bjarne Henning-Jensen made *To Be Young (Naar man kun er ung)*, with Astrid serving as his assistant. This first feature, according to Ib Monty, was 'a light, everyday comedy, striving for a relaxed and charming style, but it was too cute, and it was politely received.'[24] Their second fictional effort marked a proud moment in the postwar Danish cinema. *Ditte: Child of Man (Ditte, menneskebarn, 1946)* distilled the tragic fate of a young country girl brought alive in the pages of Martin Andersen Nexø (another of his suite of novels, *Pelle the Conqueror* inspired Bille August's 1987 release). The Danes, having recently escaped from the shadow of the Occupation, could appreciate the bitter experiences of young Ditte (Tove Maës), and the film made more money at the box-office than any other Nordisk release of that year. ASA, which had joined Nordisk and Palladium as the most active studios, also enjoyed a popular success with *The Red Earth (Den røde enge, 1945)*, which won a minor prize at the first Cannes Film Festival for its directors Bodil Ipsen and Lau Lauritzen Jr., who had made a not unworthy historical epic during the war (*Princess of the Suburbs [Afsporet, 1942]*. *The Red Land* dealt with the Resistance movement in Denmark, as did *The Invisible Army (Den usynlige hær, 1945)*, directed by Johan Jacobsen. Nothing could match the versimilitude of Theodor Christensen's documentary record of the Resistance, entitled *Your Freedom Is At Stake*, which gave audiences a glimpse of footage they could never have believed they would see.

From Documentary to Naturalist Drama

Although the crowded islands and peninsulas of Denmark have inspired many a fine documentary, the country's most distant possession, Greenland, still intrigues the Danes even more. Bjarne Henning-Jensen made *Where Mountains Float (Hvor bjergene sejler, 1955)* and another documentary on location in Greenland. **Jørgen Roos**, arguably the most distinguished documentarian in the Nordic cinema of the past twenty years, has also focused on Greenland, observing the daily battle for survival among the islanders, and seizing in unostentatious imagery their courage and cheerfulness in the face of an immense natural environment that can never be tamed. Like Lehmuskallio in Finland, he writes, directs, edits and almost invariably photographs his documentaries, which owe their ancestry to Flaherty.

One man transcended his documentary roots to become a major force in Nordic cinema. **Henning Carlsen** served his apprenticeship with Theodor Christensen, and spent the 1950's producing cinema commercials and documentaries, with Grierson's *Drifters*, Basil Wright and Harry Watt's *Night Mail*, and other British essays in the genre as his benchmark. In 1958 he was making a documentary on a Danish heating company in South Africa and happened to observe Lionel Rogosin's team at work on *Come Back Africa*. Four years later, with the aid of a family legacy, Carlsen returned to South Africa for three months of clandestine shooting in Johannesburg. The result was *Dilemma*, a feature based on Nadine Gordimer's novel *A World of Strangers*, and it won first prize at the Mannheim Film Week in 1962.

Like Dreyer an eager traveller, Carlsen has worked in Sweden and France. Even in a grim, Zolaesque film like *The Cats (Kattorna, 1964)* he examines female problems with an acuity and relentlessness that recall the early Bergman. There is a vehemence in this study of women working alongside each other in a laundry, a sense of disillusionment that mirrors the postwar mood in Scandinavia. *Hunger (Sult*, 1966) plumbs even grimmer depths than *The Cats*, but its heightened naturalism is more than worthy of Knut Hamsun's novel about a starving writer in 19th-century Norway. As Pontus, Per Oscarsson staggers like a scarecrow through the autumnal streets of Christiania (later to become Oslo). Reduced to gobbling dust from cupboard shelves, chewing paper, and begging a bone from the local meat market, he soon succumbs to his hallucinations. The weird and terrible masochism *cum* pride, so common in Strindberg and Bergman, is evident in the way Pontus treats traders and potential helpers with a sneering, patronising disdain. He dispenses all he needs to other, startled beggars. He rejects the refuge offered by the Alms House.

The dialogue in *Hunger* does not draw attention to itself. Instead, the film hinges on the reactions of Pontus to the claustrophobic world around him – 'That strange city,' wrote Hamsun, 'which no man leaves before it has marked him for life.' His quest for fame as an author gives way to

a passion for the elegant woman (Gunnel Lindblom) who perambulates along Karl Johan's Street like some tantalising ideal. Eventually he is graced with her affections for a brief hour, but so blurred is the border between fantasy and reality that one cannot be certain if this act of fulfilment is an authentic incident or merely a figment of Pontus's deranged imagination.

Carlsen's willingness to tackle the most precarious of subjects has not always reaped success. *People Meet and Sweet Music Fills the Heart (Mennesker mødes og sød musik opstar i hjertet*, 1967) and *A Happy Divorce (En lyykkelig skilsmisse*, 1975) boast an audacious comedy flourish, but their satire often flies wide of the mark. Much more poignant, in spite of its many moments of laughter, is *Oh, To Be on the Bandwagon (Man sku'være noget ved musikken*, 1972), which chronicles the frail ambitions and petty frustrations of a group of bar-flies in Copenhagen. They gather at all hours of day and night to commiserate with one another over a drink. One plays the piano, one is a butcher, one an old-age pensioner, another the local

Per Oscarsson in Henning Carlsen's *Hunger* (1966)

window-cleaner, and so on. The butcher dreams of becoming a famous opera singer and like everyone in the film makes a desultory attempt to escape from his or her slot in life. Four of them even try to buy a restaurant; but the project fails for lack of finance. Carlsen watches their jaded efforts with a compassionate, understanding camera, his zoom lens creating intelligent space within the cramped cafés, and his use of music contributing to the mood of wistfulness and regret. In its low-keyed manner, *Oh, To Be on the Bandwagon?* expresses a cogent condemnation of modern consumer society, with its emphasis on material rather than spiritual satisfaction.

Did Somebody Laugh? (Var der ikke en, som lo?, 1978) recalls *Hunger* in subject-matter if not in tone. '*Hunger* deals with the dissolution of an intellectual,' said Carlsen, 'whereas [*Did Somebody Laugh?*] describes the *resignation* of a working man. I don't want to be a prophet; I want to address the subconscious. In the 1930's, people felt that nobody was to blame for their being unemployed. Today, they believe that society has rejected them.' Like Pontus in *Hunger,* the young hero of this later film is naive and diffident, tossed aimlessly about like a boat cut free of its moorings. He too walks through the dismal streets and kips on park benches. He too grows infatuated with a particular girl, only to realise that she is deceiving him. 'If only it would snow,' he mutters, hoping for labour in clearing the roads. But of course the snow, which at the close of the film covers him like a fresh mantle − a re-birth − brings work only as long as the snow itself endures. . . . *Did Somebody Laugh?* breathes a consummate wisdom and tolerance, and its sense of fantasy illuminates even the tiniest exchange of dialogue. Characters reach out to touch one another in the grey misery of 1935, with news of Hitler, Franco, and Mussolini on the radio; and a shared meal of gruel achieves somehow the dimensions of a sacrament − all without a wisp of rhetoric or affectation. . . .

Youth in Focus

The increased government subsidies for film production that flowed via the Danish Film Foundation (later Institute) in the mid-1960's and 1970's ensured that several young talents came to the fore, in tune with their contemporaries in other Nordic countries. Danish directors tended, however, to concentrate their attention on children and young people much more frequently than those in Sweden, Norway, or Finland. By the early 1980's, indeed, some 25% of the state subsidy for film production was earmarked for movies about children or young people.

Palle Kjærulff-Schmidt, in partnership with the fruitful novelist Klaus Rifbjerg, made a series of quiet-spoken, keenly-observed films about the crucible of youth. *Week-end (Weekend,* 1962) contains some of the clichés associated with Nordic films: couples wrangling and rutting, their inhibitions loosened by alcohol and the natural surroundings. Yet its naturalist texture gives it an undeniable persuasion. Four years later, the same duo produced their most appealing work: *Once There Was a War (Der var engang en krig,* 1966). Tim, the 15-year-old hero of the film, grows up during the Occupation years of 1940-45. As he plays with his friends in Copenhagen and listens grudgingly to his parents' admonitions, he learns that Germans should be hated. But Tim is more curious and imaginative than that: the echoes of war earn only a small place in his dreams of heroism and romance. Through an accumulation of incidents in this boy's life, Kjærulff-Schmidt and Rifbjerg provide what is surely a definitive picture of Denmark during the war. The nights sheltering in the basement, the surreptitious films mocking the Nazis, the dowdy clothes: these are registered subjectively through Tim's eyes, but they are never exaggerated, nor freed from the nagging implications of the war.

Spontaneity and inspired improvisation lift many a Danish 'youth' film to an agreeable level. *Leave Us Alone (La 'os være,* 1975), directed by Lasse and Carlsten Nielsen, follows the example of *Lord of the Flies* in analysing the behaviour of a group of children alone on a Danish island. The message of this and many other Nordic films in this genre suggest that youngsters will, if left to their own devices, come to terms with life's crucial phases in a more profound and ultimately satisfying way than if they cling without question to their parents' example.

His work may be too self-effacing to attract large audiences outside his own society, but the quiet, sensitive mise-en-scène of **Nils Malmros** qualifies him as one of the top half-dozen in the Nordic region over the past fifteen years. Malmros, like Truffaut, knows how to evoke memories of childhood, and to use his own experience filtered through an adult vision. In each of his major films, his leading characters have grown older and older, from the fifth-grade Ole in *Lars Ole 5C* (1973) to the somewhat confused young film director figure in *Århus by Night* (1989). Overt sex education in the primary school might appear to be the norm in Scandinavia, but *Boys (Drenge,* 1976) suggests that there still remain more subtle ways of entering adulthood, with the guilt an inevitable concomitant to the thrill attached to each youth's mysterious discovery of sex. Like Malmros himself, Ole (who travels in the film from childhood to his early twenties) is curious and tolerant. He does not speak much, and Malmros lets the intervals between conversations elapse naturally, leaving one to imagine the perplexed and darting thoughts that come to Ole as he sits beside a girl or − in the haunting final shots − wades fascinated through the flooded basement of his family home. Ole progresses through the various stages of boyhood only to return to his infancy, as though Malmros were hinting that all one's later life may be affected by those bizarre initial revelations about one's own body and one's reactions to it.

In *The Tree of Knowledge (Kundskabens træ,* 1981), the kids have reached 8th and 9th grade. Malmros adds a special poignancy to his story by setting it at the end of the 1950's, at a period when even public schooling still contained some element of discipline and formality, so that much of the youngsters' development evolves *within* the framework of the class and its ritual excursions. Malmros lets his boys and girls unravel their emotions behind the backs of their elders.

His unforced use of symbols (the fish, for example, passed round the table at summer camp) typifies a Malmros film, as does the innate sense of humour that time and again disperses any hint of pedagogy. As they dance in fumbling intimacy to the recorded music of Chris Barber, and stray near the illicit pleasures of sex and smoking, these characters emerge from the chrysalis of childhood into the quirkish individuality of their teens.

Even more committed to the children's cause, **Søren Kragh-Jacobsen** began his career as head of children's programmes at the Danish TV. In 1978 he made his feature debut with *Wanna See My Beautiful Navel? (Vil du se min smukke navle?)*, a lively and relaxed snapshot of youngsters on vacation, discovering more about themselves than the world around them. Kragh-Jacobsen's sense of fun colours every scene, and if his second feature, *Rubber Tarzan (Gummi Tarzan,* 1981) moved down from, as it were, the second stage of puberty to the first, it sparkles with the same inventive wit. The diminutive 'Tarzan' of the title alternately baffles and amuses his elders with his antic behaviour in the suburbs of Copenhagen. The Swedes and the Norwegians have made films about children, too, but invariably their innocence is streaked with darker implications. The Danes perceive the true nature of childhood, a state of being in which anything is possible until it is proved otherwise, and in which fantasy prevails over adult rules and regulations.

Both *Emma's Shadow (Skyggen av Emma,* 1988) and *Shower of Gold (Guldregn,* 1988) reinforce Kragh-Jacobsen's claim to be the foremost Nordic director of films concerning children. In the first, 12-year-old Emma runs away from her upper-class parents during the 1930's and makes friends with a Swedish immigrant who works in the sewers of Copenhagen. In the second, a group of kids discover a box in the woods near their homes. It is stuffed with banknotes, and when the children learn that a post-office has been robbed, they are uncertain what to do. Edited down from its original form as a TV series, *Shower of Gold* proves yet again that Kragh-Jacobsen can coax spontaneous, unaffected performances from his young actors.

A contemporary of Kragh-Jacobsen's, **Morten Arnfred**, has worked in the same idiom but has also ranged beyond childhood experience into the problems of early manhood. *Me and Charly (Mig og Charly,* 1978), which he co-directed with Henning Kristiansen, charts the on-off friendship of two teenage boys, and *Johnny Larsen* (1979) uses one of the same characters (at the age of 18) to focus on the generation gulf as well as the difficulty of finding work and coping with the rigours of conscription during the 1950's. Arnfred extends his wise and sympathetic attention to all three generations in *Johnny Larsen*: to the old grandma whose sagacity often defuses a domestic squabble during the ritual gatherings at Easter and Christmas; to the father, who has always 'doffed his cap' to anyone in authority and who has been a loser all his life; and to Johnny himself, the non-conformist whose shyness with girls and occasional outbursts of wilful temper lead him away from the family hearth. Arnfred has a potent grasp of the rough pleasures of

working life, the food, the drink, the sex, the laughter with comrades. The Army scenes come across with a particular authenticity, perhaps because Arnfred himself had been drafted — and had dared to say 'No'.

Heaven and Hell (Himmel og helvede, 1988) concerns a similar rejection of established values. Maria's parents have immigrated from Poland and want to better themselves according to bourgeois standards. Their bitterness contrasts with the youthful ideals of the late 1960's, the period in which the film is set, and Maria's journey towards self-fulfilment takes her beyond the closet homosexual, Joni, who charms her away from her parents' household. In the words of Ebbe Iversen, 'The film is not a political tract but an intimate study of Maria's soft and gentle insecurity, her struggle to come to terms with her own personality and her growing, painful insight into the mysteries of human nature.'

Arnfred has also directed one of the most unusual of modern Danish films – *Land of Plenty (Der er et yndigt land,* 1983). Despite its modest surface area, Denmark depends upon agricultural produce for much of its indigenous income. Danish bacon, cheese, and butter grace tables throughout the Common Market. The protagonist in *Land of Plenty* strives to run his own farm, but finds himself sinking in a quicksand of debt. His loyal and hard-working wife suffers alongside him, and the mounting pressures on a seemingly perfect marriage make a mockery of the complex, bureaucratic subsidy system that bedevils modern agriculture in Europe. Arnfred's sober direction, and his eye for the flat arable landscapes of Denmark, allied to the heartfelt acting of Ole Ernst and Karen-Lise Mynster, transcend the depressing theme.

Three years younger than Arnfred, **Bille August** has chosen his material with such care, and devoted such attention to the organic growth of each film within himself, that he has risen irresistibly to the top echelon of Nordic film-makers. His training as a cameraman served him well on his first independent feature, *In My Life (Honning måne,* 1978), which had the courage to undermine the conventional optimism enveloping suburban, middle-class marriage. The two 'ordinary' young people who wed in August's film do not perhaps have enormous expectations. Their relationship deteriorates almost subliminally, inch by inch, behind the prim lace curtains of their first mutual home. Compassionate, shrewdly observed, and yielding to no soft centre, *In My Life* marked the arrival of a major new talent in the Danish cinema. Five years elapsed before August could confirm his promise. *Zappa* (1983) punctures the illusions of charmed adolescence as devastatingly as *In My Life* does for marriage. Three boys in the Denmark of 1961 are joined by friendship but also by a need for petty thrills and cruelty towards others who cannot defend themselves. When one of them kills an otherwise innocuous fat boy's budgerigar, he is given a terrible beating. The contrast between the classes exerts a powerful hold over the film, which echoes William Golding's novel, *Lord of the Flies*, in its understanding of the bizarre and often twisted morality of the adolescent mind. August's fascination with the macabre also colours *Twist and Shout (Tro, hab og kærlighed,* 1984)

Bille August's *Twist and Shout* (1984)

which again looks back to the early 1960's when the director himself was growing up to the sound of the Beatles. The film's structure suffers from a certain schematism, and divides the narrative into two parallel stories. This sets up a confrontation between the two extremes in Danish life, from the prim, chic, squeaky-clean world of the bourgeoisie to the sordid back streets where an abortion may take place on a kitchen table. Some of the domestic scenes in *Twist and Shout* are patronising in tone and waxen in formality. It is the one film to date in August's career that shows signs of contrivance.

Buster's World (Busters verden, 1984), originally a TV series directed by August, flows more freely and unpretentiously than *Twist and Shout*. Mads Bugge Andersen gives a performance of irresistible charm as the sky yet precocious little boy whose talent for magic gets him into — and out of — several awkward situations. Buster possesses quite a egotistical streak beneath his chirpy manner, and cannot abide anyone upstaging him, and that includes the young girl pianist for whom he nurses an incipient passion. Yet even when he flouts convention

Buster, one feels, does not comprehend his own motives, selfish though they may be.

Bille August achieved his definitive breakthrough with *Pelle the Conqueror (Pelle erobreren*, 1987), which won a host of awards, both inside Scandinavia and abroad (the Palme d'Or at Cannes, the Oscar for Best Foreign Film in the United States), as well as crowning the acting career of Max von Sydow, who was also nominated for an Academy Award in Hollywood. Throughout its running time of more than 150 minutes, *Pelle* runs the risk of tipping into sentimentality; it is, after all, the story of a small boy arriving with his destitute father in the Denmark of the 1890's. Father and son find work on a large manor, but must endure humiliation and rejection at every step. The core of the film concerns Pelle's relationship with his father and reveals how, in recognising that the old man is a coward, he himself gains a measure of tolerance and a wise perspective on the world. August's epic, photographed in lush, golden tints by the Swedish cameraman, Jörgen Persson (who made his first great impression in *Elvira Madigan*), transcends its Nordic setting and affirms the humanist ideals that

42

underscore similar frescoes of the past such as *The Emigrants* and *1900*. If *Pelle the Conqueror* does fall short of the best that Bille August may be capable of, it is because of its episodic form form, which leads to a certain tedium during the final forty minutes. This in turn stems from the source of the film, Martin Andersen Nexø's suite of four novels which deal, in the words of the author, with 'the human being itself who, naked, endowed solely with health and appetite, reports for duty in life. [The books are] about the broad path on Earth of the labourer on his endless, semi-conscious wandering towards the light.'[25]

August has laboured diligently on a screenplay for a film of Isabel Allende's triumph of magic realism, *The House of the Spirits*, but the financial packaging has not been assembled. Instead, Ingmar Bergman requested him to direct a mini-series (which will also receive cinema release) about the Swedish maestro's parents, entitled *Best Intentions* (*Den goda viljan*, 1991). In many respects a companion piece to *Fanny and Alexander*, this period tapestry explores the different perceptions of love in a formal community. Bergman's screenplay starts in 1909 and ends some ten years later, as the young pastor (Bergman's father) and his wife await the birth of their second child — who would be Ingmar.

Analyst Extraordinary

The work of **Jørgen Leth** defies ready classification. His films, both short and feature-length, are not quite documentaries. Yet rarely do they belong to the realm of fiction. All of them reflect this director's exceptional range of passions — sport, poetry, ballet, anthropology, and above all human behaviour in the everyday, formalistic sense.

Leth is something of a cinematic scientist, analysing the system that governs our responses, whether it be on a racing bike or on a dance floor. These thoughtful essays are leavened with humour and moments of spontaneous joy. As a Dane, Leth reflects many of his country's traditions, but he remains an inveterate voyager to all quarters of the globe, from China to Haiti, from Texas to northern Spain. His films emerge as subjective reactions to such journeys. His people respond to the landscape embracing them, like the farmer in his field or the tennis maestro on his practice court. Leth fails only when his self-consciousness intrudes on dramatic material, as happened in *Haiti Express* (*Udenrigskorrespondenten*, 1983).

Life in Denmark (*Livet i Danmark*, 1971) evokes the tranquil, open tracts and long sea strands, interleaved with tableaux of family groups and farming folk from the countryside that Leth knows so well. The use of still, or rather posed, imagery is a regular feature of Leth's technique. In *Good and Evil* (*Det gode og det onde*, 1975), the tableaux illustrate rubrics such as 'Good Thoughts', 'Bad Thoughts', 'Words', 'Necessary Actions', etc. In *66 Scenes from America* (*66 scener fra Amerika*, 1981), Leth isolates the intrinsic properties of the United States from one side of the continent to the other, with its garish urban architecture and its enormous skies and horizons.

Curiosity provides the energy source for most of Leth's films, and in particular his open-minded documentary, *Notebook from China* (*Notater fra Kina*, 1986), and his mind-stretching, kaleidoscopic *Moments of Play* (1986), which describes children and adults at play in different cultures and countries. The physical mechanics of sport, as well as the commitment involved in its players, fascinate Leth in documentaries like *Chinese Pingpong* (1970), *Pelota* (1984), and *Motion Picture* (1970). Human exertion and physical discipline respond to Leth's scrutiny in the profile of *Peter Martins, Dancer* (*Peter Martins, en danser*, 1978) and the documentary on the legendary choreographer August Bournonville and the Royal Danish Ballet, *Bournonville* (1979).

His studies of professional cycling, however, reach a visionary level that assures Leth a place in the annals of Danish cinema. *Stars and Watercarriers* (*Stjernerne og vandbærerne*, 1973) follows the three-week Tour of Italy, and *The Impossible Hour* (*Den umulige time*, 1975) charts the attempt of Ole Ritter to smash the one-hour professional bike record in the rarefied air of Mexico City. *A Sunday in Hell* (*En forårsdag i Helvede*, 1976) is a pièce de résistance, more than a hundred minutes of finely-calculated suspense that leave the viewer limp from vicarious excitement. Using 27 cameras, Leth attacks the Paris-Roubaix classic from every angle — from pre-dawn preparations to the cooling luxury of post-race showers. Helicopter shots, to a choral accompaniment, trail above the skein of riders. Ominous timpani on the soundtrack signal the arrival of the dreaded country roads with their choking dust and vicious ruts, while police escorts loom through the yellow clouds like Cocteau's guardians of Hell. Unlike many more glamorous sports movies, *A Sunday in Hell* never neglects the minutiae of the business: the massage of spindly legs before the start, the wheels changes in less than ten seconds, the skill of the managers, and the shrewd tactics of the top riders as they let their mates in the peloton do the initial work before surging inexorably to the front.

The Appeal of the Past

Gabriel Axel had to wait until his seventieth year to achieve with a single film the fame that has eluded all Danish directors since Dreyer. *Babette's Feast* (*Babettes gæstebud*, 1987) suffered from a scornful reception at the hands of the Danish critics, but festival screenings resulted in sales to numerous countries, and the winning of a Hollywood Oscar one year later set the crown on a film which throbs with warmth, humour and compassion. Set (apart from some awkward scenes in Paris) in the Jutland farming region that Dreyer consecrated in *The Word*, the film recounts the story of a seemingly destitute Frenchwoman, fleeing from the Paris Commune of 1871, and her triumph in preparing a gourmet dinner for rich and poor alike. Axel's style does not pretend to be imaginative or experimental; his classical narrative dotes on each luscious detail of the feast Babette concocts in the country kitchen, using her winnings in the French lottery to do so.

Stéphane Audran in Gabriel Axel's *Babette's Feast* (1987)

Yet the film discreetly underlines the parallels between Babette's endeavours and those of the artist who yearns to express his utmost. The historical basis of Karen Blixen's story recedes into the background, while the tactile delights of the cuisine bring colour and sensuality to the grim rooms of the vicarage on the windy dunes of Jutland. Stéphane Audran invests Babette's personality with the same resolute humour and dignity as Nina Pens Rode brings to Dreyer's *Gertrud*, escaping the spiritual repression that a male-dominated society, despite all its gallantry, exerts.

Max von Sydow assumed the role of director for the first time at the age of 58, when in *Katinka Ved vejen*, (1988) he brought to the screen a 19th-century novel not altogether removed in spirit from *Babette's Feast*. Herman Bang's work has inspired many Scandinavian directors, among them Dreyer, Stiller, and Cornell. Von Sydow has remarked that 'Bang had a very modern style. His sentences were as short as Hemingway's. He never tells you what his characters think or feel, he just tells you what they *do*, but you understand all the time what they *are* thinking and feeling. This particular little novel was described by Claude Monet as "the first Impressionist piece of literature".'[26] Like Babette and Gertrud, Katinka reacts against her destiny as a woman. When she fells under the spell of the handsome stranger, Huus, she must repress her impulse to abandon her jovial husband, the stationmaster in the small community where they live. Von Sydow's unostentatious direction captures the rhythm of everyday life in the Danish provinces, and the relaxed bonhomie of the people as they sit and smoke their cigars and gossip about their friends and neighbours. Beneath this ordered surface of things, there runs a bright thread of passion that emerges in quick glances, shy gestures, and in moments like the excursion to the local fair, where Huus and Katinka gaze at miniature dioramas of Sorrento and the Bay of Naples, or the Jungfrau in Switzerland, and imagine themselves escaping their frustrating situation.

Danish films frequently sift through the country's past in order to pass comment on national traits. If Katinka reproaches the vacuity of bourgeois life, and Babette expresses antipathy towards the strait-laced prudery of Lutheran existence, then Palle Kjærulff-Schmidt's *Peter von Scholten* (1987) traces with solid if uninspired confidence the career of Denmark's last governor in the Virgin Islands. Von Scholten's determination to emancipate the islands' slaves appears to stem from the tension in his private life, for he maintained a wife and family in Copenhagen and a black mistress in the Caribbean.

Rites of Passage

Astrid Henning-Jensen has continued to fine-tune her cinematic craftsmanship until her late seventies. *Winterborn* (*Vinterbørn*, 1978) has distinct affinities with Bergman's *So Close to Life*. As in the Swedish film, the acting assumes more importance than any other aspect of the drama. True, the situation resembles *Grand Hotel*, with a variety of human types locked together in Copenhagen's National Hospital, united by the single miracle of child-birth. Each personality flowers, however, in a different, more mysterious manner; one is a diabetic, another a working-class mother who agrees to sterilisation for her husband's sake, and yet another, a Turkish woman, understands scarcely a word of Danish. Over them all, as in *So Close to Life*, looms the cool, sometimes insensitive figure of the doctor, who admits to a terrifying ignorance in the face of Nature's whims. Sometimes a baby just plops out merrily into the world; on other occasions the process becomes a nightmare. Henning-Jensen orchestrates these facts and fantasies with a compassionate hand and communicates both the fear and ecstasy of parturition, and shows how it brings people together, however briefly, in a mood of awe and expectation.

The Moment (*Øjeblikket*, 1980) breathes with the tolerance, humour and optimism acquired by Astrid Henning-Jensen through some forty years of documentary and feature production. The subject – a young married woman dying of cancer – is bleak. But without in the least trivialising the prospect of death, this film sings of hope. Line's discovery that she has been stricken by this mortal enemy sparks a new energy in her hitherto bland existence. Her husband begins to appreciate her as never before, even if he turns for physical consolation to a mutual friend, Anne. Infidelity shrinks in this context to a mere natural reflex, underlining Henning-Jensen's belief that human life is a ceaseless process of decline and renewal. Line grows philosophical as her condition worsens, and she emerges from the shadow of her despair. She revels in her small children and their promise for the future, in the verdant, burgeoning landscape of Denmark in spring and summer.

In her swansong, *Early Spring* (*Barndommens gade*, 1986), Astrid Henning-Jensen summons up the memory of her own youth after the First World War, in a gentle adaptation of Tove Ditlevsen's novel. The warmth of her vision and the sensitivity of her direction outweigh the sentimentality of the picture.

Such rites of passage fascinate many Danish film-makers. Leven and Sven Grønlykke, for example, sing a poignant, vibrant melody over the fate of an 18-year-old boy in rural Denmark in their 1969 release, *The Ballad of Carl-Henning* (*Balladen om Carl-Henning*). He perishes at the hands of forces he cannot comprehend, and his naïveté is echoed to some degree in *Re: Lone* (*Angående Lone, 1970*), directed by Franz Ernst. Only the style is different – stark and quasi-documentary by comparison with the soaring impressionism of *The Ballad of Carl-Henning*. Lone is a teenager whose family background has distintegrated. Like the doomed heroine of Agnès Varda's *Sans toit ni loi*, she resorts to petty theft to survive. The impact of *Re: Lone* stems in large measure from the realistic description of contemporary Copenhagen, whose inhabitants want nothing to do with a truculent rebel. Ernst's film belongs with Finland's *Little Red Riding-Hood* and Sweden's *Love Me!* as a corrosive critique of the complacency so endemic to Nordic society.

The interplay between film and literature functions at a profound level in the first two films in **Henrik Stangerup's** brief career behind the camera. A prize-winning novelist and *enfant ferrible*, Stangerup has spent much of his life in France and does not shirk from criticising his home country's moeurs. He made his debut in 1970 with *Give God a Chance on Sunday (Giv Gud en chanse om Søndagen)*, which examines the relevance of a young person's role in modern Denmark. Young Niels discovers that he needs to be much tougher and more zealous than he is capable of being. If at the end, as he blunders down a city street towards the camera, Niels is on the verge of abandoning his vocation, then it is more a failure of belief than a failure of office.

Stangerup's discreet and sensible style avoids the ethereal formalism of Bresson and the wider metaphysical anguish of Bergman (whose *Winter Light* has a similar purpose and starts, like the Danish picture, with a prolonged church service). A few unhurried shots conjure up the bucolic atmosphere — straw burning in the fields, a plough turning over fresh earth, a breakfast in the garden.

The director's second film, *Dangerous Kisses (Farlige kys, 1973)*, also concerns inadequacy. Birte kills her husband by accident during a domestic quarrel. Traumatised, she is sent by the tribunal to a psychiatric clinic, and there strikes up a sort of friendship with one of the doctors, Torben. But even he cannot prevent Birte's inexorable drift, Lilith-like, into madness, with darkness closing around her head in the final shot. Stangerup's characters are intelligent, easily recognisable victims of modern-day pressures. *Dangerous Kisses* utters a cry of despair, the cry of everyone who has stretched out a hand to a drowning man and seen him disappear beneath the waves. What place, asks Stangerup, remains for the individual who dares to differ from the social norm, whether it be a wife driven to the edge of insanity or a doctor at odds with his committee-room colleagues?

Stangerup suffered a monumental failure when he made a screen version of the Danish theatre classic *Erasmus Montanus* by Ludvig Holberg, and has since concentrated on novels — with conspicuous success. A contemporary of his, **Christian Braad Thomsen**, has also remained outside the main stream of Danish cinema, writing about films, importing art movies to Denmark, and every few years directing a personal, rough-edged film of his own. A disciple of Godard and Fassbinder, Braad Thomsen focuses on emotional commitment in modern life, and his first film, *Dear Irene (Kære Irene, 1970)* encapsulates his quirkish, truculent, and ultimately romantic vision of things. *Dear Irene* allows its triangle drama to unfold in a rambling, Cassavetes-like manner, while its characters engage in debates that catch the free-spirited fervour of '68. *Children of Pain (Smertens børn, 1978)* aches with feeling, and recalls Chris Marker in his less polemic moments. Taking the form of a children's fairy-tale, Braad Thomsen interviews a number of adults and persuades them to summon up memories of early youth. For some, the conversation becomes an evocation of a vanished state of grace; for most, however, childhood reverberated with panic and fear, as parents elevated peccadillos into moral sins. Braad Thomsen has explored this theme of childhood

in other films, notably *Knife in the Heart (Kniven i hjertet, 1981)*.

Other Danish films contend that life contains other crucial phases — for example, the thirties. Henning Kristiansen's *Per* (1975) is a polished thriller, sustained more by its players than by its plot — which creaks badly. But Ole Ernst, as the coarse, lovable Per, whose lack of funds drives him into crime, and Agneta Ekmanner, as the elegant bourgeoise who responds to his charm, both act with wit and intelligence. At the heart of the film lies a series of long scenes at a cottage hideaway across the water in Sweden. The social divisions between the lovers prove too deep to negotiate, and they part in the cold aftermath of a long night's argument.

Esben Hoilund Carlsen's *Stepping Out (Slingrevalsen, 1981)* has been compared to Neil Simon's theatre work, concealing a kernel of melancholy behind its outer shell of bonhomie and sexual liberation. Various couples meet and interact; all are in their dangerous thirties, trying to cope with a new morality and with the failure of earlier relationships. Gazing back at youth from an even later vantage point, Kaspar Rostrup's *Waltzing Regitze (Dansen med Regitze, 1989)* studies the development of an ordinary, affectionate marriage that starts during the German occupation of Denmark. Unpretentious, but also sentimental, *Waltzing Regitze* earned Denmark a third successive nomination for the Best Foreign Film Oscar in Hollywood.

The Idiosyncratic Eye

When Danish film directors take risks, they do so with more verve and courage than their Nordic neighbours. Apart from Astrid Henning-Jensen, women film-makers have enjoyed some triumphant moments in the last fifteen years. *Take It Like a Man, Madame (Tag det som en mand, frue, 1975)* lashes out with irresistible humour at the stereotypical image of women in society, and owes its champagne fizz to the collective team known as the 'Red Sisters': Mette Knudsen, Li Vestrup, and Elisabeth Rygard. More recently, Helle Ryslinge's *Cœurs flambés (Flamberede hjerter, 1986)* paints a vivid, coarse-grained portrait of an extrovert young woman who assimilates one disappointment and rejection after another and still comes up smiling. 'I'm a great believer in humour and irony,' says Helle Ryslinge, 'the blacker and drier, the better. With the help of humour a person can, if not directly prevent sorrow, make it easier to deal with that sorrow. Humour, by giving us another perspective, has the potential to transform sorrow, perhaps make it funny, or even put it into the realm of the festive.'[27] Few scenes in modern Nordic film are so hilarious as the dinner scene when Kirsten Lehfeldt deliberately ruins a boyfriend's attempt to impress his foreign business guest.

Ryslinge followed up this vitriolic debut with a satirical portrait of a young man — the obverse of the Lehfeldt character in *Cœurs Flambés*. In *Syrup (Sirip, 1990)*, Lasse tries to take the short cut to success as a painter. For quite

Erik Clausen's *The Dark Side of the Moon* (1986)

a while he prevails, but when his lack of genuine talent emerges, the director comes down hard on him. *Syrup* is a caustic, rough-edged film that manages to transform everyday Copenhagen into a wild, extravagant location.

Individualists have always been welcome in the Danish studios. Jens Ravn, for example, brings a chilling mood to his science-fiction film, *The Man Who Thought Things (Manden der tænkte ting,* 1969), which he directed from a script by himself and Henrik Stangerup. A demonic surgeon succeeds in creating a kind of phantom human being, a 'double' for another surgeon, who is even more intelligent than the 'original'. The glaring whites and gleaming blacks of the film endow it with the aspect of a nightmare.

As late as 1984, **Lars von Trier** also resorted to monochrome, in *The Element of Crime (Forbrydelsens element)*, 'rinsing' his images in a urine-yellow light. This harsh, sexual fantasy charts a murder investigation in the Stygian Europe of some distant future. The narrative itself is hopelessly convoluted; the dialogue verges on the risible. But von Trier's film, however repellent, emits a siren call as persuasive as Godard's *Alphaville*. The dangers of such a style becomes apparent in the director's second film, *Epidemic* (1987), which plunges into self-parody.

Working with a larger budget in *Europa* (1991), von Trier again caught international attention at the Cannes Festival, winning two prizes in the process. As in *The Element of Crime*, the accent is on the *look* and *sound* of the film rather than its emotional heart. Shot in 'scope, *Europa* sucks us back into the gritty aftermath of the Second World War in Germany, where Nazi factions continue to operate in clandestine mode. Von Trier deploys all manner of technical tricks to hold the spectator's interest (not least the mesmeric voice of Max von Sydow, offscreen, as he dictates the destiny of the young hero, played by Jean-Marc Barr). The predominately black-and-white imagery recalls the German cinema of the 1950's, and evokes the sense of postwar futility most effectively.

Erik Clausen made his name by travelling through Denmark as an entertainer, and was almost forty by the time he directed his first feature film. *The Casablanca Circus* (1981) draws on some of his picaresque experiences, as does *Rocking Silver* (1983). *Felix* (1982) trembles with unconcealed compassion for an elderly lady and the cat she adores. But *The Dark Side of the Moon (Manden i månen,* 1986) reveals an altogether more sombre aspect of Clausen's personality. Unredeemed by laughter, the film follows the melancholy destiny of a middle-aged man emerging from prison, after serving a sentence for murdering his wife in a fit of anger. Clausen deliberately makes it hard for his audience to identify with this social leper, while at the same time he pricks our conscience for refusing to fathom the minds of our criminals. Peter Thiel as John lurches like a zombie through the inimicable streets and alleys of Copenhagen, finding work in a grim restaurant kitchen that is lit and shot by Clausen and his camera crew in extraordinary tones. Not even Bergman has created such a convincing sense of Hell on Earth.

Lone Scherfig made a spectacular start to her career with *The Birthday Trip (Kajs fødselsdag,* 1990), which won the

47

top prize at the Festival du Cinéma Nordique in France. In describing an excursion to Poland by a group of young Danish men, Scherfig reveals a sensitive, tolerant eye. 'The film is about our fundamental longing for someone with whom we can share our live and experiences, whether this someone be friend or lover,' she says. Another recent debut of note is Eddie Thomas Petersen's *Spring Tide (Springflod*, 1990), charting the relationship between two teenagers from very different backgrounds. Their love builds against a rural setting (Jutland) and the tensions that come from society's wary attitude to foreigners and refugees.

The career of **Jon Bang Carlsen** continues to go up and down like a roller-coaster. His award-winning short documentaries such as *Hotel of the Stars* (1981) rank with the best of Nordic films in this genre. *Hamlet − Ophelia Comes to Town (Ofelia kommer til byen,* 1985) sketches an intriguing picture of life in an isolated part of western Denmark, but *Time Out* (1988) fails altogether to penetrate the atmosphere of another remote community, in New Mexico, where a young Danish lad is seeking his long-lost father. Jon Bang Carlsen's obsession with the effects of solitude bear richest fruit in *Baby Doll* (1988), which presents a compelling study of spiritual tension. A young mother revisits a farm where she spent much of her childhood, and tries to recapture the mood and warmth of her memories. If not typical of the Danish cinema, *Baby Doll* belongs to a long line of Nordic films that have explored the fine line between past and present, memory and oblivion, madness and sanity, fantasy and reality.

1 Maurice Drouzy, in *Le Cinéma danois* (Paris, Editions du Centre Pompidou, 1979)
2 Ron Mottram, *The Danish Cinema Before Dreyer* (Metuchen, New Jersey, Scarecrow Press, 1988)
3 Maurice Drouzy, *op. cit.*
4 Ron Mottram, *op. cit.*
5 Ebbe Neergaard, quoted by Ron Mottram, *op. cit.*
7 Id., *ibid.*
8 Ib Monty, in *The Macmillan Dictionary of Films and Filmmakers, Volume 2: Directors;* edited by Christopher Lyon (London, Macmillan, 1984)
9 John Gillett, in programme brochure for the National Film Theatre (London, January 1988)
10 Georges Sadoul, *Histoire du cinéma* (Paris, Flammarion, 1949)
11 John Gillett, *The Night of Revenge*, in the programme of the National Film Theatre (London, 1988)
12 Marguerite Engberg, quoted by Ron Mottram, *op. cit.*
13 Henri Langlois, quoted in the *Cahier no. 9* of the festival of La Rochelle 1988
14 John Gillett, in programme brochure for the National Film Theatre (London, January 1988)
15 Carl Th. Dreyer, interview in *Cahiers du cinéma* (Paris, no. 170, September, 1965)
16 Armond White, quoted by Edvin Kau in *Dreyers Filmkunst* (Copenhagen, Akademisk Forlag, 1989)
17 Carl Th. Dreyer, interview, *op. cit.*
18 André Bazin, in *Le Cinéma danois, op. cit.*
19 Miles Coiner, *Dramaturgy and Theme: A Comparison of* Day of Wrath *and* Anne Pedersdotter (Salisbury, Maryland, *Film Literature Quarterly*. Vol. 17, no. 2, 1989)
20 Edvin Kau, *Dreyers Filmkunst* (Copenhagen, Akademisk Forlag, 1989)
21 Carl Th. Dreyer, interview, *op. cit.*
22 Id., *ibid.*
23 Ib Monty in *Factsheet Denmark/Danish Film* (published by the Danish Ministry of Foreign Affairs)
24 Ib Monty in *The Macmillan Dictionary of Films and Filmmakers, op. cit.*
25 Martin Anderson Nexø, quoted in the pressbook for *Pelle the Conqueror* (Copenhagen, Per Holst Filmproduktion)
26 Quoted by Peter Cowie, in *Max von Sydow* (Stockholm, Swedish Film Institute, 1989)
27 Helle Ryslinge, quoted in *Danish Films 1986/87* (Copenhagen, Danish Film Institute, 1986)

Carl Th. Dreyer (centre) surrounded by his team of actors and technicians for *The Passion of Joan of Arc* (1928). Maurice Schutz is seated, with Rudolph Maté, cameraman, standing behind him; while Antonin Artaud is second from the left and Michel Simon at the extreme right of the picture

Erkki Karu's *The Village Shoemakers* (1923)

Finland

When the itinerant Lumière film show presented fifteen short films in Helsinki on June 28, 1896, Finns were already exposed to three major cultural currents: from Russia, because the country belonged to the Tsarist Empire; from Sweden, which had controlled the country for several centuries before losing it to Moscow in 1809; and from the gathering nationalist movement in Finland itself, symbolised by the literary works of Aleksis Kivi and J.L. Runeberg.

Not surprisingly, given this energetic cultural climate, Finnish cinema soon took root. By December 1904, the first three films shot in Finland were screened: *The Students of Nikolai Street's School during the Recreation, Life Among the Esplanades,* and *Students of the Finnish Normal School.* The pioneer personality, K.E. Ståhlberg, founded the Apollo Studio, and concentrated on newsreels and bucolic films. By 1907, Apollo had produced the first Finnish dramatic film, *The Moonshiners (Salaviinanpolttajat).* Four years later, the same company released *Sylvi,* which has some similarities with Sjöström's *Ingeborg Holm* (1913) in Sweden in its attack on the injustices of society. But in 1912, Apollo closed its doors. Other studios sprang up to take its place: Finlandia Film, Lyrra Filmi, and the Pohjoismainen Biografi Komppania.

By 1917, Finland's fledgling cinema had produced some 350 films, of which 28 were full-length. On paper, they should have scored the same impact as Sweden's output across the Gulf of Bothnia. But Finland lacked the equal of Charles Magnusson as a producer and of Victor Sjöström and Mauritz Stiller as directors. Nor did the momentous events of 1917-18, when Finland seized her independence in the wake of the Bolshevik Revolution, and then plunged into a civil war of her own, yield any great works. Instead, the cinema concentrated happily on comedies and rural melodramas. Some of the most talented figures of the period, such as Mauritz Stiller and Gustaf Molander, abandoned the country of their birth to move to Sweden.

Not that the quality of film-making in Finland lacked distinction. The Lumière influence proved long-lasting. Oscar Lindelöf, one of the Apollo cameramen, was as adventurous as Julius Jaenzon, as his extant images of swimming, skating, and crowds in Helsinki clearly testify. Sakari Pälsi took his camera to the remote stretches of Siberia and the Bering Straits, and initiated a genre that still bears fruit today in the work of Markku Lehmuskallio and Rauni Mollberg.

Like Svensk Filmindustri in Sweden, the company that would exert the dominant power over its national cinema in the decades to come was founded in 1919, and called Suomi-Filmi. One of the founders was Teuvo Puro (co-director of *The Moonshiners*); another was **Erkki Karu**, destined to become the first portal personality in Finnish film. Equally adept at both business and film directing, he produced films that reflected the rollicking humour associated with 19th-century Finnish country life. Aleksis Kivi had resorted to humour as a salve for his intense literary commitment (which drove him insane, and to an early grave at the age of just 38). His books were enormously popular in Finland, and Karu's first version of *The Village Shoemakers (Nummisuutarit,* 1923) captures the physical exuberance and motley characters of Kivi's world. Esko (played by Axel Slangus, who would appear at the age of seventy in Bergman's *The Virgin Spring*) is a simpleton bachelor who never manages to find the bride of his dreams. Like the peasants in Kivi's great novel, *Seven Brothers,* Esko resorts to violence at the drop of a hat, and in one hilarious sequence in the film he wrestles with a young fir-tree after failing to locate an opponent of flesh and blood in the local forest. Erkki Karu turned his satirical eye on the prohibition laws then prevalent in Finland, showing how liquour could overcome pain in *When Father Has Toothache (Kun isällä on hammasärky,* 1923). In the same busy year, this irrepressible man shot *The Logroller's Bride (Koskenlaskijan morsian),* using six cameras for a sequence describing the boiling rapids that the logrollers must negotiate. This audacious approach to film-making contrasts with the pedestrian narrative of a rural melodrama like *The Northerners (Pohjalaisia,* 1925), directed by Jalmari Lahdensuo.

Finnish films of the silent period rarely travelled beyond the country's borders. During the early years of independence from the Soviet Union, the Finns developed a cautious, pragmatic approach to foreign affairs. Their security depended upon a harmonious relationship with the U.S.S.R. on the one side and their Nordic neighbours on the other. The cinema, even without prompting from the censor's office, tended to avoid subjects touching on international affairs. The topographical disposition of the population placed a further limitation on Finnish film-makers. Most Finns lived in the countryside; to have fed them social propaganda would have been to court financial disaster at a time when films could hardly expect support from official bodies. As late as the 1950's, film remained the ugly duckling of the arts in Finland. Most screenplays were based on literary originals, while the acting relied heavily on stage technique.

Karu continued to dominate the Finnish cinema as it approached the 1930's. One of his last silent productions, *Our Boys (Meidän poikamme,* 1929) shows his professional verve at its best. A military comedy, *Our Boys* is the first in a number of warm and observant films about army life that have emerged from Finnish studios. The arrival of the talkies was delayed by the effects of the worldwide stockmarket crash, and the career of Erkki Karu came to a swift and melancholy end. He quarrelled with his colleagues at Suomi-Filmi and, in late 1933, established a rival concern, Suomen Filmiteollisuus. But he made only three more pictures, including a pale sequel to *Our Boys,* before dying in 1935 at the age of just 48.

Two powerful figures stepped into the breach left by Karu's demise. Neither possessed the inventive gifts of this great pioneer, but each in his way brought an energy and a productivity to the Finnish cinema that would sustain its independence for the next twenty-five years. It can be argued that both men, **Risto Orko** and **T.J. Särkkä**, were more influential as producers than as directors. Orko had succeeded Erkki Karu as head of production at Suomi-Filmi, and Särkkä took over Suomen Filmiteollisuus and soon built it into the most powerful film company in the land. Orko and Särkkä quickly perceived the public's desire for fast-moving, amusing, and patriotic films. *The Steward of Siltala (Siltalan pehtoori*, directed by Orko in 1934) became the first Finnish film to attract more than one million spectators – remarkable in a country that had at that time only some 4.5 million inhabitants. Its appeal lay in its dashing narrative, its romantic charm, and its country-house setting. Finnish audiences revelled in the red-blooded story of an affair between the self-assured, arrogant woman who owns the estate of Siltala, and her 'steward' who turns out to be a man of means and fine pedigree. *The Steward of Siltala* may be no superior to the American soap-opera of today, but in the mid-1930's it enthused the Finns with its images of a lifestyle beyond the ken of most of them, and its comforting message that pretensions and appearances were not to be trusted.

Orko felt at home among officers and gentlemen, and his two most impressive films both convey the excitement and intrigue of the military life and the espionage that so often sustains it. *The Infantryman's Bride (Jääkärin morsian*, 1938) charts the development of a conspiracy in Latvia, with Finnish soldiers returning from Germany in 1916, where they had been fighting for the Kaiser. *The Activists (Aktivistit*, 1939) betrays Orko's right-wing views, as it celebrates the endeavours of the young bourgeois 'activists' who seek to weaken the Russian hold on Finland in the early years of the 20th century, and who became the 'Whites', or rightists, who would win the bloody civil war that divided Finland after the Bolshevik Revolution. *The Activists* took Finnish cinemas by storm when it was released in April 1939, while relations with the Soviet Union were deteriorating dramatically. Orko's identification of the 'Red menace' matched the mood of the hour, and not surprisingly the film was banned after the Continuation War with the U.S.S.R. in 1944. Political censorship has hampered the Finnish cinema much more than any restrictions on sex or violence.

Särkkä shared with Orko an affection for big party scenes, opulent décor, and the tapping of a profound national pride that courses more strongly through the Finland of the past seventy years than it does in any other Nordic country. Särkkä's *The February Manifesto (Helmikuun manifesti*, 1939) was premiered just two months before Orko's *The Activists*, and struck a similar chord. When Tsar Nicholas II insulted the Finns, reminding them of their minor status as a mere Grand Duchy within the Russian Empire, half-a-million Finns signed a petition, the 'February Manifesto' in February 1899, and 15,000 more refused to serve in the Russian army. A general strike lengthened the protest, and the Cossacks were despatched to Helsinki to quell this mutinous behaviour. Särkkä's flamboyant, melodramatic film suffered the same fate as *The Activists* and could not be screened publicly after the war.

The links with imperial Russia have fascinated Finnish audiences throughout the history of the cinema (as late as 1982 *Flame Top* revived the theme). The allure of life in St. Petersburg, symbolised in the career of Field-Marshal Mannerheim, who holds in Finnish history a place similar to that of De Gaulle in France or Churchill in Britain. Mannerheim's dignity and sophistication, beyond the reach of ordinary Finns, have always been regarded in an ambivalent light. On the positive side, he withdrew from public life when he found his government developing close ties with Nazi Germany. Recalled in the twilight of his career, to serve as President in 1944, Mannerheim assuaged some of the bitterness that Finns held against him because of his role as leader of the 'Whites' in the civil war of 1918. Even a frivolous confection like Särkkä's *The Vagabond's Waltz (Kulkurin valssi*, 1941) begins in the exotic whirl of St. Petersburg, with the Clark Gable of Finnish cinema, Tauno Palo, playing a baron forced to flee from Russia after winning a duel, and then taking refuge in a gypsy camp. But however entertaining, such a film pales beside the most unusual and haunting work of the period – **Nyrki Tapiovaara's** *Stolen Death (Varastettu kuolema*, 1938). Closely resembling *The Activists* in subject matter, *Stolen Death* refuses to compromise its approach to one of the most nerve-wracking spells in modern Finnish history. In a sombre, almost sinister Helsinki, passionate young people take enormous risks to undermine the Russian hold over Finland at the dawn of the 20th century. Vigilantes prowl the empty streets, false passports and subversive leaflets are concocted in cluttered basements rooms, and stolen guns are smuggled through the streets in a coffin. Tapiovaara relieves the tension of these circumstances with an erotic atmosphere rare in Nordic cinema of the late 1930's. Tuulikki Paananen as the coquettish Manja flits dangerously from one side to the other, from the activist Robert Hedman to the villainous Claesson who wants to betray the Finnish cause.

Tapiovaara by no means scorned the melodrama so endemic to Finnish cinema of the period. But he brought to all his work an idiosyncratic, quirkish eye, a tongue-in-cheek wit, and a disrespect for orthodox narrative that rendered him the Godard or Makavejev of his day. In a tragically brief career he completed just four features; a fifth, *The Way of a Man (Miehen tie)* was edited posthumously and appeared in September, 1940, a few months after Tapiovaara himself had vanished, presumed dead, while on patrol during the Winter War with the Soviet Union. His film-making retains an innocence and a zest unique in the annals of the Finnish cinema. As a controversial young critic, he commented on films for Finnish radio, and also in the columns of *Kirjallisuuslehti*. 'I believe in the vitality of film,' he wrote in 1936. 'I believe that it is only waiting for young people, free from the chains of money and with no instructions to smear love on every reel, simply to speak the truth, to show the world as they see it. That will be beautiful.'

He boldly turned his hand to every genre available. *Juha* (1937) proved a sparkling début. Based on the same novel that had inspired Stiller's *Johan* in 1919, *Juha* deglamorises the Nordic notion of the Dark Stranger who comes to rescue the long-suffering Wife from her domestic servitude. Walle

Tauno Palo in *The Vagabond's Waltz*, directed by T.J. Särkkä in 1941

Saikko as Vallavan, the Stranger, may be good-looking in an Olivier-like way, but his cynicism and complacency make him an unpleasant hero. Juha himself (Hannes Närhi) does not attract much sympathy either; he is the typical Finnish smallholder, suspicious of change and material progress, and dominated by his mother (a theme that colours one of the most enduring series in Finnish cinema – the *Niskavuori* saga). As in *Stolen Death*, Tapiovaara flouts the conventional rules of film-making, using slow-motion without warning, and cutting against the natural beat of the action. He does so again in *Two Henpecked Husbands (Kaksi Vihtoria*, 1939), a drawing-room comedy about a middle-aged man who takes advantage of his domineering wife's absence on business to enjoy himself. The material could not be thinner, but the brio with which Tapiovaara presents this collision between youth and age, liberty and repression, transcends its limitations. Swedish audiences adored the boulevard farce during the 1930's, and

Tapiovaara in Finland demonstrated that such a genre could still breathe fire.

The Way of a Man, completed after Tapiovaara's death by Erik Blomberg and Hugo Hytönen, turns to another favourite genre, the pastoral drama fuelled by class conflicts. Until the 1960's, the Finnish loyalty to the countryside and to everything it entailed (including a diet all too rich in milk and red meat) was unshakable. A film set amid the rolling fields of Häme province (home of Aleksis Kivi) would always attract more spectators than a more realistic drama unfolding in the streets of Helsinki, Turku, or Tempere. Tapiovaara knew how to exploit this obligatory environment. The romantic ecstasy experienced by the unfortunate farmer, Paavo, assumes a subversive role in opposition to the ruthless old Jaskari who tries to ruin his son-in-law. The music, the daisies everywhere in full flower, and the play of sunlight, are all elements in this rhapsody. Tapiovaara and Blomberg between them evoke the rotation of farming life and the turn of the seasons. A solitary ploughman and his horse move through the morning mist. Haycocks stand like soldiers in the fields at dawn. A montage of shots reveals the land in the grip of winter snow. . . .

Tapiovaara's legacy continues to grow because he refused to succumb to the dictates of his time. He has much in common with Jean Renoir – the pantheistic outlook on life, the untidy, instinctive technique, the distrust of crassness and pretension, the belief that chance (however melodramatic) interferes in human destiny more than moralists might ever guess. So it was with his own death in early 1940. Had he lived, he would still be only just over 80 years of age, and might have transformed the face of Finnish cinema. More than any director before or after, Tapiovaara had the latent genius to become a figure as formidable as Sjöberg or even Bergman.

The Bucolic Idiom

Other directors took their countryside stories more seriously than Tapiovaara, and to them and their audiences the worsening relations with the Soviet Union, and the Finnish government's marriage of convenience with Hitler's Germany, seemed remote. Teuvo Tulio became the third director (after Stiller and Molander) to tackle Johannes Linnankoski's novel, *The Song of the Scarlet Flower (Laula tulipunaisesta*, 1938). Tulio concentrates on the log-floaters's unerring skill in negotiating the boiling waters of the northern rivers, leaping from log to log as expertly as he flits from mistress to mistress. But as so often in Finnish cinema of this period, the acting weighs down the action, and the technical quality of the film betrays the lack of investment from which the local studios suffered. With no ready export market to hand, Finnish producers focused on a domestic public more eager to identify with favourite

Stolen Death (1938) by Nyrki Tapiovaara

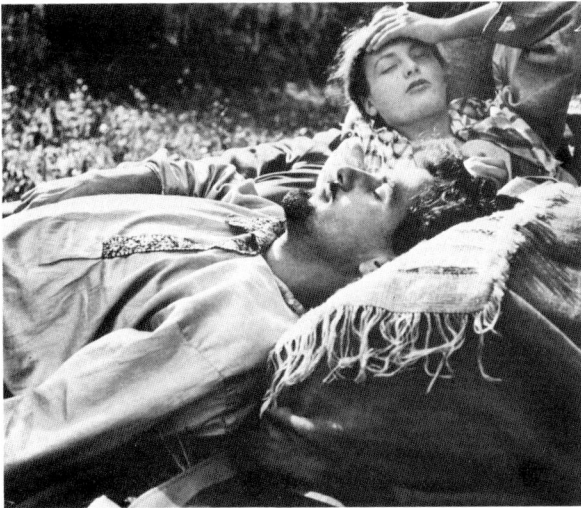

Juha (1937) by Nyrki Tapiovaara

People in the Summer Night (1948) by Valentin Vaala

characters than to compare Finnish films with those from Hollywood.

Valentin Vaala emerged during the 1930's as the most talented of the new generation apart from Tapiovaara. He too exploited the bucolic genre. In *Hulda from Juurakko (Juurakon Hulda*, 1937) he adapted the play by Hella Wuolijuoki about a girl from the countryside who makes an hilarious impact on Finnish bourgeois society. This play also inspired the Hollywood production, *The Farmer's Daughter*. The following year, Vaala turned to Wuolijoki again, with *The Women of Niskavuoren (Niskavuoren naiset)*, and thus launched one of the Finnish audience's most beloved series. Beneath the soap-opera histrionics there runs a powerful social critique. Wuolijoki, like her close friend Bertolt Brecht, saw the rigid class barriers that governed Finnish life in the prewar period, and her *Niskavuori* saga revolves around the hard-working yet avaricious Heta, who marries beneath herself in the social scale, and spends her life seeking revenge on relatives and neighbours alike. Like Capra and Clair, who he admired, Valentin Vaala's work lacked relevance for postwar Finnish cinema audiences, although he would return to the *Hulda* theme in *Come Back Gabriel (Gabriel, tule takaisin*, 1951), showing how the suave, urban ladykiller (Tarmo Manni) could be thoroughly out-manoeuvred by the apparently slow-witted rural citizens.

The quintessentially Finnish novels of Aleksis Kivi (*Seven Brothers, The Village Shoemakers*) and his more introspective 20th-century counterpart, F.E. Sillanpää (*Silja, People in the Summer Night*) provided a rich vein of rustic material for the film-makers to mine over decades. Tapiovaara adapted the Sillanpää novel, *The Way of a Man*, and Valentin Vaala turned to *People in the Summer Night (Ihmiset suviyössä*, 1948). Teuvo Tulio made the first version of the same author's *Silja — Fallen Asleep when Young (Nuorena nukkunit)* in 1937, and Jack Witikka the second in 1956.

Sillanpää, who won the Nobel Prize for Literature, abhorred the coarse-grained humour of Kivi; he weaved a delicate mood of sensuality and natural processes. The mysterious beauty of Finland's myriad lakes, fringed with low-lying clusters of birch and pine, casts its spell over Sillanpää's prose. Although in his old age he would become irascible and disenchanted (see Matti Kassila's 1988 release, *The Glory and Misery of Human Life*), Sillanpää never lost his pantheistic vision of life on earth. In *People in the Summer Night*, he writes: 'Of what account were one generation and its descendants? Innumerable ones have sprung up and died away. From here I can see tilled fields and farmhouses; I can see forests melting into the morning haze on the horizon; I can see an intricate pattern of lakes and streams with ridges in between, all created together. Mother Earth, whose surface a man has cleared with his axe, then furrowed with his plough, and at last sown with seed, before gathering the harvest and then dying. So what am I worried about?'

Like Kivi, Sillanpää had a life full of emotional suffering. The son of a farmer, he thought of becoming a doctor, but he decided to pursue his literary bent. In spite of his success as a writer, he harboured a marked inferiority complex, and when Viktor Sundvall in *Harvest Month* begs for a swig of the bottle, there is a distinct suggestion that the writer is portraying his own addiction. Sallanpää's marriage, to a country girl from his own area (near Tampere), was happy but she died without warning and Sillanpää never quite recovered from the loss. His best novels are coloured by a weariness, a resignation in the face of an inexorable metabolism. The painter (called 'the artists') in *People in the Summer Night* reflects and wallows contentedly in a wave of melancholy: 'Is it possible that anyone is satisfied with his own youth? Any more than with the rest of his life? The pain of knowledge lies in the awareness of one's own imperfection.'

Valentin Vaala's version of this novel adhered to Sillanpää's notion of country life as a constant flow of characters coming together, drifting apart, against an immutable round of dawn, day, dusk, spring, summer, autumn, winter. . . . Even a murder can be assimilated by this immutable rhythm of life: the death of the drunken Mettälä is cancelled out by the birth of Hilja's baby. The same local doctor inspects the deceased man's corpse and welcomes the new-born infant. The next morning heralds a fresh working week, with the haymaking to be done.

Sillanpää admitted to being sentimental, a trait that sets him apart from superficially similar writers like Emile Zola or Thomas Hardy. Tulio's version of *Silja* traces the unfortunate path of a country girl who loses both parents in childhood, and earns her keep as a farm labourer while the civil war of 1918 rages around her. Silja, like the flowers and tall grasses around her, springs from nature and her premature death belongs to an inevitable cycle. *Silja — Fallen Asleep When Young* was produced by a new company in the Finnish firmament, Adams Filmi, which would also develop into a major exhibition chain.

Escapism and the Aftermath of War

Swedish cinema of the 1940's reflects the country's guilty conscience about her neutrality in the Second World War. Norway, Denmark, and Iceland all learned to live, at different stages, with occupation by one side or the other. Finland's situation, however, was the most unnerving. After the bruising clash with Soviet forces in the winter of 1939-40, she had to recognise two facts of life. First, the war with the Soviet Union would escalate, and second, an alliance with Nazi Germany was obligatory. The terrible irony was that while Finns were being slaughtered in the tens of thousands on the Karelian front with Russia, the Nazi forces had percolated north through Finland. Once the Russians had repulsed Hitler's attempt to seize Moscow, they could turn their firepower on the Finns, and by 1944 the situation was grave. Viipuri, capital of Karelia, fell to Soviet tanks; Finland's President Ryti resigned in confusion as the country rejected its ties with Berlin; and the supreme commander of the army, Marshal Mannerheim, assumed the role of President in order to sue for peace with the Soviet Union.

Finland reeled in the wake of a traumatic defeat. She had not been overwhelmed by the Russians, but her losses ran to around 100,000 men, while another 400,000 refugees from Karelia had to be assimilated. There were severe reparations to be paid to the Soviet Union and, later, war debts to the United States. Scarcely a family in the land remained untouched by the pain and the humiliation.

During the war years, Finnish film production maintained a remarkable level of output — 113 features released between 1940 and 1945 inclusive. With rare exceptions (like Risto Orko's documentary on Helsinki under bombardment [*Our Struggle*, 1940]), audiences lapped up a steady diet of comedies, melodramatic romances, and thrillers. No major director tackled the fundamental issues of the war. As with the U.S. and the Vietnam War much later, the Finns would as a result of turning a blind eye to their struggle spend literally decades in examining the rights and wrongs of the period. It took a full ten years before Finnish producers dared to cope with the burden of suffering that weighed on almost every Finn in the Second World War. Under the circumspect guidance of President J.K. Paasikivi, Finland began to recover her self-respect, even if her foreign policy depended on friendly relations with the big neighbour to the East.

The triumph of **Edvin Laine's** screen version of Väinö Linna's novel, *The Unknown Soldier (Tuntematon sotilas,* 1955) opened the floodgates for others to confront the sound and fury of the war. This is not the sort of film that Risto Orko or Toivo Särkkä would have made during the 1930's. Officers and gentlemen are conspicuous by their absence. Linna's novel focuses on a single platoon, representing the courage and earthiness of the average Finn's response to the war. The comforting words of the Army Chaplain cannot protect these young recruits from the savage gunfire that rips through the forest and reduces their numbers inexorably. Trees, like soldiers, are struck down. In its best moments, Laine's film conveys the pain of a country whose very nature is under assault. As the ceasefire comes, like the bell that signals the end of a terrible boxing match, the smoke clears and the surviving men can hardly believe the

Edvin Laine's version of *The Unknown Soldier* (1955)

news. 'The Soviet Union won,' jokes one infantryman, 'but second place was earned by a small country called Finland.' Such lines, and Laine's invocation of Sibelius's 'Finlandia', serve to emphasise the patriotism of the film. With Särkkä's Suomen Filmiteollisuus producing *The Unknown Soldier*, the intention is to revive a nation's flagging pride in itself. When Rauni Mollberg came to make a new version of Linna's epic, he would eschew all hint of heroism (see page 68). Laine never questions the nature of war as such; if battle is joined for a just cause, then a loss of life is inevitable.

Such an attitude can be condemned with hindsight but, given the political reality of the time (the height of the Cold War), Laine and those who now began to deal with the legacy of the war may be forgiven for seeking to hearten their audience. Nor should such considerations detract from the narrative verve of *The Unknown Soldier*. The three hours race past, enlivened by a series of three-dimensional portraits. Åke Lindman's Lehto, shooting himself in the mouth after being wounded; Veikko Sinisalo's Lehtinen, covering his comrades' retreat in heroic fashion; Reino Tolvanen's captious Rokka, whose roots lie in the Karelian isthmus that the Finns realise they cannot save from Russian invasion. *The Unknown Soldier* impressed audiences throughout the world, playing in cities where no Finnish

film had ever been released before. In West Germany alone, 34 copies of the film were distributed. At home, Laine's epic joined *The Steward of Siltala* and *The Vagabond Waltz* as the films that had attracted more than a million spectators on the domestic circuit.

The following year, in *Evacuated (Evakko)*, **Ville Salminen** turned attention to one of the most tragic consequences of the war — the forced migration of thousands of Karelians in the shadow of the first 'Winter' war with the Soviet Union. Neither heroism nor cowardice struts his hour upon the stage in these circumstances. Instead there is the overwhelming sense of a people deracinated. Panic spreads as local folk hear that the Nazis have invaded Poland, and then that Finland has withdrawn its diplomats from Moscow. Nothing must be left for the invader from the East. Houses are burnt and boats sunk. Some Karelians refuse to leave (one man must be roped up before being loaded on to a sledge in the all-pervasive snow), and when they do arrive without ceremony in towns like Kouvola, they are like refugees of all periods and of all wars: hungry, humiliated, and devoid of a place in society. The announcement of peace brings a cathartic relief to *The Unknown Soldier*, but not to *Evacuated*, for the price of peace is the irrevocable surrender of Eastern Karelia to the U.S.S.R. Few moments in Finnish cinema are imbued with

Evacuated (1956) by Ville Salminen

such poignancy as when the leader of the voluntary reserve, who has piloted the refugees to some kind of safety, flings himself on his bed and weeps with grief at the news.

The Underestimated 1950's

By the early 1950's, Finland was recovering its self-confidence after the grim years of war with the Soviet Union. Between 25 and 30 feature films were produced by the domestic industry during the middle years of the decade, and audiences supported them eagerly. New directors emerged to work alongside older colleagues like Toivo Särkkä, Valentin Vaala, and Teuvo Tulio. This new generation breathed fresh life into conventional genres. They took more risks than the previous generation had done. They responded to influences from abroad (much of Matti Kassila's output, for example, is in tune with the early 1950's work of Ingmar Bergman).

Escapism continued to colour the routine films from Finnish studios, but **Erik Blomberg** infused *The White Reindeer (Valkoinen peura,* 1952) with such lusty vigour that its fantastical story gripped audiences at home and abroad with all the appeal of an action thriller. *The White Reindeer* is a Lapp saga, and proves the argument that the greatest films are not necessarily the most 'international' in character. Nothing could be more Finnish than the foreboding imagery of this legend, about a lonely, seductive woman who turns into a witch by night, in the manner of *Doctor Jekyll and Mr. Hyde* or *Cat People.* Supple and athletic, Pirita takes the form of an alluring white reindeer. One herder after another follows the creature into the 'Evil Valley', only to find the reindeer transmogrifying into a vengeful Pirita, who kills them on the spot.

Blomberg emphasises the stark contrast between the gleaming white of the snow and ice by day, and the darkness of the Arctic night. He gives the film a powerful surface texture, integrating character and landscape in a sensual ballet (Pirita lopes through the snow in slow-motion, hinting at her 'other' identity, that of the reindeer). Where many a film-maker of the period would have opted for studio decor to illustrate such a ghost story, Blomberg took his cameras north to Lapland. His tiny crew consisted of his wife, Mirjami Kuosmanen (playing Pirita and also functioning as scriptgirl), a cameraman and his assistant, three professional actors, a driver, and Blomberg himself. From the exhilarating opening sequence, with Pirita competing in a sledding race, to the melancholy finale as Pirita's husband realises that he has killed the dreaded 'white reindeer' and thus his beloved wife, Blomberg's film captures the harsh purity of the Finnish winter, and the intrepid zeal that enables the Finns to cope with it.

The White Reindeer won a prize at the Cannes Festival of 1953, but Blomberg did not match the quality of this film in any of his four future features. His name, if not his masterpiece, was overshadowed by a more consistent talent, **Matti Kassila**. Although he pleased audiences in Finland with his detective films, *Radio Commits Burglary (Radio tekee murron,* 1951) and *Radio Goes Crazy (Radio tulee*

The White Reindeer (1952) by Erik Blomberg

Blue Week (1954) by Matti Kassila

58

halluksi, 1952), Kassila did not invest them with the passion and lyricism he would bring to his great works of the 1950's. These early comedy-thrillers confirm his facility with dialogue and characterisation, and imbue the drab postwar streets of Helsinki with a grimy magic of their own. *Blue Week (Sininen viikko*, 1954) traces the aching progress of an affair between a married woman and a footloose young man, during one of those brilliant summers that lure Finns to lakes and islands in a hectic attempt to banish the memories of the long winter months. Desire and season become as one, and the inevitability of autumn's approach rhymes perfectly with the dying fall of the affair, which ends when the woman's husband takes his own life. Osko Harkimo's cinematography resembles the subtle use of natural light and shade being achieved by Gunnar Fischer for Bergman in contemporary films like *Summer with Monika* and *Summer Interlude*. Allied to this exquisite visual gloss is a sensitive use of open-air sounds — small stones clattering over rocks like a harbinger of remorse or retribution, and scurries of wind that signal the end of summer's optimistic weather. . . . The abiding strength of *Blue Week*, however, derives from Kassila's refusal to censure the clandestine relationship between the two lovers, she a sophisticated, frustrated wife, he the reckless yet intuitive young man who is a cut above the 'beach bum' personality one might expect to find in such a situation. *Blue Week* retains, therefore, a whiff of danger, of a young couple playing with fire and of someone (the husband) suffering as a consequence. The film throws out a challenge to the grey routine of its period, turning to Finland's natural beauty to sustain his expectancy. Like *Elvira Madigan*, Kassila's most beguiling film celebrates the sensual, erotic allure of high summer.

Two years later, Kassila endowed *Harvest Month (Elokuu)* with another, more voluptuous conception of summer. The mood in this adaptation of F.E. Sillanpää's novel about harvest-time in the lush province of Häme is almost other-worldly. The borders of day and night dissolve. As in *Smiles of a Summer Night*, the traditional hours of darkness are replaced by an unbroken, dreamlike opalescence. These are the 'white nights' referred to by Norwegian novelist Knut Hamsun. Daily routine degenerates into a kind of torpor. There is nothing to do but sit and gaze, and bicker, and drink. Veteran lock-keeper Viktor Sundvall has a craving for the bottle, a weakness inflamed by the arrival of his old sweetheart. 'Harvest Month is a film of many borderline feelings, borderline events,' Kassila has said. 'Summer is ending, along with a man's life.'[1] The film has closer affinities with the traditional pastoral cinema of Finland than *Blue Week*. Where it demonstrates Kassila's maturity as a director is in its brilliant use of the close-up. Sundvall (played by Toivo Mäkelä) cannot escape the inquisitive eye of the camera as it prowls and pivots. No other film has caught so exactly the spiritual pressure of Sillanpää's work. Viktor tries in vain to recapture his vanished youth, and in so doing hastens his demise. The weather provides a counterpoint to the emotional drama. The oppressive heat builds into a storm. When it has passed, people and fields alike remain trapped in a curious twilight zone. The canal,

which through *Harvest Month* has served as a reminder of the passage of people and things along the stream of life, inspires the final sequence. The regular Tampere boat passes the scene of Sundvall's death, and Kassila's camera wheels gravely like some dispassionate observer from outside Time. Then, as it proceeds on its way, another vessel emerges from the mist protecting the innocent lake. It is an image of tranquillity that balances the film's opening shot of gleaming, untrammelled water.

In all Kassila's major films of the 1950's, young people offer a source of hope for the future. In both *Blue Week* and *Harvest Month*, the actor Toivo Mäkelä plays an elderly man who perishes in the face of young love and a psychological acceptance of failure. Kassila has commented on the part of Sundvall in terms that might equally be applied to Siiri's husband in *Blue Week*: 'The decline of peasant culture is best seen in the most highly developed individuals, those who crumble first: the strands that bind them to the old, vanishing world are so complex and delicate that they suffer the most. Sundvall is not gifted enough to reach any outstanding position: basically his talents and resources are only middling, and he declines into the life of a petty official and dies in an atmosphere of stew and dirty washing.'[2]

Topi, the ill-fated hero of Kassila's *The Red Line (Punainen viiva*, 1959) falls into the same category. Topi believes in the victory of the working classes in the elections of 1906. His intelligent wife attends political rallies, but must witness the death of her children from sickness and malnutrition. Topi himself is mauled to death by a gigantic bear near his forest hovel. The symbolism burdens *The Red Line* with a doctrinaire didacticism, and Topi's death arouses not so much a sense of catharsis as a mood of defeat. Kassila matches Sweden's Alf Sjöberg in addressing ideological issues in the cinema, but his more lyrical films have survived the passage of years better than the grim schematism of *The Red Line* (which would be made into an outstanding opera by Aulis Sallinen in 1979).

Edvin Laine's versatile gifts make him a director worthy of comparison with Kassila, and his stirring rendition of *The Unknown Soldier* can never be underestimated. Well-known for his monolithic, Gabin-like performances as a screen actor, Laine brings to his mise-en-scène a similar ponderous strength. Retribution and social indignation run through his numerous films of the postwar period, from *In the Shadow of Prison Bars (Ristikon varjossa*, 1945) to *The Price of One Night (Yhden yön hinta*, 1952). His outstanding work of the 1950's, *Black Love (Musta rakkaus*, 1957) looks as though it had been made a full decade earlier. Its description of life in the Tampere working-class district of Pispala breathes an air of postwar depression. Laine himself plays the proletarian father-figure who tries to stall his daughter's love for a young student whose university education conflicts with the blue-collar traditions of the father's family. This is not a documentary polemic about factory conditions. Laine's radicalism is of a different tinge. He is most fascinated by the emotional claustrophobia that breeds violence and an inevitable dependence on drink.

Alcoholism and its attendant problems cast a shadow over

Toivo Mäkelä in Matti Kassila's *Harvest Month* (1956)

several films of the 1950's, a decade in which Finnish cinema may be said to achieve what other countries, less crippled by the aftermath of war, had already done in the 1940's. The mauling administered by the might of the Russian artillery had inflicted on Finland a spiritual defeat from which it took many years to recovr. In film after film, characters lose confidence in their ability to cope with the pressures of everyday existence. The evils of excessive drinking feature in films from the other Nordic countries, but only in Finland is alcoholism such a recurrent metaphor for the flight from boredom to conformity. This phenomenon belongs by no means exclusively to the postwar period. A film like Jaakko Pakkasvirta's *Poet and Muse (Runoilija ja muusa*, 1978) shows that composer Jean Sibelius and poet Eino Leino would drink themselves into a stupor for days at a time when they went out on the town. And the use of illicit 'stills' for producing a primitive kind of substitute liquor have been celebrated throughout the history of Finnish cinema, from *The Moonshiners* in 1907

to Mikko Niskanen's *Eight Deadly Shots (Kahdeksan surmanluotia*, 1972). To analyse the reasons for this dependence on hard liquor among Finns would require an entire book of its own, and it is all too easy to invoke clichés such as the grim climate, the sparse population in agrarian areas, or even an authoritarian government policy that permits Finns to purchase alcohol only at specified government stores. To the bourgeois Finn, heavy drinking remains anathema — 'a vice rather than a sickness, to be condemned rather than pitied. This explains the motivation of many films on the subject, films that chart the inexorable expulsion from society of those who succumb to the bottle's allure. The Finn usually drinks in order to get drunk, seeking release and oblivion. He does not grow merry, as his Latin cousin does after a few glasses of wine. He become morose, truculent, bitter, and even violent.

Kassila alone has lent this ugly condition a certain wistful poetry, in *Harvest Month*, but other films of the 1950's took a more didactic, moralistic tone. **Jack Witikka**, whose

Mikko Niskanen (in doorway) in his own *Eight Deadly Shots* (1972)

droll, whimsical fable *The Doll Merchant (Nukkekaupias ja kaunis Lilith*, 1955) had impressed critics at the Berlin Festival, turns a harsh spotlight on the divisive consequences of alcoholism. Eero (Kaarlo Halttunen) tries to banish his memories of the war against the Russians by drinking with his friends in Helsinki, while his wife and children wait anxiously at home. Forced to borrow, and finally steal, in order to finance his craving for vodka, Eero finds himself out of work and out of sympathy with the society around him. Even when he returns from a 'cure' at one of the country's clinics, he cannot shake his habit. Witikka observes the man's decline with a surgeon's baleful eye, recognising the inevitability of his hero's fate yet siding, one feels, with the character played by Tauno Palo, who listens to Eero's problems and shares his recollections of battle in Karelia.

A jocular approach to the liquor problem may be found in **Roland af Hallström's** *Joseph of Ryysyranta (Ryysyrannan Jooseppi*, 1955). The original novel by Ilmari Kianto is set

in 1924, and this gives the story of woodcutter Joseph an almost nostaligic quality. Joseph is a hunchback, and turns to moonshining in order to provide for his starving family during the harsh winters. Outwitting the Prohibition laws of the period delights both Joseph and his eager clients for the alcohol – who include the local sheriff and the local pastor (who quotes the Bible in justification of the occasional tipple). Such antics belong to the tradition established by Aleksis Kivi's *Seven Brothers*, where the brothers carouse the night away while their freshly-built house burns to the ground.

*　　　*　　　*

Literary adaptations helped to sustain the output of Finnish studios during the 1950's. Walentin Chorell's novel, *Miriam*, found a sensitive screen director in **William Markus**. The film, like the book, accentuates the class consciousness of a country that, despite its republican

61

status, took longer than Sweden to shed such distinctions. Miriam makes the mistake of falling in love with the son of the household where she acts as maid. The parents determine to prevent the affair going any further and although the film does not end on a happy note, Markus manages to expose the hypocrisy of the schoolmaster and his snobbish wife.

The same ingrained prejudice inflames *Loviisa*, which Valentin Vaala directed from the play by Hella Wuolijoki. A landowner (Tauno Palo) enrages his mother by preferring a local milkmaid to the well-to-do Loviisa. So as to retain his property, he agrees to marry Loviisa, but his heart remains with the milkmaid, and he finds himself trapped in a relationship that embodies all the cant of an agrarian society still rigidly obedient to its historical configuration. Another film inspired by Wuolijoki's fiery writing, *Heta from Niskavuori (Niskavuoren Heta*, 1952), describes a similar predicament. Heta marries beneath her, and defies the ill-feelings of her family by helping her simple-minded yet affectionate husband to build their own home, and then to give birth to several children, thus founding a dynasty that would continue to fascinate Finnish filmgoers (who must rely for soap-operas on American imported TV series) up to the mid-1980's, when Matti Kassila made the enjoyable (if uninspired) *The Tug of Home (Niskavuori*, 1984).

Aleksis Kivi's prolific career as a writer has also provided rich source material for the Finnish cinema, although no single film has tapped the dark reservoir of despair lying deep within this jocose writer's œuvre. Like Hans Andersen, his Danish counterpart, Kivi knew the pangs of unrequited love, and never found a woman to marry. Aapeli, the tailor in *The Betrothal (Kihlhaus*, 1955), cannot keep pace with his termagant of a young wife, and loses her irrevocably to her rich friends and relatives. Erik Blomberg handles the story with deftness and compassion reminiscent of Stiller in *Thomas Graal's First Child* (1918).

The 1950's mark the apotheosis of the Finnish 'bucolic' film. By the 1960's, the centre of attention has shifted to the cities, and to a generation beginning to benefit from the economic miracle that before long would make Finland's economy the most prosperous in the Nordic region.

The Challenge of Youth in the 1960's

Apart from *The Unknown Soldier*, few Finnish films had appealed to foreign distributors or audiences. Most of the heavyweight directors who had dominated production during the 1930's, 1940's, and 1950's, were now growing old and often out of touch with the rapidly changing face of the nation. Risto Orko, T.J. Särkkä, Valentin Vaala, Teuvo Tulio, and Edvin Laine were still active behind the camera in one capacity or another, but their finest work lay behind them. Finland's nouvelle vague in the 1960's followed the example of young French directors of the period in seeing the film-maker as a true *auteur*, writing and directing from an original idea, and escaping from the sterile world of the studios into the streets and suburbs of an urban society that was attracting increasing numbers of Finns from the rural areas.

The rapid development of new talent in Finland during this decade depended upon private initiative and investment, however, while in neighbouring Sweden (and Denmark) the establishment of quasi-state institutions for the stimulation of domestic film production gave those nations a head start. Individual Finns — Maunu Kurkvaara, Risto Jarva, Jörn Donner — chose an independent route in order to break with the conventional means of screen expression. Kurkvaara owned a colour laboratory from 1963 to 1970, and for several years earned his living as a designer of boats and toys. Risto Jarva began by making short, often sponsored documentaries, and then established the independent production company, Filminor, with his colleagues and friends. Jörn Donner returned from a spell as a critic and film-maker in Sweden to found his own company, Jörn Donner Productions, which supported not only his own work but also that of others like Mikko Niskanan, Erkko Kivikoski, and Timo Bergholm.

New actors, actresses, and technicians appeared to give impetus to this vanguard. The cinematographers Kari Sohlberg and Antti Peippo, for example, and committed performers from the stage like Kirsti Wallasvaara, Kristiina Halkola, and Liisamaia Laaksonen, brought an energetic new stimulus to the Finnish cinema. Not until the late 1960's did any of this activity result in recognition outside the country, but the momentum gathered pace, and Niskanen's *Skin, Skin (Käpy selän alla*, 1966) was sold to more than 30 countries; Donner and his partner, Arno Carlstedt, used the profits to invest in further offbeat films, under their FJ-Filmi banner.

Influences from abroad can be readily detected in the work of Finnish directors of this period. Just as Widerberg in Sweden responded to the free-wheeling style of Cassavetes, Godard, and Truffaut, so **Maunu Kurkvaara** acknowledged the spell of Antonioni. His uncompromising approach to narrative form marks *Darling (Rakas*, 1961), which penetrates its characters' feelings as they seek an escape from traditional family and conjugal ties. In observing the undemonstrative behaviour of the two lovers in *Darling*, Jaska and Sini, Kurkvaara confirms his skill as a cameraman, with long, languid travelling shots and huge close-ups that map the landscape of the human face in all its moods and seasons.

Kurkvaara says that he had not seen any films by Antonioni when he made *Darling*, but concedes that they shared a certain mind-set. Both men are painters in their spare time, and share a fascination with the sea. Another common trait is the disappearance, and even suicide, of a principal character in a film. *Private Property (Yksityisalue*, 1962) pieces together the strange life of an architect who is found dead in his cottage one winter. In *Redhead (Punatukka*, 1969), the suicide of her flatmate triggers a fundamental change in the approach to life of the main character, Tuija. Kurkvaara's strength as a director resides in his subtle involvement of people and their environment. Sophisticate though he may appear to be, he exhibits many ties with the great Nordic cinema tradition of Sjöström and Stiller, with landscape and seascape exerting an influence on human behaviour.

Kurkvaara's work attracted some favourable notices at festivals, but lacked the commercial elements necessary for exhibition to a wider public. As a director, however, he earned the respect of his peers in Finland, and was an early recipient of the national film prizes that were introduced in 1961 to encourage artistic cinema. He also made no concessions to the 'new' medium of television, which reached Finland only in 1958. Nor was he in tune with the radicalism that coloured so much of his contemporaries' work in the 1960's. An aesthete to his fingertips, Kurkvaara also knew how to regulate sound and image in a bewitching ensemble.

For Finnish cinema to make a distinct impact abroad, however, a more aggressive language was necessary. By his own example as a director, and through imaginative marketing outside Finland, **Jörn Donner** succeeded in achieving this breakthrough. His career in Stockholm [see SWEDEN, page 147] had entered a cul-de-sac, and he wisely returned to his native Finland. *Black on White (Mustaa valkoisella*, 1968) reveals more of Donner's true personality: ironic, impudent, and anti-bourgeois. By playing the leading role in this and other films, Donner betrays a narcissistic trait, while at the same time associating himself unmistakably with a liberated sexuality opposed to the discreet good taste of traditional Finnish cinema. *Black on White* is a brisk movie, superficially a commercial for Finnish standards of living, but more subtly a condemnation of a society that draws its sustenance from glamour and egocentricity. Its story of a businessman's infidelity could have been snatched from the front page of a dozen women's magazines − an 'imitation of life' where cash has been replaced by credit cards and discussion by public-relations chatter. Donner's ensuing films, *69* (1969) and *Portraits of Women (Naisenkuvia*, 1970) dug a frivolous finger into the pulse of contemporary Finland, measuring the hypocrisy of its moral codes, and testing the resolve of the women's liberation movement. *Fuck Off! Images of Finland (Perkele! Kuvia Suomesta*, 1971) constituted a sort of Finnish *I Am Curious − Yellow*, including 'live' interviews with politicians and prostitutes.

Donner is more persuasive when poking fun at society than he is when reaching for the poetic or grandiloquent pronouncement. *Anna* (1970), although by far the most controlled and sophisticated film of Donner's middle period, lacks some essential optimism. It resembles the chamber cinema of Ingmar Bergman, and in particular *Through A Glass Darkly*, but the inner throb of Bergman's anguish is missing. Donner rarely seems to suffer alongside his characters, or to smile wryly with them. For those who read Swedish, his talent flourishes best in his novels and essays, where his laconic, austere writing eschews the temptation of epithet and metaphor and achieves a distilled truth worthy of Hemingway, or of Norman Mailer at his best.

The films which Donner helped to produce and market abroad laid the pattern of Finnish cinema in the 1970's and 1980's. *Little Red Riding-Hood (Punahilkka*, 1968) compels the spectator to identify with a tough young woman whose years spent in reform school have made her cynical and derisive. Anja (Kristiina Halkola) expresses the pent-up resentment and immaturity that typified much of the 'spirit of '68'. Timo Bergholm, the director, refuses to sentimentalise the situation (even when Anja weeps, her tears are those of exasperation, not sorrow), and his wife Eija-Elina Bergholm's screenplay has a refreshing candour and freewheeling verve.

Erkko Kivikoski's *Hot Cat (Kuuma kissa*, 1968) offers an equally impressive female character, but this time a demure young schoolteacher in the provincial town of Lahti. She seems awkward, and wary of men, until she develops a relationship with a student that nourishes her self-confidence. She discovers not only that she attracts the opposite sex, but also that the received ideas purveyed by her fellow teachers are out of tune with the times. Her student friend rails against the school platitudes: 'They jaw on about the mercy of God and Bless This House and Glorious Fatherland, but how can you love the fatherland when you don't even know how many political parties we've got? Or where babies come from? Or how to stop them coming if you don't want them?'

Mikko Niskanen's *Skin, Skin* appeared in 1966 and does not aspire to any political comment. Two boys and two girls spend the summer camping in the Finnish lakes. Nevertheless, a wind of change rustles through the film, heralding the gales of two years ahead. When Leena, the would-be writer, is frightened by a horse, there is the implication that sex and its repercussions hold similar terrors for her. When a small girl on a nearby farm suffers a bite from a snake, the incident symbolises the emotional dangers that none of the friends will acknowledge. The changing morality of the 1960's dictates the tone of Niskanen's film. 'If youth is the best time,' says Leena, 'how difficult it will be to grow old.'

Niskanen had made his debut four years previously, with *Boys (Pojat*, 1962), and its *triste* complexion derives as much from the director's two years study at the Soviet film school, VGIK, as it does from the subject: a group of children in northern Finland coming to terms with the Nazi occupation of 1944. Parallels with Niskanen's approach may be found in other Nordic countries − in Laila Mikkelsen's *Growing Up* (see NORWAY, page 97), and Palle Kjærulff-Schmidt's *Once There Was a War* (see DENMARK, page 40). For the 'lads' of Niskanen's generation, the war created a forcing house in which the innocence of ordinary childhood soon evaporated. One of the most sympathetic boys, Jaakko (Vesa-Matti Loiri), is deserted by his mother, who runs off with a German officer while her husband is away on the Karelian front fighting the Russians.

Another significant film of the Finnish nouvelle vague which suggests the changes afoot in a society increasingly confronted with material comforts is **Jaakko Pakkasvirta's** *Grass Widow (Vihreä leski*, 1968). Pakkasvirta had started his career as an actor, in films like *Man From This Planet* and *Darling*, and his friendship with Risto Jarva had taken him behind the camera as co-director of *Night or Day* (see below). *Grass Widow* staggers somewhat beneath its load of clichés: the bored housewife in a luxurious modern suburb, the insensitive husband, the innocuous lover. But the central message carries a warning note to viewers of the 1960's: the traditional role of a woman is no longer relevant, and women must learn to deal with the new-found freedom and potential. Eija Pokkinen, as the lonely young woman, had, like other contemporary Nordic actresses (Vibeke Løkkeberg, Agneta Ekmanner) spent time in Paris as a mannequin, and brings to *Grass Widow* a grace and sophistication unusual in Finnish cinema of the 1960's. The protagonist in Pakkasvirta's next film, *Summer Rebellion (Kesäkapina*, 1970) is in fact a photo mannequin who loses sight of her true identity as she tries to live up to the ideals of the consumer society. 'Pakkasvirta shows first how Susanna becomes an alien to herself, the conflict between her real self and the self engaged in publicity. This private aspect is expanded gradually, and is converted by Pakkasvirta into a general criticism: Susanna's conflicts are not solely her own, she is no more than a typical example of a human being who, exposed to the prevailing economic

system, sells herself bit by bit, and is exploited to provide support for the illusion of welfare.' (Sakari Toiviainen, in *International Film Guide 1971*, London 1970).

Risto Jarva

Some film-makers are significant despite the commercial failure of most of their work, and the lack of any indisputable masterpiece in their œuvre. **Risto Jarva** belongs among them. During the 1960's and 1970's, until his brutal death in a traffic accident coming home from a preview of his final film, *The Year of the Hare (Jäniksen vuosi*, 1977), he expressed the eagerness of his generation for social change and artistic experimentation. Jarva's offbeat heroes try to stake out for themselves a measure of independence within the economic system. His films take place, defiantly, in the everyday world of the present: no flight into history for Risto Jarva. He was the first to show

Boys (1962) by Mikko Niskanen

men at work in modern Finnish factories, struggling against the mechanised routine and drab domestic rituals of urban existence. In *Worker's Diary (Työmiehen päiväkirja*, 1967), Juhani is a welder who seeks to climb up the social ladder via a marriage to middle-class Ritva. Added to his resentment at factory conditions is an inner anger (still harboured by many Finns) about the Civil War that followed the Russian Revolution and its impact on Finland. Juhani and his younger workmates resent the ageing generation who put 'country' ahead of 'people' and fought on the White side in that conflict.

In *When the Heavens Fall (Kun taivas putoaa*, 1972), Jarva switches his attention to the scandal of yellow journalism, and to the intellectuals who can perceive the flaws in their society yet lack the moral fibre required to overcome them. Although marred by the journalist's excess of self-pity, *When the Heavens Fall* proves that when Jarva wanted to, he could treat erotic scenes with skill and feeling, and also that in Antti Peippo he enjoyed the services of one of the best postwar Finnish cameramen.

One Man's War (Yhden miehen sota, 1973) turns the Finnish worker's dream of independence into a nightmare, as a construction worker attempts to set up his own fledgling business and finds himself sinking into debt while his marriage collapses beneath the strain. In films like these, Jarva's only equivalent in world cinema is the English director, Lindsay Anderson. Jarva probably shared Anderson's cynical belief that revolutionaries will always be assimilated by the Establishment. Christer Kihlman, the Finnish novelist, has written: 'There is a hard, biting, paradoxical poetry in the indescribably ugly, desolate, inhuman and degrading work camps and building sites, places which depict destruction and disintegration rather than expansion and human progress. Just as [Jacques] Tati creates poetry from the plastic and concrete sterility of modern urbanism, Jarva creates his poetry from the bleak, dirty, gouged ground in which the excavator works.' In the final shots of *One Man's War*, Erik Suomies leaves for Sweden in order to find work. This conclusion resounds with irony for Finnish audiences, for the workers migrating to Sweden in the search for a better life often return home in confusion, having been unable to set down roots in an alien land, and resenting the condescension shown towards them by their Swedish hosts. Mikko Niskanen, in *Gotta Run!* and Jon Lindström, in *Homeward in the Night*, deal with similar feelings of frustration vis-à-vis Finland and her Nordic neighbours.

It would be wrong, however, to classify Jarva as a pessimistic director. *Game of Chance (Onnenpeli*, 1965) includes some effervescent sequences worthy of Jacques Demy in his prime, and a beutifully understated melancholy as its main character (played by Jaakko Pakkasvirta) wanders pensively through the streets of Helsinki as dawn appears and he recognises that his affair with Eija Pokkinen's blonde mannequin in unlikely to progress. *Rally (Bensaa suonissa*, 1970) confirms the exuberant, fun-loving side of Jarva's nature, and charts the rise and fall of a socially-ambitious rally driver who marries into nothing less than a sausage-meat fortune. Comedies like *The Man*

Who Couldn't Say No (Mies joka ei osannut sanoa ei, 1975) and *Olympic Holiday (Loma*, 1976) did well at the Finnish box-office, and still show Jarva to have been a satirist with a sharp and affectionate eye for his countrymen's foibles. His most mature and likeable work, however, is his last. *The Year of the Hare* blends Jarva's social concerns with his fantasist's love of Nature, describing an advertising executive who takes off into the Finnish countryside as an act of rebellion against the inhuman pattern of city life. Vatanen (played by one of Jarva's favourite actors, Antti Litja) plunges into the forests to find relief from both a nagging wife and an incipient ulcer. He tosses his necktie unceremoniously into a lake, and bathes nude to his heart's content. Peippo's photography gives a visual reality to the secret yearning of most Nordic citizens, for whom water and woodland will always be more 'genuine' than concrete cities. In a predominantly flat country like Finland, the immense, unremitting extent of forests and lakes has endowed the national art with an almost palpable sense of the wilderness (illustrated through the paintings of Akseli Gallen-Kallela). Man becomes aware of his own insignificance when surrounded by such vast space; his art emerges in a more contemplative form than that of other regions.

'Green' in attitude a good decade before most film-makers in Europe, Risto Jarva does not allow aesthetic considerations to distort his basic concern for sociological, environmental, and humanist themes. He cannot match the intuitive brilliance of a Tapiovaara, and his direction lacks the rich, confident flow of a Mollberg, but he laboured to forge a new, more honest brand of Finnish cinema during one of the most uncertain periods in its history, and his example inspired numerous young directors.

Into the 1970's with the Finnish Film Foundation

On February 1, 1970, the tiny Finnish Film Foundation became a reality. Long discussed, this state organisation had many similarities to the Swedish Film Institute, established in 1963, and the Danish Film Foundation, which opened its doors two years later (see pages 160-161). The budget with which the Finnish body operated seemed pitiful — a mere $200,000. The Ministry of Education still dispensed $300,000 per annum in film awards and other grants, but for several years the concept of government support for the cinema was honoured in symbolic terms rather than in any real hope of contributing a majority of any one film's budget. Such money as was available to the Foundation flowed from a 4% levy on all cinema tickets sold throughout the country. During the early 1970's, production in Finland lurched almost to a complete halt, and in 1974 just two domestic features were released. The bulwarks of production, like Suomi-Filmi and Fennada-Filmi, concentrated on the distribution and exhibition of foreign films in order to survive. Independent producers like Jörn Donner encountered increasing difficulty in selling Finnish films abroad as the excitement and innovation of the late 1960's gave way to the earnestness of the 1970's.

In this uncertain climate, various directors made their début only to find that they could not raise the funds to shoot a second or third film. Sakari Rimminen, fresh out of a Film Studies course at the Helsinki Ateneum, persuaded Donner to finance *Castle of Pot (Pilvilinna*, 1971). Coarsely-cut, acted with the well-meaning intensity of an amateur cast, *Castle of Pot* celebrates the alternative lifestyle promulgated by the students who had been inspired by the 'events of '68'. The film won the Gran Premio at the Bergamo Festival in 1972, but Rimminen faded away into the world of sponsored films and documentaries. Seppo Huunonen delighted 350,000 Finns with *The Sheep-Eaters (Lampaansyöjät*, 1972), which satirises the conventional Nordic approach to 'hunting and fishing'. Two middle-aged businessmen decide to track down the innocent sheep (by no means common in Finland) and roast the mutton in the earth, washing it down in vodka and singing bawdy ditties all the while. Huunonen foolishly followed this unpretentious comedy with a convoluted adaptation of the Lionel White novel that had inspired Godard's *Pierrot le fou*. Shot partly on location in Spain, *Obsession (Karvat*, 1974) spins a web of blackmailing intrigue but repeatedly breaks the spell with self-conscious devices such as pixillation, slow motion, and stylised violence.

Another director who failed to go beyond his first feature was Peter von Bagh. After a promising, whimsical short film, *PockPicket* (1968), von Bagh embarked on the story of one of Finland's most notorious modern Casanovas, Pertii Ylermi Lindgren, in *The Count (Kreivi*, 1971). Despite the engaging performance by Lindgren as himself, this comedy depends for its impact on too much lavatorial humour and abandons any attempt to analyse the reasons why an alleged total of 76 women should have agreed to get engaged to a lover whose oleaginous charm looks distinctly superficial. Von Bagh contributed significantly to screenplays for both Risto Jarva and Jaakko Pakkasvirta, and has written some of the best historical surveys of the cinema available in the Finnish language.

Erkko Kivikoski's *The Brothers (Kesyttömät veljekset*, 1969) created an absorbing and entertaining framework for a debate between the two opposing currents in social thought at the turn of the decade. Eero, the one 'brother', believes in socialist ideals; Antti, the other, seeks fulfilment through establishing his own small business. Each must depart from his declared aims, on a private as much as an economic level. Kivikoski knows how to offset the dialectical nature of his subject with witty moments, and with bright, engaging imaginery recorded in the streets of contemporary Helsinki. *Gunshot in the Factory (Laukaus tehtaalla*, 1973), however, surrenders to the pessimism that forces its central character, an elderly trades union official, to shoot his boss. Two years later, in Norway, Oddvar Bull Tuhus would approach a similar set of circumstances in a more rewarding form of variation on the 'docudrama' (see *Strike!*, page 95). Like *Castle of Pot, Gunshot in the Factory* won the Gran Premio at Bergamo (Sanremo), but its failure at the Finnish box-office persuaded Kivikoski to quit the director's chair for more than seven years. When he did return, he revealed a mature, thoughtful persona. *Night by*

the Seashore (Yö meren rannalla, 1981) justifies comparison with the 'chamber cinema' of Bergman, and introduced one of the best new actresses in Finnish cinema, Eeva Eloranta. A small group of friends gather at a villa overlooking the sea. The long summer's night contains those staples of Finnish domestic drama: liquor, sauna, infidelity. Kivikoski controls his volatile material with a masterly skill, but once again the financial misfortunes of the film, allied perhaps to a lack of self-confidence, led this modest, gentle director away from the studios and into the teacher's chair.

Mikko Niskanen's *Eight Deadly Shots (Kahdeksan surmanluotia*, 1972) was originally made for television, but edited by Jörn Donner into an international version for theatrical release. The gritty, unequivocal visual style of Niskanen, a child of the countryside, attains its peak in this wrenching reconstruction of an incident in the village of Säkkärämäki in 1969. No other Finnish film encapsulates more dramatically the pressures of life in the remote north – the unforgiving climate, the smallholder's struggle for economic survival, the lethal grip of alcohol when depression demands it. Niskanen himself plays Pasi, the victim of these distressing circumstances, and does so with a compelling authority. Like Mollberg's *Earth Is Our Sinful Song* (see below), *Eight Deadly Shots* twists its spiral of emotional and psychological pressure until a violent climax becomes not just inevitable but cathartic. Niskanen and his team of three cinematographers observe the tiny, poignant details of bucolic life, so that the symbols of hope and despair do not so much obtrude as reside in the vibrant texture of the film. Niskanen has returned to agrarian themes in his films since 1972, but never with such shattering force.

Jaakko Pakkasvirta, a director accustomed to looking at life from a pessimistic standpoint, confounded the critics' expectations with his finest work, *Poet and Muse (Runoilija ja muusa*, 1978). If Aleksis Kivi and J.L. Runeberg recovered the Finnish language from cultural oblivion in the 19th century, then Eino Leino (1878-1927) soared like a bird on the winds and skies of that language. His lyric poetry is exquisitely shaped, and sparkles even in translation. Pakkasvirta finds him a colossus with feet of clay, but sympathetic in spite of his vices. Torn between a spendthrift wife and an intellectual mistress, depressed by his brother's ill-health, and intoxicated by the heady mix of Finnish nationalism and Russian socialism, Esko Salminen's Leino assumes tragic proportions.

If *Poet and Muse* marks the highpoint of Pakkasvirta's career, then *Men Can't Be Raped (Miestä ei voi raiskata)*, made in the same year, may be accounted the best film in Jörn Donner's prolific œuvre. Its source, a laconic, incisive novel by Märta Tikkanen about a 40-year-old woman who avenges herself on a man who has forced himself on her after a casual meeting, allows Donner to draw yet another of his intriguing portraits of modern women. Eva Randers does not even attempt to seek justice through the usual channels; she tracks down her foe with the cold-blooded fury of *The Bride Wore Black*. Although shot on location in Helsinki, *Men Can't Be Raped* operates on a psychological level quite different from *Beyond the Law* (1987, see

Esko Salminen and Elina Salo in Jaakko Pakkasvirta's *Poet and Muse* (1978)

below), which also tackles an individual's reaction to rape. Jeanette Bonnier, Donner's second wife, contributed to the screenplay of the film, and the dialogue is blessedly free of the stilted, monosyllabic utterances of so many of this Swedish-speaking Finn's earlier screen efforts.

Rauni Mollberg

Rauni Mollberg has made only five feature films for the cinema, but those have already established him as the most authoritative director to emerge in postwar Finland.

The art of Rauni Mollberg flows from the Finnish landscape. His characters move not against a backdrop of field and lake and forest, but deep *within* that topography. They form part of that mysterious life force we call Nature. They are born, they perish, and in between they undergo a process of spiritual growth and awareness – all registered uniquely in terms of the cinema.

Mollberg was already over forty years of age when he directed his first feature for the big screen, *Earth Is Our Sinful Song (Maa on syntinen laulu,* 1973). It proved an instant hit with Finnish audiences, attracting more than 700,000 spectators (out of a population of 4.9 million!), and raced round the international festival circuit. *Earth Is Our Sinful Song* was sold to over twenty countries. Yet prior to that, Mollberg had established a high reputation for his TV films. These included two adaptations of the fiction of Toivo Pekkanen, *My Childhood* and *In the Shadow of the Factory,* and a stunning featurette entitled *The War Recluse,* about an elderly villager caught up in the war against the Soviet Union; there are only a few lines of dialogue, the impact of the film comes from the reaction of the ailing man to his solitude and his snowbound surroundings.

Mollberg demonstrated with this TV work that he could coax from his actors a quality of performance that transcended that of the stage (where Mollberg had begun his career) and that was infinitely more eloquent than the cold, impassive acting of Miklós Jancsó's players, for example. As with all artistic magic, it is difficult to analyse the technique that results in such a quivering intensity. Part of it lies in Mollberg's way of gazing down into people's grave, disturbed, troubled faces from slightly above eye-level; his characters move heavily, as though sleep-walking, weighed down by Life's burden.

But Mollberg is by no means a pessimistic director. He believes in the potential for maturing and understanding. Like the English novelist Thomas Hardy, he sees his country folk moving to the tune of some unseen, unfathomed spiritual force. *Earth Is Our Sinful Song* and *Milka* are great films because they tap into this life-force. Siskonranta, in southern Lapland, is an island in time, an archetypal community untouched by such modern inventions as the car or plane. Life in this remote village is a ritual, a jeremiad of pain and despair, lit only by brief sparks of pleasure that the villagers snatch without thought for cost or consequence. 'The themes in *Earth Is Our Sinful Song* are universally human,' says Mollberg. 'I have made a film about feeling and emotions. Today our world of feelings is being narrowed down: it is the

technocrats who manage things, and deep human emotions are left in the background.'

Milka, made in 1980 and like *Earth Is Our Sinful Song* based on a novel by Timo Mukka, follows the spiritual yearning and sexual awakening of a young girl in the Lapp forests. She and her widowed mother both fall in love with the same man. Irma Huntus here (like Maritta Viitamäki in *Earth Is Our Sinful Song*) gives a performance of translucent ardour. Mollberg seems able to inspire his performers to *live* their characters without succumbing to the self-conscious style of the Actors' Studio.

Birth and death occur in Mollberg's world without a trace of melodrama or obscenity. In *Earth Is Our Sinful Song*, death comes to the inhabitants of Siskonranta as unaffectedly as it does to the reindeer despatched with a single expert blow in the corral. The building of coffins is routine work, part of the texture of life. Martta, the girl whose natural lustiness triggers the dramatic events of the movie, gives birth to a baby, who survives to symbolise fresh hope for the community.

Rauni Mollberg's third feature, *Pretty Good – For a Human Being (Aika hyvä ihmiseksi,* 1978) is set in a small Finnish town during the Prohibition era of the 1920's. The tone is much lighter than in his other films, and the main actors, including a nine-year old boy, are beautifully directed and allowed to express their innermost fears and aspirations. Once again, these are the less privileged members of society; Mollberg has never been attracted by the prosperous, bourgeois city-dwellers we find in so many modern Finnish pictures. Yet he does not order his work according to a socialist scheme of things; he works always from the humanist impulse. In their bucolic environment, Mollberg's characters are in closer touch with the essential rhythm of life much more vividly than they ever would be in an urban setting.

The Unknown Soldier (Tuntematon sotilas, 1985) proved almost as popular as *Earth Is Our Sinful Song*, with attendances of some 600,000 in Finland. Väinö Linna's novel about a platoon of young soldiers in the bitter Continuation War against the U.S.S.R. appeared in the 1950's, and was made into a hugely successful film by Edvin Laine. Thirty years later, Mollberg took up the challenge of adapting *The Unknown Soldier* for a new generation – a generation no longer stirred by patriotic fervour and to whom the clatter of guns was only a distant folk memory. His film is a searing indictment of war, and of the corrosive effect it has on human beings. Mollberg boldly selected a group of young and inexperienced actors, and kept them together over a period of more than a year – so that their ageing and maturing can be observed, literally, on screen during the movie. If conclusive proof of Mollberg's ability to work with actors was ever needed, *The Unknown Soldier* provided it to a remarkable degree. Caught up in the remorseless wheels of war, these young lads find time for drinking, joking, cheating, whoring, and heroism. The film begins and ends on two similar, extraordinary images: the bare, vulnerable chests of young troops. In the first shot they pulse with life, and are injected by the army doctor as part of the induction process; in the closing shot, they lie inanimate on a crude cart, just two of the hundreds of thousands of corpses wrought by the havoc of war.

Mollberg's pungent satire, *Friends, Comrades (Ystävät, toverit,* 1990) strikes a significant chord in a world so recently menaced by Saddam Hussein; but its ostensible theme of an arms magnate enjoying the tribute of East and West, Fascist and liberal, friend and foe, pales beside the craving for natural fulfilment that courses through the film like a powerful current.

Arno Jurmala, lord of his Lapland domain, extracts millions of tonnes of nickel ore from the fells, creating ammunition for the guns of Hitler, Franco, Churchill, and the oh-so-neutral Swedes. Like Coppola's Godfather, Jurmala regards the world in terms of Family, and everyone has his price. Behind the exotic celebrations that mark his birthday at the outset of the film lies a dark cloud of intrigue and coercion. Like the Godfather too, Jurmala never kills with his own hands; his gory deeds are performed by others at his command.

At the heart of *Friends, Comrades* stands a more fascinating personality even than Jurmala. Stina Ekblad's Lisa, the magnate's wife, dreams of giving birth to a son, of complying with the eternal rhythm of the Nature she sees and appreciates all about her – and which the juggernaut of war will ravage almost beyond recovery.

Nature, however, has her own means of purging such desecration, and the images one bears away from *Friends, Comrades* remain those of open skies and undulating fells. There can be no pessimism while the sun gleams on water and the virgin snow envelops the countryside and the birds rustle and sing unseen in the woods. No film-maker of our times has fingered so unerringly that mysterious pulse of things, and communicated his feelings in such mesmeric visual patterns. And for Mollberg the human animal remains the most precious of all earth's possessions, an enigma worthy of endless analysis and sympathy.

Renewal in the 1980's

While the Swedish cinema slipped off the pace in the 1980's, the Finns accelerated out of the grim economic slide of the previous decade and succeeded in reaching an international audience, most notably for the work of two brothers, Mika and Aki Kaurismäki.

Irma Huntus in Rauni Mollberg's *Milka – A Film about Taboos* (1980)

This new period enjoyed a racing start with *Flame-Top (Tulipää*, 1980) being selected for official competition at Cannes – the first Finnish film so honoured since *The White Reindeer* 28 years previously. This bold, brightly-coloured, and assured debut by a directing team (**Pirjo Honkasalo** and **Pekka Lehto**) hitherto noted for short films, charts the life of a farmer's son, Algot Tietäväinen. Hiding behind the pseudonym of 'Maiju Lassila', he flitted from a croft in the Finnish countryside to a star-spangled wedding in St. Peterburg, and from an allegiance to terrorist groups to writing pacifist novels. For Lassila, rebellion was not so much a matter of lifting a rifle as of wielding a pen. *Flame-Top* exhumes the life of this bizarre individual, making it a litmus test for Finnish responses to pressures during the 20th century. The film sweeps away any remaining doubts about the Finnish cinema's production values. From Kari Sohlberg's glowing cinematography to the blazing conviction of Asko Sarkola and Rea Mauranen as the writer and his mistress, *Flame-Top* justifies the praise that Nordic critics heaped upon it. Honkasalo and Lehto's next film, the early anticipated *Da Capo* (1985), bears the familiar mark of so many 'second' efforts in the Nordic cinema: still technically impressive, but pretentious in concept and muddled in execution. Once again they select an intriguing real-life hero, this time the brilliant young violinist, Heimo Haitto, who dazzled audiences in Finland and the United States during the 1930's. Their portrait of the young prodigy and his Svengali-like mentor should have been more fascinating than it looks and sounds on screen. The fate of Honkasalo and Lehto after this failure shows how unkind and shortsighted the economic realities of Nordic cinema can be. Neither she nor he has made another film since *Da Capo*.

As in Sweden, several new faces emerged during the 1980's, revealed great promise in a first feature, and then either abandoned the struggle to survive behind the camera, or opted for television or the theatre. **Ralf Långbacka**, had he been born in Germany, France, Italy, or Britain, would surely have been ranked with Peter Brook, Giorgio Strehler, or Peter Hall as one of the foremost stage directors of the postwar period. In Finland, his theatrical work is held in high regard, and his single feature film, *Mr. Puntila and His Servant Matti (Herra Puntila ja hänen renkinsä Matti*, 1980), contains wit and humanism. At the core of the play by Brecht and Hella Wuolijöki is the rumbustious, querulous Puntila (played with absolute command by Lasse Pöysti). Puntila drinks himself into a stupor while the shrewd young Matti watches cynically, waiting for the moment to unseat his master. Långbacka's eye for the lush rural environment liberates his film from the confinement of the stage original, and finds at the heart of the social comedy an affinity with Finnish life (much more than German).

Most of the neophyte directors of the decade were considerably younger than Långbacka, and their concerns reflected the social pressures on a generation seeking to escape the fatalism of its parents' world. No film articulates these feelings to more poignant effect than **Tapio Suominen's** *Right On, Man! (Täältä tullaan, elämä!*, 1980). Its jeans-clad teenage protagonist, Jussi, finds himself like Truffaut's Antoine Doinel at odds with society. His teachers cannot fathom him, and Jussi remains an outsider, even when seen in the company of his pals. Helsinki (and indeed all the Nordic capitals) presents a blank, inhospitable face to its denizens after Suominen's unsentimental, yet deeply-felt film reveals the gulf between consumer-oriented affluence and the introspective anxieties of adolescence. **Jaakko Pyhälä** deals with a similar vein of frustration in his nervy *Jon* (1983). Contrary to the tradition of young people migrating from the countryside to the big city, Jon forsakes Helsinki and treks to the most remote northern tip of Finnland – and then to an offshore island on the Arctic Ocean where he lives with a motley collection of dropouts and failures. Pyhälä uses the 'scope format to rich effect, showing the austere, unforgiving beauty of the 'end of the world', a far cry from the lush pastoral landscape of Aleksis Kivi or F.E. Sillanpää.

The boys in Mikko Niskanen's *Gotta Run! (Ajolähtö*, 1982) belong to that first flush of youth, midway between the schoolboy Jussi and the disillusioned Jon. Still comparatively innocent after fulfilling their army service, these three youngsters from the agrarian heart of Finland decide to take ship for Sweden and Norway in search of easy money. But their lack of academic qualifications, allied to the Finns' perennial timidity when essaying a foreign language, frustrates their attempts to settle down in either country. Niskanen relates their moments of elation and disapointment with great sensitivity, and his actors reward him with performances that light up the screen with their spontaneity. He can also coax persuasive acting from women like Sanna Majanlahti, as the young librarian in *Gotta Run!*, and Anna-Leena Härkönen, as the credulous girl in *Mona and the Time of Burning Love (Mona ja palavan rakkauden aika*, 1983). Mona embraces religion as an abstract alternative to the concrete temptations of daily life in the 1980's, but also perceives revivalism as a refuge from emotional pressures. Finns pay lip service to the Lutheran Church through their obligatory tax contributions, but in practice are more likely to respond to Jehovah's Witnesses or Pentecostalists who knock at the door of suburban apartments with a surprising success rate. For perhaps the last time in his career, Mikko Niskanen demonstrates his skill at establishing mood and intensity of feeling.

One of Finland's most versatile young directors, **Lauri Törhönen**, made a stunning début in 1984 with *Burning Angel (Palava enkeli)*, which manages to be both acutely personal and unabashedly critical of the complacent mood in Finland's mental institutions. Related in subject if not in temper to *One Flew over the Cuckoo's Nest*, this grave portrait of a young nurse (Riitta Viiperi) in an asylum inspires compelling performances from all concerned, and especially Eeva Eloranta as a demented patient. The dialogue is snappy and penetrating, not least in the scenes between the nurse and her overweening mother. *Burning Angel* occupies a similar place in Finnish cinema as Vilgot Sjöman's *You're Lying* in Swedish film, asking the eternal question, Who are really sick – the prisoners and patients, or those caring for them?

The son of Matti Kassila, Taavi, also made an assured first feature, *The Archer (Jousiampuja*, 1982). Its handsome, resolute-looking hero emerges in the opening sequence from one of the most potent modern metaphors for youthful solidarity the rock concert. Blackmailed into selling drugs (but not using them himself), Aki by chance comes under the influence of a middle-aged man ('the archer' of the title) who runs an ambulance service in Helsinki. This solid individual (brilliantly played by Åke Lindman, who first came to prominence in Edvin Laine's *The Unknown Soldier* in 1955) teaches Aki the wisdom of nurturing sufficient strength, physical and mental, to stand on his own feet. Less successful is Kassila's description of the evil drug-dealer and his cynical attitude by comparison with the help given to the sick by the ambulance service where Aki works. *The Archer* remains one of the most underestimated Nordic films of the past ten years, a victim of its own unfashionable material and its courage in exploring abstract ideas.

Even during the 1960's, films about politics and the business world have never figured prominently in the Finnish cinema. **Lauri Törhönen** made a brave stab at reviving the fierce spirit of that decade when he brought to the screen the controversial play by Raija Oranen, *The Undressing (Riisuminen*, 1986). A socialist cabinet minister meets a former mistress in the lobby of a Helsinki hotel, and they spend the night together. As in a Strindberg chamber play, the two lovers tease, torment, and assail each other until, all passion spent, they acknowledge that they have abandoned the ideals of their youth and surrendered to the corruption and sweet living of the economic 'miracle' of the Finnish 1970 and 1980's. Eeva Eloranta again asserts her status as one of the finest contemporary actresses in Nordic cinema, and Esa Vuorinen, working within the confines of a small hotel suite, displays his talent as a cameraman of international class.

The producer of *The Undressing*, Jörn Donner, himself returned to the director's chair with *Dirty Story (En smutsig historia*, 1984), an analysis of the intrigue and dissimulation endemic to 'big business'. Erland Josephson as Gabriel Berggren, the head of United Metal, one of the largest enterprises in Donner's fictional Finland, radiates a troubled nobility, a reluctance to accept the triumph of age over desire. One of the handicaps of the film is its failure to lend any erotic charge to the affair between Gabriel and a typist at his company headquarters. Shot in Swedish, like all Donner's films, *Dirty Story* has its roots in the novel *Gabriel's Day*, which had been published the previous year. The dialogue reads better on the page than it sounds on screen, but at least Donner should be praised for his rejection of the easy epithet or metaphor; no Finnish artist so accurately mirrors a society where shallow sentiment is beyond the pale.

Another Swedish-speaking Finn, **Jon Lindström**, won selection for the Quinzaine des Réalisateurs at Cannes in 1984 with *The Final Summer (Den sista leken)*. Poised geographically between Finland and Sweden, Lindström's bizarre, unsettling story unfolds in the archipelago where families live throughout the year alongside those who flee to the islands from the city each summer. Victor (Sven Wollter) is a junk-dealer who roves these skerries in search of things to sell during the winter in Stockholm. Fastening on to a chalk-quarrier and his wife, Victor finds himself increasingly attracted to their teenage daughter. His desire is unostentatious, and yet his feelings manifest themselves in Lindström's allusive imagery. *The Final Summer* does not boast the luxury of catharsis; its mood descends in an inexorable spiral towards the dark pit of despair, disgust, and death. The lonely horizons and rocky shores of the archipelago form an essential part of Victor's spiritul desolation.

In a period when most Finnish films concentrated on the urban environment, some directors breathed new life into the pastoral genre. Veikko Kertula's *Big Blonde (Iso vaallee*, 1983) tells a familiar tale of a young man obsessed with a voluptuous woman, but its every image celebrates the lush countryside of Häme province, where Kivi and Sillanpää lived and wrote. Jaakko Pakkasvirta moves farther north in *The Howling Miller (Ulvova mylläri*, 1982), an engaging modern parable about a miller (Vesa-Matti Loiri) who exasperates the local community, is marched off to the asylum, escapes into the woods, and reappears in the guise of a wolf hungry for revenge on the local sheriff. Like Jarva's *The Year of the Hare*, Pakkasvirta's deceptively sunlit film deplores the bigotry and authoritarianism of the late 20th century.

To the northwest, in the province of Pohjanmaa, 'all wisdom gathers in the old women, but the men are filled with madness,' according to a family granny in *Plainlands (Pohjanmaa*, 1988). Adapted from an outstanding novel by Antti Tuuri, this turbulent film revives the time-honoured strife among brothers and girl-friends, cousins and uncles. As they argue over an inheritance from a grandfather who has died in the United States, these hard-drinking, hard-fighting individuals behave like schoolkids playing truant from the real issues of life. **Pekka Parikka**, directing his first feature film at the age of 48 after a long career in television, coaxes daring performances from veteran actors like Esko Salminen and Aarno Sulkanen, and from newcomers like Taneli Mäkelä.

The domestic success of *Plainlands* (which also won the Prix de la Presse at the Festival du Cinéma Nordique in Rouen in 1989) enabled Parikka to embark on the first major dramatic recreation of Finland's 'Winter War' with the Soviet Union in 1939-40. And again, the basis for Parikka's work was a novel by Antti Tuuri. Made in severe conditions on location in Finland, *Winter War (Talvisota*, 1989) commemorates a desperate phase in Finnish 20th-century history. For 105 days, during the terrible winter of 1939-40, Soviet tanks, planes, and artillery bombarded the Finnish lines across the Karelian isthmus. This grim yet often moving film concentrates on an infantry platoon from Ostrabothnia which is force to join the Eastern front where Stalin's divisions are launching a pre-emptive strike against Finland. Parikka's approach shares much in common with Mollberg's in *The Unknown Soldier*. The men are flung into an inferno of pain and death, obliged to withstand the implacable assault of an army infinitely better equipped than its Finnish counterpart. Parikka focuses with relentless precision on the clumsy savagery of trench warfare, and the apprehension of the defending troops as they see a broad line of Russian tanks emerge like prehistoric monsters from a wood. Despite its length (3¼ hours) the film unfolds with a certain lumbering grace, thanks to excellent camerawork by Kari Sohlberg, whose vision of war is couched in livid almost cadaverous tones.

Two other recent films have harked back to the 'Continuation War' of 1941-44. **Timo Linnasalo**, a disciple and colleague of Risto Jarva, focuses on an unfamiliar aspect of the conflict in *Guarded Village 1944 (Vartioitu kylä 1944*, 1979). It observes the sleepy, ominous life of a village on the Russian border, across which guerillas, saboteurs, and fifth columnists slip almost unnoticed. War afflicts this village like a virus, sapping the energy of the inhabitants and spreading distrust throughout the community. Jaakko Pakkasvirta's *Sign of the Beast (Pedon merkki*, 1981) destroys for once and for all any remaining vestiges of satisfaction among Finns with the country's official alliance with the Nazis during the 'Continuation War'. The Finnish officer corps appear craven and disorganised. Corpses are buried with unseemly haste. Hope of victory over the Soviets has long evaporated. The mood of resignation fuels a chaotic orgy of violence and indulgence. Meanwhile, in Lapland, the German presence is tolerated on more humane terms, in *Angela's War (Angelan sota*, 1984), directed by Eija-Elina Bergholm from Jörn Donner's novel about the misplaced love of a Finnish nurse for a Nazi officer.

The late **Heikki Partanan** served his apprenticeship years in documentary, but was always involved in children's films, too. *Pessi and Illusia (Pessi ja Illusia*, 1984) is based on a book that was actually written on the battlefield by Yrjö Kokko. Part fairy tale, part anti-war allegory, its delicate texture owes as much to the cinematography of Henrik Paersch as it does to Partanen's restrained direction. *Pessi and Illusia* uses the landscape of Finland at various stages of the year to suggest hope and despair, bitterness and warmth. 'The presence of war is one of the strongest and most impressive factors in the film,' said Partanen. 'It's true that *Pessi and Illusia* is a fairy story, but it contains much so-called "more significant" material, i.e. reflections of a pacifist nature, and lyrical images of Nature, which at certain junctures aspire to the level of mature metaphysics.' Standing shyly in the margins of contemporary Finnish cinema, **Markku Lehmuskallio** has devoted his obsessive gaze to all manner of flora, fauna, and social outcasts. Few Nordic directors have equalled his studies of men in the Lapp wilderness: *The Raven's Dance (Korpinpolska*, 1980), and *Skierri — Land of the Dwarf Birch (Skierri — vaivaiskoivuven maa*, 1982). Lehmuskallio transcends the limits of the conventional documentary, however, showing his human characters as part of the natural cycle, somewhat in the idiom of Sucksdorff or Troell in Sweden. His most mesmerising film remains *Blue Mammy (Sininen imettäjä*, 1985), strives to penetrate the hermetic world of a deaf mute artist whose inspiration comes from the forest and lakes in which he lives.

*   *   *

In an inevitable reaction against the benevolent despotism of state aid for the arts, some directors in Finland resolved to make their films outside the system. None has done so with more ingenuity and pertinacity than **Anssi Mänttäri**. He began with a bitter account of a modern Finnish family being subverted by alcohol: *The Holy Family (Pyhä perhe*, 1976). Despite the central performance by Lasse Pöysti, the film wore an air of déjà vu. For six years Mänttäri stayed in the wings. Then, in 1982, he slipped on-stage again with *Toto* (1982), using the female pseudonym, Suvi-Marja Korvenheimo. Within 24 months Mänttäri had shot and released three more features, returning to his own signature with *The Clock (Kello*, 1984). As prolific as Godard or Fassbinder, Mäntärri during the mid-1980's seemed to stand at the centre of all intellectual controversy in Helsinki. But the public did not patronise his films, and the critics reacted with lukewarm enthusiasm to his flippant approach. 'I make subjective films on my own conditions,' said Mäntärri. 'If people like them, that's fine, but if they don't, it upsets me only from an economic point of view.' He received hardly any financial support from the Finnish Film Foundation during this period. Mnttäri appears to have burned himself out, although his most recent feature for the cinema, *Mother Wanted (Anni tahtoo äidin,* 1989), is a relaxed, enjoyable exercise in musical comedy, with a young girl trying to find a partner for her shy, single father. Anssi Mänttäri has turned his hand to every genre imaginable, even adapting Aulis Sallinen's and Paavo Haavikko's opera, *The King Goes Forth to France (Kuningas lähtee ranskan*, 1986). At his worst, his narcissism becomes insufferable. He grafts his personal complexes on to everyday situations in contemporary Helsinki, and does so without much visual invention or narrative thrust. Occasionally, he can make a film that engages everyone's fancy, such as *Nothing But Love (Rakkauselokuva*, 1984), which deals with a couple who cannot have children on account of the husband's sterility. In exasperation, they accept the idea of a surrogate father, and this man strikes up a strange, poignant relationship with the wife. Mänttäri's middle-class characters rarely arouse such audience sympathy as do Liisa Halonen, Markku Toikka, and Antti Litja. In the words of Kari Uusitalo, '*Nothing but Love* is as unassuming, warm, and rough-edged as life itself.'

Two other free spirits have manifested themselves in recent seasons. **Ilkka Järvi-Laturi** won the Nordic Film Prize for his first feature, *Homebound (Kotia pain*, 1989). A bleak, spare, haunting film set in the northern town of Oulu, *Homebound* bears the trademark of a fresh and gifted new director, even if its picture of Finnish provincial life owes more to fantasy than to reality. Drenched in pessimism, Järvi-Laturi's work possesses a saving strength and resilience akin to the Kaurismäki brothers. The other new talent is **Juha Tapaninen**, whose background in TV commercials adds zest to his resurrection of small-town dreams during the grim-faced 1960's, in *Prince of the Hit Parade (Iskelmäprinssi*, 1991). This was the decade of cut-rate screen musicals in the Finnish cinema, and from this dross Tapaninen has fashioned something of more precious metal.

Guarded Village 1944 (1979) by Timo Linnasalo

Brothers in Revolt: Mika and Aki Kaurismäki

The cinema has not spawned many partnerships between brothers, at a creative level. Even the famous Soviet pair, 'The Brothers Vasiliev', were not in fact related. The only contemporary parallel is the work of Paolo and Vittorio Taviani in Italy, or Joel and Ethan Coen in the United States. **Mika** and **Aki Kaurismäki** are unique, however, in that each of them makes his own films. When they first embarked on their whirlwind assault on Finnish cinema and its conventions, they helped each other on everything, from writing the screenplay to handling production duties. Aki even acted in Mika's first medium-length work, *The Liar (Valehtelija* (1981). Now they have followed their individual creative paths, while retaining a close fraternal interest in their company, Villealfa Productions, and in the art cinemas which they own in Helsinki.

When they started, the brothers were treated to condescension by most film observers. Their nihilism and constant references to American film noir and the Godardian pranks of the French nouvelle vague seemed likely to restrict their audience to a few perennial movie buffs. Their first feature, *The Worthless (Arvottomat,* 1982) performed respectably in the big city movie theatres, and was selected for festival screenings. Though dismissed by some as a replicant of the German gangster movie (and of Wim Wenders' *The American Friend* in particular), it crackles with an anarchic humour all its own. Besides, the spirit gliding over the Kaurismäki world is that of Erich Maria Remarque, aided and abetted by Patricia Highsmith. The novels of Remarque, say the brothers, 'contain an all-pervasive melancholy and their message is that if you try to attain happiness you destroy everything.'[4] Their anti-heroes are forever on the run, fleeing from the big city towards some earthly paradise beyond — and rarely arriving. Manne, the down-at-heels loser of *The Worthless*, gets on the wrong side of some mobsters. Like the Kaurismäkis themselves, he flouts all the rules, and

73

Pessi and Illusia (1984) by Heikki Partanen

cheerfully so. He is the outside who defies the reality of Finnish life. Everyone knows that you cannot buy hard liquor at a roadside café in Finland — so Manne promptly orders a Calvados. Manne also typifies the Kaurismäki world with his yen for the Ideal Blonde, a dumb broad who looks good and who invariably survives the final shootout, even if she loiters light-years away from today's feminist. The brothers deplore the corrosive influence of American and Swedish culture on their native land. 'Finnish architecture as such has been totally obliterated,' complains Aki Kaurismäki. 'In all our films you will find glimpses of the way Helsinki used to look.'[5] One of the favourite Kaurismäki districts is Eira, in the south of the capital, and in *Calamari Union* (1985), seventeen characters called Frank (plus one named Pekka!) traverse the city from Kallio

to Eira; the film amounts to a dark, inchoate, yet often witty valentine to Helsinki.

When Aki made his début as a director at the age of 26 with *Crime and Punishment (Rikos ja rangaistus*, 1983), he surprised observers with his choice of such a familiar novel. The film's controlled understatement instantly distinguishes it from anything else in the Finnish cinema, however. *Crime and Punishment* progresses with austere rigour towards its ineluctable conclusion. The characters are ultra-modern (the murderer is a law student who earns his money by working in an animal slaughterhouse), but the streets and restaurants of Helsinki are transmuted by Kaurismäki into the landscape of nightmare. One of the abiding strengths of this team has been their ability to shoot on location and yet invest each image with something of the romantic and the bizarre.

Blue Mammy (1985) by Markku Lehmuskallio

Unlike Anssi Mänttäri, the Kaurismäkis have secured a reasonably large audience for their work, and have also made a breakthrough on the screens of Paris, London, and Berlin. Mika is the lighter-hearted of the two, although even his best work is shot through with a fatalistic streak. In *The Clan — The Tale of the Frogs (Klaani — tarina Sammakoitten suvusta,* 1984), a strange agglomeration of petty criminals and social rebels cling together in the outskirts of the city, the enveloping verdure a symbol of the unpolluted life they crave in some obscure, unarticulated manner. This 'family' idiom returns in Mika Kaurismäki's *Helsinki-Napoli — All Night Long* (1987), where a cab-driver in West Berlin finds himself involved in some hilarious mayhem and needs the help of his family to survive. If the Kaurismäkis had done nothing else, they could be praised for nurturing the talent

of Kari Väänänen, whose versatility has brought him roles in a wide variety of Finnish films, from *Jon* to *The Unknown Soldier.* Väänänen brings a convincing blend of naiveté and passion to the name-part in *Rosso,* directed by Mika Kaurismäki in 1985. As an Italian hit-man assigned to kill an unidentified enemy of the Mafia in Finland, he travels on a dark yet often amusing odyssey around the country. As in *The Worthless,* the mournful fields and forest-limned horizons of southern Finland suggest the solitude of the soul in its eternal wandering (the film is prefaced with a quote from Dante's *Inferno*). The Kaurismäkis look upon their country's landscape with the elated, curious eyes of an immigrant.

Aki Kaurismäki, in his trilogy, *Shadows in Paradise (Varjoja paratiisissa,* 1986), *Ariel* and *Match Factory Girl (Tulitikkutehtaan tyttö,* 1990), regards the city as a cold, inhospitable prison, occupied by cheats and felons. To survive, to escape: these become the essential aims of any Kaurismäki character. Aki's assets are a crisp, laconic narrative line, and a minute attention to the details of working existence. His plots seem snatched from the pages of David Goodis or Jim Thompson. Underscoring this like a growling bass motif is the director's resentment of menial labour. Work in a prison plant in *Ariel* looks no worse than the anti-hero's girlfriend's 'legitimate' work in a meat factory, or the supermarket environment in *Shadows in Paradise. Match Factory Girl* opens with a montage of the assembly-line process in match-making, suggesting an environment inimical to emotion or human warmth. In many respects this third film in the trilogy is at once the most austere (in a Bressonian sense) and the most eloquent. The loss of parental love and the cynical deception of a man she meets at a dance bar combine to provoke the unnamed young woman at the centre of the film to take her revenge in a manner worthy of Patricia Highsmith.

Aki, the colder and more subtle of the brothers, has achieved cult status in many cities over the past few years. He has demonstrated a nice line in comic-strip satire in *Leningrad Cowboys Go America* (1989). Shot mostly on location in the United States, the film charts the chaotic progress of a Russian pop band through the American deep south, and does so with bone-dry wit. *I Hired a Contract Killer* (1990) contains many a mordant line, but hovers uneasily between black comedy and poetic realism. The Kaurismäkis have done their best work in their native country, and just as *I Hired a Contract Killer* looks ill at ease in the London docklands, so *Amazon* (1990) transplants Mika's favourite themes to the jungles of South America without enhancing their significance one iota. *Amazon* is redeemed by a bravura central performance by Robert Davi, as a world-weary adventurer who befriends a Finnish businessman who has, one assumes, fled to Brazil to escape some ugly incident in his past, but the ecological 'message' of the film does not carry conviction. Mika has taken a step forward in his career with *Zombie and the Ghost Train (Zombie ja kummitusjuna,* 1991), which was selected for the New York and San Sebastian festivals and conjures up moments of real feeling from a hotch-potch of 'booze, rock 'n roll, Helsinki, and Istanbul'.

Markku Toikka in Aki Kaurismäki's *Crime and Punishment* (1983)

The Kaurismäkis offer the best hope for the Finnish cinema's establishment of a bridgehead in cinemas around the world. Each brother can on occasion produce an image of authentic resonance and imagination (the burial scene in the countryside in *Rosso*, or the death of Mikkonen in *Ariel*, pressing with his last gasp the button that brings the jalopy roof gliding over his head like a shroud). But if they are to join Mollberg, Jarva, and Kassila among the giants of the postwar Finnish film, they must relinquish their childish jocularity and improve on their comic-book character-isations. Finland in turn needs to encourage their prolific production schedules, and to welcome their encouragement of other young directors, at a time when almost all the major production and distribution companies in the country have closed their doors or been swallowed by Finland's last remaining giant of the movie industry, Finnkino — itself compelled to merge with Denmark's Nordisk. To a large degree, the activity of the Kaurismäkis encapsulates the entire history of film in Finland: stories with old-fashioned values, tinged with pessimism, and made on minuscule budgets.

1 Quoted by Peter Cowie, in *Finnish Cinema* (London, The Tantivy Press, 1976)
2 Id., *ibid.*
3 Extracted from *Cahier no. 10*, published by the Festival of La Rochelle, 1989
4 Quoted in *Brothers in Revolt*, in *Look at Finland* (Helsinki, Finnish Tourist Board, no. 1, 1986)
5 *Ibid.*

Matti Pellonpää in Aki Kaurismäki's *Shadows in Paradise* (1986)

Beneath the Glacier (1989) by Gudny Halldórsdóttir

Iceland

Step by step, year by year, the Icelandic cinema, like some glacier descending from the mountains, leaves its mark on the world scene. This fledgling film industry remains apart from its Nordic neighbours by its language (even if it is basically Old Norse, the 'Latin of the North') and minuscule economy. But on closer inspection the Icelandic cinema appears as an extremely durable creation – the creation not so much of movie moguls as of movie maniacs. Film-makers in Reykjavík still mortgage hearth and home in order to realise their dreams, and audiences in the 1980's cheerfully paid more for a ticket to a domestic film than for routine foreign fare from Hollywood or Europe.

In the space of a decade, Iceland has established an instant tradition. Statistically, this does not sound very impressive: two or three feature-length films each year, serving the islands' population of around 240,000. But at least two Icelandic directors, Ágúst Gudmundsson and Hrafn Gunnlaugsson, have earned a reputation on the festival circuit, and some of their films have been screened in art-houses and on television outside the Nordic area. Reykjavík, the capital, contains a mere 90,000 inhabitants but as films like *Jón Oddur and Jón Bjarni* and *Inter Nos* have demonstrated, here may be found the urban pressures and complexes that afflict Paris or New York.

Thanks to co-productions with Sweden, Norway, and Denmark, the Icelanders have managed to sidestep the inevitable financial exigencies of a tiny nation which, even if it boasts its own international airline, does not have the resources to invest heavily in the cinema.

The landscape is conducive to outdoor film-making. In winter, Iceland actually records a higher mean temperature than either New York or Vienna, while its long, clear days and nights in spring and summer fulfil the cinematographer's dream. Much of Iceland's natural beauty is mirrored in those films released in recent years: its rolling uplands around Reykjavík, with black volcanic soil peering through the crusted snow like the slag from some Valhallan coalmine; the pastoral valleys where remote farms survive on slender resources; the glaciers and *geysírs* that lend a sense of danger and impermanence to the Icelander's way of life; and the calm lakes and tranquil inlets.

Budgets are trimmed to the bone in Iceland. Ágúst Gudmundsson made *Land and Sons* in 1979 for a mere $130,000. Thráinn Bertelsson's suspense thriller, *Twilight*, cost $200,000. Actors and actresses, of whom there only about 200 in the entire country, receive modest stipends. Studios as such do not exist. *The House*, one of the most professionally-shot of Icelandic features, made use of a warehouse in Reykjavík harbour for its interior sequences.

Before the Revolution

Icelandic cinema begins in 1906, when a three-minute documentary was shot in the country by the Dane, Alfred Lind (Denmark having owned Iceland for some six centuries by that stage). The first movie theatre opened in Reykjavík on November 2, 1906. Not for almost a dozen years did native film production get under way. In 1919, a team from Nordisk Film Kompagni in Copenhagen came to Iceland to shoot *The Story of the Borg Family (Saga Borgarœttarinnar*, 1921). Filming took place in a small town just 10 km outside the capital, and excellent use was made of a local wool-market, as well as the craggy rock formations that distinguish the Icelandic landscape. Based on a popular Icelandic novel by Gunnars Gunnarsson and starring an Icelandic actor, the story adumbrated one of the themes that has percolated Icelandic cinema itself in recent years: the conflict between the desire to travel abroad in search of fame and fortune, and the need to remain at home to tend the ancestral estate.

Hadda Padda, co-directed in 1923 by **Gunnar Róbert Hansen** and **Gúdmundur Kamban**, features one of the most respected of Danish actresses, Clara Pontoppidan, and its final reel proves that Victor Sjöström by no means stood alone as the only Nordic silent director capable of handling outdoor suspense. Clara Pontoppidan, dangling on the end of a rope above a treacherous chasm, tries to drag down the man whose love for her has now ended. After a desperate struggle with her emotions, she cuts the rope and plunges to her death in the foaming waters below. The sequence calls to mind Sjöström's narrow escape while shooting *The Outlaw and His Wife*, and Miss Pontoppidan confirmed in an interview that a double was only used in certain shots.

Such films merely confirmed the Icelandic environment as uniquely exotic. Local film-makers remained in the shadow of the better-equipped Danes who visited the country regularly. Abroad, Jacques de Baroncelli made an impressive screen version of Pierre Loti's *Pêcheur d'Islande* in 1924.

Loftur Gudmundsson (no relation to Ágúst Gudmundsson) forms the bridge between the silent and sound periods in Icelandic film history. In 1923 he made *The Adventures of Jón and Gvendur* on 35mm, but then withdrew from the fray until 1948, when he resurrected some documentary footage he had shot on 16mm in 1924 and developed his material into the country's first colour talkie, *Between Mountain and Shore (Milli fjalls og fjöru)*.

It is a 19th-century story again reminiscent of *The Outlaw and His Wife*, describing the romance between Ingólf, a poor farmer's son, and a wealthy merchant's daughter. Some heads of slaughtered sheep are discovered, and the young man is arrested and flung into an open-air wooden cage. The real thieves are caught red-handed soon afterwards as they prepare to escape in a boat laden with more sheep (next to fish, Iceland's most precious living commodity). The film suggests that the merchant takes sides with the poor, which was certainly not always the case in real life, although *Between Mountain and Shore* is based on a true incident.

With Iceland achieving independence from Denmark at last in 1944, a new spirit of national pride in the arts took hold. The prolific Óskar Gíslason directed several films on 16mm during the 1950s, including *New Role (Nýtt hlutverk*, 1954), the story of an old harbour worker who has nothing to do when he retires. Mixing documentary and dramatic scenes (the film opens with the old man attending his wife's burial), *New Role* gives a lively impression of the Icelandic herring fishing tradition.

Gabriel Axel brought some vigour (if also some unconscious humour and bathos) to the saga form in *The Red Mantle (Den røde kappe*, 1967), with Gunnar Björnstrand and Eva Dahlbeck involved in love, treachery and death in medieval Iceland. Shot in 'scope, *The Red Mantle* took full advantage of its locations on Iceland without persuading its audience that this tale of revenge was anything other than a costume spectacle on a par with Hollywood's cloak and sandal epics.

Much more intriguing, and serving as a harbinger of good things to come, is **Reynir Oddsson's** *Murder Story (Mordsaga*, 1977). Wickedly satirical, as dry as a good martini, and audacious in its use of long takes, *Murder Story* seems strongly influenced by the work of Claude Chabrol. Oddsson takes delight in mocking the garish, American-style furnishings of the Icelandic bourgeoisie. A young office worker lives with her horrid father and meek mother. The man listens to Wagner's *'Tristan and Isolde'* on disc while his wife quaffs cognac furtively in the bathroom, and indulges in sexual daydreams. The film reaches its high point during a grotesque dinner party at which the guests pay lip-service to the chichi names of the hour, whether they be Haydn or Dean Martin. It breaks up in disarray when one of the guests tries to seduce the host. The ensuing murder, and the bizarre attempt to dispose of the corpse, is filmed by Reynir with guile and professional skill. Not surprisingly, he left for Hollywood soon afterwards, and worked for a while in American television.

The Breakthrough

In April 1979, the Icelandic Film Fund was launched and dispensed some 30 million Icelandic crowns – less than half the cost of a single feature. Shared out among several applicants, this sum did however act as a trigger for a release of cinematic energy unequalled in the Nordic region since the establishment of the Swedish Film Institute in 1963. Independent producers came forward; directors invested their salaries and arranged leasing of their films to the country's various movie theatres (there is no distribution system *per se* in Iceland). Technicians performed more than one chore. Actors came from the streets and hills as well as from the stage.

By the late 1970's, several of Iceland's brightest young artists were coming home from studies abroad (Ágúst Gudmundsson, for example, had graduated from Britain's National Film School), and joined with friends who had been working in television. They rejected the easy option – the cloning of the Hollywood commercial movie – and instead brought their talents to bear on local subjects, local traditions, and local cultural impulses. Although the Icelandic sagas have inspired three or four films during the past decade, the emphasis has been on modern topics, on

themes that flow without affectation from the everyday lives and concerns of Icelanders.

Ágúst Gudmundsson emerged first from the starting gate, with the premiere of *Land and Sons (Land og synir)* on February 25, 1980. Almost half of the country's entire population flocked to see the film, a remarkable figure even for Icelanders, who attend the cinema ten times each per annum. Much of the credit must go to Ágúst's shrewd choice of subject-matter. *Land and Sons* deals with the economic depression of the 1930's, when farmers suffered from sheep disease as well as financial hardship, and the migration to Reykjavík and other coastal towns in Iceland gathered pace. Indridi G. Thorsteinsson's novel focuses on a lone farmer and his son, trying to eke out a living in a mist-shrouded, isolated valley. Book and film delineate the ideological and emotional differences between father and son – the one tied to the farm and the local community, the other tempted to seek new values in an urban environment. *Land and Sons* has the tang of a pastoral Western. The smallholding on the lush hillside evokes *Shane*, but in place of marauding cattle barons there is penury and deprivation. The son despises the rustic routine. 'Our inheritance is economic crisis and disease,' he complains. When the father succumbs to a heart attack while raking hay in the fields, the son reconsiders his position. Saddled with debts, he sells the farm and the sheep, digs a grave for his favourite horse and shoots it the next morning. The boy waits for a bus to take him and his girlfriend to the city. But the girl fails to arrive, and the young man, leaving his dog with a hotel-keeper, boards the bus alone. . . .

Ágúst displays a sure grasp of narrative line in this début feature. Using long-shots (which usually decelerate a film's progress) to fix the characters in their wilderness landscape, he relies on brief spurts of laconic conversation to give the audience the facts it needs. Certain key sequences, such as the father's collapse, contain virtually no audible dialogue. Significant issues like the development of the co-operative movement, which the father helped to establish in the district, are not permitted to dominate the human tragedy of the film, which amounts to the inevitable dissolution of family ties in the face of hardship and solitude. *Land and Sons* signals the flight of younger folk to the towns, rearing in turn a succession of urban problems.

The first film of Ágúst's contemporary, friend and rival, **Hrafn Gunnlaugsson**, bears a singular resemblance to *Land and Sons* in thematic material. The conflict between duty and ambition gives *Father's Estate (Óðal feðranna*, 1980) its impetus, as a widow tries to prevail upon one of her two sons to return to the countryside and care for the family estate. Where Ágúst's film closes on a note of liberation, Hrafn's shows the university student effectively trapped on the farm with his ailing mother and his handicapped sister. *Father's Estate* is based on the director's original screenplay, and takes place in a contemporary Iceland where the farmer's life is regarded by many city-dwellers as a sentence of death. The contrast in style readily distinguishes these two films, however. Hrafn's work, dark of hue, boils with a restless energy like the huge hot-water spring, Geysír, that figures in his second film, *Inter Nos*. Ágúst's approach is less ostentatious, allowing the theme to percolate into the viewer's subconscious, so that images and morsels of dialogue linger long after the film has ended.

Hrafn has, in his 'modern' films, displayed a fascination with the disintegration of the family unit. *Inter Nos (Okkar á milli*, 1982) identifies with a middle-aged man, an engineer who has lost his bearings. His children are leaving home, and he and his wife no longer enjoy any meaningful life together. The power stations which he helped to manage and improve now strike him as futile. He yearns for a fresh start. . . . In the words of Thór Vilhjálmsson, the award-winning poet and novelist, *Inter Nos* is 'an aggressive work, attacking via the senses in an attempt to overwhelm and thus incense, eventually achieving a kind of catharsis, symbolised in the ejaculatory jet of the Geysír. The audacious director handles such themes as the meaning of life, love, sex, national values, as well as faith itself.'[1] But while its theme commands interest, the realisation of *Inter Nos* is too rash and over-heated to carry conviction. Benedikt Árnason, in the leading role, fails to suggest the current of dissatisfaction that must be coursing through this victim of the male menopause; and Hrafn's use of a zoom lens and a hand-held camera induces nausea instead of emotional anxiety. One must give credit, though, to Hrafn for his dark vein of humour, a satanic cackle of glee as a counter to the reality of the stifling, almost incestuous, loyalties of a small community.

Not all Icelanders fling themselves against the tides of life with such mercurial zest as Hrafn Gunnlaugsson. Nor yet are they so dour and humourless as many Scandinavians. One of the characteristics of an Icelander remains his quixotic spark of adventure, the antic smile that countenances risk without trepidation. **Thráinn Bertelsson**, a graduate of the Dramatic Institute in Stockholm, has, like many Icelandic directors, worked for television, directing a two-part study of *Sporri Sturluson*, the 13th-century author. Thráinn attracted more widespread attention with his feature film based on the best-selling suite of novels, *The Twins (Jón Oddur og Jón Bjarni*, 1981), written by Gudrún Helgadóttir. Two blond twin boys grow up in a modern household on the fringe of Reykjavík; mother is a nurse and father a teacher. Granny drives a jeep and goes under the nickname of 'Grand-dragon'! Like all children, the twins cherish their fantasy world, and during summer camp they take off with a couple of pals. None of their escapades is too dramatic, but therein lies the appeal of this deceptively bland entertainment. Thráinn's touch captures the everyday rhythm of childhood, and perceives adults through the refracting gaze of boys whose thoughts are more quicksilver than their demure smiles would suggest.

With so few film-makers active in Iceland, the critic may be tempted to regard their work in auteurist terms. This would be unfair to the inventive courage of the Icelandic director, who seizes any change to tackle a fresh genre, even if part of that motivation may be prompted by expediency, the need to survive in a brutally small marketplace. The thriller, often laced with supernatural overtones, has attracted various writers and directors. **Egill Edvardsson**, coming from a background in documentaries and TV commercials, has not received due recognition in Iceland for *The House (Húsid*, 1983), although the film did win three Gold Awards at the 1983 Fantasy Festival in Brussels. This supernatural tale throbs with something of the same quality as Nicolas Roeg's *Don't Look Now*, and boasts a superb performance by Lilja Thórisdóttir, as a young teacher sucked into the past by gremlins in a Reykjavík house which she has purchased with her husband. By relinquishing special effects, Edvardsson makes the situation more uncanny than the 'Old Dark House' formula generally permits. Snorri Thórisson's camera patrols the dim rooms of the couple's home with fluency and sinister authority.

Thráinn Bertelsson essays the same genre in *Twilight (Skammdegi*, 1985), shot in the western fjords of Iceland. Ragnheidur Arnarsdóttir seems perfectly cast as the dark, sensual, guileful young widow who hatches a scheme for swindling her in-laws out of their share of the family fish-farm. *Twilight* was inspired by a genuine poltergeist outbreak, and Bertelsson marshalls his natural assets — the perilous landscape of ice and snow, the loneliness of the farm, with its incongruous swimming pool illuminated by night — only to let the dramatic tension uncoil in scene after scene. When violence does break out (a snowmobile charging out of control, or a blaze at the shack beside the pool), the film exerts a weird intensity. It also shows how the 'foreigner', the visitor from abroad or even from Reykjavík, experiences vibrations of hostility and deracination in the remote areas of Iceland.

Psychological isolation also grips the neophyte novelist, Helgi, in Hilmar Oddsson's *The Beast (Eins og skepnan deyr*, 1986), when he returns to his childhood home out near the fjords. He is haunted by the dream of shooting a reindeer, and the borderline between fantasy and reality blurs as the film progresses. The film suffers from similar problems to those that vitiate *Twilight*. Sinister openings to sequences sputter and die; tension fails to accumulate. The narrative line wavers and drifts into meditative confusion long before the young anti-hero succumbs to his deep-seated anger.

Swedes have a word for imagination that translates literally as 'fantasy full', which is exactly applicable to **Lárus Ýmir Óskarsson's** splendid début, *The Second Dance (Andra dansen*, 1982), made for the Swedish company, Sandrews, in association with the Swedish Film Institute. Critics have tarred Óskarsson's effort with the brush of Wenders, Polanski, and Antonioni; but throughout this road movie for women lurk constant flashes of inspiration so enigmatic, so magical, and so impish that they mark the Icelander as one of the most original voices of his generation. Two women meet outside Stockholm. Jo, the younger one, gives Anna a lift in her battered Citroën. While Anna is bold and assertive, quick-thinking and shrewd, Jo lingers in the background, recording incidents with her camera. Anna dreams of a father and the legacy that might be hers; but, as in all classic road movies, the journey, not the arrival, matters. In a hotel worthy of Hitchcock or Nemec, an impromptu drinks party goes sour; an ugly black raven watches balefully in a nearby room. In a bizarre, floodlit mansion, both Anna and Jo dress up in ball gowns and then flee from the distraught owner of the property. *The Second Dance* uses monochrome cinematography to transmute the virgin landscape of northern Sweden into a dream zone, in which people become dark shadows, of themselves and of their past and future.

After a frustrating decade, spent mostly in Sweden, Lárus Ýmir returned to his roots with *Rust (Ryd, 1991)*, a film full of technical panache yet altogether lacking in narrative verve or conviction, dwelling uncomfortably on the sins of a ruthless garage owner named, appropriately, Baddi.

All of these films function on a more subtle level, than the loud and abrasive *Foxtrot* (1988). Its director, Jón Tryggvason, is too reliant upon his experience of TV commercials, and piles one climax atop another until a plateau of absurdity is reached. Even the bizarre configurations of the Icelandic landscape lose their atmospheric quality as the film develops into a crude B-movie about two half-brothers driving across the country with a truckful of money. Both men, and the girl they meet en route, assume comic-book proportions, while the cliché-ridden dialogue, and the heavy lather of violence applied to scene after scene, only reinforces the American idiom.

Violence spatters the pages of every Icelandic saga, yet it remains comparatively rare in those local films dealing with contemporary issues and relationships. **Fridrik Thór Fridriksson** introduces shooting and gore into *White Whales (Skytturnar, 1987)* and does so with some justification. The entire film amounts to a roar of fury, tracking the destiny of two simple-minded seamen after they come ashore from a whaling expedition. Away from the heaving deck and the lashing seas, Grímur and Bubbi cannot cope with life. They make pathetic efforts to ingratiate themselves with people in Reykjavík, but the scorn and hostility of the inhabitants towards them provokes a lethal outburst of anger. Fridriksson passes withering judgement on the small-minded attitudes of his countrymen where the fishing industry is concerned, and by the climax of *White Whales* has succeeded in engaging the audience's sympathy for his maverick protagonists. Ari Kristinsson's photography makes no pretence at sophisticated lighting or crystalline focus; the movie looks like a newsreel, and the grainy texture of its visuals counterpoint the harsh naturalism of the story.

There is violence of a sort in Fridrik Thór's second film too: *Children of Nature (Börn náttúrannar, 1991)*. Focusing on the emotional and physical frustrations of old folk in Iceland, this engaging quasi-melodrama makes full use of the island's fierce and other-worldly landscapes, without yet persuading us that Fridrik Thór is a true *auteur* in the class of Gudmundsson or Gunnlaugsson.

The Atomic Station (Atómstödin, 1984) journeys back to the postwar years to re-evaluate Iceland's attitude to the foreign powers trying to manipulate its future. The original novel by Nobel laureate Halldór Laxness appeared in 1948 and its controversial rhetoric does not sound so compelling as it did then. Left-wing Icelanders still regard the American base at Keflavík with barely-disguised revulsion, although the summit between Gorbachev and Reagan in 1986 diluted

such feelings to a certain degree. But in the final analysis, *The Atomic Station* fails to speak with a commanding voice because of a fundamentally pedestrian mise-en-scène by Thorsteinn Jónsson. The period detail is established with meticulous care, and occasionally Jónsson introduces a visual frisson (such as the poles for a perimeter fence being driven into the cold earth around Keflavík like nails into a coffin) commensurate with the rich, resonant dialogue of Laxness.

The film also stresses the contrast between the ideals of the countryside and the cynical, opportunist aims of the city. Torn between these two ways of life, the pugnacious Edda finds herself caught up in the political intrigues sweeping Reykjavík, and recognising the sinister implications of sententious remarks such as, 'A small defenceless nation must be realistic to survive.' Laxness describes Edda's father building a church with his own hands in the desolate beauty of southern Iceland, while a whore in Reykjavík declares her eagerness for the atom bomb to be stored on Iceland because soldiers will pay for sex. Indeed, *The Atom Station* evinces a truth that Icelanders may take for granted but that to the outsider is quite striking — namely the strength and assertiveness of the island's women, inured by long centuries of having to care for themselves and their dependents while the menfolk went out to fishing on the high seas.

This promising dialectic never quite ignites, and the impoverished acting of Gunnar Hafsten Eyjólfsson as the weak, mealy-mouthed Member of Parliament handicaps many crucial scenes. The fate of *The Atomic Station* encapsulates the reality of film-making on Iceland. Its producer and his colleagues mortgaged the very smoke from their chimneys to make the film on a budget of $500,000. A year or so after its release they were forced into bankruptcy, despite the rare prestige of a screening at the Directors' Fortnight in Cannes and a professional publicity campaign.

The Comedy Element

Ágúst Gudmundsson has created a peculiarly zany kind of comedy that reflects the Icelanders' refusal to kowtow to social convention or to foreign influences, whether they be cultural, political, or economic. His musical comedy, *On Top (Med allt á hreinu, 1982)*, attracted audiences of more than 100,000 — almost incredible in a total population of less than 250,000. Its effervescence is hard to resist, however. The film sets out on a cheerful odyssey round the townships of Iceland in the company of two rival pop groups. The lead singers in each band have had a lovers' tiff — one of the funniest quarrels imaginable, filmed by Ágúst with slapstick gusto — and resolve to thwart each other. Such is the mirror that *On Top* holds up to the competition between the sexes in the contemporary world. The music bounces along, and is performed with professional brio; the direction is as light as a soufflé. At the film's première performance outside Iceland, Ágúst and his fellow scribe, Valgeir Gudjónsson, literally 'sang' a translation of the lyrics and dialogue over the headphones so that an audience unfamiliar with the tufts

Lilja Thórisdottír in *The House* (1983) by Egill Edvardsson

and thickets of the Icelandic language could appreciate the felicities of this offbeat musical. Apart from some over-emphatic emoting by the players, *On Top* sustains a deftness of touch and gaiety of mood rare in world cinema — and virtually unknown in Nordic films.

In *Golden Sands (Gullsandur*, 1984), Ágúst exhibits a flair for satirical film-making of the Ealing or *Clochemerle* brand, although the common threads linking all Ágúst's work are an emotional warmth and idiosyncratic outlook. On a remote stretch of Icelandic coastline, the local inhabitants are puzzled by the appearance of a tiny task-force from the American base at Keflavík. The soldiers seem to be burrowing into the sand for something or other, and the locals start holding their own council of war. Their reaction remains quite lethargic until it suddenly emerges that the Yanks may be digging for gold. Ágúst takes a sly dig at his fellow countrymen for their complaisant attitude to the

military implications of the American presence, while simultaneously applauding their natural response to the prospect of a gold rush on the neighbouring beach.

The film nourishes more ambitions than just that, however. Ágúst draws a parallel between today's events on the sands and the volcanic eruption that took place some two centuries earlier in the same region, and one of his main characters is busy writing a screenplay about the heroic parson who refused to quit his church and halted the larva by sheer force of personality. Less pretentious, and more amusing, are the director's sly glances at the contradictions inherent in Icelandic life: the farmer who listens to grand opera in his cowshed, and milks beneath the approving glare of a Karl Marx poster; or the running gag about a black stripper whose audience is whittled away by the lure of the Golden Sands.

Thráinn Bertelsson has mined another, more facile vein of

comedy, in his series about a pair of young scoundrels, Thór and Danni, who cause chaos in the fishing factories of the Westman Islands *(New Life)*, the farming community *(Pastoral Life)*, and the forces of law and order as they don police uniform *(Policeman's Lot)*. The gags are repetitive and the acting coarse-grained; Thráinn's talent extends much further than this genre of provincial farce, as *Magnús* (see below), nominated for the Best European Film of the Year award, makes plain.

Message to Sandra (Skilabod til Söndru, 1985) stems from the energetic team of Kristín Pálsdóttir (directing) and **Gudný Halldórsdóttir** (screenwriter and producer). Its blend of social comedy and artistic self-reflection does not quite succeed, but the first section of the film, observing a middle-aged writer's attempt to get to grips with a screenplay out in the wilderness, while also coping with the disarmingly ironic remarks of the young woman he has employed as housekeeper, possesses a satisfying interior rhythm. The uncertainties of the male menopause, however, tend to be obscured by the melodramatic development of the story, involving illicit sex video-cassettes and a climactic flight to Greece, where the writer becomes a café-proprietor capable of writing naught but a letter to the girl he has left behind.

Gudný Halldórsdóttir stamps her screenwriter's presence very firmly on another comedy, *The Icelandic Shock-Station (Stella í orlofi*, 1986). Chaotic, disjointed, yet undeniably amiable, this farce makes fun of the archetypal Swedish drunk. 'Salomon Gustavsson' arrives at the airport in search of a cure for his liquor problem. Instead, he finds himself at the mercy of the lusty, invigorating, endlessly inventive Icelandic housewife, Stella. Even in such a crude face, the Icelandic propensity for exaggeration, taking risks, and celebrating human clumsiness acquires an appealing aspect.

Black without Sugar (1986) takes its title from the name of an itinerant Icelandic theatre group. Directed by the young German, Lutz Konermann, and shot in black-and-white 'scope, the film is, to quote Ingólfur Margeirsson, 'a charming and ambitious film combining the road movie à la Wenders, with elements of comedy and romance. Beneath the story lies the director's requirement to make associations with different cultures, to draw social and historical parallels in order to understand the relations and connections that bind people and places together.'[2] As the troupe drift with their play through Italy, from the bustle of Rome to the tranquillity of Orvieto, Konermann manifests a distinctive skill at composing visuals and establishing a mood with the strains of a Verdi extract or the wistful dreaming tones of a tenor sax.

Living History

Icelanders regard the sagas as their national heritage. This universal literature, dating mostly from the 13th and 14th centuries, has been described by Thór Vilhjálmsson: 'The "Eddas" created for the entire North the finest pheno-menon of literary creation, one of the ageless treasures of the imaginary museum of Mankind. It flourished during a period of moral decay, a disintegration of the singular social structure, established by the settlers on a republican basis, centred around the first parliament (still in existence) founded in 930 A.D. Power in the 13th century had become concentrated in the hands of a few families madly struggling for predominance, even sovereignty, contrary to the balance of authority, responsibility, and realisable justice decreed by law, a sensible constitution that served the period so well and endured some centuries.'[3]

Ágúst Gudmundsson plunged into the thick of this vibrant literature with *Outlaw (Útlaginn*, 1981). Made almost wholly on location, the film charts an individual's clash with society, maintaining and protecting his values 'unto death'. *The Saga of Gísli* remains popular reading in Iceland even today, and in spirit Ágúst's approach to its story of a brother's loyalty cannot be faulted. The film lacks, however, the conviction of a period piece like *The Seventh Seal*. The characters are ill-defined and hard to distinguish from one another. The costumes and makeup fail to conceal the modern actors' way of delivering lines or cocking a stance. Against these flaws must be set the appealing simplicity of the images — a funeral beside a mountain tarn, or a boat burning like the pyres on the banks of the Ganges.

In Hrafn Gunnlaugsson's *The Raven Flies (Hrafninn flýgur*, 1984), the visual conflict between an unfettered seascape and a lofty, rearing line of mountains along the shore acts as a paradigm for the struggle between the outlaws and the film's young protagonist from Ireland. Certain either to exhilarate or enrage the foreign viewer, *The Raven Flies* is without doubt the best rendition to date of the Icelandic saga form, with the short sentences of that unique narrative species transmuted on screen into terse, abbreviated sentences and ejaculations of dialogue. In presenting this story of revenge, involving an Irishman who sails to Iceland in search of two villainous Vikings, Thór and Erik, Hrafn parades his admiration for both Kurosawa (*Yojimbo* in particular) and Sergio Leone. Gigantic close-ups, strident music, and majestic travelling shots along the barbarous coast give the tale the dimensions of a Western, which might be more aptly titled *Once upon a Time in the North*. Hrafn contends that in his epic he has sought to drain the myth away from young people's conception of the Viking era. Life in medieval Iceland was nasty, brutish, and short, and Helgi Skúlason's bristling performance as the villain embodies this reality. As philosophy, *The Raven Flies* may be closer to *Conan the Barbarian* than to Njal's or any other saga, but for a country with such a tiny population and such a fledgling film 'industry', Hrafn's work is a remarkable achievement. Its skills found recognition the following winter, when Hrafn won the Gold Bug for Best Director in Sweden (Stockholm-based Viking Film having contributed to the production). 'Making that film was like a military campaign,' recalls Hrafn. 'It was madness. You gamble everything, your physical and mental well-being, all your money, to make a film. In the end it was like being cast ashore in a storm; you don't give a damn what happens to the ship, even whether it is smashed on the rocks.'[4]

Hrafn has pursued his exploration of the medieval era in a Swedish TV film, *The Headsman and the Harlot (Bödeln och skökan*, 1986), which paints a ferocious picture of bigotry, betrayal, and sexual prejudice. He spent some two years, however, in concocting a sequel to *The Raven Flies*, the financial success of which in Scandinavia ensured Hrafn an easy passage when he needed to raise $2 million for *The Shadow of the Raven (I skugga hrafnsins*, 1988).

The Western, with its tight-knit family gangs and feuds, resembles the dramatic content of the Sagas. 'John Ford, for example, expresses himself with such simplicity that it verges on the fairytale,' says Hrafn, 'but he makes every line count. And my way to the Icelandic Sagas is not that of a professor of Old Norse, but working as a catalyst.'[5] Set in 1077 A.D., *The Shadow of the Raven* is made with more technical assurance than its prequel, and feeds on a constant dialectic of sea versus land, religion versus paganism, good versus evil, pacifism versus violence. A gigantic stranded whale on the seashore provides an excuse for three days of hand-to-hand fighting; a bath-house is sealed and its occupants boiled alive. The ubiquitous knife is at once a weapon and a token of power.

If one takes issue with Hrafn's version of medieval life, it is not because of the undiluted savagery, but rather because the actors seem to be straining beyond realism into a grotesque, even risible, form of expression. Sune Mangs, as the scheming bishop, and Helgi Skúlason, as the vicious steward, become symbols of evil instead of the human figures who bestride the pages of the Sagas.

Limping into the Future

Icelandic cinema has reached a critical stage in its development. During the 1980's, domestic (and foreign festival) audiences rallied to its cause out of curiosity, and sympathy for the courage of directors like Ágúst Gudmundsson and Hrafn Gunnlaugsson. Now, despite increases in the level of government support, economic difficulties assail the small band of film-makers on Iceland. The stories of bankruptcy have gone beyond a joke. Production has diminished to two or three, even one film each year. Casualties include **Thorsteinn Jónsson**, whose *Dot, Dot, Comma, Dash (Punktur, punktur, komma, strik*, 1981) augured a promising career, only for his progress to be halted in mid-flight by the debacle of *The Atomic Station*. The mixing of artistic media has tempted Icelandic film-makers, usually with disastrous results. Some critics welcomed **Kristín Jóhannesdóttir's** debut as a director, with *Rainbow's End (Á hjara veraldar*, 1983). Kristín studied cinema in Paris, and introduces into her film some of the eternal avant-garde pretensions familiar in painting, music, and literature the world over. The dialogue is incantatory, the gestures histrionic. Somewhere in the midst of this intellectual ceremonial lies the germ of a story, with a mother from the north of Iceland who has settled down as a housewife in Reykjavík and in the process has lost her gift of singing. The alluring camerawork redeems the film's inchoate form, and the whiff of the occult that seasons *Rainbow's End* links it also with works such as *Twilight* and Gudný Halldórsdóttir's *Beneath the Glacier* (based on Halldór Laxness's mystical novel about a bishop's emissary who investigates some bizarre occurrences at Snæfell's glacier).

The past two years have brought much-needed encouragement to the Icelandic film community. Thráinn Bertelsson's *Magnús* was one of the six final nominees for the 'Best European Film' award in Paris. The director's alter ego (same surname, same age) reacts with understandable shock and dismay to the news that he is suffering from cancer. Like the heroine of Astrid Henning-Jensen's *The Moment*, he tries to look calmly at his mortal situation, and to cope with the overwhelming confusion that his disease wreaks in his family. This deeply-felt film marks a major step forward in Thráinn's career, and proves that Icelandic cinema can set its sights extremely high, however hazardous the financial risks. Fridrik Thór Fridrikson's sensitive *Children of Nature* (see above) won the Felix for best music score in 1991, and received another nomination at the European Film Awards.

1. Thór Vilhjálmsson, in *International Film Guide 1984* (London, The Tantivy Press, 1983)
2 Ingolfur Margeirsson, in *International Film Guide 1987* (London, The Tantivy Press, 1986)
3 Thór Vilhjálmsson, 'Iceland – Really!', in *The Scandinavian Guide 1987* (London, The Tantivy Press, 1986)
4 Quoted in 'Once Upon a Time in the North' by Solveig K. Jónsdóttir, in *Iceland Review* (Rekyjavík, no. 4, 1987)
5 Id., *ibid.*

Madame Visits Oslo (1927) by Harry Ivarson

Norway

Time and nature have achieved an even distribution of the arts among the Nordic communities. Finland has always been to the fore in music and architecture, Denmark in philosophy and ballet, Sweden in film (and runner-up in just about everything else), and Norway in painting and − through Ibsen − in drama.

Not until the 1980's, however, did Norway excel in the art of the cinema. Indeed until the early 1970's, lack of adequate government funding meant that the domestic film industry was languishing in anonymity and mediocrity. Jan Erik Holst has pointed out the relatively large number of companies involved in production in Norway. 'A consistently recurring feature is that often a company was formed in order to make a single film: during the period 1908-75, 314 full-length films were produced by 105 companies. This remarkable distribution can be ascribed mainly to the economic factors which have played a decisive part in film production in Norway; during the early years the industry was dominated by purely commercial considerations.'[1]

A few months after the Lumière brothers' first projections in Paris, the German pioneers Max and Emil Skladanowski presented their 'bioscop' at a circus in Oslo (then known as Kristiania). According to Nils A. Klevjer Aas, 'For the next ten years itinerant cinema exhibitors roamed the country setting up their gear at fairs and following the fishing fleet and the construction crews on railways, roads and building projects. Most of these early cinema pioneers were foreigners, as were their films − French and German, Swedish and Danish.'[2]

No individual, however, seized the initiative as Ole Olsen did in Denmark or Charles Magnusson in Sweden. Norwegians remained content in regarding the movies as a pastime pure and simple, and ironically the first recorded 'Norwegian' film, a tense, quasi-documentary entitled *The Dangers of a Fisherman's Life − an Ocean Drama (Fiskerlivets farer − ett drama på havet*, 1908), was directed by the Swedish cameraman Julius Jaenzon − with funding from Hugo Hermansen, the 'Cinema King' who at that juncture owned 26 movie theatres. This one-reeler described a fisherman whose son falls overboard in high seas. He and his wife try in vain to save the boy. He is pulled on board, but too late for him to be saved. The sea features strongly in Victor Sjöström's screen version of *Terje Vigen* (see SWEDEN), but not so frequently in Norway's own films through the decades. The mountains that run like a curved spine up through the country have attracted the film-maker much more often.

Judgement on the work of Norway's lone pioneer before 1920, **Peter Lykke-Seest**, can never be definitive, for virtually all his films have been lost. He had begun his career as a screenwriter in Sweden, and he established the embryonic studio, Christiania Film Compagni, in 1916. He turned his hand to any reasonable story: the gypsy lad in search of happiness in *Paris* (1916), the romantic lovers in *Young Hearts (Unge hjerter*, 1917), or the industrial strike in *Heroes of Our Time (Vor tids helter*, 1918). According to Jan Erik Holst,[3] Lykke-Seest's most interesting film may well have been *The Story of a Boy (Historien om en gut*, 1919). Christiania Film Compagni closed its doors after failing to sell sufficient of its products on the lucrative American market.

In 1913, the Norwegian government passed the Film Theatres' Act, which not only comprised rules pertaining to censorship but also the stipulation that the country's municipal councils alone had the right to license the public screening of films. 'Municipal cinemas were established,' according to Klevjer Aas, 'first to combat opportunistic exploitation, second to employ the new mass medium in the cause of popular enlightenment, and (only) last with the expectation that the enterprise would be financially self-supporting or even bring a profit to the municipal coffers.'[4]

In practice, however, the authorities tended to invest the income from the cinemas into the building of new schools and other educational activities, and the fledgling Norwegian film industry began to lag behind its Nordic neighbours, where the major chains ploughed back much of their profit into film production.

Despite a resolute campaign by the film distributors, the municipal cinema system survived and indeed became entrenched. Even the radical new Film and Video Act of 1987 failed to change the basic principle upon which the showing of films has always depended in Norway: the local municipality has the right to sanction every public showing of film in whatever form.

Rasmus Breistein led Norway's effort to establish a national cinema during the 1920's. He had started life as a musician, and then enjoyed a spell as a stage actor. The energy and competence of his first film, *Anne the Gipsy-girl (Fante-Anne*, 1920) came as a surprise. Piling on one melodramatic plot twist after another, Breistein traces the story of the gigsy-girl Anne who has been brought up as a foster-child on a large country estate. Her childhood sweetheart, Haldor, is the son of the estate-owner, and is not permitted to marry Anne. In a fit of jealous fury, she sets fire to the house with Haldor and his bride-to-be inside. One of the estate workers, Jon, justifies his secret affections for Anne by assuming blame for the arson. Years later, after he has been released and made his fortune in the United States, Jon returns to claim Anne.

Breistein, like Sjöström and Stiller in Sweden, exploited to the full the natural locations his country offered. Studio interiors were few and far between in these early films, which were usually shot in high summer with mountains and fjords as a background. Many historians have attributed the popularity of pictures like *Anne the Gipsy-girl* to their romantic image in the eyes of the working-class people who viewed them, eager as they were to escape the dark, drab routine of life in the cities. Perhaps audiences had grown weary of the films with working-class settings which had dominated Norwegian production during the years 1912-20. Ten years later, Breistein demonstrated how skilled he had become at dealing with human predicaments in a natural landscape. *Kristine, the Daughter of Valdres (Kristine*

Valdresdatter, 1930) again comes to the defence of a young woman, a cow-hand on a country farm who is left pregnant by a visiting British aristocrat. She abandons her baby daughter, who grows up ignorant of her parents' identity. The film closes, according to contemporary convention, with a reconciliation between age and youth, as the dying English lord identifies himself to his long-lost daughter and leaves his money to her and her husband-to-be.

Two other surviving melodramas of the silent period merit attention. *Pan*, direct by Harald Schwenzen in 1922 from a novel by Knut Hamsun, uses a military background to unfold a tale of passion and jealousy that ends with a murder during a hunting trip in Algeria. *The Magic Elk (Troll elgen*, 1927) bears some resemblance in tone to Erik Blomberg's Finnish masterpiece, *The White Reindeer* (see FINLAND), in that the 'magic elk' is a reincarnation of a dead man, and invokes the fear and wrath of the local farming folk.

Harry Ivarson's *Madame Visits Oslo (Madame besøker Oslo*, 1927) is a lively comedy about two swindlers who try to steal the property of a wealthy banker who has just died. The film's leading lady, Naima Wifstrand, became familiar to a whole new generation of filmgoers during the 1950's, when she worked with Ingmar Bergman on stage in Malmö and on the screen in such films as *Smiles of a Summer Night* and *The Face*. Carl Dreyer's *The Bride of Glomdal (Glomdalsbruden*, 1925) far outshone anything being made in Norway during this period (see DENMARK, page 32).

One of the last silent films made in Norway has withstood the test of time. *Raid on the Bergen Express (Bergenstoget plyndret i natt*, 1928) is nothing more or less than a fast-moving soap opera, with the rivalry between its two main men similar to the struggle between the siblings in *Dynasty*. The director, Uwe Jens Krafft, handles the opening sequence at the National Ski-Jumping Championships with great aplomb. Aud Richter's chocolate-box beauty makes her Grete an object of desire for both Tom and the young army officer, Lund. As Grete's father is General Manager of the Norwegian State Railways, Tom must achieve a stunning coup if he is to win her hand. So he stages a robbery of the Bergen express. outwits Lund and his pursuing troops, and then hands over the loot to Grete's father in a gesture that even the old man applauds – not least because of the fabulous publicity accruing to the railways. Locations enhance the quality of this film considerably, compensating for the frivolity of the upper-class dialogue (although Hollywood was indulging in identical charades like *Show People* and *It* at around the same time). When Lund and his men fan out in search of Tom near Geilo, they ski by the light of flares against the hard-packed snow.

The silent epoch in Norwegian cinema lacks distinction. Unlike the films made in neighbouring Denmark and Sweden, Norwegian productions contained no spiritual dimension of the kind furnished by the literary sources of Selma Lagerlöf or Hjalmar Bergman in Sweden; and none of the troubling ambiguity upon which the imagination of the spectator might feed, and which is so manifest in the work of Benjamin Christensen, for example. Nor, apart from *The Magic Elk*, do Norwegian films of the period look to the supernatural for an idiom of expression. They seem content to serve the appetite of audiences who had a loyalty to cinema as a medium, if little respect for it as an art form.

The Early Sound Period

The volume of film production in Norway during the early 1930's did not exceed one or two features per annum. Pathetic though this appears by comparison with the other Nordic countries (excepting Iceland), the output is not without significance. The establishment of Norsk Film A/S in 1932 (with shares owned by 52 of the country's municipalities), and the opening of that company's studios at Jar outside Oslo in 1935, provided a basis for production that would survive into the 1990's.

The decade also yielded at least half-a-dozen films worthy of comment. **Tancred Ibsen** dominates the scene, due in part to the wealth of practical experience he had gained in Hollywood and Sweden. The grandson of the dramatist Henrik Ibsen, he accompanied Victor Sjöström to America as the Swede's assistant. After two years he returned to Scandinavia, and in 1931 directed *The Big Baptism (Den store barnedåpen)* alongside Einar Sissener. The influence of the French cinema is immediately apparent. The unemployed Harald cares for the lonely Alvilde's baby, whose sailor papa has perished in a storm at sea. As in Clair's world, the characters are viewed with intense sympathy. The grim reality of factory life, and the poverty of the rooming-house where Harald lives, seem mitigated by the jolly music and the cheerfulness of the people. Einar Sissener himself plays Harald with the gentle, self-deprecating charm of an Albert Préjean; his natural patience enables him to look after the baby while Alvilde goes out to work.

Ibsen shows his enterprise from the opening sequence of *The Big Baptism*, emphasising the rhythmic sound of the machines as they start up in the textile factory. By 1934, when he directed Victor Sjöström in *Synnøve Solbakken* for the independent Swedish company, Irefilm, Tancred Ibsen had become a master of his craft. The most influential of Swedish critics, Bengt Idestam-Almquist, wrote with some irony that it was 'the cows, the bucolic imagery, Victor Sjöström and Hugo Alfven [the composer] that save this Irefilm.'[5] But the Swedish press has never been kind to directors from other Nordic countries.

The perception of Tacred Ibsen as a director steeped in the countryside traditions of Norway may not, however, be so far from the truth. In *Fant* (1937), he made an effervescent screen version of Gabriel Scott's novel about Norwegian fisherfolk. Alfred Maurstad stars as the roguish 'Fant' who takes advantage of a young girl (Sonja Wigert) aboard his tiny boat. His reckless behaviour contrasts amusingly with the conventions of the tight-knit community, and when he plays his guitar and springs his practical jokes it is difficult not to like Fant, who resembles somewhat the personality of Michel Simon in *L'Atalante*. His death by drowning, following an accidental 'murder', allows Sonja Wigert's Josefa to return to the arms of her 'decent' lover. But Fant, like the dark, handsome stranger who pops up in so many

Nordic films, has given her a taste of another lifestyle. Through her involvement with him she can appreciate more keenly the sensual pleasure of open-air dances beside the jetty, and the glistening undulations of the water beneath the summer sky. Such imagery outlasts the slapstick quarrels that Ibsen includes to cater for his audience's expectations. One of the most popular films of the 1930's proved to be *Two Living and One Dead (To levende og en død*, 1937), which revelled in the thriller genre in telling of a post-office employee who, on the verge of retirement, is robbed one night and finds himself sucked into psychological complicity with the criminal after he has moved to Oslo.

Gjest Baardsen, Ibsen's most accomplished film, appeared at Christmas 1939, not long before the Nazi occupation of Norway. Its 19th-century hero is a blend of Robin Hood and Harry Houdini. In the briskly-edited opening scene he escapes from prison and takes to the fells. Gjest represents the ordinary people's cause in the face of the arrogance and corruption of the Law. When the local Customs officer's daughter seems about to fall into the arms of the crooked Warden of Bergen, she is rescued by Gjest Baardsen, who sweeps down like Superman to save this damsel in distress. In similar circumstances, Sjöström's characters decided to accept the destiny Nature reserves for them. Not so Ibsen's. Gjest and Anna give themselves up to the police and serve their sentences. 'I intend to pay my debts to society,' declares Gjest, tongue-in-cheek. At their trial, he denounces the Warden for his villainy, and although sentenced to life imprisonment he and Anna are set free by the magistrate.

Gjest Baardsen suffers from several naive close-up shots of faces in reaction poses, and it brims with melodrama in scenes like the discovery by Anna's father that the money has been stolen. Against that must be set Ibsen's delightful

Tancred Ibsen's *Two Living and One Dead* (1937)

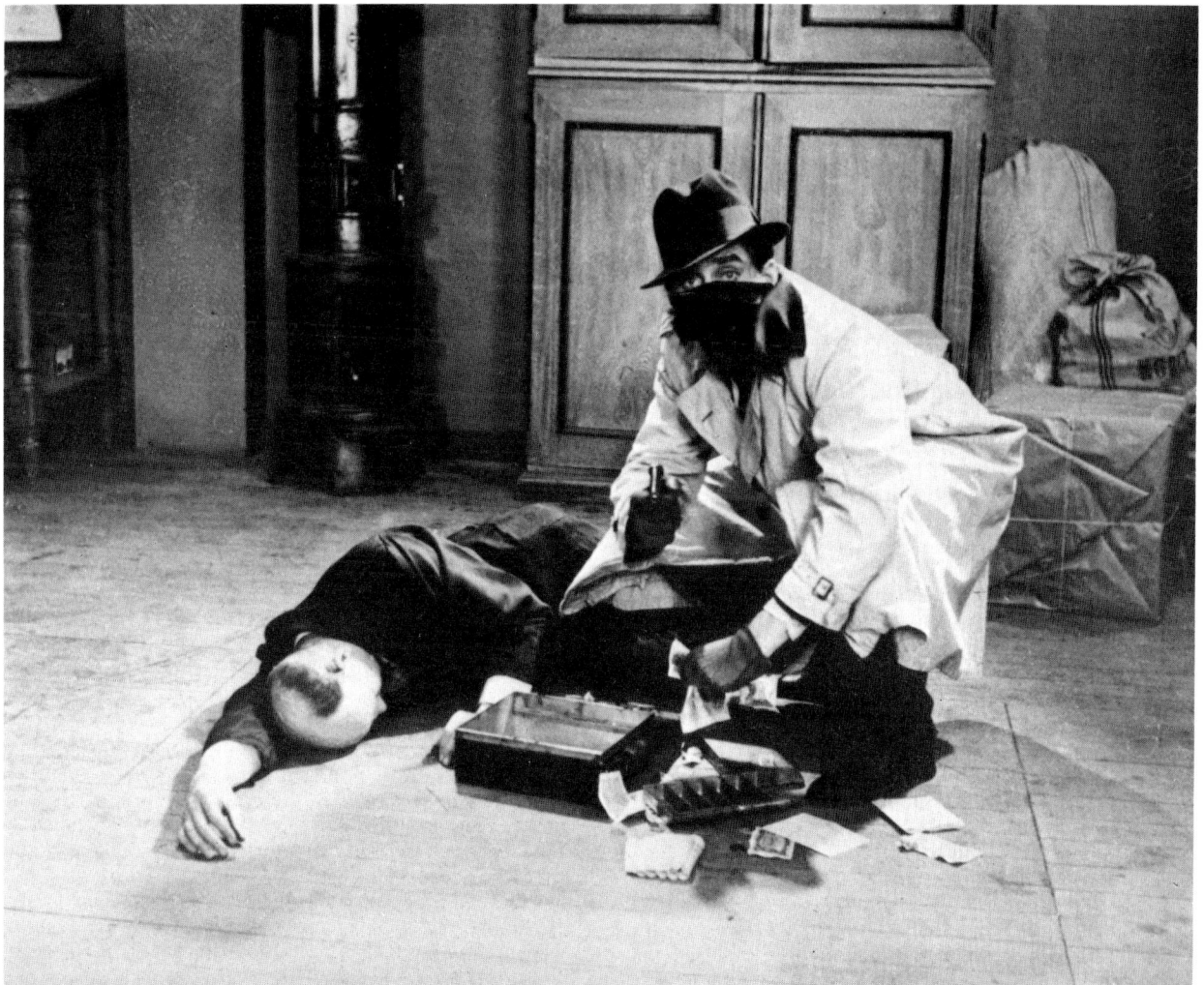

use of the Bergen locations, from the narrow streets of the town, with their wooden houses, to the brilliant scattering of trees in blossom on the hillsides, and the snow-clad fells further up.

Leif Sinding, who shot his first film in 1926, came to prominence for his adaptations of Norwegian novels. His sympathetic treatment of the gipsy community in *The Gipsy* (*Fantegutten*, 1932) brings into sharp focus the prejudice with which outsiders are treated in Norwegian society: gipsies still during the 1930's, Middle Eastern immigrant workers in the 1980's. Even Sinding seems to suggest that gipsies should be tolerated but held down as second-class citizens. Iver, the baby gipsy boy who survives an avalanche in which his mother perishes, grows up on a farm and longs to wed the insouciant Ragnhild. Caught like a half-caste between the two communities to which he belongs, Iver recognises that in the eyes of Norwegian society he wears the mark of Cain, while at the same time he finds himself captivated by the sexual charms of a gipsy girl in the locality. In a powerful climax, he must intervene to stop this girl being whipped in her own encampment for having seduced him, and his quandary is complete.

Like Ibsen's *Fant*, this film contains romantic musical numbers, presumably aimed at domestic audiences who, as in Sweden and Finland, expected such interludes when they went out to the cinema in the 1930's. Leif Sinding felt more confident about tackling social issues when he brought to the screen Gabriel Scott's novel, *The Defenceless* (*De vergeløse*, 1939). The abuse of child labour colours this picaresque story of an adolescent Albert, whose mother is a whore and who is forced to work from morning to night with other similarly deprived children on a rudimentary farm in Norway. This latter-day version of slavery cannot be entirely blamed on the farmer, who earns more money from the government for every orphan he accepts. The daily round is a tough one, interspersed with corporal punishment meted out by the old dragon of a woman who runs the domestic side of the farm.

If on the one hand Sinding adopts a critical stance to his material, in the idiom of Sweden's Hampe Faustman, on the other he develops the notion of rebellious young love that Bergman makes his own a decade later. The film's most serious handicap is its cast. The young orphans look far too well-fed and healthy to attract our pity. Nevertheless, it is difficult to comprehend how Leif Sinding, so alert to the injustices endemic to Norwegian life, should have collaborated with the Nazis to the extent of making inane comedies and propagandist films during the wartime years.

Olav Dalgard specialised in films about the working classes in Norway in the 1930's. *Growing Up in the North* (*Gryr i Norden*, 1939) was one of several productions made for the National Unions' Congress. Dalgard reconstructs the matchmakers' strike of 1889, using a cast of semi-professional players. Many sequences look contrived and the rhetoric sounds sententious, although the sequence where the women wave triumphantly to each other from the stairways and fire-escapes of the workers' houses remains a stirring piece of agit-prop, backed with the tones of the Marseillaise.

The Shadow of Occupation

Although annual film production had climbed only to six features in 1939, the market share for Norwegian pictures reached 10.4% compared to just 0.6% three years earlier. The Nazis took less than a year to exercise control over every aspect of Norwegian film production, distribution, and exhibition. 'Exhibition was run by decree, even to the point of forbidding admission between the (German) newsreel and the main feature.'[6] The so-called 'Film Directorate' imposed on local producers a standard diet of comedies and thrillers. In the words of Nils A. Klevjer Aas, 'Escapist farces were the order of the day [during the Nazi/Quisling years]; even with words from Dr. Goebbels on the importance of films indoctrinating the Nazi creed ringing in the background, only one or two of the 23 wartime films may be said to have had an ideological slant towards Nazi ideals.'[7] Alfred Maurstad's *A Gentleman with a Moustache* (*En herre med bart*, 1942) transcended the level of most Norwegian films of the time, taking as its model the Hollywood screwball comedy.

The one undeniable step forward implemented by the Film Directorate concerned the subsidy of feature films. A tax on every ticket sold contributed towards the production budgets of Norwegian films – a concept not far removed from Harry Schein's radical policy via the Swedish Film Institute from 1963 onwards.

At war's end, a sizeable residue (10.5 million Norwegian crowns) remained in the production fund, and in 1948 the income from ticket taxes amounted to no less than 20 million crowns. It allowed the government to save the ailing Norsk Film A/S by taking a minority shareholding in the company.

The Second World War exerted an impact beyond mere economic considerations. The Norwegian authorities, despite the efforts of the Quisling regime, preferred resistance and exile to collaboration. There was a tremendous struggle for Narvik, for instance, while King Haakon's personal indignation and resolve led him to resist the invasion at all costs. In 1946, Olav Dalgard and Rolf Randall's *We Want To Live* (*Vi vil leve*) dramatised this patriotic resistance, and two years later came the widely-seen Franco-Norwegian co-production, *The Battle for Heavy Water* (*Kampen om tungtvannet*, 1948).

Directed by Titus Vibe-Müller, and supervised by Jean Dréville, this 'reconstructed' docudrama benefits from the crystalline exterior photography of Hilding Bladh (who worked with Bergman five years later on *Sawdust and Tinsel*). The non-narrated action sequences survive best as the saboteurs parachuted down on the Hardanger plateau carry out their mission to blow up the German stocks of heavy water. 'Operation Swallow', as it was known, attracted the attention of Hollywood two decades later in *The Heroes of Telemark*. Like all cosmopolitan film productions *The Battle for Heavy Water* suffers from bad dubbing and disembodied voices. The British 'stiff upper lip' philosophy intrudes almost to the point of parody ('I'd be inclined to kill myself,' says one officer as he refers to the possible failure of the mission). Celebrating Christmas in a mountain hideout in 1943 also looks and sounds too sentimental for the good of this rugged film. Vibe-Müller does achieve a certain degree of catharsis when the heavy water is finally detonated just as it is about to leave for transport by ferry to Germany in 1944 — some twenty months after the saboteurs made their first sortie into enemy-occupied Norway.

Other films revived memories of the war years — Toralf Sandø's *We Leave for England (Englandsfarere*, 1946), Michael Forlong's *The Shetland Gang (Shetlandsgjengen*, 1954), and Kare Bergstrøm and Rados Novaković's *The Blood Road (Blodveien*, 1955). As late as the 1980's, the themes of betrayal and deception during the Quisling period would surface in films like *The Reward, The Feldmann Case* and *Growing Up*.

Arne Skouen, the most assured director of the 1950's and 1960's, had lived abroad in voluntary exile during the war. A novelist and playwright by vocation, he had survived as a press attaché in the United States, and returned to his native Norway in 1946. Three years later he embarked on his first film in partnership with Ulf Greber. The immediate success of *Street Urchins (Gategutter*, 1949) established Skouen's reputation as a director of actors, and he would make a further sixteen features over the next twenty years.

Reminiscent of *Sciuscià*, released by Vittorio De Sica in 1946, *Street Urchins* offers a more congenial vision of its street urchins. These kids wear baggy shorts and shirts, and large caps on their heads, as they dash through the streets of Oslo in the 1920's. Their crimes are petty by comparison with those of Buñuel's *Los Olvidados*, for example, and amount to stealing fruit from the harbour, or sacks of cocoa beans from a passing truck. The grim reality of strikes, lock-outs, and domestic poverty colours the background of the film like a poster, but the wish-fulfilment of childhood takes precedence — and no more poignantly so than in the final scene as Gotfred and Sofus gaze in wonder at the street-lights being switched on at dusk.

Many of the boys in *Street Urchins* pursued their acting career and Pål Bang-Hansen, playing the chubby little guy who is taught the rules of survival by his older pals, became a director and a TV commentator in subsequent years.

Comedy continued to attract the Norwegian public more than any other genre, and Nils R. Müller found his inspiration in the state of marriage, with films that echoed the laughter of Stiller's *Thomas Graal* satires (see SWEDEN): *We're Getting Married (Vi gifter oss*, 1951), and *We Want a Divorce (Vi vil skilles*, 1952). The Danish director, Astrid Henning-Jensen, contributed a richly-mannered, delicately-observed comedy to the Norwegian cinema in 1951, with *Krane's Tea-shop (Kranes konditori)*, which brings to life the gossip and peccadillos of a small coastal town. It introduced one of Norway's great actresses, Wenche Foss, and boasted cinematography by Arthur J. Ornitz, one of the most distinguished of Hollywood cameramen.

The Individual Perseverance of Arne Skouen

Until the late 1960's, Norwegian cinema appears to have

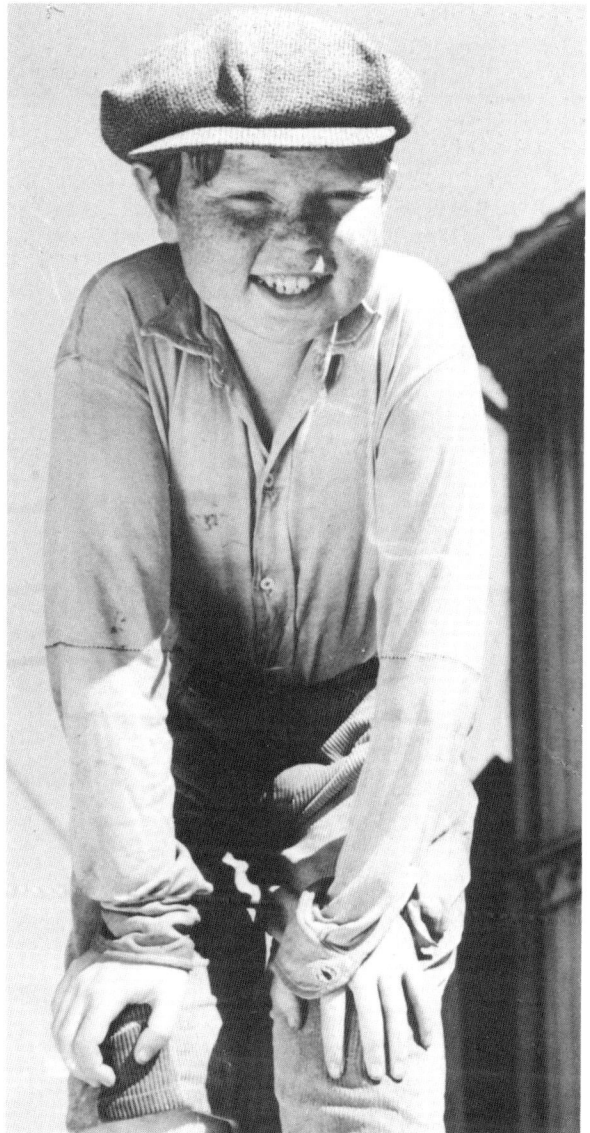

Pål Bang-Hansen in Arne Skouen's *Street Urchins* (1949)

remained almost immune to trends and forms being developed in other countries. Erik Løchen's *The Hunt (Jakten*, 1959) is said to anticipate the temporal experiments of Resnais and Robbe-Grillet, but Norwegian directors tended to react first and foremost to the requirements of their domestic audience, and only then to an inner compulsion to express their feelings on film. Arne Skouen may be regarded as the country's first genuine auteur, for he wrote the screenplay for all seventeen of his films save one, and towards the end of his career established his own production company to ensure him even greater independence.

Jack Fjeldstad in *Nine Lives* (1957) by Arne Skouen

Skouen's protagonists often transgress the rules of Norwegian society. They are not so much outsiders as insiders who through their actions and attitudes extrude themselves from their community. They turn to murder (in *The Return of Pastor Jarman [Pastor Jarman kommer hjem*, 1958]), to arson (in *The Flame [Det brenner i natt!*, 1955]), to poison pen letters (in *The Master and His Servants [Herren og hans tjenere*, 1959]), and − in Skouen's films about the Occupation − to treason and treachery.

In his quest for realism, Skouen shot most of his films on authentic locations, using the fells and villages of Norway as effectively as the larger urban environments. In the tradition of Sjöström and Stiller, he regards Nature as a crucial factor in deciding Man's destiny. His characters grapple with the elements for survival, in films such as *Nine Lives (Ni liv*, 1957) and *An-Magritt* (1969). Bo-Christer Björk[8] has also pointed out that Skouen's actors were selected carefully to suit their roles, not to placate the star system. In films like *Forced Landing (Nødlanding*, 1952)

and *Surrounded (Omringet*, 1960), he insisted on using Germans in Nazi roles.

Wind and snow provide the symphonic bass line for Skouen's masterpiece, *Nine Lives*. Based on the true exploits of Jan Baalsrud, as described in David Howarth's book, 'We Die Alone', *Nine Lives* brings its indestructible hero into direct conflict with the Nordic winter. Baalsrud falls into the hands of the Germans when he and a group of commandos try to land in occupied Norway in March, 1943, and are betrayed by a local shoemaker loyal to the Quisling regime. He escapes, and tries to remain unidentified in his native country, sheltering with various families and trying to link up with other resistance fighters. Told in one long flashback from Baalsrud's Swedish hospital bed, the film gallops along at breakneck speed, whipped forward by the music of Gunnar Sønstevold. The beaches, fells, mountains, and fjords set their hostile face against the fugitive, and soon Baalsrud falls victim to snow blindness. At last, with gangrene attacking his leg, and hallucinations clouding his vision, he takes refuge in a 'grave' hollowed out from the snow on a mountain slope. As he waits near the Swedish border for help to reach him, Baalsrud goes delirious, fantasising his own death and seeing his corpse borne over the mountains in a cortege. Few Nordic films have realised the visual potential of the mountain landscape with such distinction as *Nine Lives*. Unclogged by dialogue, Skouen's narrative proceeds with classical simplicity against the stark natural landscapes. When Baalsrud begins to go blind, he uses snowballs to guide him as he lurches forward, and Skouen edits this sequence with lyrical intensity, dissolving the frontiers between sanity and delirium. Later, as screaming winds force back a rescue party from Sweden, Baalsrud's refuge is buried by the gusting snow, in as emotional a scene as the climax of Sjöström's *The Outlaw and His Wife*. The film triumphs by virtue of the visual and aural language that Skouen conjures up to match the almost mystical quality of Baalsrud's defiance of his fate.

For his swansong, *An-Magritt*, Skouen called on the services of Liv Ullmann, by that time established as the most famous of Norwegian actresses through her work with Ingmar Bergman, and of the cinematographer Sven Nykvist, also associated with the Swedish maestro. Based on a best-selling novel by Johan Falkberget, *An-Magritt* recounts the ordeal of an orphaned girl who must fight for her basic rights in a primitive 17th-century community. Her mother commits suicide because the child is the consequence of a rape attack. An-Magritt survives from sheer indignation and persistence. Forced to labour in a stone quarry, denied even a modicum of food, she clings for friendship to Johannes, a German migrant artist. Her natural intelligence comes to her rescue, and when she learns to read she finds herself appointed leader of a workers' protest to Chancellor Bjelk in nearby Trondhjem. Skouen's control of the action sequences in *An-Magritt* lacks the delicate touch that so enhances *Nine Lives*. Liv Ullmann, too, exaggerates the frustration and anger of the heroine and is less convincing in moments of hysteria than in her soliloquies. The epic sweep of the story remains undeniable, and some scenes, such as the ox's plunging through thin, melting ice, are all the more persuasive for being filmed on location. *An-Magritt* also emphasises the role of the church in Norwegian history, and has affinities with Rauni Mollberg's *Earth Is Our Sinful Song* in this respect. In both films, the legacy of enforced solitude cause human beings to turn their emotional gaze inwards instead of relating to those around them. The cold freezes spirit as well as body. Ideals become distorted. Superstition takes hold. The constant repression of feelings finds inevitable compensation in outbreaks of violence.

A New Wave at Last

Throughout the 1960's, European cinema was in a state of flux. Sweden, through Widerberg, Sjöman, and Donner; and Finland, through Kurkvaara, led the Nordic countries in response to the new film language promulgated by Godard, Antonioni, and Cassavetes. Denmark and Norway proved slowest in following these trends. To some extent, the reason may have been administrative and economic. Norsk Film did not have a film-maker on its board until 1966, when Erik Borge became Managing Director. Television was reaching 70% of the population by 1960, and a majority of the country's movie theatres were suffering as a result of waning attendances.

Young film-makers toiled hard during the 1960's to escape from the traditional methods of production. Knut Andersen, Knut Bohwim and Mattis Mathiesen founded Teamfilm A/S in 1962, and sustained a steady flow of productions over the next two decades, even if most of these did not pretend to be anything other than local comedies. Others, more exasperated by the domestic situation, travelled abroad, or only as far as neighbouring Stockholm, to study film. Anja Breien enrolled at IDHEC in Paris, Pål Bang-Hansen at Centro Sperimentale in Rome.

The break with the past in terms of film language and choice of subject matter occurred in 1967, when **Pål Løkkeberg** directed *Liv*, a freewheeling study of a mannequin, played by his then-wife Vibeke Løkkeberg. Sharply influenced by the spirit of Godard, *Liv* may also be compared to Nordic films of the same decade such as *The Pram*, *The Mistress* and *Grass Widow*. The acting may be self-conscious, and the photography off-balance or out-of-focus, but outweighing such aesthetic faults is a palpable sense of contemporary reality. The immediate experience takes precedence over formalism and literary narrative.

Løkkeberg's career in the cinema failed to progress, and he has found more rewarding work in the theatre and television. Vibeke Løkkeberg, however, emerged from her chrysalis as a sex symbol to become one of the key personalities in the Norwegian cinema of the 1980's. Other young enthusiasts attempted to reach foreign audiences, without much help from official quarters (the Norwegian Film Institute suffered from lack of funds and authority prior to the late 1980's, and the country's films rarely appeared at film festivals during the 1960's and 1970's). Ragnar Lasse Henriksen, with *Love Is War* (1970), won a Silver Bear at the Berlinale and demonstrated his gifts as a virtuoso cinematographer. *Love Is War* suffers from an excess of rhetorical dialogue and self-conscious psychedelic effects, but Henriksen's exuberant approach captures the cinema's unique propensity for showing both the bright and the sombre sides of life.

One Day in the Life of Ivan Denisovich (*En dag i Ivan Denisovitsj' liv*, 1970) showed that Norway could participate in an international co-production with honour. Casper Wrede, known for his stage work, wrote and directed this austere screen version of the autobiographical novel by Solzhenitsyn about conditions in a Siberian labour camp. The photography by Sven Nykvist and the music by Arne Nordheim add conviction to Wrede's account of the remote, icy prison where Tom Courtenay's Ivan struggles to preserve his self-respect while compromising with necessity.

Anja Breien, returning to her native land after assisting Henning Carlsen on *Hunger* and *People Meet and Sweet Music Fills the Heart*, adopted a less aesthetic stance in discussing flaws and injustices in contemporary Norway. Her first feature, *Rape (Voldtekt*, 1971), aims to switch attention from the victim of a rape to the suspect attacker himself, and thereby to test the flexibility of the legal system and to expose its inadequacies. In certain phases, the film looks like a dossier, shot in unrelenting black-and-white tones, with long speeches into camera by prosecutor and defence counsel. At other moments it launches into subjective flights of fantasy.

Nothing in this grim-faced docudrama, however, suggested that Anja Breien's next film, *Wives (Hustruer*, 1974), would be such a sparkling, extrovert satire on the role of women in the modern consumer society. Not for many years had a Norwegian film proved such a hit at home, and even in certain territories outside Scandinavia. An undisguised homage to Cassavetes' *Husbands*, this story of three women who quit their men and their families to face an uncertain future on their own contains numerous barbed references to the complacency of Norwegian life. Women are tolerated so long as they do not interfere with male prerogatives. A rising standard of living has provoked many people to question traditional values and vested interests. Norway, for so long the most isolated of the Nordic countries in terms of culture and consumerism, now faced an abrupt transition. 'The real theme of this film,' says Anja Breien, 'is the conditioned sexual roles we are all expected to play — and our conditioned assumptions are, of course, undermined, as so often happens when we see the normal order of things turned upside down.' The wives' three-day binge acquires greater significance with each passing argument and experience; they find themselves in the male zone, with its privileges, its liberties, and its fundamental lack of domestic responsibilities.

The dialogue in *Wives* was improvised with the help of the three excellent actresses used by Breien: Frøydis Armand, Katja Medbøe, and Anne Marie Ottersen. The team had toured Norway with a play on a related theme. After each performance the actresses and director discussed the

Wives (1974) by Anja Breien

problems involved with the audience, and discovered in the process that a gulf existed between so-called 'enlightened' feminism, and the majority of ordinary people's perception of what issues were at stake.

Per Blom had helped on the screenplay of *Rape*, and in 1973 made his own debut behind the camera with *Anton*, a sensitive portrait of a fifteen-year-old boy in a small rural community. The following year he confirmed his talent with *Mother's House (Mors hus)*, which tackled the theme of incest with even more courage than Vilgot Sjöman had in *My Sister, My Love*. When Petter leaves his studies in Oslo, abandons his fiancée, and takes the train back to his home town in the provinces, his journey assumes a compulsive dimension. His 'mother's house' is a villa set apart from its neighbours in Gjøvik, at once refuge and trap. The subtle means by which the mother undermines Petter's relationship with a girl in the same town are registered in cinematic terms by Blom. The intimacy between mother and son runs like a dangerous current beneath the placid, formal surface of everyday Norwegian life, with its courtesies and rituals (such as the sharing of Christmas gifts), so well suggested in the accompanying Pachalbel 'Canon'. The androgynous Petter tries with increasing desperation to establish a 'normal' relationship with the aptly-named Eva, but his true desires overwhelm him when Eva announces that she is pregnant. In a closing sequence of soaring catharsis, Petter leaves the arms of his girlfriend, rushes home, and flings himself into the ample embrace of his mother. Their love-making represents release for both of them, and a victory for the mother. *Mother's House*, a miracle of innuendo and sly observation (Petter's girlish coiffure, for example), may also be regarded as a commentary on the taboo of homosexuality, to which Norway has reacted with much less tolerance than, say, Denmark.

Other hidebound attitudes come under fire during the mid-1970's, from film-makers more confident of their ability to transcend the frivolous image of cinema in Norway. State guarantees mounted in size and scope; more risks could be taken in the interests of artistic expression. Oddvar Bull Tuhus embarked on *Strike! (Streik!*, 1975) with the help of NRK, the national TV corporation, and a script by himself and Lasse Glomm from a book chronicling the bitter strike at the Sauda factory (an industrial firm owned by the giant Union Carbide). Recreating the various stages of the dispute in the spring of 1970, Tuhus and Glomm examine the tension that emerges between the unions at local and national level. By 're-staging' the fierce debates that took place behind closed doors among the union members, the film peers beneath the outward show of unity to discern the divisions between young and old workers, and between Marxist-Leninist dialectic and unadorned protest. The fear of a written ballot, imposed by central government, surfaces repeatedly. *Strike!* stares back through time at a dispute settled five years earlier, yet the film itself may now be viewed in an historical light too, from a perspective in which the unions have changed many of their fundamental attitudes to disputes with management.

Halvor Næss's photography contributes significantly to the absorbing quality of the film, especially during the union debates, when telephoto lenses view the proceedings from a subjective angle. Tuhus and his team falter when they try to dramatise the pressures on the strikers outside the factory; the housewives have their say, and the leading militant turns to drink. Nevertheless, *Strike!* takes an honourable place among the many Nordic protest films of the late 1960's and early 1970's. It could not have been made in the Norwegian cinema of any previous decade, which in itself underlines the enormous strides made by the younger generation during this period.

Social criticism gathered momentum in the Norwegian cinema of the 1970's and 1980's. **Lasse Glomm**, who co-wrote *Strike!* and Anja Breien's *The Inheritance*, delivered a stinging rebuke to bourgeois complacency and urban authorities alike in *Stop It! (At dere tør!*, 1980). Two youngsters steal a car late at night, and in a shootout near the airport, one of them is killed by a policeman. Reinert, the survivor, must face trial and the film concentrates on his response to the emotional and psychological pressures that accumulate in the months prior to his appearance in court. Few Norwegian films had dared to focus on the problems of unemployment, drug abuse, and single parent homes. In *Stop It!* we can recognise the same disenchanted youths who people the films of Stefan Jarl, Tapio Suominen, and Morten Arnfred. They suffer not from the genuine poverty of the Developing World, but rather from a fatal lack of motivation and the disinterested attitude of their elders.

Sølve Skagen's *Hard Asphalt (Hard asfalt*, 1986) deals with a similar situation, although with more gritty and aggressive exuberance. Drug addiction and alcoholism, the twin vices of Nordic life in the affluent 1980's, scar the lives of two young people (played with remarkable commitment by Frank Krog and Kristin Kajander). Mutually dependent, they laugh, quarrel, and commiserate with each other, surviving thanks to a series of cynical petty thefts. Skagen (working from an autobiographical novel by Ida Halvorsen) etches in raw detail the seamy underside of Oslo, its back streets frequented by drug addicts and child prostitutes. *Hard Asphalt's* bleak implications are rendered bearable by the moments of fun and satire at the expense of a society which takes itself rather too seriously. The film notes with irony that whisky is priced at excessive levels, while alcoholism on the streets appears more acute than in other countries.

Not all socially-engaged Norwegian films adopt this naturalistic texture. *Madness (Galskap!*, 1985) offers its central character, a middle-aged mother named Marianne, the refuge of insanity. It creeps up on Marianne almost without her being aware of it. Her teenage daughter has left school early and drifts around Oslo, unemployed and ready to join in spontaneous acts of protest and violence. Egil Kolstø's film views these familiar circumstances with an ambiguous eye. Instead of standing shoulder to shoulder with her husband in defence of bourgeois values, Marianne embarks on her own rebellious journey, joining the disarmament movement and quarrelling with her reactionary husband. Her spiralling descent into 'madness', to quote the sardonic title of the movie, becomes ludicrous when she escapes from hospital wearing her daughter's punk outfit. Kolstø fails to digest the heavy slices of pacifist monologue required to bolster his heroine's attitude, and *Madness* falls victim to ponderousness and didacticism. Its premise – the political conversion and liberation of a middle-aged woman – cannot be ignored, however, and stakes out the same kind of claim as *Wives*.

Alcoholism, drug addiction, and prostitution have been confronted by Norwegian film-makers, but a more recent menace, radial prejudice, has not been so easily addressed. **Gianni Lepre**, an Italian based in Oslo, had created a stir with his bizarre debut, *Henry's Back Room* (*Henry's bakvæ-relse*, 1982, see below) and for his second film turned to a controversial issues that many Norwegians would prefer not to acknowledge. *Landscape in White* (*Øye for øye*, 1985) tells a squalid story of arson and blackmail as an unscrupulous businessman frames one of his employees, an immigrant worker from the Middle East. The coarse-cut characters and the bitter tone of the film recall the work of Rainer Werner Fassbinder, while the melodramatic interplay of action and dialogue owes more to the Hollywood film noir (e.g. Ophuls's *The Reckless Moment*). Most startling and disquieting of all, *Landscape in White* unfolds in the city of Drammen which with 50,000 inhabitants is the fifth largest conurbation in Norway. The intensity of racial prejudice in the community, as much as the individual loneliness that it engenders, may not be entirely realistic, but there is no denying the force and feeling of Lepre's achievement. For him, the snow-covered fields of Norway in winter symbolise hostility rather than purity.

Political and Military Issues

As a somewhat reluctant member of NATO, Norway has felt self-conscious in the eyes of its neutral neighbours Sweden and Finland, and film-makers have addressed the country's military involvement in a critical light.

In *Remonstrances* (*Motforestilling*, 1972), Erik Løchen applies an experimental aesthetic form to a deeply provocative film about Norway's security police, its role in NATO, and the relationship between Norway and the superpowers. In the words of Jan Erik Holst, Løchen 'shows that filmic reality is equal to everyday reality. The main questions for Løchen are: what do we see, and what do we not want to see?'[9]

Hans Otto Nicolayssen adopts a more coherent narrative line in *Poachers* (*Krypskyttere*, 1982). The son of a sheep-farmer rebels against his superior officers while on military manoeuvres, because his father's traditional grazing grounds are being hived off to the army and, by extension, to the NATO forces based in Norway. Mixing comedy and melodrama with a predominantly documentary idiom, *Poachers* touches an exposed nerve in Norwegian life, and also anticipates the 'green' movement with its emphasis on the preservation of the natural wilderness environment. Nicolayssen, who has since turned to production, is one of the few Norwegian directors to have used the 'scope format (in black-and-white) to imaginative effect.

The young politician in **Pål Bang-Hansen's** *The Crown Prince* (*Konprinsen*, 1979) finds himself ensnared in a sordid intrigue when he expresses public support for Norway's NATO membership. The Labour Party in which he is one of the most promising figures has no compunction about sacrificing him when a scandal involving CIA penetration of the party threatens to cause a storm in parliament. Bang-Hansen discusses the conflict between public attitudes and private convictions, and his film indicates that beneath the sober if pragmatic face of Norwegian politics there often run currents of duplicity and cynicism.

Ola Solum, who learned his craft as a director of films for children, burst upon the international scene in 1985 with *Orion's Belt* (*Orions belte*). This political thriller won four major Amanda Prizes (the Norwegian equivalent of Hollywood's Oscars), and found eager buyers in numerous territories. Working from a novel by Jon Michelet, Solum treats an alarmingly realistic 'incident' between the superpowers with all the pace and action of a James Bond thriller. Three Norwegians stumble across a Soviet 'listening post' in a cave on the uninhabited coastline near Spitsbergen. Their immediate detection by a Soviet helicopter in the area unleashes a storm of violence and killing. The sentiments in this hot-blooded film are expressed in rough and ready terms. The Soviets blow up a motor boat without compunction. The Norwegian 'secret service', the tacit servants of NATO, behave in a manner worthy of the Mafia or the KGB. The lone survivor of the incident vanishes in a crowd of revellers in Oslo, pursued by agents of his own government who want to obliterate all traces of the unfortunate boat's crew.

Orion's Belt stands as an important landmark in the development of the Norwegian cinema. In artistic terms, it lacks subtlety and dips too easily into melodrama. But for perhaps the first time a Norwegian director shows himself capable of injecting a relentless drive into his narrative, and the four main actors perform with passion and persuasion. By revealing that each of the men on the doomed tramper makes a living from illicit smuggling, Solum's tempers the audience's shock when confronted with their fate. He exploits his locations (on Spitsbergen and off the coast of Finnmark) with professional zeal. The terrible cold, and the palpable solitude of the surviving man and his dog, is communicated in bravura film language, while the montage thrusts events forward like an express train.

Norwegians take pride in the glittering success of *Orion's Belt*. As its country's most expensive production to date (15 million crowns), the film reflects credit on the technicians and actors involved in it. But the heady cocktail of violence, prejudice, and staccato action serves only to trivialise the underlying theme. If *Poachers* is a muted moan of exasperation against Norway's membership of NATO, then *Orion's Belt* amounts to a shrill scream of protest, which numbs any attempt at analysing the political implications. The characters cannot escape their comic-book context, even if Solum's film should not be denied credit for daring to address a controversial issue. The irony is that the 'shooting war' it describes with such gusto could not take place in such simplistic terms in the post-Cold War 1990's. Solum's latest film, *The Wanderers (Landstrykere,* 1989), avoids overt political issues and emerges as an imaginative, vigorous screen version of Knut Hamsun's novel about life in a small coastal village during the 1860's.

Leidulv Risan's *Rubicon (Etter . . . Rubicon,* 1987) strives to replicate the commercial triumph of *Orion's Belt.* Its heroes and villains, however, do not wear such easily identifiable labels as they do in Solum's thriller. At the end of the day, the NATO connection may be discerned, for the Norwegian authorities try to hush up an outbreak of radiation sickness that accounts for two young boys who happen to be sheltering on an island in the vicinity of a sinister freighter. Although it is never directly shown, a neutron explosion of some kind eliminates the vessel's crew. Like *Orion's Belt,* the film surrenders all too often to melodrama, but establishes a haunting mood in its exploration of the deserted, flooding vessel. The climate of fear and apprehension is reinforced by various unusual metaphors (for example, a stricken cat's bleeding on a white sheet as a doctor attends to it). When *Rubicon* strains credulity is in its presentation of every official in the Hammerfest area as a sinister agent of some foreign power or 'authority' bent on silencing the doctor who tries to help the victims of the explosion. Both *Rubicon* and *Orion's Belt* may be viewed as prisoners of the 1980's, just as Don Siegel's *Invasion of the Body Snatchers* belongs to the paranoid 1950's. They cater to the essential conservatism of the Norwegian public, while their ambivalent endings symbolise the country's divided loyalties – on the one hand, to NATO and a 'hawkish' political stance towards Moscow; on the other, to her Scandinavian neighbours with their liberal, neutralist traditions.

A link surely exists between this discomfort with contemporary alliances, and the retrospective guilt that surfaces in films about the conduct of Norwegians during the Second World War. *The Reward (Belønningen,* 1980), written and directed by Bjørn Lien, dramatises the discovery of a man who seized the chance to make money illicitly during the Nazi occupation. Reidar's arrest after a quarrel with a former workmate leads to a trial and imprisonment. The drab, ordinary lineaments of Reidar's personality suggest that he represents all too many who profited from his country's misfortunes. At the same time, the film implicitly criticises Norway's inability to come to terms with its past.

More ambitious, and flashing back and forth in time between 1942, 1947 and 1985, **Bente Erichsen's** *The Feldmann Case (Over grensen,* 1987) peels away the layers of shame and guilt that lurk beneath the placid surface of a small Norwegian community. Its factual basis shields it from the kind of strident melodrama that mars *Rubicon,* for instance. Considerable attention is given to the tiny details of clothing, decor, and speech that evoke a specific time and place. *The Feldmann Case* investigates the murder of a Jewish couple, Rakel and Jacob Feldmann, whose bodies are found in a lake. When two guides confess to the crime,

they find themselves acquitted in court after their defence counsel argues that they were only trying to prevent the Germans discovering the Resistance's escape route to Sweden. Erichsen's calm, watchful film allows people to reveal their petty-mindedness and instincts for self-preservation. The taint of anti-Semitism emerges both from the court proceedings and from the inquiries of the journalist assigned to cover the case for a newspaper.

The film was made under threat of legal action from the two surviving guides who found the corpses of the Feldmann's. Bente Erichsen adopts a tone of regret rather than hysterical accusation (although the music is too overweening). She focuses her attention on the tight-lipped sentiment of the postwar period, not on the inidividuals whose arrest appears to close the case. She also implies that during the war Norwegians may have turned a blind eye to the fate of the Jews. Nearly half of the 1,800 Jews living in Norway in 1940 suffered deportation and certain death in Nazi concentration camps, by comparison with 1.6% of Jews who died in Denmark.

This slow process of purgation has helped many Norwegians to accept the reality of the Quisling era. One film, *Little Ida (Liten Ida,* 1981), surpasses all others in the genre. **Laila Mikkelsen's** first feature, *Us (Oss,* 1976) presents a nightmarish vision of the future, as city people are compelled by food shortages to work the fields with their own sweat and muscle, and thus confront the inequities and artificial structures of urban society. Her second film, *Little Ida* (also known as *Growing Up),* marks a giant step foward in her career. In the closing days of the Second World War, seven-year-old Ida starts to recognise that weakness provokes intolerance, and survival depends on minding one's own business. Norway is occupied but not truly at war; a country in which impotence in the face of Nazi might turns to bitterness and resentment. Ida's mother works for the Germans, and has an affair with one of their officers. She does not flaunt her behaviour, but the brunt of the community's scorn falls on Ida. Other children shun her, and she wanders on her own through the streets and fields, drawn by curiosity to a German interment camp where men with shaven heads toil in silence. When peace comes, and the enemy has departed, Ida watches her mother being taken away for punishment as a collaborator.

This screen version of Marit Paulsen's novel is directed with consummate sensitivity and even-handed irony. No accusation sounds too strident, no defeat appears too sentimental. Ida and her mother are two unfortunate creatures tossed by the tide of war and struggling to find their balance. Laika Mikkelsen's little masterpiece transcends its specific setting to become a universal lament for innocence defiled, and for a generation that must accept the bitter truths that those who 'transgress' are often victims of those who do not.

Focus on Women's Roles

Anja Breien and Vibeke Løkkeberg have remained loyal to their primary concern, the attitude expressed by a male-

Laila Mikkelsen's *Growing Up* (1981)

dominated society towards women, both past and present. *Games of Love and Loneliness (Den alvarsamme leken*, 1977), directed by Anja Breien in Sweden, emphasises how sorely constricted human emotions were in turn-of-the-century Scandinavia and is based (like Mai Zetterling's *Doctor Glas*) on a novel by Hjalmar Söderberg. Breien treats the romance with considerable respect, but beneath the grave progression of the narrative ('And the years passed . . .') runs a dark, surging current of feeling that does justice to Söderberg's recognition of the eternal clash between security and contingency in the realms of love.

Next of Kin (Arven, 1979) remains the most subtle of Breien's films, owing much to Ibsen while aiming its critique at the mournful, rigid, and hypocritical ethos of Norwegian society. A wealthy shipowner dies, leaving his relatives an ostensibly impeccable will, according to which his vast empire must be administered by a united family. But envy and ambition by degrees assert themselves, and the family circle, held together hitherto by a mood of armed neutrality, breaks up in censure and prevarication.

Although *Next of Kin* concludes on a dubious *coup de théâtre*, there is no denying the two graces of Anja Breien's achievement: her sense of humour, which resounds most effectively in the sequence when the relatives strip the dead man's villa of its furniture and heirlooms to the accompaniment of Rossini's 'Thieving Magpie' overture; and her refusal to introduce flashbacks, in a story that might be expected to rely heavily upon them. Anita Björk, Sjöberg's Miss Julie of thirty years earlier makes a particularly sensitive impression as the late magnate's sister-in-law, striving to be the last to conceal the one excess of passion that has blemished her otherwise faultless commitment to the bourgeois ideal.

In 1981, Anja Breien ranged back in time, to a century — the 17th — often ignored by Nordic artists, who tend to opt for the Sagas and medieval times, or to stay firmly rooted in the modern era. At the outset of *Witch-hunt (Forfølgelsen*, 1981) a woman arrives in a remote community in the mountain wilderness of Western Norway. She takes work at one of the local farms, sleeps with a handsome cowhand,

Lil Terselius in *The Witch-Hunt* (1981) by Anja Breien

and provokes a breeze of gossip. The country folk dread her independence and lack of shame, brand her as a witch, and receive the blessing of the local authorities for doing so. Dialogue and characterisation leave much to be desired, but the director's eye for landscape, and for an atmosphere of intolerance, sustain this paradigm for the contemporary world in which women's rights are distrusted with equal vigour.

Elisabeth Mortensen plays a young lawyer in Breien's *Paper Bird (Papirfuglen*, 1984), a woman determined to unravel the mystery surrounding her father's dramatic death. In discovering the truth about an individual so closely related to her, she also must acknowledge the gulf that yawns between men and women. The irony of the situation is heightened by the fact that the father was a famous actor, accustomed to wearing a psychological mask to shield him from both the public's curiosity, and the incestuous nature of his own family life.

Anja Breien does not advocate a war to the death on behalf of women's rights. Her indignation has softened through the

years, and at the end of *Wives, Ten Years Later (Hustruene ti år etter*, 1985) her three friends return home to their waiting menfolk. Elegance and discretion, indeed, mark her recent film, *Twice upon a Time (Smykketyven*, 1990), about a stage designer who, despite his popularity with women, finds himself unable to commit to any one relationship. **Vibeke Løkkeberg's** approach has, on the contrary, grown more severe during the two decades she has been active in the Norwegian cinema as actress and director. Her early shorts deal with topics such as abortion and the role of the unmarried mother, and in 1975 her medium length film, *Rain*, introduced what was to be the setting of her two principal accomplishments, *The Betrayal (Løperjenten*, 1981) and *Skin (Hud*, 1986): the coastal town of Bergen, where Løkkeberg grew up during the postwar years. The picture she paints in *The Betrayal* is a harsh one, castigating the petty-mindedness of a town scarred by wartime memories. Food is in short supply, collaborators are still being tried, and the influence of American culture and commerce is gaining hold. The children, each seven years of age, manage amid this turmoil to create some kind of human relationship, even though both are subjected to domestic violence and social degradation. Løkkeberg's gift for perceiving everyday settings and incidents through a youngster's eyes elevates *The Betrayal* beyond the grimy environment of a cold Norwegian port into the realm of a fantasy where innocence cannot be numbed by a lack of parental affection.

Løkkeberg's influence may also be detected in *The Head Man* (*Høvdingen*, 1983), which she wrote in collaboration with her husband, Terje Kristiansen, who directed the film. Its partly tongue-in-cheek description of a *macho* Norwegian pater familias only serves to emphasise the obsolescence of traditional power distribution in the family circle. Much more ambitious in scope, Løkkeberg's *Skin* mixes reality and symbolism in a turbid tale of incest in a small trading-post in 19th-century Norway. The film possesses certain affinities with Bo Widerberg's *The Serpent's Way* in its charting of a sexual obsession in a world devoid of love. Vilde's destiny is dependent uon the will of her 'guardian', to whom she has been pledged by her dying father.

The underlying themes of child abuse and female subjugation emerge from the film in sharp profile and at the expense of the narrative, which is confused − even in the original release version running more than three hours. Vilde's father resorts constantly to masculine excuses: 'You must try to understand me'; 'You must not leave me'; 'It's your own fault, you made me do it, you were born to it [incest]', and so on. This rhetoric assumes a haunting resonance in the natural ambience of the sea and the shoreline outside Bergen. Stones, in the photography of Paul René Roestad, appear alive and tactile. A ship's figurehead becomes a recurring symbol of Vilde's trapped, sculpted beauty. A broken doll lying on the rocky headland seems to embody the anguish and violation of the innocent child. A wedding gown floats briefly on the water before sinking like a dying aspiration. A mysterious painting of an island in the ocean fascinates Vilde, giving her a vision of what might lie beyond the menacing authority of her husband.

Abetted by the music of Arne Nordheim, *Skin* coils itself about the patient spectator, smoothly slipping from past to present, from one generation to another. Vibeke Løkkeberg herself plays Vilde as though numbed by centuries of sexual injustice, yet still retains her determination to resist her step-father's will. The film's overriding mood of hopelessness reaches its climax when Vilde kills her husband and, led away to prison, gazes back to see her daughter, face horribly titivated, in the arms of the man who had abused her when *she* was a child.

In visual and thematic terms a sequel, *Seagulls* (*Måker*, 1990) confirms Løkkeberg in both her faults and virtues − a brooding melodrama, slumbrous in form, evoking the atmosphere of the Norwegian coastal communities in the 19th century.

In Search of New Idioms

As young Norwegians returned from film schools abroad in the early 1970's, they brought with them a desire to experiment with new forms. Haakon Sandøy, who had served as assistant to Witold Leszczyński on the Polish adaptation of Tarjei Vesaas's novel, *Days of Matthew*, made his own debut with a screen version of another book by Vesaas. *The Fire* (*Brannen*, 1973) deals in symbols, and 'consists of different strands which create a unique frame around a young man's lack of relation to the technological society'.[10] Sandøy returned to Poland three years later toi make a sympathetic film concerning the life of Edvard Munch's friend Dagny Juell [*Dagny*, 1977].

Gianni Lepre, an Italian-Canadian resident in Norway for several years, brings the principles of Antonin Artaud's 'Theatre of Cruelty' to bear on a bizarre incident in one of Norway's smaller towns. In *Henry's Back Room* (*Henrys bakværelse*, 1982), a barber discovers that his teenage daughter has killed herself because she was dependent on drugs and had been forced to become a prostitute. Henry turns into an avenging angel. He takes prisoner the pimp responsible for his daughter's despair, and tortures him in the basement of his barber's saloon. Lepre's film exhibits an obsessive quality rare in Norwegian cinema, as well as an uncanny grasp of the calculated cruelty that lurks in even the most innocuous of individuals − especially when the public surrounding him behaves so callously.

Some measure of darkness also inhabits the flagrant world of **Svend Wam** and **Petter Vennerød**. Like the Kaurismäki brothers in Finland, Wam and Vennerød have worked fruitfully and impudently outside the mainstream of production in their country. They established Mefistofilm in 1976, and in a dozen films since have addressed the issues and the disillusionment that accrued from the events of '68. *Open Future* (*Åpen framtid*, 1983) examines the doubts and tribulations of a teenage boy about to leave high school in the late 1960's. *Castle in the Air* (*Drømmeslottet*, 1986) follows the fortunes of six friends of that same generation who, during the 1970's, buy a large house and move into it with their children in the vain hope of creating an ideal commune. *Goodbye Solidarity* (*Adjø Solidaritet*, 1985) looks at the materialist, self-obsessed decade of the 1980's. The two principal men in this film have abandoned the high ideals they embraced in 1968, settling instead for comfortable jobs and luxurious standards of living. This cannot conceal, however, their abject failure in relationships with parents, lovers, and children alike. In the words of Jan Erik Holst[11]: 'The film depicts, in bold anarchistic and surrealistic tones, a world in dissolution, which the lives of the main characters so vividly illustrate. Themes dealt with include the demise of human fellowship, the conflict between left and right overshadowed by re-emergent fascism, and with the encroachment of privatisation in a social democratic society.[12]

Wam and Vennerød's cinema sometimes suffers from a narcissistic streak, as well as a frivolous attitude towards heterosexual relations. This can be ascribed in part to their prolific output, but films like *Hotel St. Pauli* (1988) descend into a vortex of absurdity and gratuitous violence. Mocked and spurned though they are by Norwegian critics, Wam and Vennerød undoubtedly know how to grip an audience by the throat in the opening sequences of a film, and their

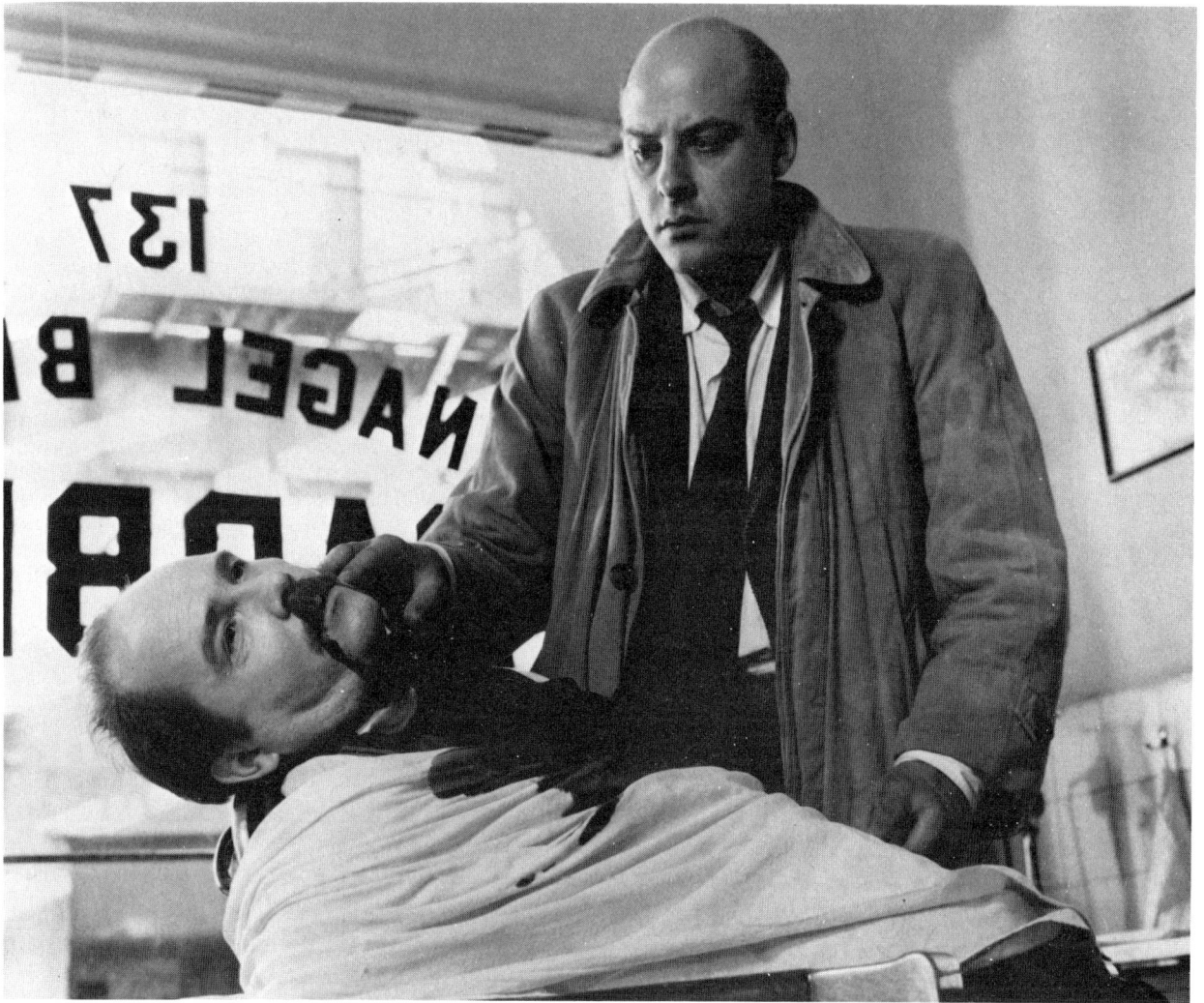

Blackout (1986) by Erik Gustavson

audacious use of music and effects lends credence to their concentration on sexual taboos and frustrations.

Norwegian directors do not often succumb to the allure of pastiche. *Blackout* (1986) resurrects the Hollywood film noir with meticulous devotion. A balding private eye finds himself diverted from retirement in Argentina by just one last job – tracking down a gangster in what looks like San Francisco's Chinatown. The offscreen monologue echoes Raymond Chandler: 'I chucked my badge in the sea and began to go through other people's dirty washing. It was a good time for bad news. . . .' Backed by a mood indigo jazz score, and rich in offbeat characters (including an undertaker who is also a drug addict), **Erik Gustavson's** affectionate homage to the 1940's falls short of its target on account of its self-conscious *mise-en-scène* – a plethora of overhead crane shots and excessive attention to details of

design and lighting. *Herman* (1990), however, suggests that Gustavson may be a force to be reckoned with. He directs his young boy actor, Anders Danielsen Lie, with consummate sensitivity in this bizarre (but good-natured and, finally, poignant) story about a child who loses his hair from a rare disease. *Herman* paints a convincing and heartening portrait of family life in the Norway of the 1960's, and fills it with quite unexpected humour.

At the opposite extreme of the spectrum stands **Oddvar Einarson's** *X* (1986), which won a Silver Lion at Venice. If this film may also be considered pastiche, then the influence is that of Antonioni. But in 1986 the theme is not romantic love of the kind that beguiled Monica Vitti and Gabriele Ferzetti in *L'Avventura* but an uninspiring relationship between a taciturn photographer and a fourteen-year-old girl in Oslo. Einarson's trademark becomes the long-held shot, underlining the slow development of the link between the young man and his friend. The girl is hardly a nymphette, and the photographer seems immature for his age, so that occasionally the traditional roles are reversed (as of course they were, in an altogether more scintillating way, by Nabokov and then Kubrick in *Lolita*). Reticent, phlegmatic, etiolated almost to breaking point, *X* signals the arrival of a talent comparable to Aki Kaurismäki in Finland and Kay Pollak in Sweden. All three directors analyse loneliness as a phenomenon of the consumer society.

In Einarson's second feature, *Karachi* (1989), two people also take refuge from the outside world, but for more mundane reasons. A young woman drug courier hides in a cop's shabby apartment at Oslo while being pursued by the drug barons she has betrayed. The subtle interplay of feelings in the relationship contrasts with the violence of the external narrative.

Erik Borge, who had revealed himself a shrewd observer of the female psyche in *Blackbird in the Ceiling Lamp (Trost i taklampa*, 1955), served as head of Norsk Film A/S for many years before retiring and writing the original screenplay for *A Handful of Time (En håndfull tid*, 1989).

Directed by Martin Asphaug, *A Handful of Time* breathes something of the same delicate mood as Bergman's *Wild Strawberries*, as an old man strives to relive a vanished love, and to expunge his feelings of guilt about a relationship that ended half a century earlier.

The Lapp Connection

Norwegian films have attracted increasing attention at festivals during the past dozen or so years. Anja Breien's *Next of Kin* featured in the Competition at Cannes, as did Vibeke Løkkeberg's *Skin*. Oddvar Einarson impressed the jury at Venice, and Per Blom's *The Ice Palace* was selected by several major festivals.

The most impressive product of the entire period, however, has never appeared at a top festival, because its producers wanted to sell it direct to audiences around the world. *Pathfinder (Veiviseren*, 1987) was nominated for Best Foreign Film in the Academy Awards in Hollywood, but lost to *Babette's Feast*. Its director, **Nils Gaupe**, comes from the Lapp region of northern Norway, and *Pathfinder*

Oddvar Einarson's *X* (1986)

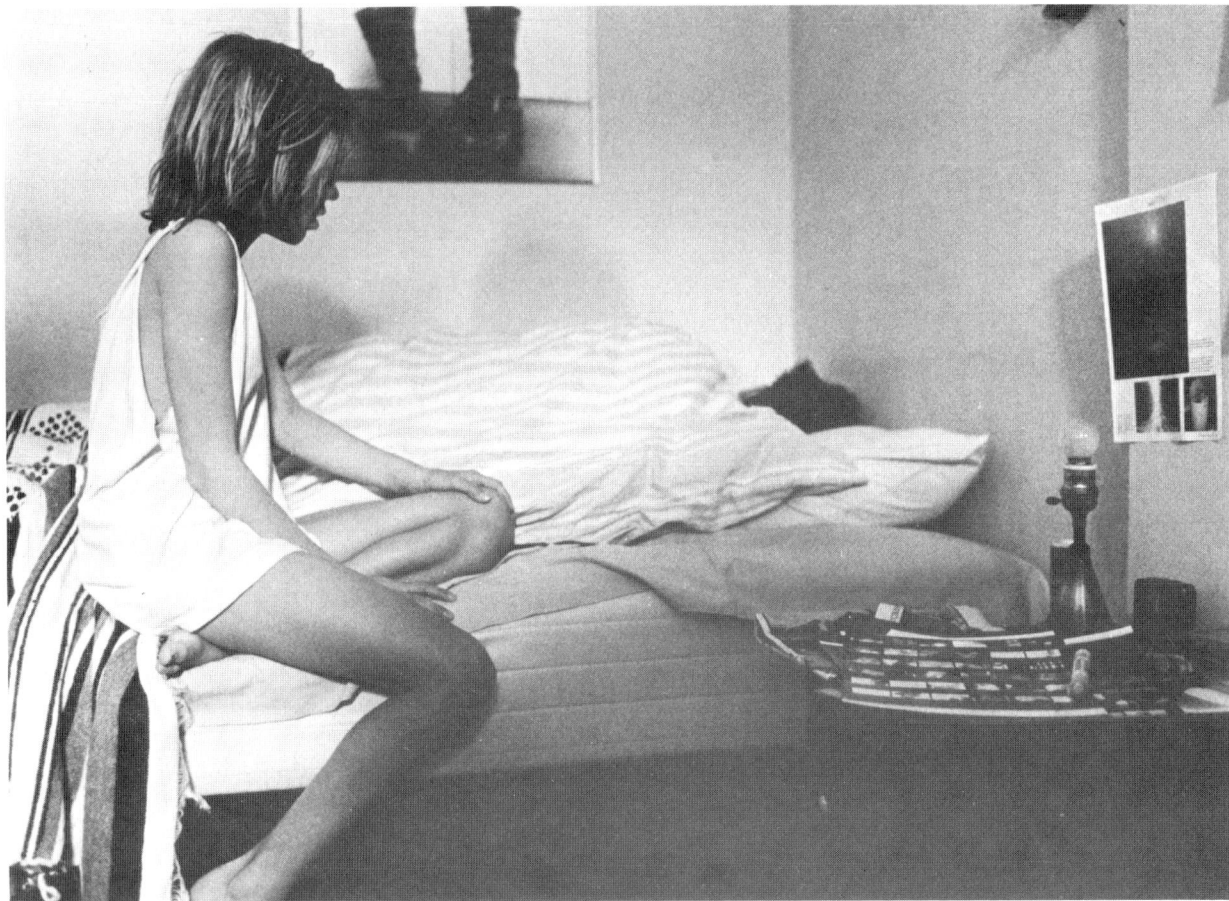

takes its inspiration from a 12th-century Lapp legend. The sparse lines of dialogue are in Sami, the Lapp language (although the marauding Tchude tribe seem to be speaking in an invented tongue), and the Panavision 'scope format allows Erling Thurmann-Andersen's camera to take full advantage of the flat, horizontal tundra landscapes.

Pathfinder touches on various aspects of Lapp culture and legend. Aigin, the teenage hero of the film, returns from a hunting expedition to find his parents and younger sister slaughtered by a band of sinister, ruthless tribesmen known as Tchudes. Now he must survive in a hostile environment where the snow rarely relents and Lapp encampments are few and far between. He responds intuitively to the symbols and supernatural signs that govern the Lapp culture: to the local *noaidi* (holy man), who counsels him against seeking revenge; and to the bull reindeer which appears to him in a vision after he has tricked the Tchudes into plunging to their death down a precipitous cliff-face. At every stage of his struggle for survival, Aigin finds himself accompanied by the accoutrements of his ancestors − rings, a drum, teeth on a string. Birds and animals become as significant as human beings, from the dog transfixed by an arrow in the opening

scene, to a huge hawk floating balefully over the tundra. The Tchudes themselves flounder like black beasts in the all-pervasive snow, and have learned to travel in single file, roped together in order to negotiate the rugged mountains and treacherous slopes.

Gaup displays an economy of statement rare in a debutant. He employs imagery rather than words to communicate the essential themes of his film: the peaceful nature of the Lapps by comparison with the barbaric Tchudes; the innocence of the women and children when faced with an all-male fighting force; the desperate aggression of the Tchudes deriving from their loss of bearings and, by extension, their separation from the 'brotherhood' in which all things are joined. When the film does adopt more conventional means of expression, the spell weakens. The dialogue in the Lapp tents, and the glib closing exclamation of one old woman ('We'll *always* have a pathfinder!'), undermines the harsh, unforgiving naturalism of the rest of the narrative.

By leading his adversaries into a lethal trap, Aigin at once avenges his murdered family, saves the innocent Lapps sheltering on the coast, and acquires a personal maturity (termed by Tim Pulleine 'the boy's rite of passage into

A Handful of Time (1989) by Martin Asphaug

manhood, italicised by the supernatural overtones attaching to the tale'[13]). *Pathfinder* stands alongside Erik Blomberg's *The White Reindeer* and Rauni Mollberg's *Earth Is Our Sinful Song* as one of the most impressive films made about the Nordic wilderness and its inhabitants. Its appeal to quite large audiences outside Scandinavia may also stem from its superb technical construction. The sound effects, enhanced by an antiphonal score, give a three-dimensional quality to the images, from the whirr of a hostile arrow to the thundering onset of an avalanche. Gaupe tends to accentuate the visceral outbreaks of violence with too self-conscious a glee, and he relies too often on close-ups. But nothing can detract from his command of film language and from his comprehension of the Nordic relationship to Nature.

It will be interesting to see if he can refine his style still further, after his adventure with Walt Disney Productions in 1990. The American company financed *Shipwrecked (Håkon Håkonsen)*, a seafaring adventure set in the 1860's and aimed at a younger audience.

Lasse Glomm also attempts to capture the mystique of the remote Norwegian wilderness in a film set during the 1860's: *Northern Lights (Havlandet*, 1985). Heikki is a small, watchful boy who leaves the hardship of his family farm and traverses the frozen wastes in his quest for the fabled 'Northern Lights', and the land of plenty where fish may be found in abundance. Glomm's film contains some spectacular imagery, and he adroitly alternates moments of tranquillity with bursts of roaring turbulence. *Northern Lights* encapsulates the Nordic yearning for freedom — from pitch-black nights, from ceaseless snow, from oceans that freeze over — in short, from a Nature that holds its human inhabitants forever in thrall.

Through the Child's Eye

Like Denmark, Norway has long placed commendable emphasis on the production of films for and about children. Sometimes this can lead to confusion. Per Blom's *Silvermouth (Sølvmunn*, 1981) baffled both critics and the marketing department of Norsk Film. In one respect it is a children's movie — the protagonist is a tubby, irresistible little boy — and in another it constitutes an adult entertainment, charting the passage of a divorce and a deserted husband's attempt to introduce a new girlfriend to his son. Blom directs the film with appropriate humour and sensitivity, forcing the audience to reconsider its views of marital conflict, and reminding it that in moments of crisis children can be at once weaker and stronger than their seniors. In Knut Andersen's *Friends (For Tors skyld*, 1982), a slightly older boy runs away from home in the hope that his father will give up his heavy drinking. The lush summer countryside, where father and son have enjoyed happy interludes, plays a major role in this engaging film, restoring the will to live and develop in the mind of its young hero.

Nature can on the other hand strike children as a terrifying challenge. In both *Zeppelin* (1981) and *The Ice Palace (Is-slottet*, 1987) youngsters must confront the mystery evinced by an alien Nature. Nina, the susceptible little girl in Lasse Glomm's *Zeppelin*, makes friends with a homeless boy, and runs after him into the depths of the forest, testing her own courage as much as searching for someone to whom she feels drawn. In Per Blom's *The Ice Palace*, two pre-pubescent girls respond to an unspoken, mutual attraction. Unn, the more fey of the pair, vanishes into the heart of an 'ice palace', where the tumbling waters of the mountainside have congealed into a cathedral-like shrine. Glomm suggests with discreet sounds and images the secret symbiosis between the two girls, culminating in a remarkable cut from Unn's dead features in the ice palace to Siss's face floating above the surface of her bathwater at home. *The Ice Palace* eschews dramatic incident, evoking instead the haunting beauty of the fells and mountains in winter, and lacquering the visuals with an ethereal music score that lulls and hypnotises the spectator into compliance with a story that shifts constantly between fantasy and reality.

If children themselves could vote for the best of all Norwegian films, they might well plump for *Flåklypa Grand Prix* (1975), a delightful puppet extravaganza directed by the single-minded, meticulous craftsman Ivo Caprino. Its combination of model care, cleverly-designed decor,m and a snorting, snarling soundtrack give this motor-racing drama a charm unmatched by any form of animation in the Nordic countries. The attendance figures for *Flåklypa Grand Prix* (2.1 million out of a national population of 3.8 million) demonstrate that Norwegians *do* support their national cinema on occasion! It is a hopeful sign for the future that Norwegians visit the movies more frequently than any of their Nordic neighbours.

1 Jan-Erik Holst, *Film in Norway* (Oslo, Norwegian Film Institute, 1979)
2 Nils A. Klevjer Aas, 'Cinema in Norway: 70 Years of a Singular System', in *International Film Guide 1988* (London, The Tantivy Press, 1987)
3 Jan-Erik Holst, *op. cit.*
4 Nils A. Klevjer Aas, *op. cit.*
5 Quoted by Bengt Forslund, in *Victor Sjöström, His Life and Work* (New York, New York Zoetrope, 1988)
6 Nils A. Klejver Aas, *op. cit.*
7 Id., *ibid.*
8 Bo Christer Björk, *Den nya norska filmen* (Helsinki, Walhalla, 1982)
9 Jan-Erik Holst, in *International Film Guide 1974* (London, The Tantivy Press, 1973)
10. Id., *ibid.*
11 Jan-Erik Holst, in *International Film Guide 1986* (London, The Tantivy Press, 1985)
12 Id., *ibid.*
13 Tim Pulleine, in *Monthly Film Bulletin* (London, British Film Institute, September 1988)

Helge Jordal in Ola Solum's *The Wanderers* (1989)

The Prisoner of Karsten's Fortress (1916) by Georg af Klercker

Sweden

The exceptional achievement of the Swedish silent cinema emerged from a long learning phase. The beginnings were cautious and somewhat ponderous, like many a Scandinavian response to new artistic movements. In February, 1895, the Edison 'Kinetoscope' was unveiled to audiences in Stockholm (and Rune Waldekranz[1] has reminded us that the German film pioneer Ottomar Anschütz sent his famous 'Schnellseher' to the first photographic exhibition at the Stockholm Palace of Industry in November of the previous year). The Court photographer, Ernest Florman (1862-1952) made two short farces in 1897, and six years later shot a series of 'song' films in which the first hint of the Swedish dramatic cinema could be discerned. These entertainments, consisting of filmic accompaniment to songs performed on a photograph disc, were screened for the future Danish King, Christian X, in Helsingborg during June of that year. Further north, in Stockholm, the Swedish monarch, Oscar II, found his visit to the Jubilee Exhibition recorded on film by one of Lumière's cameramen, Alexandre Promio, while above Blanch's Café in the Salon International some of the films of the English pioneer, Robert William Paul, were projected. Just as Denmark had the portal figure of Ole Olsen, so Sweden produced one of the truly great personalities of the silent era: **Charles Magnusson** (1878-1948). As a young man, he attended the first showings of Lumière films in Malmö in 1897, and resolved to become a cameraman. By 1905 he had made his mark as a newsreel photographer of considerable courage and integrity. He shot the state entry of King Haakon of Norway in Kristiania (later Oslo) on November 25, 1905, and despite thick fog produced a report superior to any filmed by those foreign cameramen present at the occasion.

In the early months of 1909, Charles Magnusson joined a youthful company known as 'Svenska Bio' in Kristianstad in southern Sweden. Launched in February 1907 by some enterprising businessmen, headed by Nils Hansson Nylander, Svenska Bio would, in 1919, be incorporated into the world-famous name of 'Svensk Filmindustri' (SF). From the start, Svenska Bio bolstered its activity by acquiring 19 movie theatres in 15 major towns and cities, thus providing a ready outlet for its own productions − a tradition that continues to this day in Sweden. According to Rune Waldekranz[2], the fledgling company was spurred to produce its own films by the worldwide success of Ole Olsen's Nordisk Film in Copenhagen.

Although Kristianstad was then the main centre of film activity in the country, the work of Erik Dahlberg in Stockholm should not be overlooked. Dahlberg's most impressive effort, *Gustaf III and Bellman (Gustaf III och Bellman*, 1908), used genuine locations such as the 'Gröna Lund' funfair.

Magnusson's restless ambition could not be contained for long in the provincial environment of Kristianstad. In his quest for good directors, he hired even actors like Carl Engdahl to work behind the camera. In productions like *The People of Värmland (Värmlänningarne), The Tales of Ensign Stål (Fänrik Ståls sägner),* and *Wedding at Ulfåsa (Bröllopet på Ulfåsa)*, all shot in 1909, may be found the first evidence of the bucolic, folkloric tinge that would colour so much of Swedish cinema in the years ahead. The following year, Gustaf 'Muck' Linden, a theatre director, joined Svenska Bio to film a pair of historical melodramas, one of which *(Regina von Emmeritz and King Gustaf III Adolf)* ran for 45 minutes − a substantial length for the period − and contained scenes shot on location at Maltesholm Castle.

In countries beyond Scandinavia, the primitive cinema was content with reproducing the virtues of the theatre. Staging was all. Magnusson, however, felt that both the visuals and the performances on screen should be free of the limitations of stage productions. A former cinema-owner and film reporter, he knew his profession by heart, but he also possessed a rare vision of things to come. He recognised that the public must be absorbed in what occurred on screen: 'The action is the motion picture's Alpha and Omega. It should [. . .] give opportunities for intensely exciting and interesting situations.' Remarking on the freedom granted to his directors, he said: 'The film producer must be the supreme ruler. He alone decides [. . .] but after he has given the starting signal, he should leave the director in peace. If the director is unworthy of this confidence, he is not fit to be a director.'

In the late autumn of 1910, Magnusson brought **Julius Jaenzon** (1885-1961) into the studios as his chief lighting cameraman, and thereby initiated a standard of visual excellence that would distinguish the entire Swedish silent cinema and remain unmatched by any Nordic country. Jaenzon took a unit to the United States and around the principal European cities, photographing backgrounds that could later be used in Svenska Bio productions. Two lively and amusing featurettes emerged as a consequence of this trip: *Kolingen's Galoshes (Kolingens galoscher)* and *The Adventures of Two Swedish Emigrants in America (Två svenska emigranters äventyr i Amerika)*.

Meanwhile, a pioneering woman director was experimenting with the new medium. **Anna Hofman-Uddgren** (1868-1947), with a career in cabaret behind her, delighted in filming on locations in Stockholm in, for example, *Only a Dream (Blott en dröm*, 1911), which gave the young Gösta Ekman his first big screen role, and *The Sisters (Systrarna*, 1912), which focused on the contrasting destinies of two sisters, one who lives with a wealthy protector and the other who joins the Salvation Army. In collaboration with her husband and screenwriter, Gustaf Uddgren, Miss Hofman embarked on a series of Stringberg adaptations − with the blessing of the dying dramatist himself. *Miss Julie (Fröken Julie)* and *The Father (Fadren)* both included authentic location scenes and, in the words of Rune Waldekranz, '[Anna Hofman-Uddgren] had an intuitive feeling that film possessed its own artistic resources free of all constraints of time and space.'[3] In *Miss Julie* especially, she insisted on shooting sequences in and around the Uppland castle of Stora Wäsby. But this talented woman withdrew from the movie fray in 1912, expecting her sixth child and caught up in the necessities of raising a family.

*   *   *

By 1911 Charles Magnusson had expanded his production range to include a series of travel films, shot mainly by Julius Jaenzon, and later that year Svenska Bio took the plunge of moving to Stockholm. In the spring of the following year, a splendid glass-roofed studio complex had been built in the suburb of Lidingö, and Magnusson once again cast round for good directors. The first man he contacted was **Georg af Klercker**, who had been born in Kristianstad and had served as a lieutenant with the aristocratic Svea Life Guards in Stockholm. Klercker functioned as head of the Lidingö studios until he broke off on his own initiative and joined the Hasselblad organisation in Göteborg. None of his films from the Svenska Bio days are intact — not even the immensely popular *Death Leap from the Big Top (Dödshoppet från cirkus-kupolen*, 1912) — but when one inspects the few films of Klercker's that *have* survived (all from the Göteborg period) one is forced to acknowledge that here was a major talent, a man who, had he somehow been able to work in conjunction with Mauritz Stiller and Victor Sjöström, might have enjoyed as great a renown as they did.

Several of the 27 features completed by Klercker at Hasselblad were enhanced by the ethereal beauty of Mary Johnson, an actress in the mould of Lillian Gish; she would reach her apogee as Elsalill in *Sir Arne's Treasure*. Mood and composition, however, distinguish Klercker's work more than performances. In *The Victory of Love (Kärleken segrar*, 1916) he anticipates the deep-focus photography deployed by Renoir during the 1930's. Using a system of lenses perfected by Hasselblad, Klercker seems equally at ease with natural or artificial light. In *The Mystery of the Night before the 25th (Mysteriet natten till den 25:e*, 1917), the atmosphere recalls the tongue-in-cheek thrillers of Louis Feuillade. This is a three-act 'sensational drama' featuring Cony Hoops, a celebrated detective akin to Hick Carter. Hoops finds himself trapped in a dark cottage by the so-called 'Black Band', and their dastardly leader, Craig, places a time-bomb beside him as he sits bound to a chair. The cottage is blown to smithereens but of course Hoops pops up unscathed, and is soon embroiled again with the Band at Valincourt Castle. In its wealth of bizarre incident, and its flavour of malevolence, the film now calls to mind the work of Sir Arthur Conan Doyle. The jovial, cigar-smoking Hoops may not be so suave as Sherlock Holmes, but there are several aspects of the plot that are worthy of Holmes: the death of de Valincourt from some mysterious odour, the snake which is lowered into a bedchamber, and the plethora of disguises that eventually deceives even the audience.

As one fantastic and mesmerising episode succeeds another, Klercker's ingenuity yields constant surprises. There are the fluorescent shots of a torch pointed into the camera as Craig advances down a narrow staircase, and the cunning visual deceptions of the secret 'mirror door' in the castle. This fascination with mirrors and decor colours all Klercker's cinema. In *The Prisoner of Karlsten's Fortress (Fången på Karlstens fästning*, 1916), this maverick director achieves a perfect balance between claustrophobic, carefully-lit interiors and open-air locations in and around the port of Göteborg. The narrative hinges on a melodramatic intrigue: the urbane, ruthless De Faber chloroforms a famous Professor and steals his blueprints for an 'explosive substance'. The pace accelerates relentlessly. De Faber kidnaps the Professor's daughter and hides her in an old fortress on Cliff Island outside the city. Klercker conveys the maritime environment with vivid skill. The message that the imprisoned girl manages to send out in a bottle is a facile plot gimmick, but the climax of this film matches anything being done in the international cinema in 1916. The girl leaps to freedom from a rampart, injuring her ankle, and is at last rescued from a dangerous sea inlet, while De Faber drowns in the swirling waters. As in *The Mystery of the Night before the 25th*, Klercker and his cameraman Gösta Stäring experiment with restricted lighting, to such a degree that a torch flashing along a castle passageway or strips of sunshine pouring between the bars of a window carry a tactile, threatening force.

*   *   *

Although Charles Magnusson followed his entreprenurial instincts and moved Svenska Bio to the nation's city capital, he felt more closely tied to the Swedish countryside than to the urban areas with their theatres and music halls, and he resolved to make more films on location. His employment of Victor Sjöström and Mauritz Stiller does not wholly explain the sudden improvement in quality of the Swedish cinema. Magnusson created a climate in which anything was possible, and in which each director could develop his skills and conceptions. Kenne Fant, for many years the head of Svensk Filmindustri in the 1960's and 1970's, has commented: 'Maybe here in Sweden the artistic integrity of our film directors is rather unique, but probably it is owing to the fact that most of them come from other branches of art — the theatre, literature — where their freedom is a matter of course. Besides, there is the fact that Swedish film production by tradition has accepted that every artist must work with the greatest possible freedom. Because of that, the managing directors of the important production companies have very often been people with clear practical experience of artistic work.'[4]

This refreshing laissez-faire attitude on Magnusson's part would be enhanced by the outbreak of the Great War in 1914. The influx of foreign films into Sweden diminished to a trickle in the wartime conditions, thus offering a considerable advantage to domestic film-makers, while the quality of the Swedish production attracted distributors in numerous countries overseas — even in nations like France and Germany which stood on opposing sides in the conflict. The opening of the luxurious 'Röda Kvarn' cinema in the centre of Stockholm in 1915 symbolised the prosperity of the Swedish film industry.

Victor Sjöström

The Swedes assumed the leading role in Scandinavian cinema at this juncture because Sjöström and Stiller seized the initiative and worked confidently and unremittingly. They learned the tricks of the trade as they went along, and did not pause to study the films of contemporaries like Griffith or Chaplin. Instead they created an altogether fresh visual language of their own, filling the screen with intense, bucolic, and sometimes spectacular imagery that warmed the heart of every Swede confused by the onset of the industrial revolution in the country. Sjöström and Stiller evoked nostalgia for a world and a way of life already slipping into the past. As C.A. Lejeune wrote in 1931: 'With the Scandinavians, as with no other people in the world, we get a vivid sense of inborn life in every stick and stone; the craftsman merely gives utterance to a mute energy, develops a power already lying dormant.'[5]

Magnusson hired Stiller in late 1911, but it was not until the spring of the following year, when **Victor Sjöström** joined Svenska Bio, that the partnership began in earnest. (Stiller's engagement in 1911 had been rather vague, based on some screen tests he had done as an actor.) Sjöström, who at the age of 32 had established a reputation as an actor in both Sweden and Finland, plunged happily into his new career. He accompanied Magnusson to Paris to visit the studios of Pathé Frères:

'We watched a scene with Mistinguett, I remember. Lehman, the comedian, came in with a bunch of flowers and stumbled over the famous legs of the diva. It was of course enormously amusing, but personally I was more interested in the construction of the studio. I strolled around on the sly and made sketches of the set and how they were built.'[6]

'The thing that brought me to film making,' he would remark later, 'was a youthful desire for adventure and a curiosity to try this new medium of which I then did not have the slightest knowledge.' He made his début for Svenska Bio in Stiller's *The Vampire (Vampyren)*, released in 1913 following a battle with the censors on account of its cruel climax in which Sjöström's character is tempted to drop a stage curtain on the girl who has ruined his life.

Sjöström's solid good looks, and the zeal he projected, assured him of prompt success with the Swedish film-going public. As a performer he would soon prove as intrepid as Douglas Fairbanks or Errol Flynn, with an added capacity for suggesting nobility, dignity and emotional stress. He took charge behind the cameras on *The Gardener (Trädgårdsmästaren)*, one of five productions he would helm during that hectic summer of 1912 (Stiller exceeded his output with six films!) He himself appeared in the unsympathetic title role, as a brutal head gardener overcome by jealousy of a pair of young lovers (Gösta Ekman and Lili Bech – the latter a Danish actress brought from Denmark by Charles Magnusson and something of a vamp on screen and off, her turbulent marriage with Sjöström lasting a mere two months). The film survives today and reveals Sjöström immediately as a director of fantasy and compassion. The paucity of intertitles shows that audiences of the time were quite accustomed to forming their own mental associations when presented with a strong narrative. The use of outdoor locations, that hallmark of the Nordic silent cinema, is also prominent, with Jaenzon's photography taking advantage of bright sunlight to create a lustrous background over the lake where much of the action unfolds. Lili Bech's vigorous performance as the bereaved young daughter flung out into the street by Sjöström gives great poignancy to the final scenes when she returns to go berserk inside a greenhouse and then fall dead of a heart seizure. A resonant and allusive work, *The Gardener* heralds the themes that would concern Sjöström in the years ahead: the injustice shown towards unmarried women in Swedish society, the lethal influence of alcohol – alleviating pain, inducing melancholy, and finally leading to death; and the involvement of landscape and natural surroundings as a personality in the drama. What other European film of 1912, for example, contains such a bewitching shot as the one near the close of *The Gardener* when Lili Bech, poised in the bow of a rowing boat, with the camera directly looking over her shoulders, glides over the lake towards the gardens that she once knew and loved?

A fire at the Lidingö Studios in 1941 destroyed a majority of the films made by Sjöström and Stiller during this period, but fortunately the most important of all the early productions, *Ingeborg Holm* (1913), survived. Sjöström's first authentic masterpiece may be scrutinised and defended as the most thoughtful and controlled of all films made prior to Griffith's *The Birth of a Nation* two years later. Based on a stage play about a woman who falls foul of the public welfare authorities in Helsingborg, *Ingeborg Holm* provoked a furious controversy in the press. The cruelty of a widow's having her child snatched from her side by the welfare authorities after the death of her husband, resulting in the woman's own descent into madness, placed the Poor Law Commission in an extremely bad light. On October 27, 1913, a reviewer in Göteborg wrote: 'We have seen good films made by Swedish artists, but none that can compete with this.' The screenwriter, a schoolteacher named Nils Krok, deserved much of the acclaim. He explained his motives in a letter to *Stockholms Dagblad* on November 10, 1913:

'[Twenty years ago] I first attended a Poor Welfare meeting. It made an indelible impression on me. For several weeks I could not rid myself of the images. There came timid old women, whose cheeks trembled as they stood before the Board, and vagabonds appeared, clamouring in demand of their rights. [. . .] Some seven years later, there came before the session a young woman who had seen better days. Her husband was dead, she had five children and no resources; nor could she work, for she had arrived straight from hospital, where she had been suffering from a gastric ulcer. That was when I got the idea of writing my play, *Ingeborg Holm*. The whole drama is built around the point when Ingeborg Holm enters the sessions room and has not yet uttered a word. It is the most powerful scene in the entire play.'[7]

Sjöström refused to tone down the reality of such circumstances. He depicts the widow in the Poor House, growing more and more distraught as her children are torn

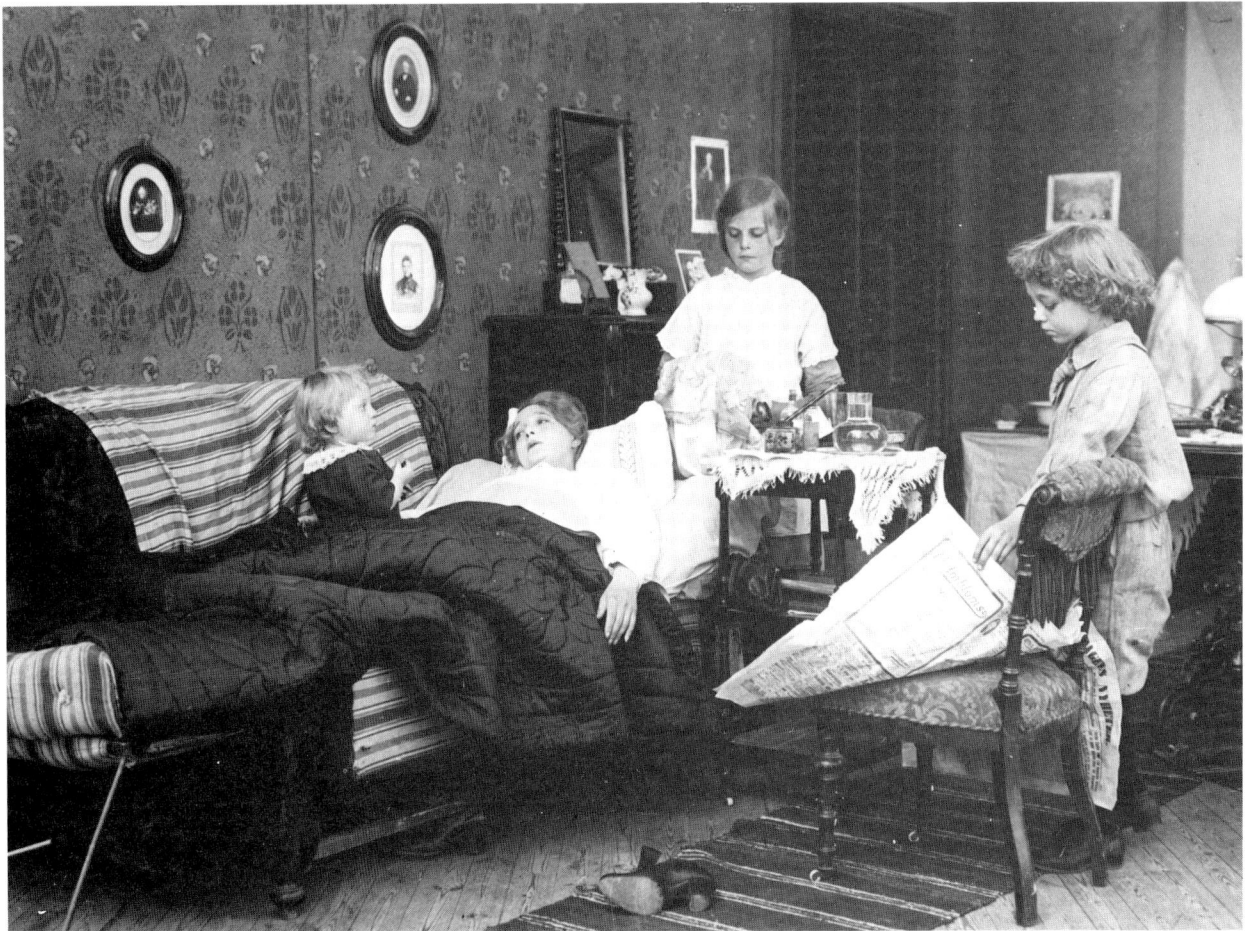

Ingeborg Holm (1913) by Victor Sjöström

from her one by one. She learns that her daughter is ailing, and she escapes from the police in a futile effort to reach the girl. But she is found and brought back to the hospice. She wanders to and fro before the camera, white-haired before her time and caressing her apron or a piece of wood as though it were her baby. When this and other productions reached France, it was not surprising that comparisons were made between Sjöström and Victor Hugo. Both artists shared a profound compassion towards the downtrodden and deformed; both men relished every chance to set their dramas in authentic surroundings. Their heroes live off the land and the sea, by the example of their toil and suffering call attention to the failings of society. With a restraint and eloquence worthy of Mizoguchi, Sjöström shows Ingeborg Holm in long shot, rushing down a muddy slope and then scaling the fence that surrounds the hospital where her child lies sick. . . . As Bengt Forslund has noted in his biography of Sjöström, the director 'described [Ingeborg's suffering] as an equally sober and inexorable process. No one is really bad, everyone feels pity for Ingeborg and her offspring,

they pat the children on the head and Ingeborg on the shoulder — yet at the same time spread their hands: what can they do? They have their instructions, and must obey them. It was not the first time that one had been shown social evils on the screen. American movies, for instance, often featured 'society's unfortunate children', but this was the first time that it was done without sensationalising, in order to move and involve the spectator. *Ingeborg Holm* was in fact the first Swedish film to have exerted a direct influence on society.'[8]

Between *Ingeborg Holm* and *Terje Vigen* (shot in 1916), Victor Sjöström underwent a change of outlook. He was always enthusiastic about the indigenous advantages of working in the Swedish landscape, and directed his actors on location in Gotland and in Northern Sweden. But he objected when Magnusson wanted him to film two works — one of them *Terje Vigen* — by Ibsen. He did not see how the philosophical style of Ibsen could be reconciled with the predominant vogue for comedies and thrillers. Then came a transformation, uncannily like that experienced by Isak

Victor Sjöström in his own *Terje Vigen* (1916)

Borg in Bergman's *Wild Strawberries*. He made a sentimental journey to the province of Värmland where he had been raised. He met his old nurse, who told him of his gallant mother, who had worked in the harbour with the infant Victor on her arm after her husband had left for the United States. Continuing his journey by bicycle he reached Grimstad, on the Norwegian coast, where Ibsen had been inspired to write his epic poem about Terje Vigen, the sailor who defied the English blockade during the Napoleonic Wars. From this point onwards Sjöström's attitude assumed a pantheistic tinge. God, like good and evil, was ever-present in Nature, which in turn exerted a powerful influence over Man's existence.

Accordingly, when he returned to Stockholm in mid-August, 1916, he was more disposed to direct Magnusson's dream production. By the standards of the day it could have proved the *Heaven's Gate* of Svenska Bio. The budget climbed to 60,000 crowns (three times the usual sum for the period) and production took a mammoth three months. The gamble succeeded, however. Not only did *Terje Vigen* open

to ecstatic reviews in Sweden, but it sold 43 prints abroad, bringing in revenues of around 100,000 crowns. Sjöström found himself hailed as the leading director of his time, and he had cause to look back always with happiness at the summer of 1916, for during the shooting of the film he had met Edith Erastoff, an actress who would remain his wife for almost three decades.

In *Terje Vigen*, for the first time in the cinema the natural background reflects the struggles between the characters and within themselves. The film is described by René Jeanne and Charles Ford as a kind of 'intimate *Song of Roland*, celebrating the sea and the men who live with it, denouncing the wickedness of war and the ambitions of dictators, and pitying the lot of the man whom war has removed from all her holds dear and who finds himself alone.'[9] The poem, verses from which are used as inter-titles by Sjöström, tells of an intrepid fisherman, Terje, who slips through the line of English ships in order to bring back provisions from Denmark for his starving family. But after a protracted chase he falls into the hands of an English

111

frigate and is flung into prison. When the war ends, he is released and returns to his village, only to find that his wife and baby son have died of malnutrition. He retreats in misery to a lonely island. Then, during a terrible storm, he has to rescue the crew of a small boat, and discovers that he has saved the English captain who captured him so long ago. His first impulse is to let him drown; but when he catches sight of the baby in the arms of the captain's wife, he relents, and suddenly his loathing of life abates.

The film is swept along by the feeling for landscape and atmosphere, by the almost prehensile attacks of the sea, and by the brilliantly syncopated editing which is at its most impressive in the scene where Terje rows desperately away from the frigate's boat. Sjöström alternates close-ups of Terje's weary arms heaving the oars back and forth, with shots of the well-drilled English crew slipping easily through the breakers. The sea remains Terje's real foe, and there is a magnificent rear view of Sjöström shaking his fist at the boiling waves. This defiance in the fact of Nature runs through many of the best Scandinavian films.

When *Terje Vigen* reached the United States in 1920, one reviewer wrote, 'Victor Seastrom [as Sjöström was called there] should come to America and teach his competitors how to make films.'[10]

During the spring and summer of 1917, Sjöström shot two films back to back. Each took his career a step further; each promulgated his increasingly determinist approach to life. *The Girl from the Marsh Croft (Tösen från Stormyrtorpet)* was the first film he adapted from the literary work of Selma Lagerlöf, and marked also the arrival of Lars Hanson (later the husband of Karin Molander) as an important star. Selma Lagerlöf (1858-1940) came from Värmland, and her lyrical, impulsive imagination took fire from the legends and folk-tales of the province. With the success of *Gösta Berling's Saga* in 1891, she was able to leave her teaching post and become a full-time writer. The Royal family expressed much interest in her novels, and she would be one of the early winners of the Nobel Prize. Unfortunately her most spectacular achievement, *The Ring of the Löwenskölds* (1928), appeared too late to be filmed by Sjöström or Stiller.

In *The Girl from the Marsh Croft* Sjöström again demonstrates his skill at recreating scenes from rustic life. This film's slender fabric of plot is chequered with domestic details and local events. A girl gives birth to an illegitimate child. The father denies any links with the affair, and the girl becomes a pariah in the gossip-ridden community. Then the son (Lars Hanson) of a neighbouring landowner takes pity on her, and persuades his mother to take her into their household as a servant. His fiancée reacts with some displeasure and a thinly-disguised expression of jealousy. But in the end she owes a great deal to the 'girl from the Marsh Croft', who gives evidence that enables her lover to go free after he has been charged with murdering a local man in a pub brawl.

Natural scenery is used throughout the film with a subtlety unequalled by anyone else at the time, (although Dreyer, who admits he was influenced by Sjöström, shot *The Parson's Widow* in Sweden also in 1917 and brought the spirit of a rural community similarly to life). The valley is a symbol of felicity and hope to the woebegone girl up on the mountainside. For a brief period she experiences real happiness in the landowner's house; she is not so much ambitious as eager to be playing a positive role in life. She loses her fear of rearing her child alone. Sjöström reveals this change of attitude by directing the early scenes in a heavy, lugubrious tone, emphasising the overcrowded hut where the girl's parents eke out their living, and then lightening the atmosphere as her life seems to bloom more significantly.

The Girl from Stormycroft called attention to the plight of the peasant classes in Sweden, and Sjöström's achievement lies in his ability to handle these outlandish scenes with a fidelity that must have been extremely moving at the time. The brawl at the tavern, the scores of minor characters who move in the background of the film, and the concision of the inter-titles, suspend one's disbelief and demand a more personal involvement on the part of the spectator. And that splendid moment when Hanson is chopping wood and bids a terse farewell to the girl from the Marsh Croft after she has been driven out by his fiancée's family, offers some idea of just how great a 'sound' director Sjöström would have been. Physical movement and exertion reflecting mental turmoil; from *Terje Vigen* to *The Wind*, this was always his forte.

The Outlaw and his Wife (Berg-Ejvind och hans hustru) appeared on New Year's Day, 1918. It pursues the line of *Terje Vigen*, championing the individual's struggle against a hostile society and a relentless adversary — Nature herself. As the Icelandic outlaw forced to climb even higher into the mountains to evade capture by the region's sheriff, Berg-Ejvind (played by Sjöström himself) is a forerunner of the Knight in Bergman's *The Seventh Seal*, refusing to succumb to the inevitable, and he joins his dead wife in a snow-covered grave. He survives to this point by virtue of his physical courage, illustrated in a vivid sequence when he dangles on a rope over a high cliff and is hauled to safety just in time (during filming, Sjöström almost lost his life when this stunt went awry).

The everyday rhythm of pastoral life, and the pleasures and pain accompanying it, emerge with a charged brilliance in the cinematography of Julius Jaenzon. The interiors in the farm at the beginning of the film look quite authentic, as does the open-air dance that would have stirred the heart of John Ford. We see Berg-Ejvind heating water on a bubbling *geysír*, and bathing naked in the foaming waterfalls and pool where his baby is destined to drown. But this exultation soon diminishes, for Berg-Ejvind has offended society (stealing a sheep, escaping from prison) and must pay the price. Alone with his beloved Halla (Edith Erastoff), the outlaw struggles to keep warm as winter closes in. Old and bitter, the couple remember the happy days of their romance on the farm so far below. At last they perish together in the snow; the fire gutters out, and the corpses lie frozen in a perpetual reproach to the social system that has rejected them.

When this work opened in Paris, in 1921, the critics welcomed it with acclaim. Louis Delluc, having seen it two years earlier, wrote: 'Here without doubt is the most beautiful film in the world. Victor Sjöström has directed it

The Outlaw and His Wife (1918) by Victor Sjöström

with a dignity that is beyond words [. . .] It is the first love duet heard in the cinema. A duet that comprises all of life. Is it a dream? What happens in it? I don't know. Does something happen in *Romeo and Juliet*? People love each other and live. That is all.'[11] Some years later, in his pioneering *Naissance du Cinéma*, Léon Moussinac conceded that while the Americans had been the first to use Nature in the early Western genre, 'Sjöström shook us with *The Outlaw and his Wife*, which with its powerful human pathos and emotion drew its strength from Nature in a more accomplished way than did Western movies [. . .] Without copying the Americans, the Swedes have taken over the formula, but have supplemented and enriched it through their rare sensitivity.'[12] Jean Béranger, in *La Grande Aventure du Cinéma Suédois*, locates the influence of *The Outlaw and his Wife* in Jacques Feyder's *La loi du Nord*, with its sequence involving a man dangling over a precipice on a rope.[13]

Sjöström continued to adapt the novels of Selma Lagerlöf to the screen. Dreyer noted that her 'predilection for dreams and supernatural events appealed to Sjöström's own somewhat sombre artistic mind.' In *The Sons of Ingmar (Ingmarssönerna*, 1918), the director gives convincing form to the story of Ingmar, who climbs towards Heaven on a gigantic ladder in order to consult his ancestors about his emotional problems. The image is ingeniously composed; one can detect in Sjöström here a mounting interest in the 'look' of a film.

Julius Jaenzon shot some indoor scenes for the production in normal sunlight against outdoor settings on the studio lot at Lidingö. This two-part film attracted 196,000 spectators in Stockholm alone, and its huge commercial success enabled Magnusson to take over his rivals and form Svensk Filmindustri in 1919, and also to build new studios in the suburb of Råsunda. The sequel, *Karin, Daughter of Ingmar (Karin Ingmarsdotter*, 1920) again involved Sjöström in hazardous stunt work (plunging waist-deep into an icy river,

113

for example) and remains a fluent film. 'Its formal plastic qualities, and the ease with which Sjöström breaks up his sequences into very modern-looking close, medium, and long shots, make it difficult to believe that the film was made nearly sixty years ago,' wrote the English critic John Gillett in 1978.[14]

A Lutheran strain may be detected in much of Sjöström's work, even if, unlike Dreyer, he almost attempts to conceal it. Stiller, his great colleague, could thank his Russian Jewish background for his freedom from such a characteristic. In *The Monastery of Sendomir (Klostret i Sendomir*, 1920), for example, the owner of a castle discovers that his wife has been unfaithful to him, and murders her. Then he converts the castle into a monastery so that he may do penance for the rest of his life. This relentless, claustrophobic quality also inhabits *Master Man (Mästerman*, 1920), in which Sjöström himself creates a rounded portrayal of Master Sammel Eneman. This august individual lives in a coastal community, and has acquired a stranglehold over half the local population due to his financial acumen. As the principal pawnbroker in the area, he sits alone in his dark house surrounded by objects that evoke either his own days as a sailor or the possessions of once well-off people forced to approach 'Master Man' for a loan. Not that he is irredeemably evil, for one night he rescues a girl when she is set upon by two ruffians down by the shore. But like a spider he covets this new possession, and insists that the girl act as her own 'collateral', until her boyfriend has saved sufficient to reclaim her. A film that could so easily have ground to a halt in sombre interiors and an atmosphere of moralistic gloom instead under Sjöström's direction manages to acquire a champagne fizz towards the end, as 'Master Man' is increasingly mocked by the local folk, who trip him up and play pranks as he struts down the lane in his best suit, holding flowers and a necklace for the girl who he believes will have to marry him instead of her beloved Knut.

The Sons of Ingmar (1918) by Victor Sjöström

Master Man still commands attention because the locations selected by Sjöström – the woods, streams, lakes, fields, etc – do not change, while the décor and costumes do. The Swedish silent directors' resolve to use natural settings has proved to be their passage into posterity.

The crowning glory of Sjöström's career in Sweden was *Thy Soul Shall Bear Witness (Körkarlen,* 1921), which was based on a novel by Selma Lagerlöf and offered Julius Jaenzon the most taxing technical challenge he had ever faced. The story of David Holm (Sjöström once more), who is clubbed down in a graveyard on the stroke of midnight at the turn of the year, and who is resurrected by an embodiment of Death (a coach-driver emerging from the waves) to relive the crises and errors of his past existence, is narrated in a complex weave of flashbacks and superimpositions. For the sequence in the churchyard, everything had to be photographed at least twice. 'We were proud of the ghosts' consistency,' wrote Sjöström once the ticklish night shooting was over. 'They were actually not flat and misty. As a result of artful lighting they had become three-dimensional in their spirituality.'[15]

Sjöström performs the part of David Holm with dazzling ease, and without makeup. As an actor, he is often limited by his own exuberance. He flings his entire personality into a scene, and thereby sacrifices his self-discipline. In *Thy Soul Shall Bear Witness*, he ranges from cynicism and wry humour to moments of agony and bewilderment. The phantasmic scenes are even more credible because they are placed at intervals between the often savagely realistic incidents in the life of David Holm, the callous ribaldry in the taverns, and the harsh quarrels between husband and wife in front of their frightened children.

The construction of flashbacks is extremely complex, and in fact about four-fifths of the film takes place in the cemetery itself. Occasionally, as many as four images are superimposed on a single frame. The first action of the

Karin, Daughter of Ingmar (1920) by Victor Sjöström

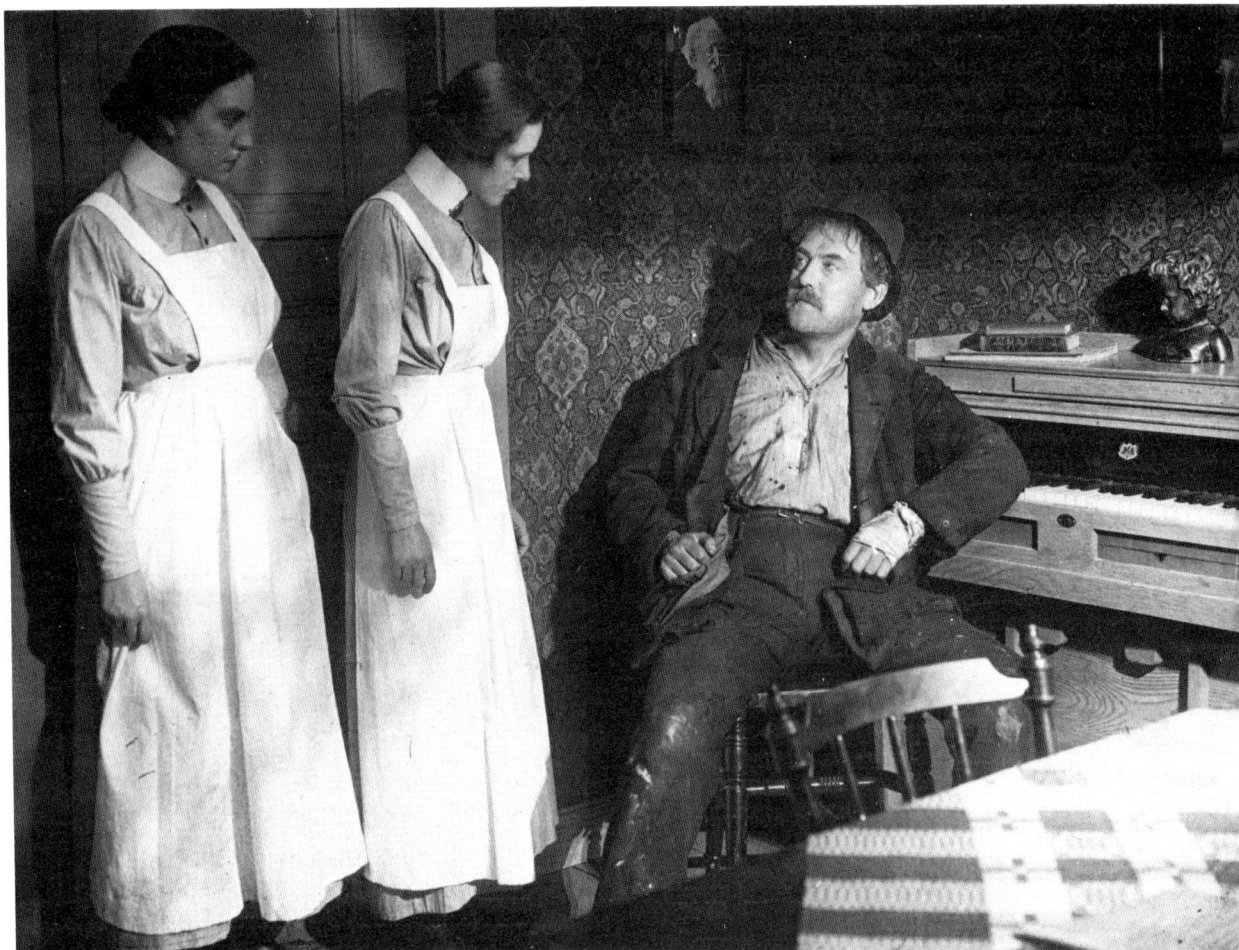

Victor Sjöström in his own *Thy Soul Shall Bear Witness* (1921)

coachman, as he carries off a wealthy man who has shot himself, looks startlingly ingenious; there seems to exist a tangible separation between body and soul. The images of the carriage moving over the waves, or silhouetted like some spectre against a twilight skyline, carry a strong appeal to the imagination. When Holm is summoned from his physical envelope to join the coachman, he puts his hands to his *ears* – a superb touch that conjures up the ghastly noise of the approaching carriage.

In 1923, Victor Sjöström sailed for America, where he would enrich Hollywood with films like *He Who Gets Slapped* and *The Wind*. When he returned to Sweden in the early summer of 1930, he would attempt to recapture the vitality of his earlier work, but productions like *The Markurells of Wadköping* (*Markurells i Wadköping*) did not even figure significantly in the output of the 1930's. As an actor, Sjöström graced some of the Swedish cinema's most solid achievements – and in particular Gustaf Molander's version of Kaj Munk's *The Word* (*Ordet*, 1943), and two of Ingmar Bergman's most appealing films, *To Joy (Till glädje*, 1950) and *Wild Strawberries* (*Smultronstället*, 1957).

Ingmar Bergman held Sjöström in enormous admiration. '[He] recognised at an early stage (much more so than Stiller) how important it was to create multi-dimensional films. I don't mean so much on a technical level as in other ways; using actors to project several things at once.'[16]

*　　　*　　　*

Mauritz Stiller

The films of **Mauritz Stiller**, habitually linked with those of Sjöström, at first bore little resemblance to the Swedish literary and pastoral tradition. But as his career advanced so the influence of the landscape and of the romantic and fatalistic traits in the novels of Selma Lagerlöf began to impinge on his work, until in *Johan* (1921) he produced a film as ardent in its harvesting of natural forces as any of Sjöström's work.

Stiller was suave, sophisticated and extremely musical. 'He'd get physically sick when he saw anything ugly,' recalled Sjöström later. To the world, he became famous during the 1920's as the mentor of Greta Garbo. Stiller was homosexual, and his relationship to Garbo was that of Pygmalion to Galatea. He never felt at home in Hollywood, and his star waned while Garbo's waxed. During the 1910's and early 1920's, however, he matched Sjöström stride for stride, and his films appear today to be the by far the livelier of the two directors'. If he ranks slightly below Sjöström in the pantheon of world cinema, it may be because his work lacks the intensity of human passion that runs through that of his great colleague.

In terms of personality the two men were as different as chalk and cheese. Had it not been for the pleasant euphony of their names in tandem, 'Sjöström and Stiller' might never have been linked, any more than Renoir and Carné in the French cinema, or Reed and Lean in the British. Sjöström did of course act in certain Stiller pictures – although that was for contractual reasons more than anything else – and the two men did not mix socially. One cannot help feeling that the cosmopolitan Stiller may have secretly scoffed at the stolid rural Swedishness of his studio rival, but there is no evidence to prove it. 'We used to talk about completely different things when we met,' said Sjöström. 'What we talked of least was film. Maybe we read each other's scripts and of course we went to each other's premieres and were pleased about each other's success – we were, and remained, friends – but that was all. There was never any kind of artistic partnership.' Bengt Forslund has noted that in Sjöström's total of almost 400 letters to his wife Edith Erastoff, the name of Stiller occurs but twice.[17]

Mauritz ('Moje') Stiller was born in 1883 in Helsinki, of Russian Jewish parentage. By the age of four he was an orphan, and emigrated to Sweden at the age of twenty-one in order to escape military service in Finland, which was still a Grand Duchy in the Russian Empire. Like Sjöström, he began his career as a stage actor, touring in Finland and Sweden, sometimes even in the same theatre groups as Sjöström. By his late twenties, he had progressed sufficiently to be given the stewardship of Lilla Teatern in Stockholm. When he applied for a post with Svenska Bio, Charles Magnusson offered him instead a position as manager. Stiller hesitated, which made Magnusson angry, and the two men parted. But some months later, in 1912, he again applied for a job at Svenska Bio, and agreed to join Magnusson as a director. 'I had studied the cinema very seriously for a whole year. But now the situation had definitely changed. They were rather cool and hesitant towards me.' But at least he was on board.

The calibre of Stiller's early output is even more difficult to gauge than that of Sjöström. Between 1912 and 1916, he directed 36 films, of which only one – *The Wings* (*Vingarne*, 1916) has survived. Gösta Werner has researched the documents concerning this period – screenplays, stills, production records, etc – and has commented that Stiller was consistently drawn towards stories taking place in upper-class surroundings. In *Mother and Daughter* (*Mor och dotter*, 1912), he describes the insane jealousy of a wealthy prima donna upon learning that her lover, a Count, prefers her daughter as a companion. In *The Black Masks* (*De svarta maskerna*, 1912), an army lieutenant is involved with a tightrope dancer and also embroiled in a secret society; the film apparently astonished the industry with its assured use of parallel action and trick perspectives that reached a spectacular climax as Sjöström and Lili Bech escaped by rope from a tall building. In *The Dagger* (*Dolken*, 1915), Lars Hanson made is début as an actor, only to perish at the hands of a well-off vamp, played by Lili Bech.

The earliest sequences shot by Stiller come from *The Model* (*Mannekängen*, 1913) and were viewed by the distinguished critic Bengt Idestam-Almquist, who wrote: 'If we did not have evidence as to the first steps in Stiller's career, we could easily make a wrong judgement. The scenes are shot in a tram. Stiller makes fun of the ladies' fashion of the period and especially the enormous hats of these women, embellished with huge pins that constituted a real danger to those next to them. He used actors who were later to be greatly appreciated in stage revues; it was all amusing, but rather simple and lacking in finesse. Stiller was capable of making much finer and wittier comedies.'[19]

Within the space of a month during the late summer of 1916, two films by Stiller were released that emphasised the range of his talent and feelings. Miraculously, both *Love and Journalism* (*Kärlek och journalistik*) and *The Wings* (*Vingarne*) have survived. The one expressed in bold, satiric terms the arrival of the 'liberated' woman; the other, based on a novel by Hermann Bang (*Mikaël*, which Dreyer also adapted some eight years later in Germany), revealed in coded language the gay disposition that Stiller had to play down throughout his life.

Stiller's gift for comedy set him apart from Sjöström who, although he could act on screen with as much skill and wit as any comedian of the time, liked to give his work a tone of fatalism that precluded levity (save in *Master Man*). *Love and Journalism*, a mere hour or so in length, remains sparklingly fresh and worldly-wise. The heroine is a young reporter who ensconces herself as a maid in the home of an Antarctic explorer in order to obtain a 'scoop' for her local newspaper. The mood of the film is established immediately when the handsome explorer (Richard Lund) fends off the arrogant inquiries of the press with the aid of his buxom old housekeeper. But Karin Molander's insouciant heroine charms her way into the vacant post of parlourmaid in the explorer's household.

Stiller's style is already fully formed at this stage. His characters are deftly-drawn, usually intelligent and full of gusto. The sexes skirmish, then retire to consider their next stratagem. But there is never the slightest hint of maliciousness in a Stiller situation, as there can be in a Bergman comedy: the lovers in his entertainments seem to be aware of the outset of their mutual attraction, but they refuse to acknowledge defeat before they have shown their mettle. Each of them is ready, and secretly eager, to enter an intimate, fantasy world. The Stiller hero belongs among the cinema's supreme romantic figures, whether he be the ingenuous Thomas Graal or the melancholy Gösta Berling.

These creations were achieved as much by hard work as by inspiration. In the words of Bengt Idestam-Almquist: 'As a director, Stiller was a Svengali, a torturing devil beyond compare, but he was loved by his sacrificial victims because he produced results.' Performers like Karin Molander and Tora Teje never excelled their work for Stiller.

In the opinion of Idestam-Almquist, *Love and Journalism* bore the hallmarks of the early Danish cinema: 'The Scandinavian cinema is a long way removed from the "Danish" source; the films featuring Danish vamps tried to achieve an up-to-date realism, but they could never free themselves from a certain staginess and the "scene, title, scene, title" syndrome. In Stiller's work, the narrative runs smoothly and without rough patches. In *Love and Journalism* the narrative is visual and so lucid that a mere 25 titles or so are necessary; furthermore, these titles are perfectly moulded into the film.'[20]

The Wings, only resurrected in 1987, presents an altogether different set of problems. In form, it belongs among the most adventurous of its period. In *Thomas Graal's Best Film*, made the following year, Stiller was one of the first directors successfully to use the 'film within a film' format. But in *The Wings* he anticipates Brecht and Godard by opening the film with scenes showing screen tests of Nils Asther and Lili Bech for a 'film' inspired by Carl Milles's sculpture, 'The Wings'. The results prove disappointing, and Lars Hanson takes the Asther role, playing Mikaël, the young painter and adopted son of Claude Zoret (Egil Eide), the 'Master' sculptor. The story, for all its velvet elegance, revolves around the betrayal of love. Zoret is courting a luscious princess, but when she meets Mikaël she switches her affections and the old Master collapses from a heart attack. On his deathbed he signs a will leaving all his possessions to Mikaël, who is clearly the object of his affections. The film suffers from stilted, even melodramatic performances. Only Lars Hanson fulfils Stiller's patent desire to *suggest* emotion rather than state it. When, for example, he learns that his Master has been stricken, he lets his hand droop to his side in a pregnant gesture, and his face reflects the sense of shock and guilt allied to loss. Another typical Stiller touch occurs early in the film when Mikaël comes into the Master's studio and perceives the Princess's cloak flung over a chair. He raises it almost, but not quite, to his lips as though it were a sacred object.

For Gösta Werner, the subject of *The Wings* is 'as in the novel *Mikaël* by Herman Bang, the story of the joy and love of being an artist. It is also a variation on the eternal triangle [. . .] In the novel, there are no allusions to Zoret's erotic attraction towards Mikaël, Irrespective of Bang's own homosexuality, there are no gay themes, even disguised ones, in the novel. This was also so where Stiller's film was concerned.'[21]

Hindsight, however, suggests otherwise. Stiller was merely obeying the custom of his period in describing a heterosexual struggle. For those wanting to find a homosexual theme, there are palpable signs and clues. Zoret's comportment implies all the frustration of someone in the grip of what Oscar Wilde termed 'the love that dares not say its name'. According to Fredrik Silverstolpe:

'In Herman Bang's novel the work of art was a painting. In Stiller's film, on the other hand, the painting was replaced by a sculpture which gave its name to the film. This sculpture is identical to Carl Milles's *The Wings*: an eagle is flying off with a young man in its grasp. The young man with the eagle is "a homoerotic icon" in the history of art. Hundreds of artists since the days of antiquity have used this theme to illustrate the myth of Ganymede — it is the story of Zeus who was so in love with the beautiful Ganymede that he transformed himself into an eagle in order to bear him to Olympus, where Ganymede became his cup-bearer.'[22]

This seems to be the only occasion in his prolific career when Stiller dated to subvert the traditional romantic circumstances of the cinema and even in *The Wings* he may have felt obliged to add the 'distancing' prologue in order to divert the authorities' attention from the true implications of the film.

Ironically, Stiller's 'troubled' films, such as *The Wings* and *Gunnar Hede's Saga*, have endured less well than lightweight comedies of the order of *Thomas Graal's Best Film* (*Thomas Graals bästa film*, 1917) and *Thomas Graal's First Child* (*Thomas Graals bästa barn*, 1918). Recent screenings and revivals of the work of **Gustaf Molander** suggest that this modest individual, whose career spanned more than half a century, may have been crucial to the success of the Swedish silent cinema. Molander, a young actor at the Royal Dramatic Theatre in Stockholm, had submitted to Magnusson a screenplay for *Terje Vigen* and when the film entered production the following year, he shared the screenwriting credit with Victor Sjöström. His second filmed screenplay was for *Thomas Graal's Best Film* and was credited to him under the pseudonym of Harald B. Harald.

Graal is a famous scriptwriter infatuated with a secretary at the studios; he concocts a screenplay around her domestic life (so, twice in the same year, Stiller revelled in the 'film within a film' mode). The very structure of the movie reflects Graal's approach to life, his devious fancies, and his disarming jokes. As the 'script' takes shape, Stiller treats his audience to scenes of melodramatic irony by which Graal imagines the poor secretary to be plagued at home by her tyrannical parents.

Thomas Graal's Best Film works primarily as a comedy of manners, but it also functions effectively as a satire on film-making, even at this early stage of the industry's development. The implication is that the cinema stands beyond reality, and as a medium attracts only the 'hammy' situation and the exaggerated personality. Victor Sjöström and Karin Molander, the one cocky, flirtatious and full of inventive little gestures, the other pert and deliciously astute, form the ideal screen couple, comparable to such later partnerships as those of Myrna Loy and William Powell, and Clark Gable and Claudette Colbert.

Their spontaneity of reaction reaches perfection in the sequel, *Thomas Graal's First Child*, in which Stiller abandons the flashbacks of the earlier film in favour of a more chronological structure. The film begins with the wedding of Thomas and Bessie. Sjöström performs a kind of agonised striptease as he temporarily mislays the ring, and an argument starts in the taxi as they leave on their honeymoon: should the firstborn be a boy or a girl? Their dispute reaches such angry proportions that they retire to separate rooms and refuse to eat or talk with each other. Then one day a passer-by catches sight of Bessie at her window and flirts with her. This incenses Thomas and he attacks the offender in the street. Bessie has to intercede, and husband and wife are reconciled. After this brilliant opening passage, the film settles down to a spirited account of the Graal marriage, the birth of a son ('Man hopes but God decides'), and the gradual lessening of friction between the married partners. When Bessie plays the piano, the baby howls with rage; Thomas takes over, and the crying changes to ecstatic approval. There are other humorous scenes, such as Thomas's return from his pseudo-'shoot', furiously counting the hares, grouse, and partridge in the back of his car, and his amusing his son by placing a wastepaper basket over the dog's head so that the basket floats mysteriously around the floor.

The domestic relationships and erotic byplay in Stiller's comedies possess an application and a validity beyond their immediate setting − and generation. Molander's dialogue sparkles with sarcastic repartee, while Stiller brings to every sequence an impeccable sense of timing (for example, the quarrel on the honeymoon, when Thomas and Bessie withdraw to their respective bedrooms in high dudgeon, the two doors slamming in significant unison). The innate flair for rhythm that serves Stiller so impressively in the subsequent *Sir Arne's Treasure* can be noted at several points in the two Graal comedies − particularly during the brawl beneath the apartment when the irate Thomas is set upon by the crowd. At such moments Stiller clearly manipulates the susceptibilities of the audience, but at other junctures his grouping of characters within the frame and in the décor is so adroit and premeditated that few cuts are necessary, thus allowing the spectator to share the comedy more closely. The overall structure of the film is so tightly constructed, and the pace so steady, that there are scarcely any *longueurs*.

Egil Eide in *The Wings* (1916) by Mauritz Stiller

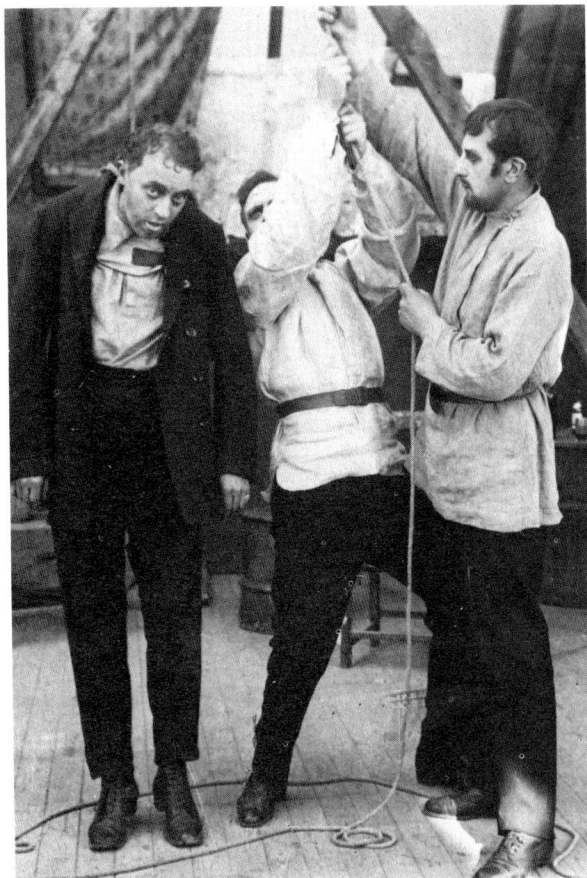

Thomas Graal's Best Film (1917) by Mauritz Stiller

In December 1920, Max Reinhardt made a guest appearance in Stockholm with his Deutsches Theater. Starved of foreign films during the Great War, the Germans found themselves stunned by the Swedish productions on view. When Reinhardt returned to Berlin, he declared: 'I was an avowed opponent of the cinema until I came to Sweden and saw *Erotikon*. This film totally changed my attitude and I am convinced that the cinema has a future [. . .] It is the Swedish cinema that is pointing the way.'[23]

Not that Stiller worked in a vacuum. Rune Waldekranz claims that his comedies revealed the influence of the satirical screenplays written by Anita Loos for Triangle in Hollywood in 1916 and 1917, especially those featuring Douglas Fairbanks and directed by John Emerson. In turn, *Erotikon* (1920) would be acknowledged as inspiring some of the work of Lubitsch and DeMille.

Despite its august reputation, *Erotikon* looks more and more musty with the passing years. There are several reasons for this. The film derived from a rather pompous 19th-century play. Gustaf Molander did not contribute to the screenplay. Stiller himself lost something of his vitality in dealing with the immense logistics of the production: 800 extras for the big scene at the Stockholm Opera, a ballet composed specially for the film, aerial sequences showing Tora Teje indulging in aeroplane excursions with her admirer. As a consequence, the characters remain undeveloped and are manoeuvred rather too obviously; indeed Stiller's groupings appear surprisingly static and formal at this stage of his career. *Erotikon* survives without question as an elegant pirouette of a movie, sensational at the time because of its lack of inhibitions and its risqué innuendo. The wife, Irene (Tora Teje), of an absent-minded professor of entomology is courted by a young sculptor (Lars Hanson) and the pompous Baron Felix. The elaborate antics of these characters emerge in their proper perspective at the start of the film when the professor makes some significant comments about 'the communal life of the striver beetle' in a lecture. Later, there is a performance at the Stockholm Opera that also reflects, or distorts, the erotic proceedings. The seduction of the Shah's wife in this ballet plays the same dramatic role as the play in *Hamlet*, although it is not arranged from within for dramatic purposes, merely included by Stiller as a typically discreet allusion.

Like Stiller's other comedies, *Erotikon* derives its humour from the mutual distrust among the leading characters. The sculptor lives in fear of Irene proving unfaithful to *him* (never mind the hapless professor), and its transpires that she in turn has been tormented by the thought of his being unfaithful to *her*. Stiller delights in sidestepping the rules of polite society. Even the movement with which Preben helps Irene into her fur coat assumes a sensual elegance. Marthe (Karin Molander), the old professor's niece, throws contemporary modesty to the winds when she is alone, lights herself a cigarette and relaxes full-length on a couch with her calves amply exposed. Stiller does not in this way vent his disapproval of the depraved upper classes; he is, if anything, endorsing their sly disregard for decorum. The arid atmosphere of the institute where the professor holds his classes represents an unsophisticated, narrow-minded way of life that invites Stiller's scorn.

When Stiller chose to leave the stuffy boudoirs and salons of high society, he showed that he could depict Scandinavian 'outdoor' themes with as much panache as Sjöström. *The Revenge of Jacob Vindås (Fiskebyn*, 1919) described the religious intolerance endemic to the fishing communities of the West coast, and the lyrical imagery and documentary realism of *The Song of the Scarlet Flower (Sången om den eldröda blomman*, 1919) recalled *The Outlaw and His Wife* (and in 1969, Jean Mitry wrote that this latter production had conserved its freshness).[24]

More dazzling in its analysis of personalities under stress, and in its technical audacity, is *Sir Arne's Treasure (Herr Arnes pengar)*, filmed over several arduous weeks during the winter and spring of 1919.

Set in the 16th century, *Sir Arne's Treasure* chronicles the flight of three ruthless mercenaries from Gripsholm Castle, after a botched conspiracy during the reign of Johan III. It introduces another distinctive Stiller quality – his skill at integrating vision with reality. After the mercenaries have pillaged the manor of Sir Arne, the sole survivor of the attack, Elsalill (Mary Johnson), relives the violence over

Mary Johnson (right) in *Sir Arne's Treasure* (1919) by Mauritz Stiller

and over again. Her nightmares, in which the spectre of her slaughtered foster-sister figures persistently, conflict with her growing love for Sir Archie (Richard Lund), the good-looking, dastardly leader of the mercenaries. This blighted romance is among the most touching in all Swedish cinema, and no death is more poignant than that of Elsalill as, thrust forward like a shield by Sir Archie, she perishes on a soldier's lance. So the winding cortège across the ice at Marstrand brings Elsalill to her final resting-place, and constitutes one of the high points of Julius Jaenzon's career as a cinematographer. This celebrated image was inspired by an illustration for Selma Lagerlöf's novel by the great painter Albert Edelfelt. The late Sergei Yutkevich told Bengt Idestam-Almquist: 'Swedish films enjoyed a remarkable success [in the U.S.S.R.]. Those by Sjöström and Stiller touched us the most. Naturally, our directors of the 1920's were influenced by them; there was no intention to copy these works, but their impact was so great that it automatically, to a certain degree, left an imprint on the Russian films. Would Eisenstein have composed his procession in *Ivan the Terrible* in quite the same way had he not seen *Sir Arne's Treasure*? This link leapt to mind immediately for me.'[25]

Sir Arne's Treasure is sustained by its mood of desperation: the mesh of conflicting desires holds the film in a taut, dramatic form. On the one hand there is the anxious longing in the mercenaries for the ice to thaw so that they can escape from Sweden, and on the other the agony of Elsalill, drawn inexorably to bind her fate to that of Sir Archie.

Johan (1921), based on a Finnish novel, underlines Stiller's keen grasp of the Nordic temperament. Fundamental to its theme is an idea that recurs frequently in Scandinavian cinema: a stranger arrives on the scene, symbolising a beacon of hope and excitement in the life of a remote community. Marit, a farmer's wife, is seduced by a passing visitor. He abducts her, and together they hurtle down a precipitous river, only to be caught by Marit's pursuing husband. The stranger is worsted but − and Stiller's understanding of human nature again comes to the fore − it is the farmer whose spirit is broken, for he realises that Marit did in fact quit of her own accord.

Stiller in this production matched Sjöström's descriptions of pastoral life and physical toil. Nor could his colleague have surpassed the editing in the lovers' trip down the river, which appears as a continuous movement, a whirling

121

The Song of the Scarlet Flower (1919) by Mauritz Stiller

Gunnar Hede's Saga (1922) by Mauritz Stiller

descent into chaos and misadventure. Nyrki Tapiovaara also seized the heart of this story in his adaptation twenty years later (see FINLAND, page 52), but failed to extinguish the memory of the earlier version.

In 1922, Stiller made his last film of genius, *Gunnar Hede's Saga (Gunnar Hedes saga)*. Again the source was a novel by Selma Lagerlöf; again Mary Johnson had a key role as the fey Ingrid; and again Stiller sought out a difficult location (Jämtland, in northern Sweden, where the reindeer scenes were filmed). The wistful protagonist in this tale ventures to the extreme limits of Lappland, where he buys a herd of reindeer. Hoping to stave off bankruptcy at the family manor, he drives them on the long trek south. An accident during a stampede almost kills him, and he suffers amnesia. Ingrid nurses him back to health until the sound of her violin playing restores his memory. The film contains none of the sardonic tones that mark Stiller's comedies. Being a musician himself he manages, as no other Swedish director could, to capture the vibrant, twilight world of the wandering players and to mould in Mary Johnson's Ingrid a heroine of infinite poise and delicacy.

Stiller cast the 17-year-old Greta Garbo in *The Atonement of Gösta Berling (Gösta Berlings saga*, 1924). Intended as the apotheosis of Swedish cinema up to that time, it became instead its swansong. The economic data alone demonstrate its failure: *Erotikon* had been bought by 45 territories outside Sweden, and yet in spite of a massive sales campaign, *The*

Atonement of Gösta Berling found release in only 28 countries. The pace of this long, elaborate film was too slow by comparison with the French and American films that were now asserting their dominance over world markets. Garbo's luminous beauty as the Italian girl who dotes on the handsome, defrocked parson, Gösta Berling, certainly distinguished many scenes. Elsewhere the film was handicapped by a lack of zest and narrative flexibility quite astonishing in a director of such energy as Stiller. The acting still looks theatrical, and scenes shot in the studios contrast embarrassingly with those out of doors (particularly in the long chase across the ice, as Lars Hanson and Greta Garbo, aboard a large sled, try to outpace a pack of pursuing wolves).

Even the discovery of Garbo, usually credited to Stiller, belonged to Gustaf Molander. As head of the Royal Dramatic Theatre's academy, he had selected her as one of the most talented of his pupils. Garbo's first appearance on film, in a publicity short for fashion-wear, shows her as unrecognisably plump and exuberant. Stiller's achievement was to isolate − and then magnify − the innate control and coolness of her expression.

Learning to Live with Hollywood

Going to the cinema as a pastime reached all-time records in Sweden as the new decade dawned. It has been estimated

Greta Garbo in *The Atonement of Gösta Berling* (1924) by Mauritz Stiller

that the number of 'visits' to the movies exceeded the number of seats available in Stockholm. Attendances topped the 8 million level, only to decline dramatically to 6.7 million in 1921. The Swedish film industry faced competition from a host of other spectacles, live shows, circuses, dance competitions and so on. But the simultaneous failure of Sweden's own film production developed from other causes.

Sjöström and Stiller, the champions of their generation, had few horizons left to conquer – at least in Sweden. Their art stagnated. Sjöström could no longer breathe life into a portentous drama like *Love's Crucible (Vem dömer*, 1922), while Stiller manifested a streak of complacency, even arrogance, in his demand for ever greater resources and budgets. Perhaps both men felt bored; they needed a fresh challenge, and the offers made to them by M-G-M offered an escape route from the drudgery and expectations of the domestic movie business.

Apart from this, Swedish films could no longer depend on a captive audience. American films were freely imported after the end of the Great War, and with each passing year the Hollywood machine strengthened its appeal, at home and throughout the world. In turn, this nurtured in Swedish film circles an overt commercialism, typified by the changes at Svensk Filmindustri. The Swedish tycoon and so-called 'Match King', Ivar Kreuger, gradually increased his shareholding in the company until his representative on the board, Olof Andersson, exerted a powerful hold over SF's policy. Charles Magnusson, the pioneer who had seen his enterprise climb to an unrivalled position in 1919, lost control as one poor season succeeded another. By 1928 he was ready to throw in the towel, and Olof Andersson took over Svensk Filmindustri on behalf of Kreuger. His departure from the scene followed a veritable exodus of talent. Not only Sjöström and Stiller had gone to America, but also stars like Greta Garbo, Lars Hanson, and Karin Molander, as well as one of the best writers, Hjalmar Bergman (even though he did not stay long in Hollywood). The political climate had also changed. Respect for artistic experiment did not distinguish Arvid Lindman's Conservative party, which gained 73 seats in the elections of 1928. Less than two years later, the Swedish economy reeled before the 'Great Depression' that swept in from the United States. Unemployment leapt from less than 50,000 in 1930 to 161,000 at the close of 1932. Kreuger's empire crashed about his ears, and he committed suicide. Ironically, attendances began to climb once more, as always happens at a time of war or economic recession. With the studios producing a stream of lightweight comedies and drawing-room romances to cope with this unexpected public demand, the character of Swedish cinema had undergone a fundamental transformation.

*   *   *

Three men, all born within seven years of one another, remained in Sweden to salvage the honour of the Swedish silent film. **Gustaf Molander**, as has already been noted, began his career as a screenwriter for Sjöström and Stiller.

John W. Brunius established his reputation in 1919 with *Synnöve Solbakken,* starring the effervescent Karin Molander and filmed on location in Norway. And **Per Lindberg**, better known for his theatre work, found himself contracted by Bonnierfilm to direct the screenplays of his brother-in-law, Hjalmar Bergman.

Rune Waldekranz has pointed out that Brunius's *Synnöve Solbakken* had been inspired by the peasant paintings of the German painter, Adolf Tidemand.[26] The following summer, he made *The Mill (Kvarnen,* 1921) in the southernmost province of Skåne. Again, melodrama and morality intermingled in a conflict between a sloe-eyed temptress (Clara Kjellblad) and an unspoilt country girl (Ellen Dall) that leads to murder, and to a climactic showdown when the old mill burns to the ground. Leif Furhammar refers to the symbolism of the animals in this Brunius production: 'Especially emphasised is the cat that always accompanies Clara Kjellblad like a symbol of Lise's uncivilised dishonesty or malevolence, and the similarly symbolic doe that follows the good, pure-hearted Anne as played by Ellen Dall.'[27] *The Mill* proved a greater critical success in France than it did in Sweden.

Brunius could certainly marshall big crowds, as demonstrated in *Johan Ulfstjerna* (1923), with its scenes of Cossack violence filmed with no fewer than six cameras in Helsinki's Senate Square, and most conspicuously of all in *Charles XII (Karl XII,* 1925). Scripted by Hjalmar Bergman and starring the top star of the day, Gösta Ekman, this historical epic about one of Sweden's best-loved kings should have broken box-office records. In fact, it lost the huge sum of 342,000 crowns – all borne by the headstrong producer Herman Rasch. Ekman's performance scarcely redeems the film when viewed today. Alternately pensive and melancholy, wild-eyed and manic, he captures the monarch's impulsive quality but little else. Charles XII had to combat Poles and Russians to the east, and fire and intrigue at home. Brunius's direction comes alive in the outdoor sequences – the hunt for a marauding bear, the charge of the cavalry in the battle with the Tsar's troops at Narva, and the numerous engagements in snow-covered terrain. Nothing daunted, Brunius survived to direct two more mammoth costume dramas: *The Tales of Ensign Stål (Fänrik Ståls sägner,* 1926) and *Gustaf Wasa* (1928), each divided like *Charles XII* into two parts. His work during the 1930's left no mark on the decade.

Gustaf Molander, however, wielded an altogether more durable talent. Throughout the 1920's, 1930's, 1940's, and even 1950's, he directed films which, while amounting to a heterogenous body of work, rarely failed to tap his unostentatious gifts.

His marriage to Karin Molander lasted only eight years, but during the 1910's he wrote some scintillating lines for her in the two *Thomas Graal* films directed by Stiller. Once he graduated to direction (from 1920 onwards), Molander adapted like a chameleon to the taste of the day. *Ingmar's Inheritance (Ingmarsarvet,* 1925), for example, deals with a complex family saga as befits an adaptation of Selma Lagerlöf's *Jerusalem,* but does so in the brisk, action-packed manner that Hollywood had already perfected. 'Lill'

Ingmar Ingmarsson (Lars Hanson) is the quiet teacher who by degrees learns to fulfil his destiny and run the family estate. He must cope with the wiles of relatives and neighbours alike, as well as the presence of the extraordinary Helgum (played by the German actor Conrad Veidt). Helgum becomes almost a parody of the 'Dark Stranger' so often encountered in Nordic film. At once a religious zealot and an ambitious farm manager, Helgum impresses the locals with his visions — which include a grisly storm with trees uprooted and split by lightning — and his memory of a shipwreck in which people behave like beasts, killing one another and forcing their victims under water.

Molander, in seeking a narrative zest, does not sacrifice his loyalty to the pastoral environment. The landscape is alive, with rivers flowing, trees swaying in the wind; you can feel the rain and the warmth of the sun.

Two years later, he used similar locations for a different purpose. *His English Wife (Hans engelska fru*, 1927) was, despite its title, a co-production between Sweden and Germany, with Lil Dagover — best known as the dark-eyed girl in *The Cabinet of Dr. Caligari* — in the title role, playing opposite the Finnish actor, Urho Somersalmi. Acting with forceful self-confidence, Dagover cuts a formidable figure as the Englishwoman who shrugs off an arranged marriage in London and travels to Norrland, in the far north of Sweden, to seduce her family's richest creditor, Birger Holm. Molander's direction fails to bring the London sequences alive, but once on home territory his flair for outdoor filming enhances the mood. Cathleen's tumbling into a turbulent river, and her rescue by the unwitting Birger Holm carries a satirical spice worthy of Stiller, and concludes with Holm peeling off the unconscious beauty's wet clothes as fastidiously as James Stewart treats Kim Novak in *Vertigo*. The film degenerates into drawing-room melodrama after Cathleen abandons her Swedish husband and returns to England. The second half of *His English Wife* owes its salvation to Lil Dagover's cheerful, energetic, and often effervescent performance as the merry widow. Karin Swanström's portrayal of the English mother underlines how significant in Nordic cinema the maternal role can be. Some Swedish actresses, from Stina Berg to Naima Wifstrand and Jullan Kindahl, specialised in playing these parts.

Indeed Stina Berg's 'Ma Catherine' in Molander's *Sin (Synd*, 1928) functions as a pivot for much of the drama, and symbolises the puritan conscience of Sweden. Strindberg's play, *There Are Crimes and Crimes*, about a reckless, susceptible writer who abandons his wife and child for a ruthless *femme fatale* (Gina Manès, in her element!), receives from Molander an urbane, even humorous treatment. The court scene at the end, with a shrewd inspector unravelling the truth that lies behind the disappearance of the hero's little daughter, grips the audience like the dénouement of a good detective story. Even in this most sophisticated of settings (Paris and its theatre milieu) Molander cannot forget his loyalty to Mother Nature, and includes some storm sequences that suggest the wrath of God in the face of the evil projected by Gina Manès's vamp.

Much less successful is *One Night (En natt*, 1931), which was directed in a French version by Henri Fescourt. Again Molander brought a certain degree of verisimilitude to a foreign setting — Finland on this occasion, in the wake of the Bolshevik Revolution. The influence of Eisenstein colours the overheated story of a young Finn, Armas, who espouses the radical cause in direct opposition to his aristocratic parents. His psychological tension is presented in arresting visuals by Molander, but the dialogue by Ragnar Hyltén-Cavallius is declamatory and bombastic. So too is the music, even if Sibelius is exploited. The montage sequences, the experimental sound, and the vigour of many of the action scenes, all demonstrate Molander's eagerness to broaden his palette, and to absorb some of the new trends that were sweeping through European cinema in the late 1920's.

Molander's sturdy commitment to certain basic principles of film-making enabled him to distinguish the otherwise mediocre Swedish cinema of the 1930's with productions featuring the talents of two key screen personalities of the era: the aging Gösta Ekman and the callow Ingrid Bergman.

* * *

The third of the directors who gave a tinge of distinction to the otherwise mediocre Swedish cinema of the 1920's had studied under Max Reinhardt. Per Lindberg remains one of the most enigmatic figures of the period. He produced many important plays during the 1920's and 1930's, worked in radio, and wrote some key books on the arts. His slender output of films comprises just nine features. Before his death in 1944, Lindberg helped to develop the concept and design of Malmö Municipal Theatre, where Ingmar Bergman would spend some of his most glorious years as a stage director.

The Norrtull Gang (Norrtullsligan, 1923) belongs among the most courageous and enjoyable films of the European decade. Films prior to 1923 had presented individual female characters of flesh and blood, but *The Norrtull Gang* established a precedent in dealing with a cast dominated by four lively women. From the opening sequence, the intertitles are unusual in reflecting a person's thoughts and memories. The screenplay by Hjalmar Bergman transcends the familiar image of women as decorative objects. The four who make up the 'gang' take city life in their stride. One loses her job after campaigning for strike action at the office. Another resigns after the boss has flirted with her once too often. The film resembles a witty book of memoirs, almost a diary. Lindberg's direction escapes the conventions of the time so that his women still look quite modern, with their no-nonsense coiffures, for example, and the minutiae of everyday life come across vividly. Seventeen years later, he would again demonstrate his gift for directing actresses, in *The June Night* (see page 130).

* * *

Swedish film production declined through the later 1920's, reaching its nadir in 1929, when a mere six features were

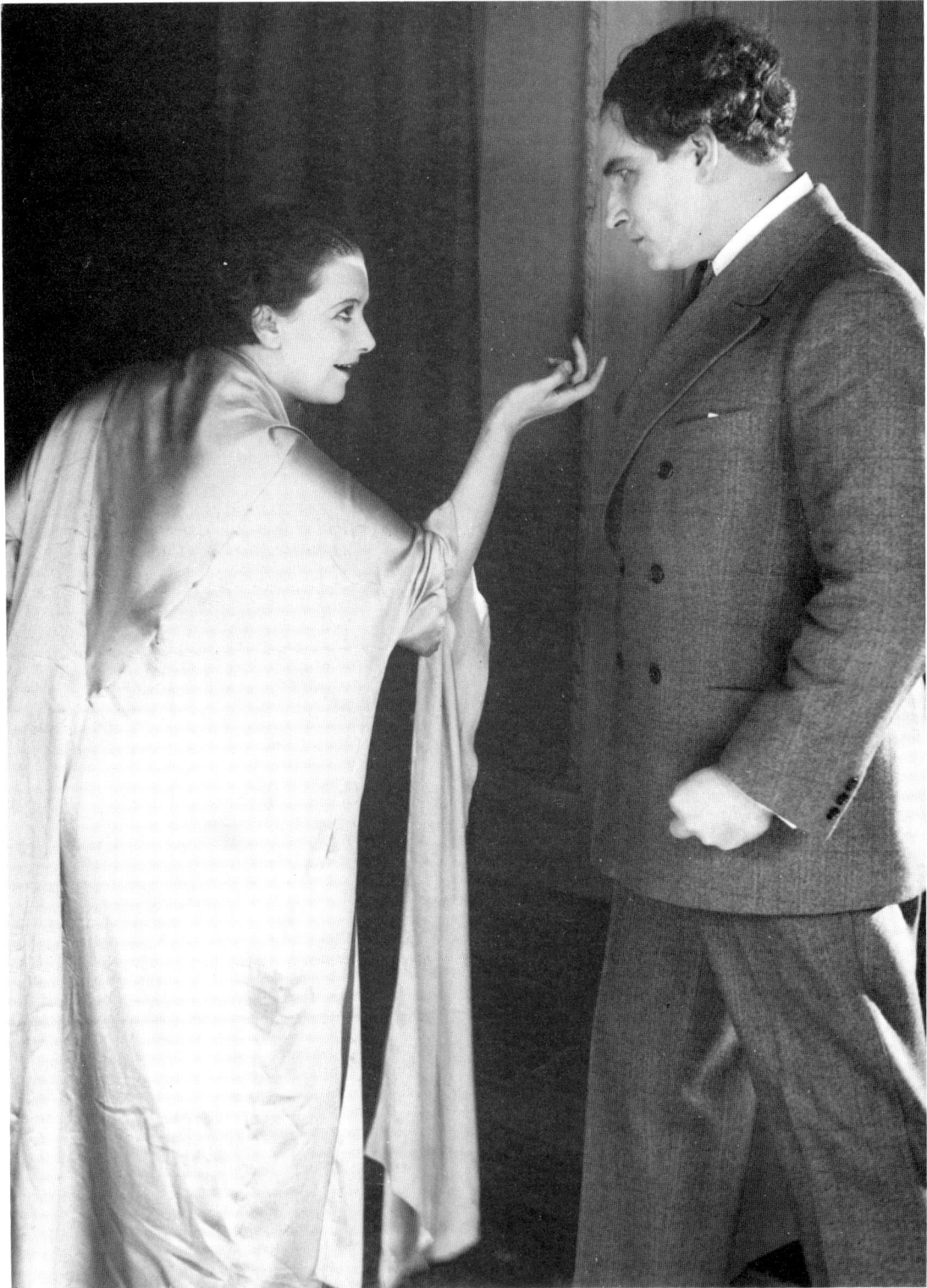

His English Wife (1927) by Gustaf Molander

released. However, as the domestic industry began to recover its poise, and to assemble vehicles more suited to the tastes of the period, so output accelerated once more, settling down at some twenty-odd features per annum.

The triumphs of Sjöström and Stiller had created a climate in which the director's role attracted some glamour. Edvin Adolphson, known as a leading screen actor, went behind the cameras and launched Ingrid Bergman on her career in *The Count from the Old Town (Munkbrogreven*, 1935). Olof Molander, who would be revered for decades as the greatest of all Swedish stage directors, made a brave stab at demythologising *The Lady of the Camellias (Damen med kameliorna*, 1925). His Marguerite (Tora Teje) displays no ecstasy in her love affair with Armand Duval (Uno Henning), nor is she the youngest of fallen women. Although the film betrays the theatrical loyalties of its director, with the camera observing most scenes from a single, rigid setup, Molander knows how to rein in the histrionics of his players (Nils Arehn, for example, creates an excellent Georges Duval), and he copes well with the outdoor scenes – the duel with rapiers in the woods can scarcely be faulted from an aesthetic standpoint.

Danish skills also brought flashes of offbeat brilliance to the Swedish cinema of the 1920's. **Carl Th. Dreyer** made *The Parson's Widow (Prästänkan*, 1920) for Svensk Filmindustri, and **Benjamin Christensen** took the first confident step into the real of 'docudrama' with *Witchcraft through the Ages (Häxan*, 1922), shot in Denmark but produced by Svensk Filmindustri.

Dreyer recognised the influence of Sjöström on his career, and *The Parson's Widow* bears the hallmarks of the Swedish master, not least in its rich evocation of the countryside. The sylvan scenery is rendered by cinematographer George Schnéevoigt with bright enthusiasm, giving the 16th-century tale a cheerful aspect. Like all Dreyer's best work, the film contains a mischievous streak, and indeed without

Lars Hanson, a stalwart of Swedish stage and screen, in Gustaf Molander's *Ingmar's Inheritance* (1925)

Witchcraft through the Ages (1922) by Benjamin Christensen

it the story of a young priest who is suddenly expected to marry an eighty-year-old widow would be implausible. Dreyer's characters speak with a gripping intensity, their faces viewed in audacious close-up. Just as Sjöström influenced Dreyer, so with his accent on the close-up Carl Th. Dreyer would leave his mark on Ingmar Bergman. *The Parson's Widow* has a special significance in terms of Scandinavian co-operation. The production relied upon Swedish funding, a Danish director, and actors from Sweden, Norway, and Denmark.

So too does *Witchcraft through the Ages*. Christensen devoted over three years of his life to this massive production (now available only in an 88-minute version), and Svensk Filmindustri purchased a studio in Hellerup outside Copenhagen; this was reserved for Christensen's film, and his alone, and Richard Louw took full advantage of the luxurious conditions, building one elaborate and meticulously detailed set after another. Christensen begins

his *magnum opus* with dioramas and drawings illustrating Man's earliest impressions of the Earth and the universe. Soon he introduces animated scenes, filled with tiny puppet figures, and then a series of luminous tableaux vivants. *Witchcraft* analyses its subject with irrepressible verve and libidinous glee. Where other directors (Dreyer included) would opt for sombre, fateful imagery, Christensen relieves the anguish of his subject by focusing on the lighter aspects: coins that engage in a pixillated dance before vanishing after an old woman's dream, or a fat friar driven so mad with lust that he pursues a woman through an orchard, or a gaggle of nuns going into hysterics after one of them acts in a lecherous manner. Even as it informs its audience of the evils of bigotry and superstitiion, *Witchcraft* leaves the impression of a forceful, even aggressive film. Time and again we are trapped into momentary belief in the power projected by evil masks or, most memorably, by the 'Devil' played by Christensen himself with much sexual innuendo.

From a Swedish standpoint, however, the freshest and most courageous film of the period was **Alf Sjöberg's** *The Strongest (Den starkaste*, 1929). It brought the decade to a close on a high note, but unfortunately did not herald a new stage in the development of Swedish cinema. Indeed, despite his acknowledged brilliance as a stage director at the Royal Dramatic Theatre, Sjöberg found himself unable to get a project accepted at the film studios during the ensuing ten years. The critical reaction was very favourable, contrasting the open-aired pastoral and maritime scenes with the plethora of stuffy, salon comedies and melodramas to which Swedes had grown accustomed in the late 1920's. *The Strongest* records a struggle between two men's desire for a farmer's daughter, Ingeborg, near the Norwegian port of Tromsö. Human rivalries and jealousies are played out in the weird, snowy landscape. Gustaf, the handsome stranger, woos Ingeborg from under the nose of stolid Ole, but to the end he remains a chivalrous figure, relishing the continual struggle with Nature and her demands far more than the duel with Ole over the girl at home. Man versus the elements constitutes the major theme of Sjöberg's assured début as a screen director. 'Here,' says the old father, 'right belongs to the strongest.' As in *The Outlaw and his Wife*, the landscape asserts its power to influence the lives of the characters in these remote regions, and the scenes of seal and bear hunting on the ice-floes may be compared to Flaherty's achievement in *Nanook of the North.*

Rising above the Lightweight

In a decade when Europa Film and Sandrew Film would establish themselves as genuine competitors with Svensk Filmindustri, two individuals at once typified and transcended the 1930's: Gustaf Molander behind the camera and Ingrid Bergman before it. Unlike Garbo, the young Bergman appeared in several Swedish films before finally moving to the United States. She worked with various directors, and her parts ranged from the tiny to the dominant.

Her début in *The Count from the Old Town* (1935) at the age of 20 brought her critical recognition, including this comment in the Social Democrats' newspaper: 'A fresh and unusually young lady, lively and confident and already well versed in film craft.' In this cheerful comedy about Stockholm in the days of 'Prohibition' (beer is the only alcohol permitted), she plays the maid at a hotel in the quaint old quarter of the city. The cinema's first glimpse of Ingrid Bergman is a shot of her looking out of a door in the hotel and taking a newspaper from the concierge with a giggle that would characterise her role and much of her life. She enjoys her romantic scenes with Edvin Adolphson, who plays the unemployed, cloth-capped Åke, flirting and stealing a kiss when the opportunity presents itself. Bergman's concerned stare, her buxom figure, and her patent sincerity cuts like a knife through the frothy artifice of the genre of which *The Count from the Old Town* is so typical.

Not that these so-called 'Pilsner' films of the 1930's should be dismissed out of hand. René Clair was signing his name to many a similar production in France, and received applause in all quarters for his work. When one re-views *The Count from the Old Town* today, one responds to the clever use of real locations in Stockholm, and to the personalities drawn like caricatures in the margins of the entertainment.

The film secured for Ingrid Bergman a contract with Svensk Filmindustri, and under Gustaf Molander's direction she blossomed into an actress mature beyond her years and looks. She overcomes the stereotypical settings and circumstances of the period, and stubbornly resists any attempt to immerse her into the bourgeois 'family' that sits at the core of most Nordic films of the prewar decade. In *Swedenhielms* (1935), she remains the only relaxed member of the household, making gentle fun of her lieutenant *beau* even when he pretends to have fallen out of love with her. Audiences flocked to see Gösta Ekman as the *pater familias* in *Swedenhielms*, a scientist whose glorious career cannot lessen the *tristesse* of his private life. Ekman is most impressive in solo scenes — when, for example, he gazes piteously up at his wife's portrait, and then returns to his armchair, a bowed figure, and extinguishes the light for the sake of peace. Around him, the younger generation complains about the rising cost of living.

The luxurious, almost stifling atmosphere of such films concealed the reality of life in Sweden, which was adjusting to the reforming zeal of a socialist administration and preparing to bid farewell to the class-consciousness exemplified in *Swedenhielms* and in *Intermezzo* (1936), which would be re-made in Hollywood as a David O. Selznick production. A certain pulse still throbs at the heart of this latter film, however saccharine its romance between a great violinist (Ekman) and his children's young music teacher (Bergman). Perhaps it is Gösta Ekman's impassioned conviction as the happily-married husband who tries so hard to wring a second chance from life. Perhaps it is Ingrid Bergman's unforced devotion as the shy young teacher, distraught at the domestic schism she has provoked. The moral guilt of the period adds a dark overtone to *Intermezzo*.

Molander continued to satisfy the public's need for superior soap-opera. At the start of *Just One Night (En enda natt*, 1939) he pays lip-service to the changes at work in Sweden. Edvin Adolphson's Valdemar Moreaux works in a fairground, and tells his girlfriend who owns the Tivoli that people can now 'find a place in society' instead of tramping the roads in poverty. But soon the film ushers us into the comfortable, invulnerable world of country mansions, where Ingrid Bergman spends her summers with her guardian, the formidable Colonel von Brede. An incipient relationship between Bergman and Adolphson is nipped in the bud by the revelation that he is none other than the Colonel's illegitimate son. The class complexes underpin the entire film, abrading even the most tender scenes between the would-be lovers. Bergman does her best to illuminate the stilted dialogue with her insouciant rendering of 'Charlie Is My Darling!' at the piano, and she brings a palpable indignation to the scene in her bedroom when, with dress torn, she tells Valdemar in furious tones that he has ruined everything between them and must leave. It's a key scene that in its rejection of uninhibited desire communicates the dying efforts of the 1930's to turn its back on the new realism that was shaping the country's future. People in *The June Night (Juninatten*, 1940) also strive to maintain a respectable front, but this time Ingrid Bergman plays the outsider anxious to conceal a dramatic shooting incident in her past. Like all 'outsiders' in Scandinavian cinema, she comes from the provinces, from Gustafssund, up north near Sundsvall. Under the direction of Per Lindberg (whose female characters are the most convincing on the Swedish screen apart from Ingmar Bergman's), the small, soap-opera issues on which *The June Night* turns assume a certain validity. The film benefits from a wealth of intimate, romantically-charged close-ups, and Lindberg's tongue-in-cheek sense of humour enlivens the trial scene at the beginning, when Kerstin (Bergman) tries to protect the seaman who has shot and wounded her in a fit of pique. Melodrama and frivolity may have sustained the vast majority of Swedish films of the late 1920's and all the 1930's, but the urgency of Ingrid Bergman's youth and the sleek professional skills of Molander from time to time breathed some life into the dross.

The Shadow of War

While most other European nations braced themselves for commitment to battle as the 1940's beckoned, Sweden concentrated instead on effecting the most radical social reforms of the century. The so-called Saltsjöbaden Agreement, signed in 1938, established a civilised relationship between labour and capital which has continued to the present day. Unemployment fell steadily. Health insurance became available to all.

Yet although Sweden's time-honoured neutrality saved her from immense losses of men and money, it could not shield her from the successive psychological effects of the Second World War: a sense of guilt, especially towards her occupied Scandinavian neighbours, Denmark and Norway, and then an all-pervasive *Angst*, which would colour the early work of Ingmar Bergman in the second half of the decade.

Film-makers responded to this ominous climate by attacking the surrogate 'Nazism' that lay ill-concealed beneath the Swedish class system. This authoritarianism could be found in the remnants of an Anglo-Saxon paternalism on a family level, in the army, the church, and education. The 'family' unit so essential to the frivolous films of the late 1920's and 1930's is challenged and flouted in the most significant productions of the 1940's. Some directors adopted a metaphorical approach to the circumstances of the time, resorting to historical costume drama to point an anti-Nazi moral (*Ride Tonight!* and *Partisans* being good examples of this quasi-genre).

Part of the mingled guilt and outrage felt by Swedish film-makers stemmed from the government's undisguised assumption that the Germans would triumph in their struggle with the Allies. Trainloads of Nazi soldiers were permitted free passage through Sweden from Norway on their way home on furlough, and the Engelbrecht division was granted the right to cross Sweden en route to Hitler's major offensive against the Soviet Union in June 1941. Swedish iron-ore and ball bearings, not to mention Bofors weaponry, contributed to the Nazi war effort until well into the war.

This atmosphere proved a stimulant for the Swedish film industry, and restored the integrity and commitment that had so distinguished the early silent work of Sjöström. The abiding link between these two eras — Gustaf Molander — could now afford to tackle riskier themes. *Ride Tonight! (Rid i natt!*, 1942) is based on an historical novel by Vilhelm Moberg that brought its author notoriety in Nazi Germany. The story offers a passionate denunciation of totalitarianism. After the atrocious campaigns of the Thirty Years' War, numerous foreign nobleman gained power in Sweden. They exercised what amounted to feudal control over their retainers, and Moberg saw in the passive resistance of these country folk a parallel for his own time, and the *budkavle* — the stick of carved wood passed from village to village when a rising was planned — became a very real symbol of the anti-Fascist feeling in neutral Sweden during the Hitler period. The blonde peasant (Oscar Ljung), who is driven from his land although he is a tax-paying member of the community, recalls Sjöström's Berg-Ejvind, an outlaw surviving in the hills and showing defiance until the very last, when he is murdered by the vicious Hangman (Erik Hell).

The following year Molander turned to a more naked examination of the war and its impact on Scandinavian citizens. *There Burned a Flame (Det brinner en eld*, 1943) follows the travails of a theatre company in Oslo during the sombre occupation of Norway by 'a foreign power' (the Germans are never specifically branded). The 'National Theatre' takes on the dimensions of a patriotic symbol, with the noble figure of Victor Sjöström as the Director being arrested for rejecting the regime's propagandist aims. The film is vitiated by its schematic plot and its black-and-white characterisation (Stig Järrel as the smug, power-hungry collaborator, Lars Hanson as the German military attaché with a heart of gold, Lauritz Falk as the young actor who sacrifices his life in foiling the enemy troops). Yet the conflict between love and political commitment sustains the film, while the hard-lit photography of Åke Dahlberg typifies the high technical standards that were once again distinguishing the Swedish cinema.

Gustaf Molander's version of *The Word (Ordet*, 1943) has paled beside Carl Th. Dreyer's adaptation of the same Kaj Munk play a dozen years afterwards, but the comparisons usually ignore the circumstances under which the Swedish film was made. While Dreyer concentrates exclusively on the mystical, even pantheistic elements in the story of a farmer's wife miraculously brought back to life, Molander finds a certain political allegory in the material. By a cruel chance, Munk (a Danish priest) was shot by the Nazis barely a week after the premiere of *The Word* in Stockholm. Like Prévert and Carné's *Les Visiteurs du soir*, made the previous year, *The Word* mixes a blend of religion, superstition, and romance to communicate a sense of social survival in the face of the forces of Evil/Death. Molander's version also provided the ageing Victor Sjöström with one of his most satisfying roles in the 1940's, as the troubled *pater familias*.

This prolific decade in the development of the Swedish cinema (386 features released during the period) may, with hindsight, be assessed in terms of the predominant auteurs – Sjöberg, Molander, Hasse Ekman, and the young Ingmar Bergman – but it would be a mistake to underestimate the shadow of war. Already in late 1939, the Winter War between Finland and the Soviet Union brought the prospect of armed conflict right to Sweden's own borders. Many Swedes felt a closer kinship with the Finns, by reasons of history and even language, than they did with the Danes or the Norwegians.

Although the Swedish army mobilised in preparation for battle, the fact that its soldiers, seamen, and airmen were not called upon to shed blood during the wartime era gave an artificial tone to the many films turned out by the studios in which military themes and personalities play a major role.

Hasse Ekman's *The First Division (Första divisionen*, 1941) resembles such British films as *The Way to the Stars* (about the R.A.F.) and transplants to the milieu of the Swedish forces all the hierarchical class tensions by now familiar from the 1930's. Certain scenes capture the sense of a communal existence as well as the enforced gaiety of the 1940's: the dinner toasts at long mess tables, with Lars Hanson in one of his final roles as the Squadron Leader; the songs in the lounge, with Gunnar Sjöberg playing the guitar; and the glimpses of each man's private life during the brief spells of leave. The flying exercises are forcefully described, fomenting tension despite the absence of real wartime engagements.

Ekman, however, whose slick, suave style was made for the glittering moment rather than satisfying any deep artistic energy, soon found that the climate of the epoch was best treated obliquely. *His Excellency (Excellensen*, 1944) drew its inspiration from the war and in particular from the *Anschluss* in Austria. An ailing poet refuses to capitulate to torture in a typical struggle between liberty and dictatorship.

More effective in reached a large audience, *Partisans (Snapphanar)*, premiered in the final days of 1941, cast one of the country's most beloved comedians, Edvard Persson, in a blood-and-thunder historical adventure movie based on the struggle between Denmark and Sweden for control of the southern Swedish province of Skåne in 1676. The film aroused the suspicions of the regime in Norway, which banned the film for nine months on the grounds that it celebrated 'partisan activity', but for most Swedes of the time it provided a feast of thrills and laughter that made reviewers look to comparisons with Zorro, Douglas Fairbanks, and Tom Mix, while simultaneously admiring the skilful screenwriting of Karl Ragnar Gierow and the competent direction of **Åke Ohberg** (hitherto known as an actor). Persson, however, looms large at this juncture because he assured the success of the fledgling film studio, Europa Film, and appealed to Swedes everywhere with his

whimsical manner, his massive girth, and his Scanian accent. In the late 1930's he had served as a comedian for the common man; throughout his work ran a profound distaste for anything or anybody with intellectual pretensions. Like Oliver Hardy he was at his best when driven to grumpiness, and at his least appealing when lapsing into the sentimental witticisms of his province. But in *Partisans* he is not allowed to dominate the cast, and indeed plays almost a supporting part as the chubby farmer who gives vent to patriotic declarations intended to encourage Swedes as the Nazis made inroads into Scandinavia. *Partisans* presents an agreeable picture of Swedish bucolic life, and recalls the spirit of Robin Hood, along with clichés of the genre such as roistering taverns and lusty wenches.

As in all the Nordic countries, escapist romance, comedy, and melodrama proved most popular at the box-office during the first half of the 1940's. Hasse Ekman answered this need with alacrity. *Flames in the Dark (Lagor i dunklet*, 1942) marked Stig Järrel as the archetypal repressed Swede. Playing with wild-eyed gusto, he brings a certain plausibility to the conduct of a provincial schoolmaster instructed by his mother on her deathbed never to marry. He does marry, but his jealousy of others' happiness spurs him into pyromania. *Flames in the Dark* may be regarded in retrospect as reflecting a deep-seated insecurity among Swedes of the period, puzzled by the sinister and lethal philosophy that seemed to be devouring all too many of their Nordic neighbours. *Change of Trains (Ombyte av tåg*, 1943) was subtitled by Ekman as 'a serious comedy' but lacks the astringent quality that would distinguish Bergman's essays in this genre during the 1950's. Nothing could be more tearjerking than this dime-novel tribute to a young actress (Sonia Wigert) who forsakes her decent local lover (Hasse Ekman himself) for the suave, cynical charms of a Stockholm matinée idol (Georg Rydeberg). Nowhere else is the influence of Hollywood on Swedish film so conspicuous. Every character is perfectly coiffed and immaculately dressed, with a new style for every scene. Ms. Wigert's health problems are worthy of Marguerite Gauthier, and the sentimentality of the dénouement, as she is abandoned, gazing out through a rainswept hotel window as her lover takes the train out of her life, answers precisely to the demands of the Hollywood 'weepie'.

Ekman did himself better justice in *The Royal Rabble (Kunglige patrasket*, 1945), which, by observing theatre life through the eyes of three generations, manages to analyse the mystique of the stage and to pin down the petty vanities and emotional fragility that its spell can expose. *Wandering with the Moon (Vandring med månen)*, made in the same year, focuses on the evanescent beauty of the Swedish summer and its luminous nights that somehow signify the ecstasies of youth.

More mature, *Girl with Hyacinths (Flicka och hyacinter*, 1950) explores the mind-set of a young woman, Dagmar Brink, who commits suicide in her shabby room. Her neighbours resolve to investigate the reasons for her death. The film becomes a mosaic of recollections through which the wan, wistful figure of Dagmar (Eva Henning) wanders as if in a trance of melancholy. Most of the people in her life smother her with their woes, never thinking to inquire about her own concerns. She strikes up an acquaintance with a drunken artist named Körner (brilliantly played by the underrated Anders Ek − Frost in *Sawdust and Tinsel* − whose hieratic gestures and bitter, twisted mouth bring a character instantly to life). Dagmar's ex-husband, a captain in the army, has left her after four years of marriage because he has discovered a love letter addressed to her and signed by an anonymous 'Alex', who turns out to have been a woman.

In *Wandering with the Moon* Ekman dwells on the delights of summer; in *Girl with Hyacinths* he drives home the extended depression of winter, and the rain falling remorselessly, and the heavy shadows of darkness filling the streets. Within, ceilings weigh on the heads of characters while they are often viewed from a sharp inferior angle. Deep-focus sets them, traps them, in their miserable surroundings. This fluent visual manner reinforces the nostalgia of the postwar period. Nothing seemed durable in the 1940's. Dagmar Brink is in no small way the conscience of a neutral Sweden.

Sjöberg's Talent Reaches its Prime

After his decade in the wilderness, Alf Sjöberg found a *Zeitgeist* to suit his prodigious gifts. The frivolous Swedish cinema of the 1930's had been anathema to him, and now his political commitment matched the hour. He was acutely conscious of the dangers of Hitlerism, and *They Staked Their Lives (Med livet som insats*, 1939) was completed just after the outbreak of the Second World War, and received its première in January 1940. Its theme, dealing with individuals caught up in a net of power and intrigue against their wishes, typifies also Sjöberg's later works, especially *Only a Mother* and *Wild Birds*. The leading characters are members of an underground movement in an unnamed Baltic country which is clearly a police state. The frequent quarrels among the agents, and the gloomy gatherings in bare rooms, underline Sjöberg's fatalism and the perplexities of a Europe drifting inexorably into war. Human relationships begin to matter again in the Swedish cinema after the long years of levity and saccharine emotion. Others felt the same impulse; in France, Carné's *Quai des brumes* and *Le Jour se lève* breathed a fatalism akin to Sjöberg's; in Britain, the novelist Graham Greene made his breakthrough with disenchanted books like *A Gun for Sale* and *The Confidential Agent*; while in Sweden itself, Anders Henrikson struck a similar chord with *A Crime (Ett brott,* 1940), which used the murder mystery format to address the break-up of the Swedish *grande famille.*

With the bit between his teeth, Sjöberg proceeded to direct a further six films before the end of 1945. In all of them may be found a current of anger at the injustice of war and class, even if Sjöberg's exasperation reaches us in tightly-controlled aesthetic terms. In both *This Blossomtime . . . (Den blomstertid,* 1940) and *Home from Babylon (Hem från Babylon,* 1941), the actress Gerd Hagman appeared as

a would-be successor to Ingrid Bergman. Her chiselled features, magnificent eyes, and statuesque figure rendered her more aloof as a personality. She never became quite the star many expected her to. Already in these films, however, Sjöberg finds himself caught between the virtues of location and studio scenes. This dichotomy haunted him throughout his film career. Scenes on the Swedish coast, and in Paris, contrast favourably with the stage-managed interiors, where Sjöberg's characters exhibit a glossy lifestyle not far removed from the familiar Hollywood whirl of nightclubs and lavish salons. At his best, Sjöberg would demythologise such sequences with his ruthless use of shadows and hard lighting.

If critics could correctly deplore the elements of melodrama and self-pity in Sjöberg's early films, none could deny the prodigious accomplishment of *The Road to Heaven (Himlaspelet,* 1942). Part allegory, part fantasy, this morality play by Rune Lindström brings to life the folklore of Dalecarlia, the province north of Stockholm that is celebrated not only for famous sons like the painters Anders Zorn and Carl Larsson but also for the most colourful handicrafts in the country (the 'Dalecarlian Horse' serves as a symbol of Sweden for many tourists). As a film, *The Road to Heaven* at once harked back to the silent screen versions of Selma Lagerlöf's religious novels, and pointed forward to Bergman's *The Seventh Seal*. Mats Ersson (played by Lindström himself) is a young Candide of a peasant who is incensed by the unjust trial and condemnation of his fiancée Marit as a witch. After she has been burned at the stake, Mats strides off on 'the road to heaven', to demand justice and recompense. Like any idealist, however, and like those Scandinavians at bay before the Nazi threat, Mats succumbs to the Devil's blandishments. He drinks and fornicates, grows rich through the chance discovery of copper ore, and is only saved on his deathbed by the Good Father, who has watched him from the outset. The stern religious message of the film may sound obsolescent now, but what endures is the panache of the 'drinking song', and Mats's headlong dash by horsedrawn sleigh across the plain to the City of Desire, as well as the pastoral contentment and quietness of scenes like the reunion of Mats with the mistress he had revelled with on his travels. Its emphasis on traditional values and the dangers of superstition bring *The Road to Heaven* close in time and strength to Dreyer's *Day of Wrath* (1943).

The Royal Hunt (Kungajakt, 1943) contains the same thinly-disguised reference to Nazism as does Molander's *Ride Tonight!* It summons up the ceremonial and dormant virility of the 18th century with an approach not far from Renoir's *La Marseillaise.* Sweden's position in the Northern firmament was uneasy circa 1775, and there were Russian efforts to overthrow Gustaf III. One loyal Swede, Rehusen, refuses to join the plotters and Sjöberg shows him as a symbol of a strong, loyal Sweden. Captured at the height of the crisis, Rehusen flings back his head scornfully and exclaims, 'You can take us to court for being unfaithful to the new government but you can never quell our spirit!'

The Royal Hunt provides further evidence of Sjöberg's graceful, felicitous gift for directing exteriors. The 'hunt' itself, for example, is a regal centrepiece, a Watteau canvas

Per Oscarsson in Alf Sjöberg's *Wild Birds* (1955)

come to life as the white horses spread over the fields to the accompaniment of Lars-Erik Larsson's martial music. There is a cavalier, gallivanting rhythm to the film at such moments that owes everything to the director's flair for inspiring his players and exercising a masterful control over the gradations of light and shade within each image.

Alf Sjöberg could take credit for the single most seminal film of the decade: *Frenzy (Hets,* 1944). Scripted by the neophyte Ingmar Bergman (who has conceded the portal role of Sjöberg in creating the finished film), *Frenzy* tuned into a new mood that pervaded Sweden towards the end of the war years. Bergman had joined Svensk Filmindustri some eighteen months earlier. It was a good period, with the enlightened Carl-Anders Dymling as head of the company and Victor Sjöström as artistic adviser. Sjöström liked this screenplay about the mental stress inflicted by a teacher on his pupils in a Stockholm high school, and Sjöberg's assured direction smoothed the immaturities in Bergman's youthful writing. Sjöberg found that the revolt of youth against the pompous characteristics of an older generation accorded with his own interest in the clash between social classes. Stig Järrel developed the sadistic, demented character he had already sketched in *Flames in the Dark,* while Alf Kjellin and Mai Zetterling emerged as the first of a new wave of popular stars in the Swedish cinema. Sjöberg lays strong emphasis on the parallels between Järrel's tyranny in the classroom and the terrifying regime still in power in Germany. The schoolteacher wears glasses similar to Himmler's, and reads *Dagsposten,* a Swedish newspaper with Nazi sympathies. From this chrysalis would be born also the vision of Ingmar Bergman, with the schoolroom and the grim family table a microcosm for 'Hell on earth'.

Alf Kjellin and Mai Zetterling proved such an appealing partnership in *Frenzy* that Sjöberg used them again in *Iris and the Lieutenant (Iris och löjtnantshjärta,* 1946), which continues the assault on the hidebound Swedish bourgeoisie. The prosperous 'family' in such 1930's films as *Swedenhielms* and *Intermezzo* offered, for all their faults, a comfortable refuge from the inequities of the outside world. But in *Frenzy, Iris and the Lieutenant,* and in an increasing number of late 1940's Swedish movies, the family is viewed as a source of bitterness and dissension, an obstacle in the path of a younger generation yearning for social — and psychological — liberty. The romance between Robert and Iris in Sjöberg's first postwar production caries its own nostalgia, like the ill-fated affair in David Lean's *Brief Encounter,* made the previous year. After their evening at the cinema, they pause on a bridge in the darkness. As Iris gazes over the rails, a ship moves silently forward over the gleaming waters of Stockholm harbour. It suggests the quintessential Nordic desire to escape — what Swedes call the *utbrytningsdröm.*

The Uncompromising Flourish of Hampe Faustman

One of the youngest most explosive talents of the 1940's in Nordic film was **Hampe Faustman** who at the age of twenty played a minor role as a revolutionary in Sjöberg's *They Staked Their Lives.* An ardent admirer of the Soviet cinema, and of Mark Donskoi in particular, he soon turned to directing. He expressed himself with passionate rigour, seeking to view his proletarian characters from angles and standpoints that would render their condition meaningful on film. He sympathised with the lot of the Swedish farm labourers in *When Meadows Bloom (När ängarna blommar,* 1946), a work that resembles the first postwar productions from Eastern European studios (Frigyes Bán's *The Soil under Your Feet,* for example). The sunny landscape of the countryside contrasts ironically with the poverty of the farm labourers. The 'New Deal' launched by the Social Democrats in the late 1930's took several years to penetrate the rural areas of Sweden, and Faustman, every inch a Marxist, uses the classical situation of a strike on which to construct his film. The landowner, with his Alsatian dog and the feather in his hat, comprises intolerance and ruthless authority. The agricultural workers huddle together in restless groups, congregating in their leader's cabin to hear a record of the 'Internationale'.

Faustman stood aloof from the absolute disillusion that alarmed most young artists directly after the war. He shared the horror of the writers of the 1940's — the so-called *fyrtitalisterna* — when confronted with the barbarities of Nazism and the potential of the atomic bomb, but he still hungered after humanistic ideals. *Foreign Harbour (Främmande hamn,* 1948) deals with the clandestine shipment of arms to the fascists, an abuse of neutrality that must have stung a government which had turned a blind eye to the trundling of trains by night through Sweden en route to Norway or Finland, bearing arms. The action of the film takes place in and around the small Polish harbour of Gdynia (although exteriors were shot in Finland), and Faustman's skill at chronicling the life of the docks and the ship's crew is masterly. High-angle shots stare down at the men in their cramped quarters and stress the sordidness of their plight as they scrabble like animals in the snow for potato peelings. The encroaching ice remains always there in the background, cutting off the crew's retreat from their misery and isolating the harbour itself so that the central issue — should or should not the cargo be accepted? — is inescapable.

In an all-too-brief career, Faustman espoused the cause of the Swedish gipsies in their efforts to gain social recognition, in *God and the Gipsyman (Gud fader och tattaren,* 1954), and made a late adaptation of Rudolf Värnlund's play about the pressures on Swedish neutrality during the war, *Submarine 39 (U-båt 39,* 1952), which Ingmar Bergman had staged in Stockholm during the early 1940's.

Passing the Torch: from Molander to Bergman

Sweden's pre-eminent place as a film-producing nation in the Nordic region may have many reasons, but none so manifest as the unbroken *tradition* in each of the professional crafts that film-making comprises. Gunnar Fischer, who would become the celebrated

Holger Löwenadler in *Iris and the Lieutenant* (1946) by Alf Sjöberg

cinematographer of Ingmar Bergman's early years, learned his skills from the veteran Julius Jaenzon. Bergman himself served as 'script boy' to the established Alf Sjöberg on the set of *Frenzy*. The greatest line of continuity, however, may be found in the work of Gustaf Molander and its 'merger' with that of Bergman in the late 1940's. By a happy chance, here was a director who had worked on the screenplay of *Terje Vigen* in 1916 and who still ranked among his country's top film-makers when Bergman conceived the idea for *Woman without a Face (Kvinna utan ansikte, 1947)*. Molander collaborated on the screenplay, and proceeded to give credence and form to Bergman's inchoate outburst of anger against a woman who had scarred his early love life. Molander paints a vivid picture of Stockholm in the grey months of 1945, where ration cards were required for that essential symbol of time, the cigarette. Gunn Wållgren brings to the part of Rut Kohler all the ice-cool scorn and calculation of the 1940's *femme fatale*. Small personal details in Bergman's own background are kept in the film by Molander (the illuminated clock at the top of Hedvig Eleanora Church, for example, which Bergman used to see as a teenager from his parents' apartment in Stockholm).

The following year, Molander directed another Bergman scenario, *Eva* (1948), and began shooting, by coincidence, in the same week as Bergman himself started directing *Port of Call*. Yet *Eva* is much the more personal of these two films. It evokes, with only a minimum of melodrama and scarcely any sentimentality, the vanished world of Bergman's pre-war childhood, when he would spend summers at his grandmother's house in Dalarna. Contrasting with Molander's affectionate depiction of the sleepy rural community is the explosive anger of Bergman's *alter ego*, Bo Fredriksson (played by Birger Malmsten). 'I hate everyone!' he exclaims as a twelve-year-old, and smashes his milk glass on the floor during the evening meal. 'Never forget,' he tells himself as he stands beside the spot where through his own carelessness a small blind girl has been killed by a passing train, 'that Death is a terrifying fate.' 'I don't believe in God!' he tells his childhood sweetheart.

Despite its flashes of cynicism, *Eva* is given a gentle temper by Molander's wise direction. When Bo plays the trumpet for his dying uncle, the scene is charged with a poignancy that Bergman himself could not achieve for many years to come. Death's curse may loom over the film, and nothing could be more characteristic of Bergman than the dead man's corpse being washed up on the seashore; yet the optimism of the ending restores Bo's faith in life. Eva gives birth to their baby son, and Bo gazes down at the infant as he stands beside the sea, 'Death is no longer a shadow at my back, but a part of life.'

Eva contains an exuberant performance by Eva Dahlbeck, an actress who would grace some of Bergman's wittiest films of the 1950's. She plays the lusty city girl who seduces the innocent Bo when he comes to stay with her and her boyfriend in Stockholm. Dressing, she lets out a scream of delight, 'Just for life!' This hedonism, which would become a significant trait in Bergman's mature work, was rare in the Swedish cinema of the 1940's. Sjöberg, in *Only a Mother* (*Bara en mor*, 1949), knew also how to tap the talent of this prodigious actress. Dahlbeck plays the gypsy-labourer's wife whose destiny is to produce one child after another, and then to die from excessive physical labour. The social conscience of a Sweden recently converted to the welfare state lies heavily imprinted on *Only a Mother*. There is a sense of one generation succeeding another in useless, remorseless succession. Death assumes a ritualistic role. Events move with such terrible speed that Rya-Rya has no time, save briefly on her deathbed, to reflect on the loathsome life she is forced to lead.

Sjöberg returns to the roots of the Swedish cinema, to the mood of bucolic fatalism inherent in *The Outlaw and His Wife* and *Gunnar Hede's Saga*. Ordinary incidents often contain a specific overture of sorrow and disaster. For example, the bellowing of the cows in the shed counterpoints the anguish of Rya-Rya just before she collapses, and the first indication of her fall is a sluice of milk spreading over the floor beneath a cow.

Ingmar Bergman and the International Triumphs of the 1950's

The films of **Ingmar Bergman** have been subject to as frequent, and as detailed scrutiny as the campaigns of Napoleon. What follows here will seek to place the greatest of all Swedish film-makers in the context of his nation's production, and to examine how far his work reflects a specifically *Swedish* or *Nordic* approach to life.

Bergman's unique film language emerged from the crucible of the *Angst*-ridden 1940's. Although not one of the *Fyrtitalisterna* ('writers of the Forties'), he found himself in eager sympathy with them. Rune Waldekranz, the doyen of Swedish critics, has summed up the movement as follows: 'The group in many ways resembled Britain's coterie of Angry Young Men, although it was possibly more vitriolic in its resentment of conservative culture and certainly more vital in its rebellion against traditional literary forms. Characteristic of the work of these new writers was an

Eva Dahlbeck in Alf Sjöberg's *Only a Mother* (1949)

absolute disillusionment, an infinite horror before the severe conditions of human life in the era of the atom bomb. Aggressively disdainful of the older general, cynical about the efficacy of humanistic ideals, and greatly influenced in their writing by the lessons of depth-psychology and radical sociology, they were able to make a sort of philosophy out of their agonised surrender to pessimism and melancholy.'[28]

This description fits Bergman's early work like a glove. In films like *Crisis* (*Kris*, 1946), *A Ship Bound for India* (*Skepp till Indialand*, 1947), and *Music in Darkness* (*Musik i mörker*, 1948), his characters rail against a cold, invisible Deity, and dismiss the habitual salves and pleasures of the world as mere impediments in the way of some abstract Truth. Bergman's anti-heroes of the 1940's and early 1950's bear little resemblance to the social reality of the period. Instead they spring fully-clad from the pages of Strindberg, the dramatist most admired by Bergman throughout his life, and owe their fantastical, abrasive wit to the works of Hjalmar Bergman, the writer who had collaborated on the films of Victor Sjöström in the early 1920's. The moments of skilfully-turned horror in Bergman's cinema may be traced back in part to the romantic agonies of the 19th-century poet and dramatist, Jonas Love Almquist, and in part also to the German expressionist cinema of the silent era (Bergman was an omnivorous film buff from his early twenties, and soon built up his own collection of classics on 16mm).

Even in *Prison (Fängelse)* and *Thirst (Törst)*, both released in 1949, Bergman could not aspire to the mellow thoughtfulness of Gustaf Molander. Once he had negotiated the torrents of youth, however, he could concentrate with all his considerable talent on the issues that concerned him most deeply. He began to appreciate the Swedish landscape, and in particular the unalloyed solitude located in the archipelago outside Stockholm, where as a boy he had spent many a holiday with his family. The sea among elements, and summer among seasons, soon figured prominently in Bergman's cinema. In this he belonged unmistakably to the heritage of Victor Sjöström and Mauritz Stiller. The titles of his films from the period mirror this obsession with the bright, sensual days of the year: *Summer Interlude (Sommarlek,* 1951), *Summer with Monika (Sommaren med Monika,* 1952), *Smiles of a Summer Night (Sommarnattens leende,* 1955), *Wild Strawberries (Smultronstället,* 1957). . . .

The climate exerts more than a mere physical impact on Nordic people. During the severe winter months (and in Finland, for example, there are days when it hardly gets light), families keep to themselves. They do not stand about in the streets for a chat as the fortunate Italians or Greeks or Californians can do. They perform their daily tasks from a kind of ritual duty, sustained by a distant prospect of summer. When that hallowed season arrives, the Scandinavians' entire attitude seems to change. People become cheerful and communicative. They flood in their thousands into the countryside, relishing the long weekends in their summer cottages. The briefness of the Nordic summer merely enhances its joy and beauty. The borders between day and night dissolve. In *Smiles of a Summer Night* and *Harvest Month* (see FINLAND), the traditional hours of darkness are replaced by an unbroken, dreamlike opalescence. These are the 'white nights' referred to by Norwegian novelist (and author of *Hunger*), Knut Hamsun. Set in such attractive surroundings, Bergman's tormented dramas proved more congenial to audiences outside his native Sweden. (As a film-maker, he has never been popular at home, and most Swedes respect him more for his work in the theatre than for his notoriety as a director of films dealing with concerns remote from their own.) Not that Bergman has ever followed the evolution of Swedish society with the keen engagement of a Hampe Faustman or even an Alf Sjöberg. When at last he came under fire from a younger generation, during the early 1960's, Bergman was criticised for devoting his artistic talents to a form of spiritual onanism far removed from the daily lives and issues of ordinary Nordic citizens.

In two significant areas, however, Ingmar Bergman touches with his films a nerve so sensitive that Swedes denounce him for it. His childhood upbringing in a parsonage has been chronicled at length by himself and many film historians. Bergman drew remorselessly on this period of his life, taking revenge on a family that had repressed and humiliated him beyond measure. Like most young rebels, he was reconciled with his parents towards the end of their

Mai Zetterling and Birger Malmsten in *Music in Darkness* (1948) by Ingmar Bergman

lives, and indeed his father, Chaplain to the Royal Court of Sweden, praised *The Seventh Seal* when it appeared in early 1957. Composites of his mother and father appear in numerous Bergman films (the three 'sisters' in *Cries and Whispers*, or the parson in *Winter Light*, for example). Only at the very end of his career, with *Fanny and Alexander* in 1982, did Bergman bring himself to accommodate in one film the extremes of pleasure and anguish that had marked his childhood. The stone-walled cruelty of the Bishop's home in *Fanny and Alexander* contrasts with the fruitful warmth and good cheer of the Ekdahl household.

The other aspect of Bergman's work that worries Scandinavians flows from that repressed youth of him. In film after film he presents characters who cannot *communicate* with one another. In *Persona*, this handicap has reached such an extreme stage that Liv Ullmann's Elisabet Vogler utters barely a word throughout the film's intense 81 minutes. In *The Silence*, the two Swedish 'sisters' cannot understand the language of the country through which they are passing. This metaphorical inarticulacy and incomprehension lead swiftly to a failure to interact on any kind of emotional level whatsoever. Repression breeds misunderstanding and, soon, bitterness. Such circumstances develop in nearly all of Bergman's major films, from *Thirst* to *The Face*, from *Through a Glass Darkly* to *A Passion*.

The couple at war: Birger Malmsten and Eva Henning in *Prison* (left) and *Thirst* (right) both released in 1949

Gunnar Björnstrand and Eva Dahlbeck in *Smiles of a Summer Night* (1955) by Ingmar Bergman

Harriet Andersson in Bergman's *Summer with Monika* (1953)

Bibi Andersson and Victor Sjöstrom in *Wild Strawberries* (1957)

Annalisa Ericsson and Maj-Britt Nilsson in Bergman's *Summer Interlude* (1951)

Such psychological repression habitually manifests itself in Bergman's world in the form of sexual frustration — for instance in the arid onanism of *The Silence*, or the desperate homicidal instincts of Peter Egerman in *From the Life of the Marionettes*. Sexual matters occupy in Bergman's cinema the same prominence as the drive for money and social power fills in Hollywood movies. Bergman talks about sex in a sophisticated, extremely intimate way. Swedes and Danes were among the first to accept the open availability of pornographic magazines and sex aids but while Danes remain relaxed about this side of life, Swedes view Bergman's unrelenting concentration on the 'squalid', realistic elements in sexual relations as something regrettable and somewhat 'un-Swedish'. The humiliation of his childhood colours much of the erotic imagery in the mature Bergman's work (the deliberate abasement of Anna at the hands of the barman in *The Silence* both illustrate this theme).

Upon closer inspection, however, these taboos, whether religious or sexual, do not belong exclusively to Ingmar Bergman. They are a constant in the Nordic cinema, from silent days to the latest wave of films. The love between Berg-Ejvind and Halla finds no sympathy in the 'Icelandic' society depicted in *The Outlaw and His Wife*. Benjamin Christensen, in *Witchcraft through the Ages*, charts the surreptitious links between sexual desire and religious fervour. Carl Th. Dreyer, in *Day of Wrath*, equates sexual expression with loyalty to the Devil. Per Blom's *Mother's House* demonstrates that even behind the clean, well-lit walls of a contemporary Norwegian town, incest can dominate the life of a mother and her sheltered son, while in Iceland Hrafn Gunnlaugsson has consciously set out to flout the taboos in a small, tightly-knit community (in *Inter Nos*, for example).

Nor is Bergman's obsession with metaphysical questions unique to him, as is so frequently charged by his detractors. Dreyer is forever his counterpart in Denmark, painting his moral and religious dilemmas in tones even more austere than Bergman's. Rauni Mollberg, in *Earth Is Our Sinful Song* and *Milka*, cuts to the quivering core an isolated rural society in Finland that responds to the church's demands with almost manic intensity. Alf Sjöberg's career contains films like *The Road to Heaven* and *Barabbas*, which debate ethical and ecclesiastical issues with unashamed vigour. In short, Bergman cannot be blamed for responding to the Lutheranism predominating in his region of the world, any more than Fellini can be chided for his perennial references to priests and nuns and the whole legacy of Catholicism.

Bergman's great achievement during the 1950's was to find a cinematic language to match his literary themes and obsessions. In *Sawdust and Tinsel* (*Gycklarnas afton*, 1953), he turned to brilliant effect his fascination with the German silent cinema and the Russian masterpieces of Sergei Eisenstein and established himself as the master of the close-up. In *The Seventh Seal* (*Det sjunde inseglet*, 1957), he brought to life the frescoes he had witnessed in the Uppland churches where his father preached in the 1920's and 1930's, and endowed everyday religious symbols with three-dimensional properties. In *Wild Strawberries*

Fanny and Alexander (1982) by Ingmar Bergman

Liv Ullmann in Bergman's *Persona* (1966)

140

Gunnel Lindblom and Gunnar Björnstrand in *The Seventh Seal*, by Ingmar Bergman

Harriet Andersson in *Sawdust and Tinsel* (1953) by Ingmar Bergman

Stig Järrel and Jarl Kulle in Bergman's *The Devil's Eye* (1960)

(*Smultronstället*, 1957) and *Smiles of a Summer Night*, Bergman paid homage to the various moods of the Swedish countryside, and to the pantheistic philosophy already implicit in Sjöström's films of the silent era. In *The Face* (*Ansiktet*, 1958), he developed the *mask* as a sign of both human vanity and inhibitions. And at the end of the decade, in *The Virgin Spring* (*Jungfrukällan*, 1960), he introduced a more severe aesthetic, placing his characters in the heart of a beautiful but indifferent Nature, and telling his story with rigorous clarity.

Against these gaunt, often repellent masterpieces must be set the delightful comedies of manners that showed Bergman as the heir to Marivaux and Wilde. In the final episode of *Waiting Women* (*Kvinnors väntan*, 1952), in *A Lesson in Love* (*En lektion i kärlek*, 1954), *Smiles of a Summer Night* and *The Devil's Eye* (*Djävulens öga*, 1960), the new maestro could be seen in ebullient mood. Again, such films do not dwell in isolation within the Swedish landscape; they descend directly fom the rich satirical talent of Mauritz Stiller in films like *Love and Journalism* and *Erotikon*.

Curiously, for all his love of Strindberg, Bergman did not attempt to bring his plays to the screen. Sjöberg's *Miss Julie* (*Fröken Julie*, 1950) and Anders Henrikson's *Married Life* (*Giftas*, 1956) proved that Strindberg's narrow, if piercing vision could be expanded to fill the more open spaces of the cinema. The fine calibre of Swedish acting is evident in the performances in *Married Life*, by Anita Björk as a glacial, frustrated young woman who fears the male sex, and by Gunnel Broström, as a stiff and masculine schoolmistress who promulgates the intellectual precepts associated with the heroines of Ibsen. Anita Björk has her finest hour in *Miss Julie*, a film that demonstrates how closely allied in spirit Bergman and Sjöberg are when dealing with themes such as sexual humiliation, self-loathing, and the psychological baggage with which childhood so often burdens the inhibited. Nor is *Miss Julie* a mere screen rendition of Strindberg's play; Sjöberg flashes back and forth in time between past and present, and he uses the expansive grounds of the Count's estates during the Midsummer Night to give the story a social and environmental context. In so doing, of course, he diminishes the claustrophobic atmosphere that the play creates on stage, where all the action takes place in a single room — the kitchen of the Count's mansion.

The struggle between the sexes, so endemic to Strinderg's dramas, looms large in the Swedish films of the 1950's. **Arne Mattsson**, a journeyman director at his best in a handful of films made during this decade, taps the tradition of Sjöström and Stiller in his *Salka Valka*, based on a novel by the Icelandic author Halldór Laxness. It is perhaps the one film of the sound period that recalls by its scenic ardour the determinism of Sjöström's *Terje Vigen*. In both films, the sea and the mountains dominate the human characters who dwell alongside them, governing the pattern of their lives. The tiny fishing village where the young Salka arrives with her mother, seasick and helpless in the fog, is soon revealed as a primitive community where thrift is the highest of all virtues; where superstition runs rampant; and

where the night brings trepidation and the morning its evanescent hopes. This tough, coarse-fibred material receives full-blooded treatment from Mattsson. Time and again he and his cinematographer Sven Nykvist choose an unusual camera angle so that the sensation of conflict, both within the chaacters themselves and in their daily confrontations, is conveyed with palpable force. Faces block out one corner or side of the frame in monstrous close-up. Figures loom over the camera, heavy with strength and emnity; or they become frail objects in their surroundings, like Sigurlina as she wanders into the breakers on a desolate stretch of beach to escape her ghastly domestic life.

Mattsson, like Matti Kassila in Finland, has continued to work until the present day, but enjoyed his heyday for a few brief years in the 1950's. *The Bread of Love* (*Kärlekens bröd*, 1953), a tightly-directed account of trench warfare in the bitter Winter War of 1939-40, and *People of Hemsö* (*Hemsöborna*, 1955), which echoes Strindberg's macabre vision of life in the Stockholm archipelago, both communicate a sense of Man absorbed by the elements. The film which brought Arne Mattsson his international audience, however, is less impressive than these. *One Summer of Happiness* (*Hon dansade en sommar*, 1951) promoted the image of Sweden as a bucolic land where young love could be consummated without fear or recourse to strict moral codes. The film mingles the saccharine romanticism of the 1930's with the freedom of expression and pictorial naturalism that was introduced by the younger directors of the postwar period. In seems unbelievable, when the film in viewed again now, that the single, short love scene beside the lake between Ulla Jacobsson and Folke Sundquist should have provoked such a sensational reaction. Bergman's *Summer with Monika*, made the following year, is much more erotic. Common themes link the work of these two Swedish directors, born less than eighteen months apart. Both men chart the plight of the individual who dares to flout the conventions of society, especially in sexual matters. Both revel in filming on location in the skerries and the unspoilt countryside of Sweden. Both men's films can betray a surprisingly tender core of emotion. When the priest at Kerstin's funeral in *One Summer of Happiness* says, 'The only truth in this earthly world lies in knowing how to love one another,' he might well be speaking in a Bergman film of the 1940's or 1950's. Where Bergman excels Mattsson, and indeed all his contemporaries of that period, is in his gift for *evoking* a specific emotion in a specific place at a specific time. *Summer Interlude* possesses a distinctive, mysterious aroma that can in part be explained by the story's belonging to Bergman's adolescence in the seemingly-vanished world of the 1930's. Through an unostentatious montage of tranquil images — glittering inlets, grassy slopes, sunlit rocks — he creates a visual paradise that is both touched by the nostalgia of memory, and yet also invested with a vivid sensuality that springs from the moment. Like all Bergman's visions of happiness, they are tinged with foreboding. Birds squawk ominously on the island where the ballerina-heroine, Marie (Maj-Britt Nilsson), relives her First Great Love. After the fatal accident in which her beloved Henrik is killed, the sun shines — only to be obscured by a sombre cloud. The opening rehearsal at the ballet is interrupted by a power failure; the stage is blacked out just as Marie begins her solo dance.

The theme that runs like a filigree through *Summer Interlude* and all of Bergman's early and middle-period films is the need for Man and Woman to cling together in order to outwit and outlast a crass, authoritarian social order. Even in his major philosophical apics, such as *The Seventh Seal*, this simple, unalloyed love serves to combat the shadow of Death and, more insidious, the cynicism so endemic to failed relationships.

While directors like Bergman, Sjöberg and Mattsson all made use of real locations to give an extra dimension to their dramatic conflicts, one Swedish film-maker, **Arne Sucksdorff**, investigated the natural world with the eye of an anthropologist. Man and Beast are both hunter and hunted; only by recognising this unalterable fact, implies Sucksdorff, can each survive in an environment of mutual respect. Quasi-documentaries like *A Summer Tale (En sommarsaga*, 1941) and *A Divided World (En kluven värld*, 1948) express Sucksdorff's avowed philosophy: 'I try to create life — at least, that is my aim and purpose. I think there is something uplifting in human endeavour that is praiseworthy, even ennobling. That is an eagerness for life, which I see as an embryo growing to life itself.' In Nature, creatures destroy one another not from malevolent desire but from an inherent necessity, and Sucksdorff's world is despite all its violence a purer place than Bergman's *huis clos* where human sadism creeps in disharmoniously. The shortness of the summer does, however, have the same connotations of ecstasy and gloom for these creatures as for the characters in *Summer Interlude* or *One Summer of Happiness*.

Anita Björk in Alf Sjöberg's *Miss Julie* (1951)

Sucksdorff, like Flaherty, remains fascinated by innocence. He finds it in childhood and in the world of Nature, and in *The Great Adventure (Det stora äventyret*, 1953), these two naturalists draw close together. The film took two and a half years to complete, and constitutes the most felicitous blend of fiction and documentary in Sucksdorff's career. Two young boys rescue and tame an otter which has been poaching a fisherman's catch during the winter, when the Swedish lakes freeze to a diamond hardness. Their mistake likes in their belief that they can deflect the course of Nature by treating the otter kindly. Soon Sucksdorff's quest for natural themes took him to Kashmir for *The Flute and the Arrow (En djungelsaga*, 1957), and the slums of Rio de Janeiro for *My Home Is Copacabana (Mitt hem är Copacabana*, 1965). In his descriptions of people and animals going about their daily activity, Sucksdorff has no peer in Nordic cinema; only the contrived nature of his 'plots', and a certain artifice in his montage, prevent him from being considered as one of the great Swedish cinéastes. Despite the tradition of using landscape and Nature as participants in Swedish screen drama, Arne Sucksdorff has few heirs, chief among them being Stefan Jarl (see page 157), while the Finn, Markku Lehmuskallio, seems also attracted to a blend of the documentary and the dramatic in his films about Lappland and northern Canada (see page 72).

Another isolated talent, whose career has flourished more in the theatre than in the cinema, is **Peter Weiss**. During the 1920's, Sweden remained out of touch with the avant-garde proclivities of the French directors. But after the Second World War a German, Peter Weiss, who had studied art in Prague, settled in Stockholm and made a series of experimental short films. In his paintings, some of which are represented in the Swedish National Museum, Weiss resembles Dali in his obsession with human limbs, heads, feet, and palms of hands. The human anatomy is equally omnipresent in his films. In *Study II*, for example, Eduard Laurot has noted that, 'the slowness of movement, the bizarre surrealistic composition, and the latent symbolism of attitudes and gestures make this film a convincing account of the hallucinatory states of half-waking consciousness.'[29] Weiss's other *Study* shorts are also semi-abstract, with frequent sexual connotations. *Enligt lag* (1957) is concerned with prison life, and its shots of corridors and of human figures eating and exercising radiate an hypnotic spell.

At the start of Peter Weiss's lone feature-length film, *Mirage (Hägringen*, 1959), a young man approaches a great city. For the first few minutes, as in Mamoulian's *Dr. Jekyll and Mr. Hyde*, the camera assumes the position of his eyes. Gradually, a surrealistic mood takes over; the film becomes a waking dream. Seeking a job, the young man finds himself first in a boxing gym, then in a morgue, and finally in a menacing building site. *Mirage* begins in the mists of dawn and ends with its ubiquitous youth retreating into the dusty fields whence he has come. Weiss was clearly responding to the avant-gardist signals of his time, and his work rhymes to some degree with the preoccupations of American experimentalists such as Stan Brakhage and Maya Deren.

The Great Adventure (1953) by Arne Sucksdorff

Nothing he achieves on the screen, however, possesses the riveting power of his *Marat-Sade*, which has been performed in theatres all over the world.

Beginning Again: the Energetic 1960's

The death in 1961 of Carl Anders Dymling, for two decades head of Svensk Filmindustri, symbolised the need for a new start in Swedish cinema. So too did the parlous economic situation in which the industry found itself. A combination of declining audiences, due in the main to the impact of TV (which had come to Sweden in 1956), and a punitive entertainments tax (25% on average), had dissuaded the independent producer from embarking on any enterprise that smacked of experiment or social comment. Nor was there a film school at which neophyte directors or technicians could be trained.

The individual who changed this gloomy situation into a flourishing climate for young directors was Harry Schein. Not a film-maker himself, Schein combined an outstanding business acumen with a perspicacious talent for film criticism. His energy and imagination forced through a major reform of the Swedish cinema, and the Swedish Film

Institute, of which he was the founder and managing director, became a model for state-supported foundations and institutions throughout Scandinavia and as far away as Australia and Argentina (see page 161 for a description of the Institute's activities). Schein's basic idea involved the substitution of a 10% levy on all movie tickets in place of the entertainments tax. The money raised in this way flowed directly to the Swedish Film Institute, which used its income to finance domestic film production through a system of *quality awards*, and to foster other areas of film activity. Schein had written a book, *Can We Afford Culture?* in which he maintained: 'The case of Ingmar Bergman – and the general development of the international film market – has taught the Swedish film industry a lesson. Its chance to survive in the harsh international climate is to invest in quality films.'

Schein's initiative released the frustration of a fresh generation of directors, most of whom felt ashamed not only of the poor quality of Swedish cinema, but also of the unquestioning praise showered upon Ingmar Bergman. Bo Widerberg, the most mercurial of the young film-makers, wrote a scathing attack: 'Bergman welcomes the coarsest myths about us and ours, emphasises the false notions which foreigners love to have confirmed.' He went on to reproach the Master for his 'vertical cinema' in which Man is either humbled or exalted. 'The book was a protest,' declared Widerberg with the hindsight of later years. 'Every new Swedish film was a disaster; it had absolutely no connection with modern society.'

Three of the key names of the period in Swedish cinema – **Bo Widerberg**, **Vilgot Sjöman**, and **Jörn Donner** – soon emerged from a background of writing about film. The fourth vital member of the new wave, **Jan Troell**, did not, but helped Widerberg with the camerawork on his early work. All responded to the changing face of daily life in Sweden, and their films dealt with such issues as unmarried maternity, teenage delinquency, divorce, and in general the taboos that even a 'liberated' society like Sweden had not yet banished. Above all, their work mirrored their own struggle to express themselves in a world suspicious of the arts and of the political engagement that would reach its climax in 1968.

Most of the new films showed the influence of the French Nouvelle Vague and of such innovators as John Cassavetes in the United States and Tony Richardson, John Schlesinger, Karel Reisz, and Lindsay Anderson in Britain. They sought to reproduce the texture of everyday life in all its haphazard complexity. Widerberg's *The Pram (Barnvagnen*, 1963) and *Raven's End (Kvarteret korpen*, 1963), Donner's *A Sunday in September (En söndag i september*, 1963), Sjöman's *The Mistress (Alskarinnan*, 1962) and especially his *I Am Curious* docudramas of 1967 and 1968, readily set aside the immaculate camerawork, flawless sound, and linear narrative construction associated for so long with Swedish cinema. In *The Pram*, for example, Widerberg constantly demands the spectator's reactions, by means of fragmented scenes and images, cutting off his characters in the middle of a sentence or gesture. The films brims with unanticipated events, abrupt exits and entrances. Moments of vicious anarchic humour punctuate the central affair between Britt and Robban, and the sequence in which Britt's other boyfriend, Björn, plays with a chewing-gum machine in the street at night is a triumph of improvisation. The modern skylines of Malmö become part of the characters' lives, emblematic of a bright new future that is reflected in the sunstruck windows as Britt pushes her pram along the streets and the film comes to its end. The nihilism and exhibitionism of Godard creep into *The Pram*, but Widerberg has a flair for making unobtrusive comment in the manner of Truffaut. The gravity of his work derives from a stern moral approach to life: 'Morals are highly important to me. In my novels I was a terrible moralist and, even if I no longer want to judge, I'm still worried by sharp and unexpected differences of opinion.' Widerberg's men and women are faced continually with a moral choice, but the morals are not necessarily those of the utilitarian society in which they dwell. They are more fundamental than that, and depend on an element of mutual respect.

Like Widerberg, Jörn Donner has always regretted Bergman's failure to treat living, dramatic crises in social terms. Birgitta and Stig in *A Sunday in September*, like Britt and Björn in *The Pram*, live and move in an urban setting. Each of the four stages in Donner's film begins with a montage of travelling shots over the city and the Swedish countryside, cut to jazz and *musique concrète*, establishing a mood and a tempo to match the period. The premature marriage between Stig and Birgitta ends in failure and disenchantment. More significant, however, is the form that Donner employs. 'It is in the nature of things,' he said at the time, 'that films of the type I attempt to make cannot have a climax and an end. My purpose is to try to tell about certain situations of choice, to try to give them a personal interpretation and thus to leave the viewer free. Life's decisions are not the simple black-and-white matters which conventional films make them out to be. In many ways life is irrational, although Man tries to conceal this aspect of life behind a mask of rational actions.'

'Marriage is only a lesson in resignation,' sighs one of the characters in Donner's second, Stillerian comedy, *To Love (Att älska*, 1964). This note of pessimism runs through most of Donner's early work. His lovers embody the *Zeitgeist* of the 1960's in their determination to live together only as long as the moment of attraction lasts, even if Anne in *Adventure Starts Here (Här börjar äventyret*, 1965) declares apologetically that she is well adjusted on the surface but ill adjusted underneath.

It seems less of a break with the Bergman tradition than a coincidental reference to the Master's early work, that the first films of Widerberg, Donner, and Sjöman should all be concerned with the disillusionment of girls faced with the inadequacies of their male partners. In Vilgot Sjöman's world, youth is seen being put to the sword of life. Preconceptions prove deceptive, and the flesh weak. *The Mistress* has a strong moral ring to it. Sexual indecision may be the theme, but the anonymous girl's enjoyment of life is severely undermined by her conscience, by a fear that she is treading outside the bounds of morality.

Thommy Berggren (left) in Bo Widerberg's *Raven's End* (1964)

Soon Sjöman was dissatisfied with treating the problems of individual lovers. In a sequence of films he launched a remorseless bombardment against the bastions of Swedish bourgeois complacency, political, social, and sexual. *491* (1964), based on a controversial anti-authoritarian book by Lars Görling, subjects both police and probation officers in Sweden to a ruthless scrutiny, as they attempt to control a group of hooligans and orphaned boys. The supervisors of the Welfare Board are seen to be more corrupt than the youths, who themselves are infected by this corruption. Shades of *Ingeborg Holm*!

Sjöman's magnum opus, pared down from 400,000 feet of film to just under four hours, emerged in two parts in 1967 and 1968: *I Am Curious − Yellow (Jag är nyfiken − gul)* and *I Am Curious − Blue (Jag är nyfiken − blå)*. The eponymous heroine, Lena Nyman, conducts a private opinion poll as to

the state of Sweden in the 1960's. She finds that thirty years of Social Democratic rule have not achieved the ideal of a classless society, and that complacency stands in the path of reform. The films bear the hallmark of documentary, and yet many sequences are improvised extensions of a dramatic situation. 'You can say that I moved in the difficult field of psychodrama,' said Sjöman soon afterwards, 'where you try to take the experience of yourself or the actors [. . .] in the making of a play or a film.' *I Am Curious* amounts to *cinéma-vérité* with a difference: it really does give the impression of a filmed *experience*, in which Sjöman is as much involved as anyone as he watches Lena's love affairs with a jealous eye. The films together promulgate the notion that private and public ethics are indistinguishable one from another, and that society's shortcomings provoke the erosion and collapse of private relationships also.

148

Lena Nyman in Vilgot Sjöman's *I Am Curious − Yellow* (1967)

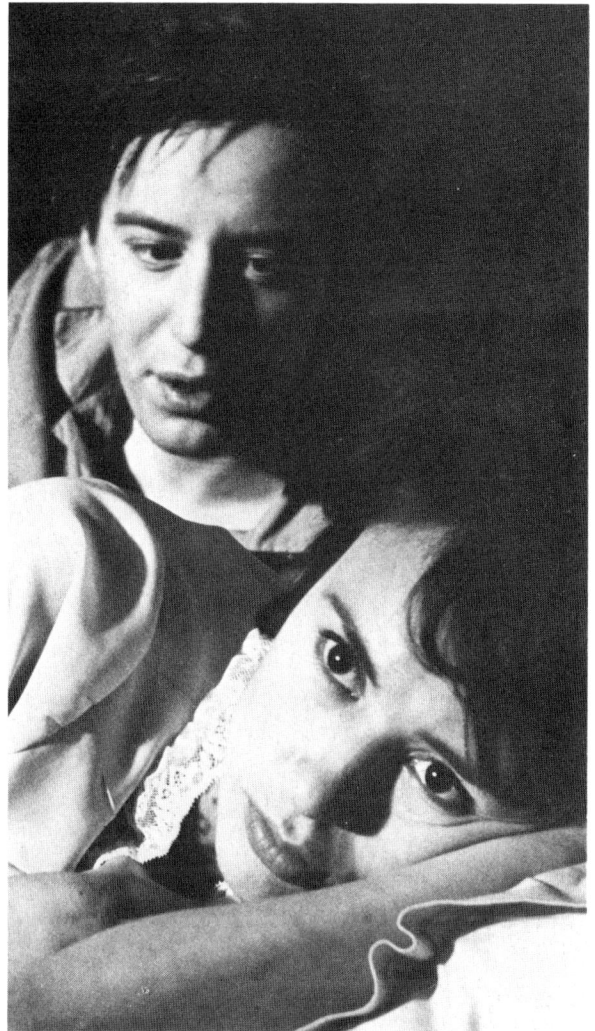
Thommy Berggren and Harriet Andersson in Jörn Donner's
A Sunday in September (1963)

Sjöman's condemnation of public institutions in Sweden caused raised eyebrows abroad as well as at home. In *You're Lying (Ni ljuger* 1969), he exposes the soul-destroying conditions prevailing in Swedish prisons. The outward face of this most modern of prison systems, its architecture, its hygiene and so on, disguises an aridity of spirit, and a numbing hostility towards the inmates that may, Sjöman argues, be more noxious than the antiquated jails of other countries. Swedish psychiatric care attracts even more withering criticism in a docudrama from the same year, *The Assault (Misshandlingen)*, directed by Lasse Forsberg. Crude as a slap in the face, *The Assault* makes no effort to clothe its fury in civilised conversation. The arguments are loud and pugnacious. The anti-hero, Knut Petersen, finds himself at first patronised and then confined to a straitjacket after he has punched a company director on the jaw in the middle of Stockholm.

When Widerberg, in *Elvira Madigan* (1967) and *The Ådalen Riots (Ådalen 31,* 1969), and Sjöman, in *My Sister, My Love (Syskonbädd 1782*, 1966), looked to the historical past for their subject-matter, the outrage in their voice in no way diminishes. In all three films, society bears down upon those who transgress its rules. The factory workers on strike in *The Ådalen Riots* are repelled with police firepower, just as the demonstrators against white Rhodesia are repelled by water cannon in the collective documentary *The White Game (Den vita sporten,* 1968), on which Widerberg also worked. The incestuous relationship of the brother and sister in *My Sister, My Love* has a vibrancy and candour at odds with the perverse formality and fin-de-siècle lassitude of 18th-century Sweden, and the illicit romance between Count Sixten Sparre and his beloved Elvira serves as a

149

stinging rebuke to a society still dependent on the church, the army, and the family hearth.

Elvira Madigan shows Widerberg in his most inspired mood, telling his tale in imagery seized from the summer fields and woods of Skåne and Denmark's North Zealand. Like Bonnard's canvases, the film communicates an intimate bliss, a sensual affection for natural light and objects, tinged with Nordic premonitions of death – the wild strawberries signalling bliss, the spilled wine prefiguring the final loss of blood and vitality. Widerberg trims each scene at the crucial juncture so that the charm lingers rather than palls. The allusions speak discreetly for themselves. There is the parallel, for example, between Elvira's precarious practice on the tight-rope and the dangerous path that these lovers tread through life. There is the sober moment when the officer places his tunic around Sixten's dripping shoulders to keep him warm, and Sixten becomes acutely conscious of his flight from family and regiment. Such intimations may be found in the great outdoor films of Sjöström and Stiller, and their presence in the innovative films of the 1960's demonstrates the resilience of Swedish cinematic tradition. *Elvira Madigan* introduced a cinematographer, Jörgen Persson, fresh out of Film School but with a flair for location shooting that marked him as the heir to Julius Jaenzon, Gunnar Fischer, and Sven Nykvist. To this list should be added the name of Jan Troell who, with rare exceptions, has photographed his own films and done so with uncompromising perfection. Troell's work has much in common with that of his contemporaries who came to prominence during the 1960's. He has criticised the Swedish school system in *Ole dole doff* (1968), and subjects his native land to a sort of mild *I Am Curious* examination in *Land of Dreams (Sagolandet*, 1988), but his principal fascination is with individuals who press against the grain of life, rather than against a particular social system. Troell's heroes tend to be outsiders, decent folk whose aspirations are conditioned by the natural circumstances in which they live.

The Emigrants (Utvandrarna, 1971) won for Troell a special reputation in the United States, where audiences saw in the 19th-century saga of Karl Oskar and Kristina the ancestors of themselves as settlers in a new country. Nothing illustrates more palpably than the opening sequences of *The Emigrants* the perennial Nordic theme of Man versus Nature. Karl Oskar struggles in vain to rid his fields of the huge boulders left in the wake of the Ice Age. The inhospitable terrain compels him to join his fellow Småland farmers and take ship for America – where the struggles begin all over again. For Troell, Man's toiling in the face of nature reflects the emotional conflicts that lie deep within him. This theme underscores two of his greatest films, *Here Is Your Life (Här har du ditt liv*, 1966) and *The Flight of the Eagle (Ingenjör Andrées luftfärd*, 1982). In the first, young Olof must learn to survive in the harsh climate of northern Sweden, helping to float logs, to saw wood, and finally to work as a railyard navvy. Only about ten per cent of *Here Is Your Life* was shot inside the studio; the bulk of the film springs as honestly from the countryside of Norbotten as did the first masterpieces of Victor Sjöström.

In the later work, Andrée's obstinate insistence on trying to reach the North Pole by balloon becomes the physical manifestation of his tormented soul and his reluctance to suffer the humiliation of failure in the eyes of admiring supporters and patrons alike.

Troell has stretched the boundaries of the regular documentary, so as to accommodate his own emotional concerns. 'As long as the film-maker sticks *to his own truth*,' he has remarked, 'I feel he is rendering an accurate picture of things, even though he may have been editing ever so much; it is when he *consciously* deviates from this truth that his film becomes, in my opinion, false – and thereby non-documentary.' Troell's is the genuine *caméra-stylo* to which Astruc referred. He registers the details that make up the weal of life with a swiftness and sensitivity that would be literary were they not so indelible in imagistic terms. In *Here Is Your Life*, the heroic vision of August leaping over the logs in midstream is followed almost immediately by shots of the old man's watch ticking away as if his spirit were still alive, and of a fly buzzing helplessly against the window pane in the hot afternoon. Thus Troell involves us in the natural cycle of things, and patiently shows how frustration and sudden extinction are suffered by every creature, not just Man.

While the zest and thematic intensity of Sjöström may be instantly recognised in the cinema of Jan Troell, the irony and sophistication of Stiller preside over the early films of **Jonas Cornell**, albeit filtered through the 'swinging' mood of the 1960's, with the surrealistic tinge that coloured the films of Richard Lester and the Beatles. *Hugs and Kisses (Puss & kram*, 1967) makes splendid use of squeaky-clean apartments and chic garb to point up the foolishness of its husband and wife, who are so preoccupied with their own good looks that they tend to underestimate the cuckoo in the nest – a bohemian writer who has been flung out (with his typewriter a short distance behind) by his previous mistress. After its fashion, *Hugs and Kisses* offers as effective a critique of Swedish bourgeois condescension as the more abrasive attacks of Widerberg and Sjöman. *Like Night and Day (Som natt och dag*, 1969) also reacts with scepticism to a Swedish society where affluence and property create a hierarchy as rigid as the English class system. Susanne, the glamorous TV announcer, Claire, her avaricious sister, and Erland, the renowned medical professor, and Rikard, Susanne's uncertain young lover, must all dance to the rhythm dictated by this system. Prosperity does not go hand-in-hand with psychological security. Cornell reproaches with these films a world in which appearances matter more than substance. The same astringent quality has given a lasting value to films like Stiller's *Love and Journalism* and *Erotikon*.

Mai Zetterling, whose films as a director have effaced many of her mediocre performances as an actress, shares Cornell's repugnance for monied hypocrisy. *Loving Couples (Älskande par*, 1964), *Night Games (Nattlek*, 1966), *The Girls (Flickorna*, 1968), and *Doctor Glas (Doktor Glas*, 1969) all revolve around a core of frustration. But Zetterling's characters suffer not only from social, but also from sexual repression. It is as a suffragette that

The Emigrants (1971) by Jan Troell

Zetterling makes her most effective contribution to Swedish cinema. The women in her films are united by their dislike and disdain for the men around them. In *Loving Couples*, the visual panache and admirable acting convey this sexual loathing in amusing, even incisive terms. But in *Night Games* and *The Girls*, the tone becomes too strident, and the emphasis on perversion too salacious. Her most controlled achievement remains *Doctor Glas*, based on the novel by Hjalmar Söderberg, which enfolds the essential Nordic sense of sin in the eyes of a Lutheran God. The respectable Glas finds his lust for the local pastor's wife so overwhelming that he must resort to violence to expunge it. Assailed by nightmares (in one, he must struggle with heavy blocks of stone in a quarry), the doctor must continue to parade through the changing streets of his city until, almost a hundred years old, he recognises that he will never enjoy the love of a woman. Ulf Palme's performance gives the film a mood of trepidation and mitigates the glacial look of *Doctor Glas*. Zetterling's only other work of interest,

Amorosa (1986), traces the life of Agnes von Krusenstjerna, who wrote the suite of novels that formed the basis for *Loving Couples*.

Some directors during this period struggled to find a distinctive voice without achieving the all-important festival breakthrough abroad. **Johan Bergenstråhle**, for example, exhibits in *Made in Sweden* (1969), *A Baltic Tragedy (Baltutlämningen,* 1970, and *Foreigners (Jag heter Stelios,* 1972) an undeniable political commitment to exposing corruption and injustice, but his imagery and narrative resources cannot endow this ideal with a persuasive cinematic force. **Stig Björkman**, gifted as a critic, has also failed to establish himself as an *auteur*. His work, always well-assembled, suffers from a paleness of complexion and a curious lassitude of spirit. His most ambitious film remains *Behind the Shutters (Bakom jalusin,* 1984), and its account of a writer's obsession with a mysterious and beautiful woman in North Africa carries distinct echoes of *Vertigo*. Reality merges with fiction when the writer begins

Here Is Your Life (1966) by Jan Troell

Foreigners (1972) by Johan Bergenståhle

to cast the girl in a new novel on which he is working, and the influence of Antonioni predominates over that of Hitchcock. Immaculate, evocative photography by the Dane, Dirk Brüel, haunting music by Ulf Dageby, and skilful acting compensate for a basic lack of inner tension in *Behind the Shutters*.

Jan Halldoff's spontaneous, unpretentious approach to teenage problems earned him good audiences during the 1960's, and a reputation in Sweden akin to Claude Lelouch's in France. His observant style ensures that his boys and girls are never loaded with a symbolic weight, and his use of music contributes to the feeling of happiness tinged with the worry of trying constantly to 're-charge life' that sparks his characters. *Life's Just Great (Livet är stenkul*, 1967), *Ola & Julia* (1967), *The Corridor (Korridoren*, 1968) and *A Dream of Freedom (En dröm om frihet*, 1969) all signal Halldoff's strength as a director of young actors, but also a poverty of visual fantasy. His richest work, *The Last Adventure (Det sista äventyret*, 1974) owes much to its source, a novel by Per Gunnar Evander about a young man who completes his army service only to shrink from committing himself to any profession. Like the irresolute young doctor in *The Corridor*, this outsider (alarmingly well played by Göran Stangertz) cannot decide on his response to the new morality.

Striving for Excellence beyond Bergman

Between the formation of the Swedish Film Institute in 1963, and the start of the 1970's, more than fifty new directors had made their debut in Swedish cinema. While Ingmar Bergman, and the most durable talents of the 1960's continued to produce estimable work up through the 1980's, there is no escaping the conclusion that Sweden, despite all its financial stimulation of film-making within the country, has failed to find any new talent to match the spirit of the times. The Danish, and even the Finnish, cinema enters the 1990's in healthier state than the Swedish. Not that the average Swedish film of the past twenty years has been outrageously bad. Some directors, like Kay Pollak, Gunnel Lindblom, and Marianne Ahrne, have manifested a gift for analysing human behaviour. Others, such as Kjell Grede, Stig Björkman, Hasse Alfredson, and Carl-Gustaf Nykvist, possess an eye for the fantastical that recalls the Stiller of *Gunnar Hede's Saga*. Still others, like Allan Edwall, Mats Arehn, and Christer Dahl, cope competently with their material and occasionally forge a passage of great quality. But few have been able to sustain their early promise, and to strike a responsive chord among foreign audiences. Even Lasse Hallström, whose *My Life as a Dog (Mitt liv som hund*, 1985) earned several million dollars in the United States, does not seem likely to consolidate his reputation. The history of the Swedish cinema since 1970 may therefore be written in terms of genres and themes rather than that of *auteurs*. Ingmar Bergman, who lived in Munich for some years during this period, retained his individual choice of subject-matter, although even he focused on a modernist topic in *Scenes from a Marriage (Scener ur ett äktenskap*,

1973) and *Face to Face (Ansikte mot ansikte*, 1976), as well as resorting to the documentary form for two studies of the island of Fårö, where he lives.

Comedy, Fantasy and Childhood

The *salon* comedy of Mauritz Stiller (and, to some extent, Bergman) has not enjoyed a revival. Instead, Swedes have flocked to see more down-to-earth humorous films, many of them anchored in Swedish customs and traditions and therefore persistently unamusing to the foreign observer. **Lasse Åberg's** satirical adventures have proved enormously popular with home audiences. In *The Call-Up (Repmånad*, 1978), *The Charter Trip (Sällskapsresan*, 1980), *SOS – Swedes at Sea (En segelsällskapsresa*, 1989), and *The Accidental Golfer (Den ofrivillige golfaren*, 1991) Åberg's Tati-like personality gives an agreeable, manic tinge to the proceedings. The team of **Hasse Alfredson** and the late-lamented **Tage Danielsson** created a series of fantastical comedies that took as their starting-point a particular foible in the Swedish personality and then spiralled away on flights of surreal whimsy. At their best, in *Go Ashore (Att angöra en brygga*, 1965) or *The Apple War (Äppelkriget*, 1971), this talented pair could bring an axe, if not a rapier, to many of the hallowed shibboleths of modern Sweden. The moments of bizarre, even macabre humour in such comedies have been developed to an often disturbing degree by Alfredson in his personal films like *The Simple-Minded Murderer (Den enfaldige mördaren*, 1982), which launched the career of the versatile actor Stellan Skarsgård, and *False as Water (Falsk som vatten*, 1985). The psychological suspense movie is a genre not often essayed by Swedish directors, and Alfredson's narrative style slips along smoothly and persuasively until a certain grotesquerie consumes the material.

Another Swedish comedian who has clearly aimed at more than mere farce is **Allan Edwall**. Without doubt a gifted dramatic actor (viz. *Winter Light, Here Is Your Life* and *The Emigrants)*, Edwall also projects immense appeal as a comic figure, sometimes in the screen versions of children's stories by Astrid Lindgren, and sometimes by representing the outsider, the unfortunate Swede who falls foul of the system, as in *Loafie (Limpan*, 1983). 'Loafie' has a weakness for the bottle and spends his time confined to a welfare clinic. Everyone, young and old alike, ridicules this engaging fellow who enjoys the company of strangers and retains a cheerful outlook on life. *Loafie* seeks the vulnerability concealed beneath most people's social airs and complexes. It also demonstrates that a class society *does* indeed exist in Sweden, and that alcoholics can be treated stupidly and even cruelly. Edwall's *Åke and His World (Åke och hans värld*, 1984), although not strictly a comedy, contains many amusing moments. Six-year-old Åke is a susceptible country boy responding to life in happy family surroundings. The film gazes back nostalgically at an inter-war period free from the cynicism and sordidity of contemporary existence.

Scenes from a Marriage (1973) by Ingmar Bergman

The Mozart Brothers (1986) by Suzanne Osten

Suzanne Osten has maintained an exciting place in both theatre and cinema in contemporary Sweden. Her humour tends to froth and bubble, and turn all too quickly into painful self-parody. Her debut feature, *Our Life Is Now (Mamma,* 1983) sung a nostalgic paean to the tenacity of her mother, a film critic much influenced by her early experiences in Paris. 'Mamma' strives to reconcile the demands of being a single parent and a fledgling film-maker. *Our Life Is Now* wallows in self-gratification and a naive acceptance of French 'culture', but amid the banality Malin Ek's central performance flares with feminist conviction. Osten's next two films, *The Mozart Brothers (Bröderna Mozart,* 1986) and *A Lethal Film (Livsfarligt film,* 1988) constitute a comic assault on the pretentious directing methods so often found in the opera house *(The Mozart Brothers)* and the movie studio *(Lethal Film)* and demonstrate the hard-edged wit of Osten's writing as well as the bravura acting of her companion, Etienne Glaser. Satire, however, is not a genre that meets with instant approval in the complacent 1980's. Suzanne Osten reached a wider circle of viewers with *The Guardian Angel (Skyddsängeln,* 1989), which was nominated for several European Film Awards and selected for the 'Certain Regard' section at the Cannes Festival. A political thriller set in the early years of this century, it works at a profound psychological level as well as giving a detailed vision of bourgeois life in town and country, even if its insistence on monochrome photography does not seem justified by the material.

More satisfying, if also more cautious, is Sven Nykvist's *The Ox (Oxen,* 1991), the cinematographer's fourth and best work as a director. Like a Zorn painting come to life, *The Ox* recaptures the mood of life in the famine-struck Sweden of 1868, when vast numbers of farming folk emigrated to America and those remaining had to struggle to eke out an existence. *The Ox* benefits from a sumptuous cast of Bergman regulars: Max von Sydow, Liv Ullmann, Ewa Fröling, Erland Josephson, and the best actor of the new generation, Stellan Skarsgård.

Lasse Hallström began making thoughtful comedies a full ten years before winning international acclaim for *My Life as a Dog.* His two rites-of-passage movies, *Boy Meets Girl (En kille och en tjej,* 1975) and *Happy We (Två killar och en tjej,* 1983) are autobiographical in tone but lacking in bite. *Father To Be (Jag är med barn,* 1979) is a pleasing confection about a young man who becomes almost more expectant than his pregnant wife when it comes to a baby, and whose hilarious antics poke sly fun at the Swedish urge for equality in domestic matters. Hallström's relaxed talent invests every scene in *My Life as a Dog* with charm and sensitivity. Though based on a novel by Reidar Jönsson, this film teems with seemingly personal recollections by the director, of a youth in the 1950's spent partly in the city and partly in the lush landscape of Småland. Little Ingemar has a wry outlook on life beyond his years, and adores his shaggy young uncle in the countryside. He has a crush on Saga, a little little tomboy who shines at both football and boxing. Over the sunlit moments looms the shadow of Ingemar's mother as she succumbs to tuberculosis. *My Life as a Dog* is blessed with a common touch, and a conviction that despite the travails and injustices of the world, human faith and humour must survive.

Much of the credit for this steady stream of Swedish films about the wonder and hazards of childhood must go to **Kjell Grede**, whose *Hugo and Josephine (Hugo och Josefin,* 1967) speaks to both adults and youngsters alike, and the late Olle Hellbom, with *The Brothers Lionheart (Bröderna Lejonhjärta,* 1977), which paints a sombre landscape against which the forces of good and evil engage in a struggle at once amusing and frightening. Grede has never forsaken his child's vision of things, in which nothing is impossible, and even the most tender of emotions can be refracted through the teasing eye of innocence. The weird assortment of painters who figure in *Hip, Hip, Hurrah! (Hip hip hurra!,* 1987) live in a soap bubble of their own creation. Life is celebrated as one long party, interspersed with fragments of reality, light and shadow. The film tantalises the spectator, leaping back and forth in time and mood, exploring the dialectic between the painter's frozen images and the hectic, unpredictable movement of real life. Certainly the film has more poignancy and antic inspiration than Grede's worthy, but leaden-footed tribute to the Swedish wartime hero, *Good Evening, Mr. Wallenberg (God afton, herr Wallenberg,* 1990).

Another veteran of the 1960's renaissance, Vilgot Sjöman, filters his memories of youth through a highly-coloured melodrama about a teenage boy being drawn into a web of eroticism and intrigue, after witnessing a murder in the Stockholm of the late 1920's. The very structure of the building where the murder takes place becomes a microcosm of the adult world, where ambition is defined by the number of steps one can climb towards wealth and an indulgence of the senses.

Another young boy, Reine, experiences a more mysterious, and at times frightening childhood in **Kay Pollak's** *Children's Island (Barnens ö,* 1980). P.C. Jersild wrote the novel on which this outstanding film is based, and Kay Pollak externalises the desires and fantasies, the fears and aspirations, of puberty. But he endows these feelings with a bewitching glow and poetry. When Reine tries to stay underwater for as long as possible, one suffers with him, one feels the pumping of the blood in one's veins and the chillness of the surrounding water. Reine's discovery of profanity, sex, jealousy, and all those other illusions and disillusions that form the process of growing up, are beautifully marshalled by Pollak.

Carl-Gustaf Nykvist's *The Women on the Roof (Kvinnorna på taket,* 1989) completes the process of coming to terms with the adult world. On the cusp of the First World War, a young girl arrives to work in a photographer's shop and studio. She finds herself fascinated by the mesmeric personality of a woman photographer, who works alone in a lofty studio and assembles weird tableaux before her camera with a calculation and intensity that would do credit to a Patricia Highsmith schemer. Although the film loses its way in a lurid climax, it taps in an extremely beguiling way some of the fundamental themes in Nordic creative art, not least the obsession with *discovery,* whether it be emotional, sensual, or supernatural in character.

Political and Ecological Commitment

The aggressive political attitudes of the 1960's may have faded from sight, but Swedish cinema has not entirely abandoned the cause of women in society, or of the preservation of our planet in the face of pollution and greed.

Stellan Skarsgård in *Hip, Hip, Hurrah!* (1987) by Kjell Grede

The Women on the Roof (1989) by Carl-Gustaf Nykvist

A background in documentaries helped **Anders Wahlgren** to give a coarse-textured plausibility to his feature-length film about the writer Moa Martinson. *Moa* (1986) recreates life in the prewar period in Sweden, where the lot of a woman novelist and poet was difficult enough without having two children drown and recalcitrant husband blow himself up with dynamite. Moa's feisty personality serves her well in coping with her second husband, the Nobel Prize-winning author Harry Martinson.

Two directors have devoted their careers to crafting small-scale, sensitive if also introspective studies of women at risk in the modern world. **Marianne Ahrne's** heroines radiate kindliness and understanding. They may move in scientific circles (a mental hospital in *Near and Far Away [Långt borta och nära*, 1976] and a natal clinic in *A Question of Life and Death [På liv och död*, 1986]), but feelings must outweigh academic achievement. The emotional fervour of Ahrne's films has proved too lush for the Nordic temperament, and her work is more sympathetically received in Latin countries. *The Walls of Freedom (Frihetens murar*, 1979) should not be underestimated. Ahrne's study of an Argentinian immigrant blundering into the crass, narrow-minded midst of Swedish petit bourgeois society glows with feeling, and a commitment to the relief of human agony that is quite without parallel in Nordic cinema.

In the same vein, but on a more dispassionate level, **Gunnel Lindblom's** *Paradise Place (Paradistorg*, 1976) and *Summer Nights on the Planet Earth (Sommarkväller på jorden*, 1986) assemble their characters during the idyllic summer weeks. An uneasy gathering of family and friends, they scratch open old sores and inflict new wounds. But the essential selfishness of the I, Me, Myself era colours all their arguments and impetuous liaisons. Less schematic than either of these works is Lindblom's second film, *Sally and Freedom (Sally och frihet*, 1979), in which the infrastructure of Swedish society is flayed with quite startling conviction. Here abortions may be obtained as easily as teeth removed. Sally (Ewa Fröling, one of the new generation of fine Swedish actors) breaks with her husband in a vague quest for freedom, but leaps almost immediately into an identical prison. Sally is too weak and immature to achieve her goal and at the end she starts over again, as she aborts for the second time, just one person in a line of beds being trundled down to the operating theatre. In Sweden, the film seems to whisper, science and technology have taken care of everything, but nobody quite comprehends that little thing called love.

Stefan Jarl began his career soon after leaving the Swedish Film Institute's Film Academy, co-directing with Jan Lindquist a scarifying documentary about two homeless youths – *They Call Us Misfits (Dom kaller oss mods*, 1968). Ten years later, Jarl took up the story of these ill-fated outsiders, in *A Respectable Life (Ett anständigt liv*, 1979), and found that one of them had died from a drug overdose. Jarl's 'green' beliefs have led him to a different type of documentary in recent years. In *Nature's Revenge (Naturens hämnd*, 1983), he sets up a vibrant dialectic between the lyrical bounty of the Swedish landscape and the threat from chemical fertilisers and toxic sprays.

Interspersing the film's evocative shots of lakes and forests are comments from conservationists who must cope with the damage inflicted by man-made chemicals. *Threat (Hotet*, 1987), made in the immediate wake of the Chernobyl catastrophe, has the severity and detachment of an early Resnais documentary. The visual material is thin – a couple of Lapps talking into camera, and some haunting images of dead reindeer being borne across a brooding sky by helicopter, plus some shots of the Lapps pursuing their eternal lifestyle. But Jarl's evident commitment to these sufferers' cause gives the film an honourable quality unmatched by similar TV programmes. Jarl's aesthetic flair enables him to convey the beauty of an environment that Man could well obliterate.

The Bergman Legacy

Ingmar Bergman retired from the cinema officially in 1982, after completing *Fanny and Alexander*. His output had continued apace throughout all the years of innovation in the Swedish film community. While many of his most celebrated masterpieces, like *Cries and Whispers* and *Persona*, transcend their Nordic origins and offer numerous avenues of interpretation, other Bergman films reflect the impact upon Sweden of the Vietnam War, and the relaxed morality of the post-1968 relationship. *Shame (Skammen*, 1968) seizes the spectator in a savage grip, dispensing with aesthetic groupings and subtle lighting in order to comprehend the unvarnished horror of guerrilla warfare. Bergman grafts on to *Shame* his personal obsession with romantic betrayal, but in showing his characters caught like flies in a conflict they do not understand, and unable to distinguish between one side and the other, he remains loyal to the Swede's neutrality complex. *Shame* reaches back in spirit to the *Angst*-ridden films of the 1940's, and to the nihilist poetry of Erik Lindegren.

Scenes from a Marriage deserves consideration as the single most important film of the past twenty years in Scandinavia. Constructed in six parts, to reach a TV audience in successive weeks, this extraordinary dissection of modern marriage also functions in its abbreviated form in the cinema. Unfolding in the bourgeois suburbs of modern Sweden, in clinical office blocks, in everyday restaurants, *Scenes from a Marriage* suggests a resolve on Bergman's part to come to terms with today's world, today's Sweden, just as Victor Sjöström did sixty years earlier, in *Ingeborg Holm*. But where, since, are the films on the scams and corruption that have scarred the industrial landscape in Sweden? On the immigrant dilemma? On the scourge of AIDS? On the implications of the Palme assassination? With Bergman now in his seventies, and working only in the theatre, there must be a unique opportunity for some major new talents to emerge and confront these issues. Meanwhile, the courage of Jan Troell in tackling the *In Cold Blood*-type of tragedy that struck northern Sweden in 1988 must be applauded; *Il Capitano* (1991) reverberates with dark, repressed forces of a kind that will always surface in counterpoint to the pristine beauty of the Nordic landscape.

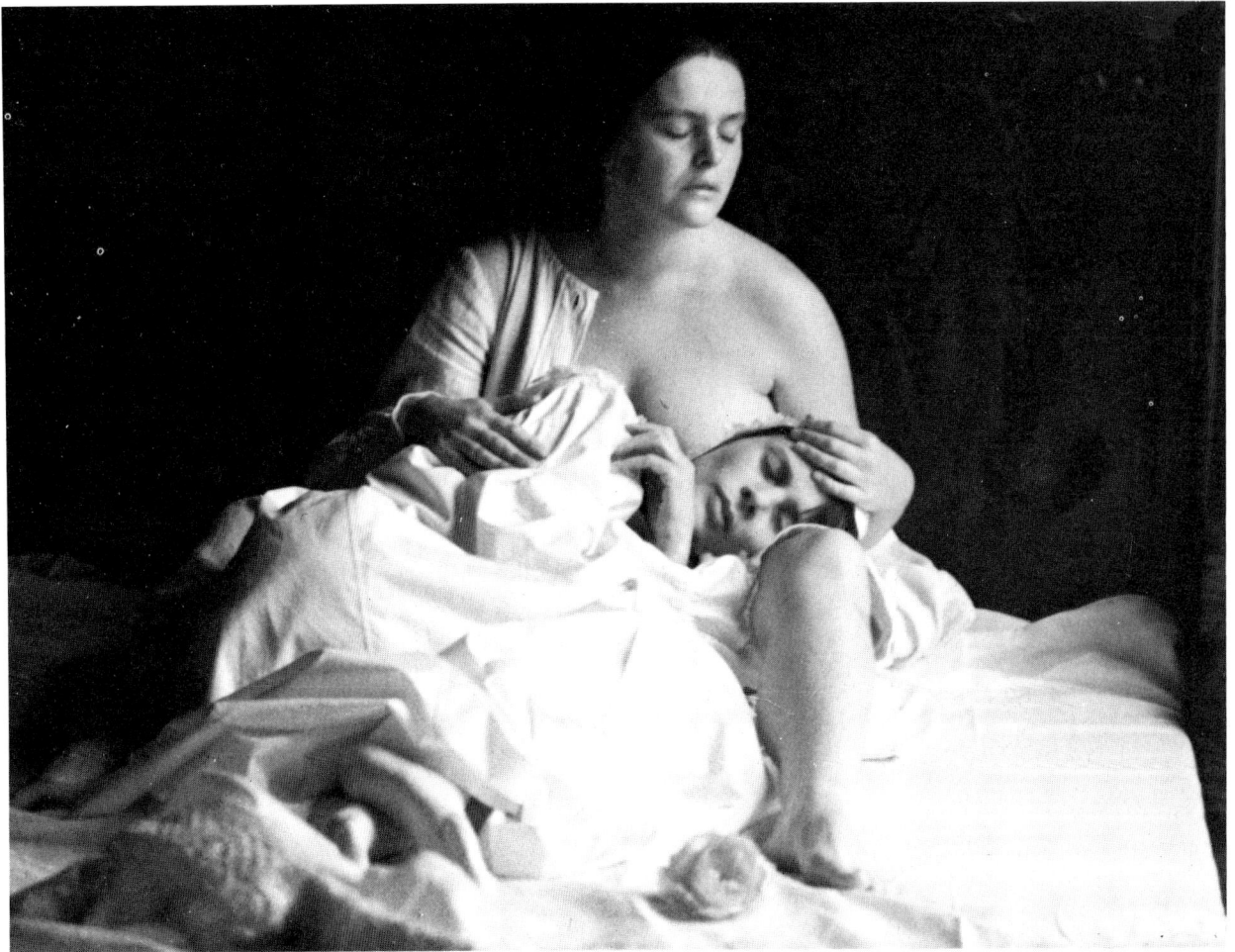

Kari Sylwan and Harriet Andersson in *Cries and Whispers* (1973) by Ingmar Bergman

1 Rune Waldekranz, 'Sweden', in *Art of the Cinema in Ten Countries* (Strasbourg, Council of Europe, 1967)
2 Id., *ibid.*
3 Rune Waldekranz, *Filmens historia, De första hundra åren* (Stockholm, Norstedts, 1986)
4 Peter Cowie, *Sweden 2* (London, The Tantivy Press, 1969)
5 C.A. Lejeune, *Cinema* (London, Alexander MacLehose & Co., 1931)
6 Quoted by Bengt Forslund, in *Victor Sjöström, His Life and Work* (New York, New York Zoetrope, 1988)
7 Quoted in *Stockholms Dagblad* (Stockholm, November 10, 1913)
8 Bengt Forslund, *op. cit.*
9 René Jeanne and Charles Ford, *Sjöström* (Paris, Editions Universitaires, 1963)
10 Bengt Forslund, *op. cit.*
11 Louis Delluc, *Cinéma et cie* (Paris, Bernard Grasset, 1919)
12 Léon Moussinac, *La Naissance du cinéma* (Paris, J. Povolozky, 1925)
13 Jean Béranger, *La Grande Aventure du cinéma suédois* (Paris, Le Terrain Vague, 1960)
14 John Gillett, programme note for National Film Theatre (London, 1978)

15 Bengt Forslund, *op. cit.*
16 Id., *ibid.*
17 Id., *ibid.*
18 Quoted by Bengt Idestam-Almquist, in *Stiller* (Paris, L'Avant-Scène Cinéma, 1967)
19 Id., *ibid.*
20 Id., *ibid.*
21 Cahier no. 8 published by the Festival of La Rochelle 1988
22 *Ibid.*
23 Bengt Idestam-Almquist, *op. cit.*
24 Extracted from Bengt Forslund, *op. cit.*
25 Bengt Idestam-Almquist, *op. cit.*
26 Rune Walkdekranz, *Filmens historia, De första hundra åren* (Stockholm, Norstedts, 1986)
27 Id., *ibid.*
28 Rune Waldekranz, *Swedish Cinema* (Stockholm, Swedish Institute, 1959)
29 Edouard Laurot, 'Swedish Cinema – Classic Background and Militant Avant-Garde', in *Film Culture* (New York, no. 4 [10], 1956.

Bengt Ekerot in *The Seventh Seal* (1957) by Ingmar Bergman.

The Nordic Film Institutes

Film production throughout the Nordic region benefits from government support, in one guise or another. Given the restricted size of the local and/or linguistic market, few domestic films can survive without such aid. The Nordic Council of Ministers has enacted legislation whereby, since January 1990, the sum of $7 million per annum will be available for the support of quality feature films to be made as co-productions between various Nordic nations. This is known as the Nordic Fund for Film and Television, and each country contributes to it.

DENMARK

The Danish Film Institute (DFI) was initially launched as a Foundation in 1965, and from its inception directed its support to the writing and producing of quality feature films (unlike its Swedish counterpart, which until 1972 rewarded quality films *after* their release). The production of films was boosted by guarantees for loans of up to 45% of the budget. This funding, as well as support for the Danish Film Museum, the Danish Film School and other related activities, stemmed via the Ministry of Cultural Affairs from a 15% royalty levied on tickets and licence fees paid by cinema-owners.

Over the intervening quarter-century, this system has undergone alteration and amendment. There is now active support for the import of high-quality foreign films, for example. A long-awaited revised version of the Film Law took effect from May 1, 1989. Under this legislation, a producer automatically receives a grant to the value of 50% of his film's costs providing he has already secured the other half of the budget from private sources. This reduces the power of the Institute's 'film consultants', who in recent years have been able to recommend to the DFI board those film projects which they feel deserve to be made.

The current production budget of the Danish Film Institute amounts to some DKK 85 million (approx. US $12.9 million), of which 25% is reserved for the making of films for children. Less than half is allocated for projects endorsed by the DFI's 'film consultants', and $2.8 million goes to productions independently set up by local private firms on the '50/50' principle described above.

The DFI also promotes and presents Danish films abroad, finances two community film and video workshops, and sponsors the publication of magazines and books on the cinema.

FINLAND

The Finnish Film Foundation was established in 1969 and was closely modelled on the Swedish Film Institute. Its income continues to be derived primarily from a levy on all tickets sold at the domestic box-office. This has increased steeply from $200,000 in 1970 to several million dollars today. Indeed, $6.6 million is available for investment in home production. Part of this money is distributed almost without restriction to producers who can raise 80% of a film's budget in advance, although the maximum per film in such cases is $100,000. The balance goes to major projects considered worthwhile by the production committee. The Ministry of Education has over the past twenty years made considerable sums available for film awards, for training and archive activity, and for pensions for film artists.

The Finnish Film Foundation serves as a nexus for Finnish film activity, and comprises editing and sound editing facilities, and an important department for the support of quality foreign film imports, the maintenance of good programmes at provincial movie theatres.

ICELAND

The Icelandic Film Fund distributed its first grants in 1979, sharing its meagre resources among several recipients. But for some years subsequently, independent film producers could rely only on token support from the Fund. In 1987 the government decided to commit support to the fledgling industry, in the wake of the break-up of the traditional state monopoly concerning TV and radio broadcasting, by obliging both Icelandic State Television and the newly-founded Station 2 (which is run privately) to contribute to the Broadcasting Stations' Cultural Fund.

The Icelandic Parliament voted 71 million crowns ($1.365 million) in subsidies for local production in 1989, to be assigned by the Icelandic Film Fund. There is no fixed percentage limit where production grants and subsidies are concerned, but in view of the island's tiny output (from two to four features per annum), support can account for half or more of a movie's budget.

NORWAY

Almost twenty years before Sweden established its trend-setting Film Institute, Norway had regarded cinema as a national cultural responsibility. Between 1945 and 1955, a modest degree of financial support was given to a film after its completion. Since then, a state loan guarantee (from 1955, slightly amended in 1964 and soon to be replaced with a direct support system) has been in operation, together with a system involving an additional subsidy for adult films equivalent to 55% of box-office income. (Children's films are supported up to 100% of their box-office returns.)

Most Norwegian feature films are produced with the aid of a state-guaranteed loan, which is granted in one of two ways: either by the state in the form of the Norwegian Film Institute, after the application has been considered by the five-member National Film Production Committee (where both film workers and producers are represented). Or the loan can be guaranteed automatically within the framework of the state subsidies that Norsk Film A/S enjoys as an independent government-owned company. The money available for such subsidies is currently in the region of $8.5

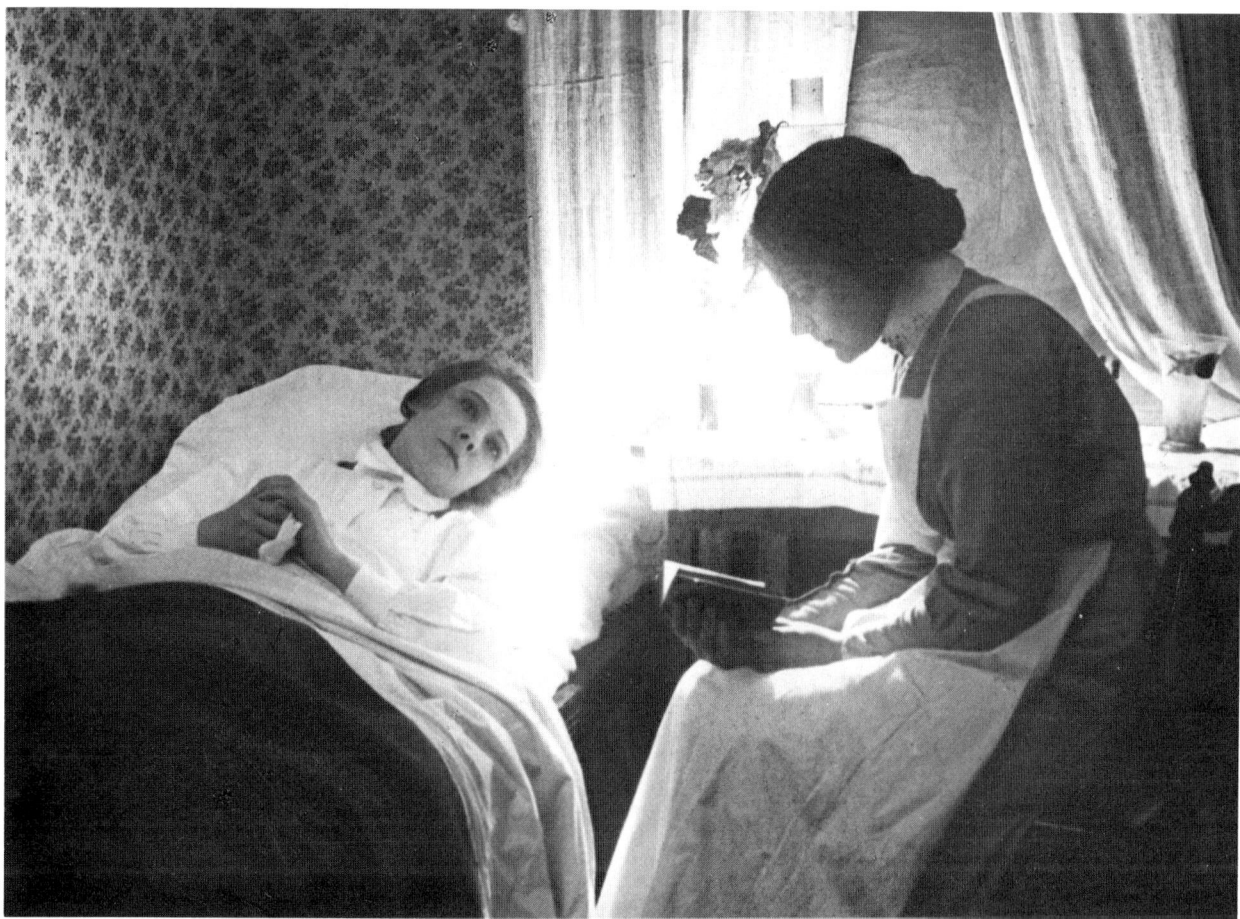

Thy Soul Shall Bear Witness (1920) by Victor Sjöström

million for feature films, including approximately $3.4 million for Norsk Film A/S, with a further $3.4 million for co-productions involving the film industry and Norwegian television (NRK).

All Norwegian full-length films receive a subsidy from the state, currently equivalent to 55% of the gross box-office income. Independent producers also keep up to 40% of the profits once their capital has been repaid by means of film rental income and the state subsidy. The powers and activities of the Norwegian Film Institute have expanded dramatically in recent years, to encompass the promotion of Norwegian films abroad as well as the management of the country's film archive.

SWEDEN

The Swedish Film Institute came into existence in 1963 as the brainchild of Harry Schein, who drafted the legislation and lobbied forcefully and intelligently for the acceptance by Parliament of the principles involved. The establishment

of SFI meant an end to a crippling entertainments tax, and replaced it with a modest levy of 10% on every ticket sold in movie theatres. The Institute could thus support various aspects of film cultural life in Sweden, from film clubs to film preservation. At first, some 30% of SFI's income was divided among all Swedish film in direct proportion to their box-office receipts, with a further 33% allotted to quality awards to Swedish features. Within a decade, the policy underwent a radical change. The Institute switched its support from post-completion awards to pre-production subsidies. In 1982 the Film Agreement again underwent revision, and SFI's income was bolstered with a levy of SEK 40 on the sale of all full-length video-cassettes. Funds available for production guarantees now amount to some $15.5 million, of which one-third is reserved for projects where the SFI itself is in charge of production.

All the other four Nordic countries have now followed the initiative of Sweden in setting up state, or quasi-state institutions through which to fund domestic film production. None, however, is so large as SFI, all-embracing in its sphere of activity.

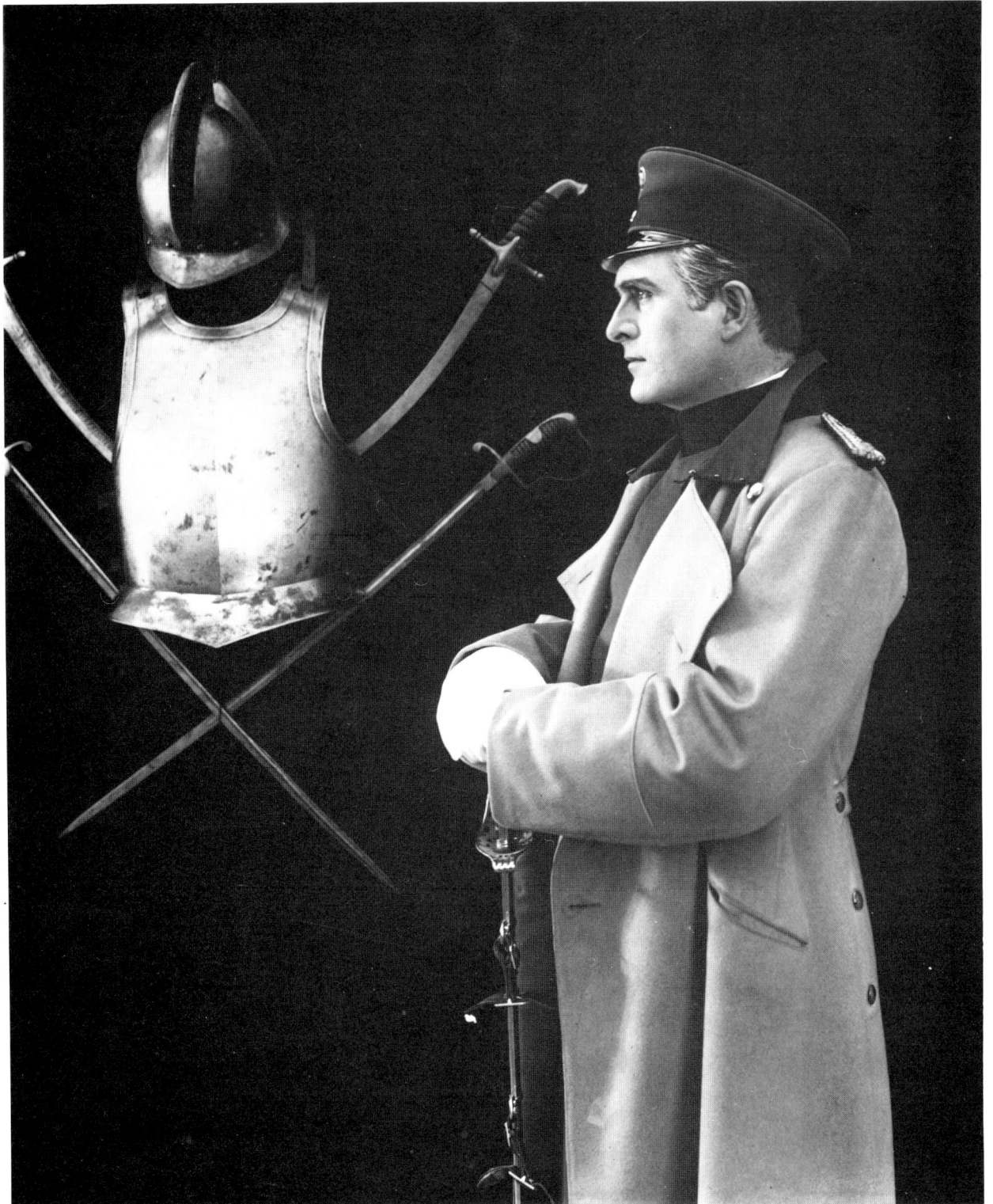

Down with Weapons! (1914) by Forest Holger-Madsen

Filmography

*Françoise Buquet, Risto-Mikael Pitkänen
and Godfried Talboom*

**Note: this is a selective list of significant films in the history
of Scandinavian cinema, and does not pretend
to be comprehensive.**

DENMARK

The Abyss
(Afgrunden)

Year of production: 1910

Production: Kosmorama; 36 mins (extant)

Release: September 12, 1910

Direction: Peter Urban Gad

Screenplay: Peter Urban Gad

Photography: Alfred Lind

Players: Asta Nielsen, Robert Dinesen, Poul Reumert, Hans Neergaard, Arne Weel, Oscar Stribolt, Emilie Sannom

A young piano teacher, Magda, leaves her fiancé (whose father is a pastor) to follow an itinerant circus performer. The affair soon goes sour, and Magda kills her lover in a violent struggle.

The White Slave Trade II
(Den hvide slavehandels sidste offer)

Year of production: 1910

Production: Nordisk Films Kompagni; 49 mins

Release: January 23, 1911

Direction: August Blom

Screenplay: Peter Christensen

Photography: Axel Graatkjear

Players: Clara Wieth, Lauritz Olsen, Thora Meincke, Ingeborg Rasmussen, Ella la Cour, Aage Brandt, Otto Lagoni, Frederick Jacobsen, Peter Nielsen, Axel Boesen, Otto Detlefsen

A young orphan, Edith, from a good family, is invited to visit her aunt in London. During the voyage, she is approached by a woman who in fact belongs to a white slave gang; on arrival in London, the gang kidnap Edith. She is eventually rescued thanks to a young man's curiosity and persistence.

The Flying Devils
(De fire djævle)

Year of production: 1911

Production: Kinografen; 880 metres

Release: August 28, 1911

Direction: Alfred Lind and Robert Dinesen

Screenplay: Carl Rosenbaum, from the novel by Herman Bang

Photography: Alfred Lind

Players: Edith Buemann, Robert Dinesen, Carl Rosenbaum, Tilley Christiansen, Einar Rosenbaum, Aage Hertel, Antoinette Winding

Four orphans grow up to become a circus act, 'The Flying Devils'. Two of them are engaged to be married, but the man cheats on his fiancée with a wealthy countess. His partner deliberately lets him plunge to his death during their trapeze act, and then flings herself after him. . . .

The Strongest
(Den stærkeste)

Year of production: 1912

Production: Nordisk Films Kompagni; 680 metres

Release: September 30, 1912

Direction: Edvard Schnedler-Sørensen

Screenplay: Alfred Kjerulf

Players: Valdemar Psilander, Robert Dinesen, Else Frölich, Anton Gambetta Salmson, Axel Mattson, Aage Lorentzen, Axel Boesen, Alf Nielsen

A proud and forceful countess is attracted to a man equally arrogant and self-assured. She tries to make him pursue her, but finally has to swallow her pride and declare her own feelings.

Atlantis

Year of production: 1913

Production: Nordisk Films Kompagni; 131 mins

Release: December 26, 1913

Direction: August Blom

Screenplay: Karl-Ludwig Schröder, Axel Garde, from the novel by Gerhardt Hauptmann

Photography: Johan Ankerstjerne

Players: Olaf Fønss, Frederik Jacobsen, Carl Lauritzen, Ida Orloff, Ebba Thomsen, Charles Unthan

A young German doctor has to send his wife to an insane asylum. He takes a voyage to the United States to recover his spirits, and falls in love with a dancer on board. She proves fickle, and eventually the doctor finds solace in the arms of a third woman.

The Strongest (1912) by Edvard Schnedler-Sørensen

Atlantis (1913) by August Blom

The White Slave Trade II (1911) by August Blom

David Copperfield (1922) by Anders Wilhelm Sandberg

The Mysterious X
(Den hemmelighedsfulde X)

Year of production:	1913
Production:	Dansk Biografkompagni; 1,977 metres
Release:	March 23, 1914
Direction and Screenplay:	Benjamin Christensen
Photography:	Emil Dinesen

Players: Benjamin Christensen, Karen Caspersen, Otto Reinwald, Bjørn Spiro, Fritz Lamprecht, Hermann Spiro, Amanda Lund, Svend Rindom, Robert Schmidt, Holger Rasmussen, Charles Løvaas

A naval lieutenant is about to leave for battle when some secret orders are intercepted by an enemy spy. The lieutenant is condemned to death for treason after a botched trial, and only the sharp thinking of his wife, acting on the impulse of a curious dream, saves him from death.

Down with Weapons!
(Ned med vabnene)

Year of production:	1914
Production:	Nordisk Films Kompagni; 1,509 metres
Release:	September 18, 1915
Direction:	Forest Holger-Madsen
Screenpla:	Carl Th. Dreyer, from the novel by Bertha von Suttner
Photography:	Marius Clausen

Players: Philip Bech, Augusta Blad, J. Fritz-Petersen, Alf Blütecher, Olaf Fønss, Carl Lauritzen

Martha loses her first husband in the war, and marries again, this time a man called von Tilling who has pacifist convictions. He wants to avoid military service, but is obliged to go to the front for financial reasons. He is wounded, and Martha searches for him among the terrible conditions of the battlefront. The war ends, and von Tilling recovers from his wounds, but a cholera epidemic follows, and Martha's sister and father die from the disease.

David Copperfield

Year of production:	1922
Production:	Nordisk Films Kompagni; 133 mins
Release:	December 5, 1922
Direction:	Anders Wilhelm Sandberg
Screenplay:	Laurids Skands, from the novel by Charles Dickens
Photography:	Louis Larsen, Chresten Jørgensen

Players: Martin Herzberg, Gorm Schmidt, Margarethe Schlegel, Marie Dinesen, Karen Caspersen, Charles Wilken, Robert Schmidt, Ellen Rovsing, Frederik Jensen, Anna Marie Wiehe, Karina Bell, Peter Malberg, Poul Reimert, Else Nielsen, Karen Winther, Rasmus Christiansen

Faithful adaptation of the Dickens classic about young David Copperfield who comes to London, stays with the indigent but kind-hearted Micawbers, and suffers all kinds of misfortunes before marrying a childhood friend, Agnes.

Palo's Wedding
(Palos brudefærd)

Year of production:	1934
Production:	Palladium; 73 mins
Release:	March 5, 1934
Direction:	Friedrich Dalsheim
Screenplay:	Knud Rasmussen
Photography:	Hans Scheib and Walter Traut
Players:	Greenlanders from Angmagssalik

Two young Greenlanders, Palo and Samo, are in love with the same girl, Navarana. She prefers Palo, and a marriage is arranged. But this provokes animosity between the two men, and Samo, made with rage, tries to kill Palo during a village celebration. But Palo recovers and retrieves his beloved Navarana, who has resisted all Samo's advances.

The Joys of Summer
(Sommerglæder)

Year of production:	1940
Production:	Palladium; 98 mins
Release:	September 26, 1940
Direction:	Svend Methling
Screenplay:	Gunnar Hansen, from a story by Herman Bang
Photography:	Einar Olsen

Players: Rasmus Christiansen, Ellen Gottschalch, Ingrid Matthiessen, Mathilde Nielsen, Sigurd Landberg, Richard Christensen, Agnes Rehni

During the early years of the century, a married couple open a guest-house in a small town in northern Jutland. They await their first tourists with restless impatience. All at once people start arriving, and it is hard to find space for everybody. Then there is a big meal, followed by dancing. Old friends run into one another, and new relationships are established. finally, the host and his wife can go to bed peacefully in their loft.

The Princess of the Suburbs
(Afsporet)

Year of production:	1941
Production:	ASA; 90 mins
Release:	February 19, 1942

Direction: Bodil Ipsen and Lau Lauritzen

Screenplay: Sven Rindom, from the play by Karl Schlüter

Photography: Rudolf Fredericksen and Alf Schnéevoigt

Players: Poul Reumert, Illona Weiselmann, Bjarne Forchammer, Eigil Reimers, Ebbe Rode, Preben Lerdorff-Rye, Johannes Meyer, Ib Schønberg, Tobe Grandjean

A rich young woman, Esther, is miserable in her marriage and when she learns unexpectedly that she is suffering from a possibly fatal illness, decides to look up a former lover. But he is married too, and in her confused state Esther wanders into the city's less salubrious areas. There she is accepted as one of their number by the prostitutes, and a young criminal is attracted to her. But one day her real identity slips out, and Esther, rather than give up her lover, commits suicide after a struggle with the police.

The Sky is Blue
(Himlen er blaa)

Year of production: 1954

Production: Europa Film; 2,835 metres

Release: March 22, 1954

Direction: Svend Aage Lorentz

Screenplay: Finn Methling

Photography: Henning Bendtsen

Players: Holger Juul Hansen, Henning Moritzen, Lise Ringheim

Early one summer morning, as young couple go out for a stroll in a park in Copenhagen. The film becomes a series of flashback episodes, triggered by everyday polite exchanges, emphasising the routine of life in a big city.

No Time for Kisses
(Ingen tid til kærtegn)

Year of production: 1957

Production: Flamingo – Johan Jacobsen; 98 mins

Release: March 1, 1957

Direction: Annelise Hovmand

Screenplay: Annelise Hovmand and Finn Methling

Photography: Kjeld Arnholtz

Players: Eva Cohn, Lily Weiding, Hans Kurt, Jørgen Reenberg, Yvonne Petersen, Annelise Jacobsen, Johns Marott, Gerda Madsen, Karen Berg, Betty Halsengreen, Preben Lerdorff-Rye, Bent Christensen, Bodil Ipsen

Neglected by her famous actress of a mother, a little girl of eight years of age escapes from her nanny, jumps on a local train and gets off at a small country station. The film tells her story from a child's point of view – his discovery of nature, of suffering, and of tenderness. Set against this is the panic of her parents as they search for her. . . .

Harry and His Valet
(Harry og Kammertjeneren)

Year of production: 1961

Production: Erik Aes; 106 mins

Release: September 7, 1961

Direction: Bent Christensen

Screenplay: Leif Panduro, Bent Christensen, from an idea by Fred Denker

Photography: Kjeld Arnholtz

Players: Osvald Helmuth, Ebbe Rode, Gunnar Lauring, Henning Moritzen, Lise Ringheim, Lily Broberg, Olaf Ussing, Palle Kirk, Aage Fønss, Einar Federspiel

Harry Adams earns his living looking after a car dump. His only luxury is the daily card game he has with his cronies. One day, a miracle occurs: Harry inherits a small fortune. Harry resolves to set about buying himself some love. He engages a valet, and proceeds to live on two different levels, one with his impoverished old pals, the other a kind of wish-fulfilment. . . .

Street without End
(Gade uden ende)

Year of production: 1963

Production: Hermes Filmproduktion; 88 mins

Release: June 24, 1963

Screenplay and Direction: Mogens Vemmer

Photography: Bent Paulsen

Players: Sunny Nielsen, Zellita Torki, Connie Ohlsen, Poul Jacobsen

Sunny is 22 and a prostitute. Already at the age of six, she had encountered a 'woman of the streets' as she sat waiting for her mother to come home one night. The film traces Sunny's inevitable decline into prostitution. . . .

Hunger
(Sult)

Year of production: 1966

Production: Studio ABC (Oslo)/Sandrews, Svenska Filminstitutet (Stockholm)/Henning Carlsen (Copenhagen); 111 mins

Release: August 19, 1966

Direction: Henning Carlsen

Screenplay: Henning Jensen, Peter Seeberg, from the novel by Knut Hamsun

Photography: Henning Kristiansen

Players: Per Oscarsson, Gunnel Lindblom, Birgitte Federspiel, Sigrid Horne-Rasmussen, Knud Rex, Hans W. Petersen, Osvald Helmuth

Harry and His Valet (1961) by Bent Christensen

Once There Was a War (1966) by Palle Kjærulff-Schmidt

Hunger (1966) by Henning Carlsen

Give God a Chance on Sundays (1970) by Henrik Stangerup

The Man Who Thought Things (1969) by Jens Ravn

Winter Born (1978) by Astrid Henning-Jensen

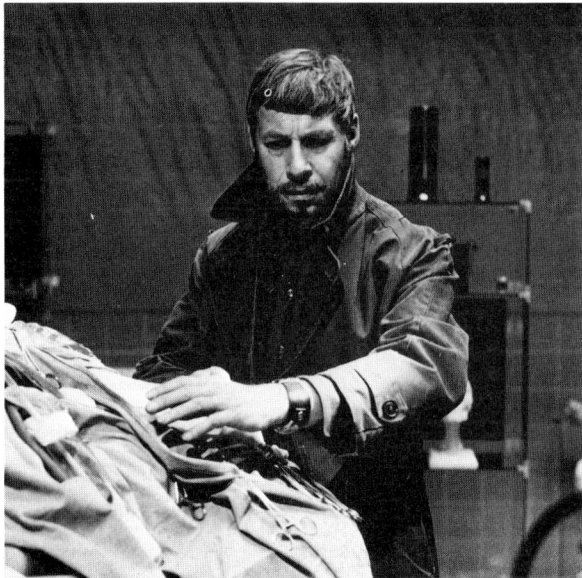

It is the autumn of 1890, in Christiania (the former name for Oslo, and capital of Norway). A gifted young writer, unable to place his work, is reduced to poverty and then a desperate search for food. He gradually succumbs to fits of insanity. . . .

A lyrical evocation of the Danish countryside, focusing on an eighteen-year-old Candide of a youngster, who is learning to be a dairyman and gets involved in some unexpectedly violent events. . . .

Once There Was a War
(Der var engang en krig)

Year of production: 1966

Production: Nordisk Films Kompagni; 92 mins

Release: November 16, 1966

Direction: Palle Kjærulff-Schmidt

Screenplay: Klaus Rifbjerg

Photography: Claus Loof, Arne Abrahamsen

Players: Yvonne Ingdal, Ole Busck, Kjeld Jacobsen, Astrid Villaume, Katja Miehe Renard, Birgit Bendix Madsen, Jen Hainig Hansen

The film recreates a period during the German occupation of Denmark, and its impact on a young boy of 15 years of age. Tim and his pals live through their schooldays, their pranks, and above all their first loves. Tim falls for a 22-year-old friend of his sister and, although she does not even notice him, Tim is profoundly affected by this infatuation. . . .

The Red Mantle
(Den rode kappe)

Year of production: 1966

Production: ASA Film Studie (Copenhagen)/Johan Bonnier (Stockholm)/Edda Film (Reykjavík); 98 mins

Release: January 16, 1967

Direction: Gabriel Axel and Frank Jaeger, from the writings of Saxø

Photography: Henning Bendtsen

Players: Gitte Haenning, Oleg Vidov, Eva Dahlbeck, Gunnar Björnstrand, Gisli Alfredson

A saga of love and hate, set in the Iceland of circa 1000 AD, and reviving the tragic story of Hagbard and Signe.

The Ballad of Carl-Henning
(Balladen om Carl-Henning)

Year of production: 1968

Production: ASA Film; 95 mins

Release: April 7, 1969

Screenplay and Direction: Lene and Sven Grønlykke

Photography: Jesper Høm

Players: Jesper Klein, Paul Hüttel, Inge Baaring, Edith Thrane, Einar Larsen, Mimi Fønss, Preben Borggaard, Kai Christofferson, John Wittig, Suzzie Müllertz, Birgitte Rasmussen, June Belli

The Man Who Thought Things
(Manden der tænkte ting)

Year of production: 1968

Production: ASA Film; 96 mins

Release: May 9, 1969

Direction: Jens Ravn

Screenplay: Jens Ravn and Henrik Stangerup

Photography: Witold Leszcynski

Players: Preben Neergaard, John Price, Lotte Tarp

Steinmetz is possessed of supernatural gifts: he can materialise thoughts and convert them into reality. He becomes rich overnight, but he yearns to create human life, and seeks the help of a celebrated surgeon. When the surgeon, appalled, refuses to collaborate, Steinmetz creates a 'double' for the surgeon, with unexpected consequences. . . .

Dear Irene
(Kære Irene)

Year of production: 1970

Production: Kollektiv Film; 100 mins

Release: February 26, 1971

Direction: Christian Braad Thomsen

Photography: Dirk Brüel

Players: Mette Knudsen, Steen Kaalø, Ebbe Kløvedal, Agneta Ekmanner, Elin Reimer, Poul Malmkjær, Erik Nørgaard, Birgit Brüel, Bent Conradi, Børge Høst, Susanne Giese

A young woman in Copenhagen is dissatisfied with her marriage, and stays with her husband only on account of their four-year-old daughter. She has a brief fling with a journalist, but this too leaves her dissatisfied, and frustrated with the lack of human feelings and development in the society around her.

Give God a Chance on Sundays
(Giv Gud en chanse om søndagen)

Year of production: 1969

Production: ASA Film Studio/Athena Film; 94 mins

Release: April 22, 1970

Direction: Henrik Stangerup

Screenplay: Henrik Stangerup, Jørgen Stegelmann

Photography: Henning Camre

Players: Ulf Pilgaard, Lotte Tarp, Ove Sprogøe, Vibeke Reumert, Ole Storm

Niels is a pastor in Jutland, and has a pretty young wife. But, knowing that orthodox religion is on the wane, he tries in various ways to revive both his own beliefs and those of his parishioners. When his audience react only indifferently to his staging of Kaj Munk's *The Word*, Niels seems to be on the point of abandoning his vocation. . . .

Oh, To Be on the Bandwagon!
(Man sku'være noget ved musikken)

Year of production: 1972

Production: Henning Carlsen/Nordisk Films Kompagni; 96 mins

Release: September 13, 1972

Direction: Henning Carlsen

Screenplay: Henning Carlsen and Benny Andersen

Photography: Henning Kristiansen

Players: Birgitte Price, Karl Stegger, Otto Brandenburg, Gyrd Løfquist, Jesper Langberg, Ingolf David, Lone Lindorff, Martin Lichtenberg, Birgit Conradi, Lene Maimu.

The film concentrates on the round-the-clock activity at a café in the Nørrebro district of Copenhagen. The characters are the café-owner and his wife, and the regulars at the bar, recounting their hopes and dreams, their disappointments and their frustrations. . . .

Boys
(Drenge)

Year of production: 1976

Production: Steen Herdel Film/EBC Film/Nils Malmros; 90 mins

Release: February 26, 1977

Direction: Nils Malmros

Screenplay: Nils Malmros and Frederick Cryer

Photography: Dirk Brüel, Morten Bruus, Morten Arnfred

Players: Mads Ole Erhardsen, Jesper Hede, Lars Junggren, Inez Thomsen, Sven Schmidt-Nielsen, Ib Tardini, Mette Marie Hede, Lone Rode, Poul Clemmensen

The film tells the story of Ole at three points in his youth. In the first episode, he is five; in the second at high school; and in the third he has reached the age of 23.

Me and Charly
(Mig og Charly)

Year of production: 1977

Production: Steen Herdel Film; 102 mins

Release: March 20, 1978

Screenplay and Direction: Morten Arnfred and Henning Kristiansen

Photography: Morten Arnfred and Henning Kristiansen

Players: Kim Jensen, Helle Nielsen, Allan Olsen, Ghita Nørby, Finn Nielsen, Jens Okking, Lise Henningsen, Else Højgaard, Erno Müller, Per Pallesen, Johnny Olsen

Steffen is sixteen years old and lives with his divorced mother, who works as a journalist on a local paper. Although he is keen on his schoolfriend Majbritt, Steffen is soon fascinated by Charly, who is in and out of reform school and has an antic, freewheeling approach to life that represents some kind of ideal for Steffen. . . .

Winter Born
(Vinterbørn)

Year of Production: 1978

Production: A-S Panorama Film; 100 mins

Release: September 1, 1978

Screenplay and Direction: Astrid Henning-Jensen, from the novel by Dea Trier Mørch

Photography: Lasse Bjørne

Players: Ann-Mari Max Hansen, Helle Hertz, Lone Kellermann, Lea Risum Brøgger, Berit Kvorning, Birgit Conradi

Some women find themselves together in a maternity hospital in Copenhagen. The film describes their hopes and anxieties when faced with the miracle of parturition and infant life.

Zappa

Year of production: 1982

Production: Per Holst Filmproduktion ApS; 103 mins

Release: March 4, 1983

Screenplay and Direction: Bille August from the story by Bjarne Reuter

Photography: Jan Weincke

Players: Adam Tonsberg, Morten Hoff, Peter Reichardt, Rikke Bondo.

A film about youngsters in the early 1960's, on the cusp of Denmark's economic resurgence. It is a world in which the adults show little or no interest in the youth around them, a state of mind that prefigures the social upheavals of 1968. . . .

The Element of Crime
(Forbrydelsens element)

Year of production: 1983

Production: Per Holst Filmproduktion ApS; 103 mins

Release: May 14, 1984

Direction: Lars von Trier

Screenplay: Lars von Trier and Niels Vørsel

Photography: Tom Elling

Players: Michael Elphick, Esmond Knight, MeMe Lai, Jerold Wells, Ahmed El Shenawi, Astrid Henning-Jensen

Fisher returns to Cairo after conducting a murder inquiry in Europe. He is confused and in need of therapy; under hypnosis, he revisits Europe, and his old police mentor whose approach has always beguiled Fisher. Little by little he is sucked into a series of bizarre murder situations. . . .

Twist and Shout
(Tro, hab og kærlighed)

Year of production: 1984

Production: Per Holst Filmproduktion ApS; 104 mins

Release: December 26, 1984

Direction: Bille August

Screenplay: Bille August and Bjarne Reuter

Photography: Jan Weincke

Players: Adam Tønsberg, Lars Simonson, Camilla Søeberg, Ulrikke Juul Bondo, Thomas Nielsen, Lone Lindorff, Arne Hansen, Bent Mejdin

Four youths in their late 'teens are starting life at university. They find themselves caught between their school outlook and the adult world, and encounter widely differing experiences when falling in love. One of the three boys, Erik, is caught up in a domestic tragedy. . . .

Cœurs flambés
(Flamberede hjerter)

Year of production: 1986

Production: Per Holst Filmproduktion ApS; 114 mins

Release: December 26, 1986

Screenplay and Direction: Helle Ryslinge

Photography: Dirk Brüel, Søren Berthelin

Players: Kirsten Lehfeldt, Peter Hesse Overgaard, Torben Jensen, Anders Hove, Søren Ostergaard, Pernille Højmark, Omgolf David, Lilian Tillegren, Hans Henrik Clemmensen, Aage Haugland, Kirsten Peuliche

An unmarried nurse of thirty wants to keep her independence. She can solve other people's problems, but when it comes to her own, things prove more difficult. The film is a strongly autobiographical satire.

The Dark Side of the Moon
(Manden i månen)

Year of production: 1985

Production: Film-Cooperativet Danmark/Metronome Productions A/S; 93 mins

Release: March 7, 1986

Screenplay and Direction: Erik Clausen

Photography: Morten Bruus, Jens Schlosser

Players: Peter Thiel, Catherine Poul Jupont, Christina Bangtsson, Kim Jansson, Yavuzer Cetinkaya, Berthe Qvistgaard, Erik Truxa, Anne Nøjgaard, Marianne Mortensen, Stig Hoffmeyer, Ramezan Arsian, Meliha Saglanmak, Roy Richards, Dogan Arslann, Elmas Yildiz

John is freed after a sixteen-year spell in prison for murdering his wife. He finds it difficult to get work, ending up as a dishwasher in a restaurant, and shunned by all save the immigrants with whom he works. One day, he meets his now grown-up daughter, but she regards him as just a murderer. . . .

Early Spring
(Barndomens gade)

Year of production: 1986

Production: Metronome Productions A/S; 90 mins

Release: November 7, 1986

Screenplay and Direction: Astrid Henning-Jensen

Photography: Mikael Salomon, Jens Schlosser

Players: Sofie Grobøl, Louise Fribo, Vigga Bro, Carl Quist Møller, Torben Jensen, Kirsten Lehfeldt, Lena Vasegaard, Benny Poulsen, John Hahn-Petersen

In the early 1930's, Ester lives with her parents and brother in a small apartment in the working-class area of Copenhaben. In the space of a few months, three important events mark Ester's life: her first communion, the arrival of her period, and her leaving school. Ester is drawn to poetry and fantasy, while her father is a committed socialist and the family languishes in poverty. . . .

Babette's Feast
(Babettes gæstebud)

Year of production: 1987

Production: Panorama Film International/Nordisk Film A/S/Danish Film Institute; 105 mins

Release: August 28, 1987

Screenplay and Direction: Gabriel Axel, from the story by Karen Blixen

Photography: Henning Kristiansen

Players: Stéphane Audran, Jean-Philippe Lafont, Gudmar Wivesson, Jarl Kulle, Bibi Andersson, Hanne Steensgaard, Bodil Kjer, Vibeke Hastrup, Birgitte Federspiel, Ebbe Rode, Lisbeth Movin, Axel Strøbye, Ebba With, Kai Kristiansen

On a stormy day in 1871, Babette arrives in a coastal village in Jutland. She has fled from Paris where she has been a revolutionary during the Commune. She shelters with two virtuous ladies, daughters of the local pastor. One day, fourteen years after her arrival, she learns that she has won a sum of 10,000 francs on the French lottery. She decides to spend the money on a surprise feast for everyone in the parish. . . .

Pelle the Conqueror
(Pelle Erobreren)

Year of production: 1987

Production: Per Holst Filmproduktion ApS/Svensk Filmindustri/ Swedish Film Institute/Danish Film Institute; 160 mins

Release: December 26, 1987

Direction: Bille August

Screenplay: Bille August, Per Olov Enquist, Bjarne Reuter, from the novel by Martin Andersen Nexø (first part)

Photography: Jörgen Persson, Rolf Lindström, Søren Berthelin, Fritz Schrøder

Players: Pelle Hvenegaard, Max von Sydow, Erik Paske, Bjørne Granath, Astrid Villaume, Axel Strøbye, Troels Asmussen, Karen Wegener, Kristina Törnqvist

One bright morning in 1890, a middleaged, widowed farmer arrives with his son Pelle in a Danish port, hoping to make a new start away from his native Sweden. Lasse is employed as a cowherd, and he and his son are humiliated by the locals. While Lasse reveals himself as a coward, his son gradually learns to cope with society and sets his sights on new horizons. . . .

Baby Doll

Year of production: 1988

Production: Crone Film Produktion A/S in co-operation with DR/Danish Film Institute; 82 mins

Release: November 4, 1988

Direction: Jon Bang Carlsen

Screenplay: Jon Bang Carlsen and Lisbet Gad

Photography: Björn Blixt

Players: Mette Munk Plum, Bodil Udsen, Birgit Sadolin, John Hahn Petersen, Lone Kellermann, Benedikte Hansen, Ricki Katharina, Morten and Jacob (babies)

Eva is 36 years old and gives birth to her first child. She decides to stay in the house of her dead grandmother, an old farm where she spent much of her childhood. But memories, fantasies, and soon nightmares begin to spoil her delight in being a mother. . . .

Heaven and Hell
(Himmel og Helvede)

Year of production: 1988

Production: Metronome Productions A/S, FI/DR, Danish Film Institute; 120 mins

Release: October 14, 1988

Direction: Morten Arnfred

Screenplay: Morten Arnfred, Jørgen Ljungdahl, from the novel by Kirsten Thorup

Photography: Dirk Brüel

Players: Karina Skands, Old Lemmeke, Harriet Andersson, Lise Ringheim, Erik Mørk, Waage Sandø, Kim Sjøgren, Judy Gringer, Anne Marie Helger, Veli Dastan, Pernille Højmark

Maria is young and beautiful. It is the late 1960's, the end of the period of rebellion and liberation. She adores the violin, and seems calm enough, but one day after a brief yet intense affair with her music teacher, she quits home. She settles down with a young waiter, but learns that he has a double life which she cannot really penetrate. Feeling trapped, she sets off on her own once more. . . .

Katinka
(Ved vejen)

Year of production: 1987

Production: Nordisk Film/Svensk Filmindustri/Danish Film Institute/ Swedish Film Institute; 96 mins

Release: August 19, 1988

Direction: Max von Sydow

Screenplay: Klaus Rifbjerg, from the novel by Herman Bang

Photography: Sven Nykvist

Players: Tammi Ost, Ole Ernst, Kurt Ravn, Ghita Nørby, Erik Paaske, Tine Miehe-Renard, Vibeke Hastrup, Henrik Kofoed, Kim Harris, Paul Hüttel, Anne Lise Hirsch Bjerrum

During the 1880's, Katinka is married to Bai, the stationmaster. But she is bored in the somewhat loveless marriage, and falls for Huus, a new man who arrives in the area. But she cannot bring herself to leave her husband and run away with Huus. Like many women of her era, she accepts her destiny. . . .

Waltzing Regitze
(Dansen med Regitze)

Year of production: 1989

Production: Nordisk Film Production/Danish Film Institute; 90 mins

Release: 1989

Screenplay and Direction: Kaspar Rostrup

Photography: Claus Loof

Players: Ghita Nørby, Frits Helmuth, Rikke Bendsen, Michael Helmuth

Based on a popular novel, the film tells the story of Regitze and Karl Aage. They are celebrating at a midsummer party and are the toast of the district, but Karl Aage is prompted into recalling various stages of their romance and married life by the revelation that his beloved Regitze is terminally ill. . . .

Twist and Shout (1984) by Bille August

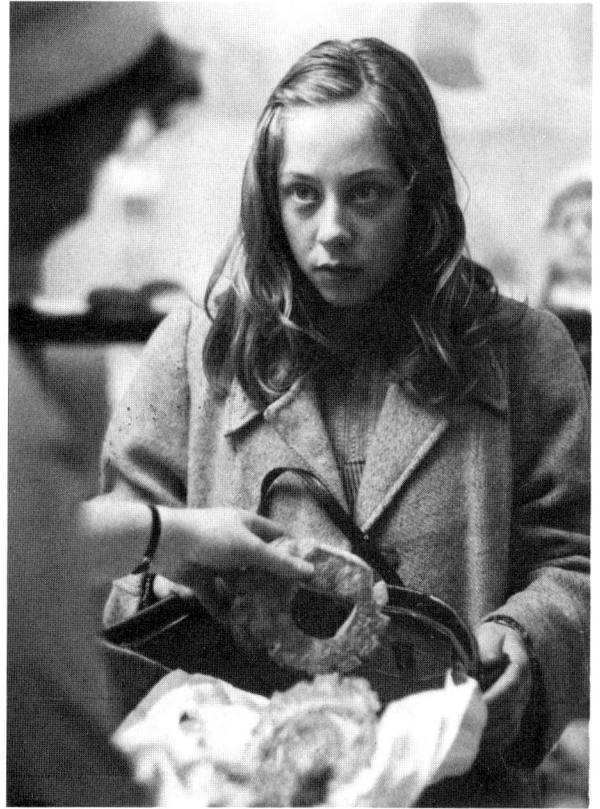

Early Spring (1986) by Astrid Henning-Jensen

The Dark Side of the Moon (1986) by Erik Clausen

Pelle the Conqueror (1987) by Bille August

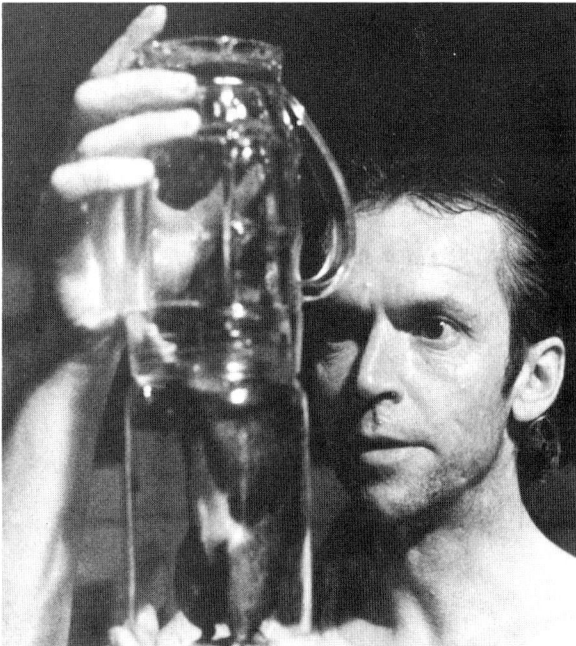

Babette's Feast (1987) by Gabriel Axel

Cœurs flambés (1986) by Helle Ryslinge

Europa

Year of production: 1990

Production: Nordisk Film and TV, Gunnar Obel, Gerard Mital Production and PPC WMG, Danish Film Institute, Swedish Film Institute, Telefilm GmbH, Eurimages; 107 mins

Release: May 1991

Direction: Lars von Trier

Screenplay: Lars von Trier and Niels Vørsel

Photography: Henning Bendtsen, Edward Klosinski, Jean-Paul Meurisse

Players: Jean-Marc Barr, Barbara Sukowa, Ernst-Hugo Järegård, Erik Mørk, Max von Sydow (voice only)

In the chaos of postwar Germany, an idealistic young American starts working as a sleeping-car attendant on the railways, falls in love with a beautiful woman, and finds himself being exploited by a neo-Nazi group known as Werewolf. . . .

Katinka (1988) by Max von Sydow

Juha (1936) by Nyrki Tapiovaara

FINLAND

The Village Shoemakers
(Nummisuutarit)

Year of production: 1923

Production: Suomi-Filmi/Erkki Karu; 76 mins

Release: November 12, 1923

Direction: Erkki Karu

Screenplay: Aetturi Järviluoma, from the play by Aleksis Kivi

Photography: Kurt Jäger

Players: Adolf Lindfors, Axel Slangus, Alarik Korhonen, Heidi Korhonen, Aku Käyhkö

The story of Esko the shoemaker's romantic misfortunes. Many sequences in this pioneering Finnish film were shot on location in the countryside.

Surrogate Husband
(Mieheke)

Year of production: 1936

Production: Suomi-Filmi/Risto Orko; 89 mins

Release: December 20, 1936

Screenplay and Direction: Valentin Vaala, from an original idea by Hilja Valtonen

Photography: Theodor Luts

Players: Tuulikki Paananen, Tauno Palo, Regina Linnanheimo, Uuno Laakso, Uuno Montonen

In order to impress her employers, a young woman is in need of a husband 'of convenience'. Valentin Vaala made his mark with this fluent comedy of manners.

Juha

Year of production: 1936

Production: Aho & Soldan; 92 mins

Release: January 24, 1937

Direction: Nyrki Tapiovaara

Screenplay: Heikko Aho, Nyrki Tapiovaara, from the novel by Johani Aho

Photography: Björn Soldan, Olavi Gunnari

Players: Hannes Närhi, Irma Seikkula, Walle Saikko, Tuulikki Paananen

Juha, a farmer, sees his young wife become infatuated with a strange visitor. The woman awakens to her new love against the backdrop of agrarian and wilderness beauty, and flees downriver with the tall, dark *charmeur*. . . .

Stolen Death
(Varastettu kuolema)

Year of production: 1938

Production: Erik Blomberg; 100 mins

Release: September 4, 1938

Direction: Nyrki Tapiovaara

Screenplay: Eino Mäkinen, Erik Blomberg, Matti Kurjensaari, from the book by Runar Schildt

Photography: Olavi Gunnari, Erik Blomberg

Players: Tuulikki Paananen, Ilmari Mänty, Santeri Karilo, Annie Mörk

Set in the early years of this century, *Stolen Death* traces the underground struggle of Finnish revolutionaries against the might of Tsarist Russia. A Russian spy allows himself to get romantically involved with the head of the independence movement. . . .

The Vagabond's Waltz
(Kulkurin valssi)

Year of production: 1940

Production: Suomen Filmiteollisuus/T.J. Särkkä; 104 mins

Release: January 19, 1941

Direction: T.J. Särkkä

Screenplay: Mika Waltari

Photography: Felix Forsman

Players: Tauno Palo, Ansa Ikonen, Jorma Nortimo, Regina Linnanheimo

The story of a young noblewoman and a vagabond who is not quite what he seems. . . . One of the most popular films of all time in Finland, attracting more than a million admissions.

Loviisa

Year of production: 1946

Production: Suomi-Filmi/Risto Orko; 90 mins

Release: December 25, 1946

Screenplay and Direction: Valentin Vaala, from the play by Hella Wuolijoki

Photography: Eino Heino

Players: Emma Väänänen, Tauno Palo, Kirski Hurme, Hilkka Helinä, Holger Salin, Maija Nuutinen

In a peasant community during the late 19th century a landowner has to answer the conflicting calls of love and social position, between his own instincts and the traditions to which he is heir.

People in the Summer Night
(Ihmiset suviyössä)

Year of production: 1948

Production: Suomi-Filmi/Risto Orko; 66 mins

Release: October 15, 1948

The Village Shoemakers (1923) by Erkki Karu

Stolen Death (1938) by Nyrki Tapiovaara

Loviisa (1946) by Valentin Vaala

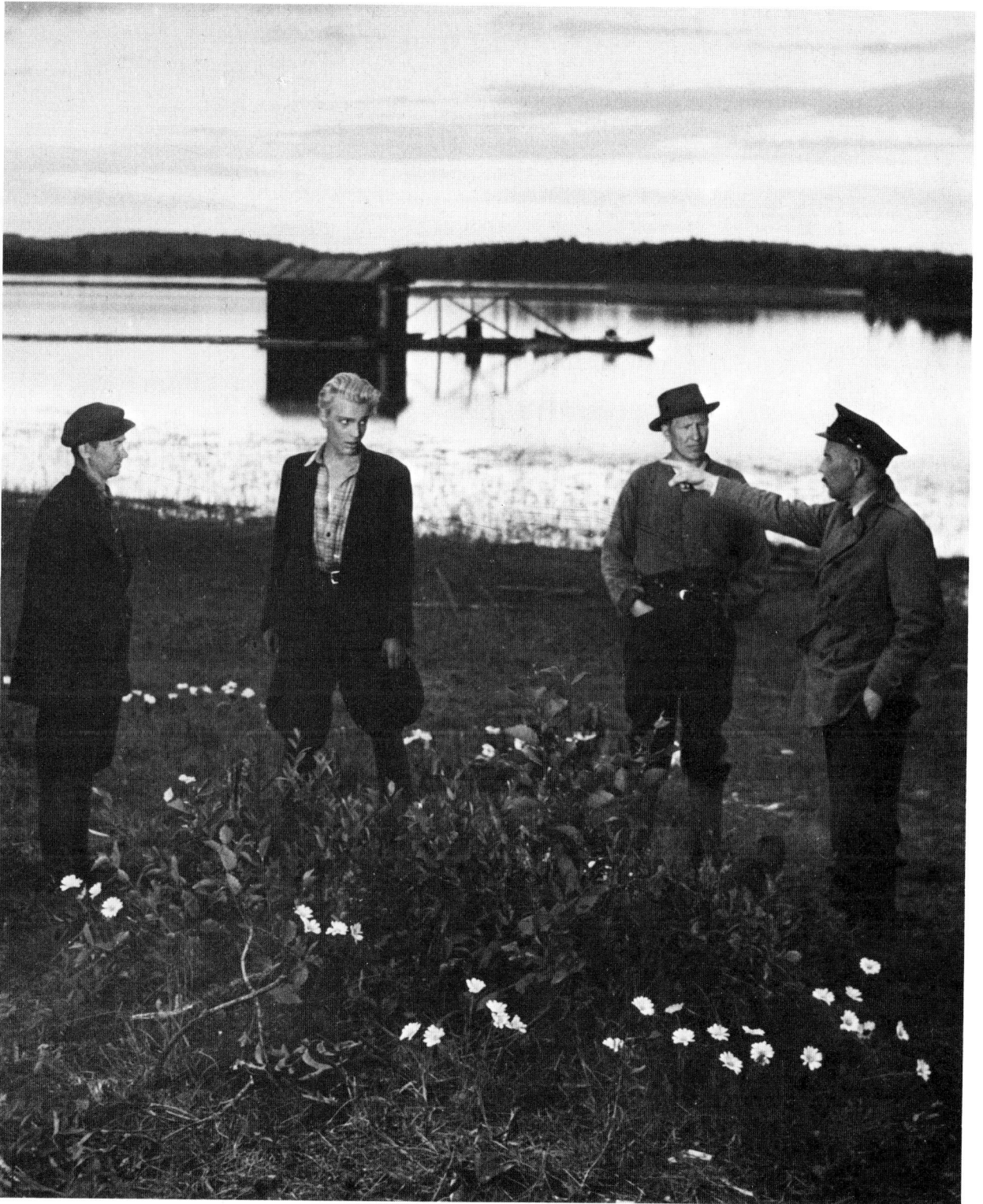

People in the Summer Night (1948) by Valentin Vaala

Direction: Valentin Vaala

Screenplay: Valentin Vaala, Lea Joutseno, from the novel by F.E. Sillanpää

Photography: Eino Heini

Players: Eila Pehkonen, Matti Oravisto, Martti Katajisto, Eero Roine, Kaisu Leppänen, Emma Väänänen

A visual poem of a film, that shows how the fate of various people becomes interlaced during the course of a long summer night.

The White Reindeer
(Valkoinen peura)

Year of production: 1952

Production: Junior-Filmi/Aarne Tarkas; 73 mins

Release: July 25, 1952

Direction: Erik Blomberg

Screenplay: Erik Blomberg, Mirjami Kuosmanen

Photography: Erik Blomberg

Players: Mirjami Kuosmanan, Kalervo Nissilä, Åke Lindman, Arvo Lehesmaa

A young woman possessed of supernatural powers turns into a white reindeer and lures men to their deaths.

Blue Week
(Sininen viikko)

Year of production: 1953

Production: Suomen Filmiteollisuus/T.J. Särkkä; 78 mins

Release: February 29, 1954

Screenplay and Direction: Matti Kassila, from the story by Jarl Hemmer

Photography: Osmo Harkimo

Players: Matti Oravisto, Gunvor Sandkvist, Toivo Mäkelä

A working lad meets an attractive woman during an excursion to the archipelago. They spend an ecstatic week together, but she is married, and when her husband commits suicide their romance disintegrates. . . .

The Unknown Soldier
(Tuntematon sotilas)

Year of production: 1955

Production: Suomen Filmteollisuus/T.J. Särkkä; 181 mins

Release: December 23, 1955

Direction: Edvin Laine

Screenplay: Juha Nevalainen, from the novel by Väinö Linna

Photography: Pentti Unho, Osmo Harkimo, Olavi Tuomi

Players: Kosti Klemelä, Heikki Savolainen, Reino Tolvanen, Veikko Sinisalo, Åke Lindman, Pentti Siimes, Leo Riuttu, Matti Ranin, Jussi Jurkka, Tauno Palo, Mikko Niskanen, Helena Vinkka

A platoon of soldiers is obliged to go to the front line in the war of attrition against the Soviet Union in the early 1940's.

Evacuated
(Evakko)

Year of production: 1956

Production: Fennada-Filmi/Mauno Mäkelä; 100 mins

Release: August 31, 1956

Direction: Ville Salminen

Screenplay: Jussi Talvi, Ville Salminen, from the novel by Unto Seppänen

Photography: Unto Kumpulainen

Players: Santeri Karilo, Linda Lampinen, Aino-Maija Tikkanen, Eila-Kaarina Roine, Matti Oravisto

At the end of the brief and savage Winter War of 1939-1940, many Finns living in Karelia were forced to abandon their homes and trek westwards to escape the invading Russians. . . .

Harvest Month
(Elokuu)

Year of production: 1956

Production: Fennada-Filmi/Mauno Mäkelä; 94 mins

Release: October 5, 1956

Screenplay and Direction: Matti Kassila, from the novel by F.E. Sillanpää

Photography: Esko Nevalainen

Players: Toivo Mäkela, Emma Väänänen, Rauni Luoma

Viktor Sundvall is a writer living in the countryside, and has taken to drink to mask his sense of failure. The arrival of an old flame stirs memories of his past. . . .

The Man from This Planet
(Mies tälta tähdeltä)

Year of production: 1958

Production: Veikko Itkonen; 96 mins

Release: November 14, 1958

Direction: Jack Witikka

Screenplay: Juha Nevalainen

Photography: Kalle Peronkoski

Players: Kaarlo Halttunen, Tea Ista, Tauno Palo, Kullervo Kalske, Jaakko Pakkasvirta

One of the first Finnish films to address the problems of alcoholism, *The Man from This Planet* traces the story of an everyday drunkard and his friends in Helsinki.

Boys
(Pojat)

Year of production: 1962

Production: Suomen Filmiteollisuus/T.J. Särkkä; 106 mins

Direction: Mikko Niskanen

Screenplay: Mikko Niskanen, Paavo Rintala, from the latter's novel

Players: Pentti Tarkiainen, Vesa-Matti Loiri, Uti Saurio, Hannu Vironmäki, Markki Söderström, Lisa Nevalainen, Kauko Helovirta

In the far north of Finland, the occupying Germans have transformed the life of a town during 1944. Each of the young boys in the film is marked by the experience. . . .

Private Property
(Yksityisalue)

Year of production: 1962

Production: Maunu Kurkvaara; 83 mins

Release: October 5, 1962

Screenplay and Direction: Maunu Kurkvaara

Photography: Maunu Kurkvaara

Players: Kalervo Nissilä, Kyllikki Forsell, Jarno Hiilloskorpi

A brilliant architect commits suicide, but his death is put down to a heart attack by his publicity-conscious family. A young assistant of the dead man starts to make inquiries, and uncovers the truth behind his master's demise. . . .

A Worker's Diary
(Työmiehen päiväkirja)

Year of production: 1966

Production: Filminor; 91 mins

Release: February 26, 1967

Direction: Risto Jarva

Screenplay: Risto Jarva, Jaakko Pakkasvirta

Photography: Antti Peippo

Players: Elina Salo, Paul Osipow, Pentti Irjala, Pertti Lumirae, Titta Karakorpi

A young blue-collar factory worker gets married to a bourgeois girl, and finds that old national scars dating back to the Civil War and the Second World War, steadily damage the relationship. . . .

Eight Deadly Shots
(Kahdeksan surmanluotia)

Year of production: 1972

Production: Finnish Television; 135 mins (theatrical version)

Release: September 15, 1972

Screenplay and Direction: Mikko Niskanen

Photography: Kimmo Simula, Juhani Vuotilainen, Seppo Immonen

Players: Mikko Niskanen, Tarja-Tuulikki Tarsala, Paavo Pentikäinen, Tauno Paananen

A docudrama based on a tragedy in 1969, when a Finnish farmer, frustrated by poverty and his own addition to liquor, killed four policemen sent to arrest him.

When the Heavens Fall
(Kun taivas putoaa)

Year of production: 1971

Production: Filminor/Kullervo Kukkasjärvi; 100 mins

Release: March 10, 1972

Direction: Risto Jarva

Screenplay: Jussi Kylätasku, Peter von Bagh, Antti Peippo, Risto Jarva

Photography: Antti Peippo, Lasse Naukkarinen

Players: Eeva-Maija Haukinen, Erkki Pajala, Heikki Hämäläinen, Matti Kassila

A yellow-press journalist resolves to destroy a woman's life by exposing her in print; in so doing he finds himself drawn into a sado-masochistic relationship with his victim . . .

One Man's War
(Yhden miehen sota)

Year of production: 1973

Production: Filminor/Kullervo Kukkasjärvi; 114 mins

Release: March 8, 1974

Direction: Risto Jarva

Screenplay: Jussi Kylätasku, Risto Jarva

Photography: Antti Peippo, Erkki Peltomaa, Juha-Veli Äkräs

Players: Eero Rinne, Tuula Nyman, Tauno Hautaniemi, Aimo Heino

A construction worker manages to get a bank loan to start his own earth-moving business. But he is overwhelmed by the economic and emotional pressures placed in his way by society. . . .

Earth Is Our Sinful Song
(Maa on syntinen laulu)

Year of production: 1973

Production: RM-Tuotanto/Rauni Mollberg; 108 mins

Release: November 2, 1973

The White Reindeer (1952) by Erik Blomberg

When the Heavens Fall (1972) by Risto Jarva

Direction: Rauni Mollberg

Screenplay: Rauni Mollberg, Pirjo Honkasalo, Panu Rajala, from the novel by Timo K. Mukka

Photography: Kari Sohlberg

Players: Maritta Viitamäki, Pauli Jauhojärvi, Aimo Saukko, Milja Hiltunen, Jouko Hiltunen, Niiles-Jouni Aikio

In a remote Lapp village, a young Lapp woman has a passionate fling with the visiting reindeer herdsman. Her family react violently, but although she loses her lover, the young woman gives birth to his child. . .

The Year of the Hare
(Jäniksen vuosi)

Year of production: 1977

Production: Filminor/Kullervo Kikkasjävi; 128 mins

Release: December 16, 1977

Direction: Risto Jarva

Screenplay: Arto Paasilinna, Risto Jarva, Kullervo Kukkasjärvi, Jussi Kylätasku, from the novel by Arto Paasilinna

Photography: Antti Peippo, Erkki Peltomaa, Juha-Veli Äkräs

Players: Antti Litja, Rita Polster, Kosti Klemelä, Jukka Sipilä, Ahti Kuoppala, Anna-Maija Kokkinen

A young man quits his advertising agency in Helsinki, and decides to spend a while in the Finnish wilderness; he finds a tame hare, brings him back to the city, and has to choose between the animal and his former life. . . .

Pretty Good — for a Human Being
(Aika hyvä ihmiseksi)

Year of production: 1977

Production: Arctic-Filmi/Veikko Korkala; 120 mins

Release: October 7, 1977

Direction: Rauni Mollberg

Screenplay: Rauni Mollberg, Veikko Korkala, Seppo Heinonen, from the novel by Aapeli (Toivo Pekkanen and Olavi Siippainen)

Photography: Hannu Peltomaa

Players: Martti Kainulainen, Railo Veivo, Mikko Nousiainen, Eila Pehkonen, Sirkka Metsäsaari, Toivo Mäkelä

A small Finnish village during the 1920's. The wounds of the Civil War have still not healed, there is prohibition and bootlegging is rampant. Mollberg's social comedy offers a subtle cross-section of this community. . . .

Men Can't Be Raped
(Män kan inte våldtas)

Year of production: 1977

Production: Stockholm Film/Jörn Donner Productions; 98 mins

Release: March 3, 1978

Screenplay and Direction: Jörn Donner, from the novel by Märta Tikkanen

Photography: Bille August

Players: Anna Godenius, Gösta Bredefeldt, Nils Brandt, Algot Böstman

A single woman meets a man at a dance-restaurant; he takes her home and rapes her. Humiliated, she resolves to take her revenge, systematically tracking the man down and humiliating him in kind. . . .

Guarded Village 1944
(Vartioitu kylä 1944)

Year of production: 1978

Production: Reppufilmi/Jouko Lumme; 100 mins

Release: November 3, 1978

Direction: Timo Linnasalo

Screenplay: Ilpo Tuomarila, from a play by Unto Heikura

Photography: Antti Peippo

Players: Markku Blomqvist, Raimo Grönberg, Kaija Kangas, Antti Litja, Tuula Nyman

Towards the end of the long war against the Soviet Union, life survives somehow along the frontier between Finland and her mighty enemy. Local intrigues, gossip, and blackmarket activity are features of everyday existence. . . .

Flame-Top
(Tulipää)

Year of production: 1980

Production: P-Kino/Jaakko Talaskivi, Claes Olsson; 130 mins

Release: October 17, 1980

Screenplay and Direction: Pirjo Honkasalo, Pekka Lehto

Photography: Kari Sohlberg, Pertti Mutanan, Raimo Paananen

Players: Asko Sarkola, Rea Mauranen, Kari Frank, Ritva Juhanto, Ari Suonsuu, Tuomo Railo

A reconstruction of the colourful, often violent life of Algot Tietäväinen, who took the pseudonym Maiju Lassila when writing. A farmer's son, he oscillated between Russia and Finland, and ended up being shot when the Finnish Civil War concluded with a rightwing victory.

Right On, Man!
(Täältä tullaan, elämä!)

Year of production: 1979

Production: Sateenkaari-Filmi/Tapio Suominen, Jorma K. Virtanen; 117 mins

Release: February 29, 1980

Direction: Tapio Suominen

Screenplay: Yrjö-Juhani Renvall, Pekka Aine

Photography: Pekka Aine, Juha-Veli Äkräs

Players: Esa Niemalä, Tony Holmström, Kati Outinen

A youngster in Helsinki plays truant from school and finds his innocence dissolving in the face of the harsh realities of urban life.

Milka — A Film about Taboos
(Milka — elokuva tabuista)

Year of production: 1980

Production: Arctic-Filmi/Rauni Mollberg; 110 mins

Screenplay and Direction: Rauni Mollberg, from the novel by Timo K. Mukka

Photography: Esa Vuorinen

Players: Irma Huntus, Leena Suomu, Matti Turunen, Eikka Lehtonen

The setting is western Lapland, close to the Arctic Circle. A young girl, Milka, and her widowed mother both fall in love with a handsome, simple-minded labourer. . . .

Crime and Punishment
(Rikos ja rangaistus)

Year of production: 1983

Production: Villealfa/Mika Kaurismäki; 93 mins

Release: December 2, 1983

Direction: Aki Kaurismäki

Screenplay: Aki Kaurismäki, Pauli Pentti, from the novel by Dostoievsky

Photography: Timo Salminen

Players: Markku Toikka, Aino Seppo, Esko Nikkari, Matti Pellonpää

A modern version of Dostoievsky's classic novel, with Raskolnikov reincarnated as Rahikainen, a slaughterhouse worker . . .

Pessi and Illusia
(Pessi ja Illusia)

Year of production: 1983

Production: Partanen & Rautoma; 77 mins

Release: January 13, 1984

Direction: Heikki Partanen

Screenplay: Heikki Partanen and his team, from the book by Yrjö Kokko

Photography: Henrik Paersch

Players: Jorma Uotinen, Annu Marttila, Sami Kangas

A film based on a book written during the Second World War by a Finnish officer, a veterinary surgeon, on the Russian front. The conflict between good and evil in a fairy-tale world is contrasted with the brutal reality of war.

Blue Mammy
(Sininen imettäjä)

Year of production: 1985

Production: Gironfilmi/Swedish TV/Helmi-Paula Pulkkinen; 98 mins

Release: September 13, 1985

Screenplay and Direction: Markku Lehmuskallio

Photography: Pekka Martevo, Markku Lehmuskallio

Players: Nillo Hyttinen, Jaakko Raulamo, Aino Lehdenperä, Kaija Kiiski, Aino-Maija Tikkanen

A deafmute painter communes in a mysterious way with his imaginery muse and the natural landscape all about him. . . .

Shadows in Paradise
(Varjoja paratiisissa)

Year of production: 1986

Production: Villealfa/Mika Kaurismäki; 73 mins

Release: October 17, 1986

Screenplay and Direction: Aki Kaurismäki

Photography: Timo Salminen

Players: Matti Pellonpää, Kati Outinen, Saku Kuosmanen, Esko Nikkari

In a grim, everyday Helsinki, romance blooms between a garbage truck-driver and a supermarket checkout cashier. . . .

The Match Factory Girl
(Tulitikkutehtaan tyttö)

Year of production: 1989

Production: Villealfa/Aki Kaurismäki/The Swedish Film Institute; 70 mins

Release: January 12, 1990

Screenplay and Direction: Aki Kaurismäki

Photography: Timo Salminen

Players: Kati Outinen, Elina Salo, Esko Mikkari, Vesa Vierikko

A factory girl lives a solitary life with her parents, cooking and caring for their every need without a word of thanks. One day, at a dance-hall, she meets a man who seems to like her, but his cynicism provokes an act of rebellion by the girl. . . .

Winter War
(Talvisota)

Year of production: 1989

Production: Marko Röhr/National-Filmi Oy; 195 mins

Release: December 30, 1989

Direction: Pekka Parikka

Screenplay: Pekka Parikka, Antti Tuuri, from the novel by Tuuri

Photography: Kari Sohlberg

Men Can't Be Raped (1978) by Jörn Donner

Right On, Man! (1980) by Tapio Suominen

The Year of the Hare (1977) by Risto Jarva

Players: Taneli Makelä, Timo Torikka, Vesa Vierikko, Heikki Paavilainen, Antti Raivio, Esko Kovero, Martii Suosalo

In the winter of 1939-40, Finland resisted the armed might of the Soviet Union for 105 days. The film follows the fortunes of a platoon of men from the northwestern village of Kauhava.

Plainlands
(Pohjanmaa)

Year of production: 1987

Production: Marko Röhr/National-Filmi Oy; 127 mins

Release: February 26, 1988

Direction: Pekka Parikka

Screenplay: Pekka Parikka, Antti Tuuri, from the novel by Tuuri

Photography: Karl Sohlberg

Players: Taneli Mäkelä, Esko Nikkari, Esko Salminen, Vesa Mäkelä, Kirsti Ortola, Tarja Keinänen, Rea Mauranen

One Sunday in summer, in the northwest province of Pohjanmaa, the Hakala family meets to divide the inheritance of a grandfather who has died in America . . .

Homebound
(Kotia pain)

Year of production: 1988

Production: Filminor/Heikki Takkinen; 90 mins

Release: March 10, 1989

Direction: Ilkka Järvi-Laturi

Screenplay: Annina Enckell, Ilkka Järvi-Laturi, Outi Nyytäjä

Photography: Kjell Lagerroos

Players: Ilkka Koivula, Jonna Järnefelt, Leena Suomu, Risto Tuorila

A film about the underworld of an industrial town, Oulu, in the north of Finland, and a young man who has come to Helsinki in the hope of leaving his past behind . . .

Flame-Top (1980) by Pirjo Honkasalo and Pekka Lehto

Friends, Comrades
(Ystävät, toverit)

Year of production: 1990

Production: Filmi-Molle Oy; 130 mins

Release: November 16, 1990

Direction: Rauni Mollberg

Screenplay: Rauni Mollberg, Joni Skiftesvik

Photography: Kjell Lagerroos

Players: Mikk Mikiver, Stina Ekblad, Hanny Lauri, Paavo Liski

Before and during the Second World War, diplomats and businessmen trek to northern Lapland to pay tribute to the magnate who controls immense quantities of nickel; but the magnate and his wife are not so fulfilled as their official appearance suggests . . .

Milka — A Film about Taboos (1980) by Rauni Mollberg

Crime and Punishment (1983) by Aki Kaurismäki

Pessi and Illusia (1984) by Heikki Partanen

Kati Outinen and Matti Pellonpää in Aki Kaurismäki's *Shadows in Paradise* (1986)

Father's Estate (1980) by Hrafn Gunnlaugsson

ICELAND

Land and Sons
(Land og synir)

Year of production: 1979

Production: Is-film s/f; 93 mins

Release: February 25, 1980

Screenplay and Direction: Ágúst Gudmundsson, from the novel by Indridi G. Thorsteinsson

Photography: Sigurdur Sverrir Pálsson

Players: Sigurdur Sigurjónsson, Jón Sigurbjörnsson, Gudny Ragnarsdóttir

A farmer and his son live in a remote valley with their debts and anxieties mounting. When the father dies, his son decides to quit the land of his youth, as well as the girl he has been courting, and sets off for the big city.

Father's Estate
(Odal fedranna)

Year of production: 1979

Production: FILM h/f and Viking Film (Stockholm); 98 mins

Release: May 21, 1980

Screenplay and Direction: Hrafn Gunnlaugsson

Photography: Snorri Thórisson

Players: Jakob Thór Einarsson, Sveinn M. Eidsson, Hólmfridur Thórhallsdóttir, Johann Sigurdsson, Gudrún Thórdardóttir.

A farmer dies, leaving his widow with the management of a farm in the Icelandic countryside. Both the sons have other interests, and when the elder one has an accident, the younger son must try to look after things . . .

Outlaw/The Saga of Gísli
(Útlaginn)

Year of production: 1981

Production: Is-film s/f; 108 mins

Release: October 31, 1981

Screenplay and Direction: Ágúst Gudmundsson, from an Icelandic saga

Photography: Sigurdur Sverrir Pálsson

Players: Arnar Jónsson, Regnheidur Steindórsdóttir, Thráinn Karlsson, Helgi Skúlason, Bjarni Steingrimsson

When Gísli's sworn brother is murdered, Gísli is sure that his brother-in-law is guilty. He slaughters him, and is hunted as an outlaw . . .

Rainbow's End
(Á hjara veraldar)

Year of production: 1982

Production: Völuspá Film Productions; 112 mins

Release: March 2, 1983

Screenplay and Direction: Kristin Jóhannesdóttir

Photography: Karl Oskarsson

Players: Arnar Jónsson, Helga Jónsdóttir, Thóra Fridriksdóttir

A family saga of sorts, drawing on classical Icelandic elements and a satirical view of the modern world. Three members of the same family try to come to terms with their past differences . . .

The House
(Húsid)

Year of production: 1982

Production: Saga Film; 101 mins

Release: March 12, 1983

Direction: Egill Edvardsson

Screenplay: Egill Edvardsson, Björn Björnsson, Snorri Thórisson

Photography: Snorri Thórisson

Players: Lilja Thórisdóttir, Jóhann Sigurdarson, Helgi Skúlason, Thóra Berg, Arni Tryggvason, Borgar Gardarsson

A young couple move into an old house. But the woman especially begins to detect weird sensations in the house itself, as though spirits from the past were pressing on her and her husband, who concentrates more and more on his work as a musician. . . .

The Atomic Station
(Atómstödin)

Year of production: 1983

Production: Ódinn Film Production; 98 mins

Release: March 3, 1984

Direction: Thorsteinn Jónsson

Screenplay: Thorsteinn Jónsson, Thórhallur Sigurdsson, Örnólfur Árnason from the novel by Halldór Laxness

Photography: Karl Oskarsson

Players: Tinna Gunnlaugsdóttir, Gunnar Eyjólfsson, Arni Tryggvason, Arnar Jónsson

An intelligent young country girl comes to postwar Reykjavik and finds work as a maid in a prominent politician's home while she studies music. But her employer is involved in secret negotiations for the establishment of a nuclear base on Iceland . . .

Rainbow's End (1983) by Kristín Jóhannesdóttir

White Whales (1987) by Fridrik Thór Fridriksson

When the Raven Flies
(Hrafninn flýgur)

Year of production: 1983

Production: FILM h/f with Viking Film and Swedish Film Institute (Stockholm); 110 mins

Release: February 4, 1984

Screenplay and Direction: Hrafn Gunnlaugsson

Photography: Tony Forsberg

Players: Jakob Thór Egill Ólafsson, Edda Björgvinsdóttir, Helgi Skúlason, Sveinn M. Eidsson, Flosi Olafsson

Set in the Middle Ages, the film tells the story of Gest, an Irishman who as a child witnessed the murder of his parents by the Vikings and who seeks revenge on Iceland . . .

White Whales
(Skytturnar)

Year of production: 1986

Production: Icelandic Film Corp.; 80 mins

Direction: Fridrik Thór Fridriksson

Screenplay: Einar Kárason, Fridrik Thór Fridriksson

Photography: Ari Kristinsson

Players: Thorarin Thorarinsson, Eggert Gudmundsson

Two friends have been working on board a whale-boat. When they come ashore at the end of the season, they find themselves at a loose end, and also treated with disdain and suspicion by the locals. Provoked, they decide to hit back . . .

Magnús

Year of production: 1989

Production: New Life Productions; 93 mins

Release: August 11, 1989

Screenplay and Direction: Thráinn Bertelsson

Photography: Ari Kristinsson

Players: Egill Ólafsson, Thórhallor Sigúrdsson, Gudrún Gísladóttir, Jón Sigurbjórnsson, Margrét Akadóttir

A press photographer in his early forties suddenly learns that he has cancer. His situation forces him to assess his life and motivations, and he relives some of the special moments in his past, from the sublime to the ridiculous . . .

Children of Nature
(Börn náttúrunnar)

Year of production: 1990

Production: Icelandic Film Corp. Max Film (Berlin)/Metro Film (Oslo); 85 mins

Release: autumn, 1991

Direction: Fridrik Thór Fridriksson

Screenplay: Fridrik Thór Fridriksson, Einar Már Gudmundsson

Photography: Ari Kristinsson

Players: Gîsli Halldórsson, Sigridur Haglin, Egill Olafsson, Tinna Gunnlaugsdóttir, Baldvin Halldórsson, Rúrik Haraldsson, Bruno Ganz, Gudbrandur Gíslason

A robust if truculent pensioner is placed in an old folks' home; there he meets a sweetheart of his vanished youth, and together they escape and head for the countryside they once knew so well . . .

Outlaw (1981) by Ágúst Gudmundsson

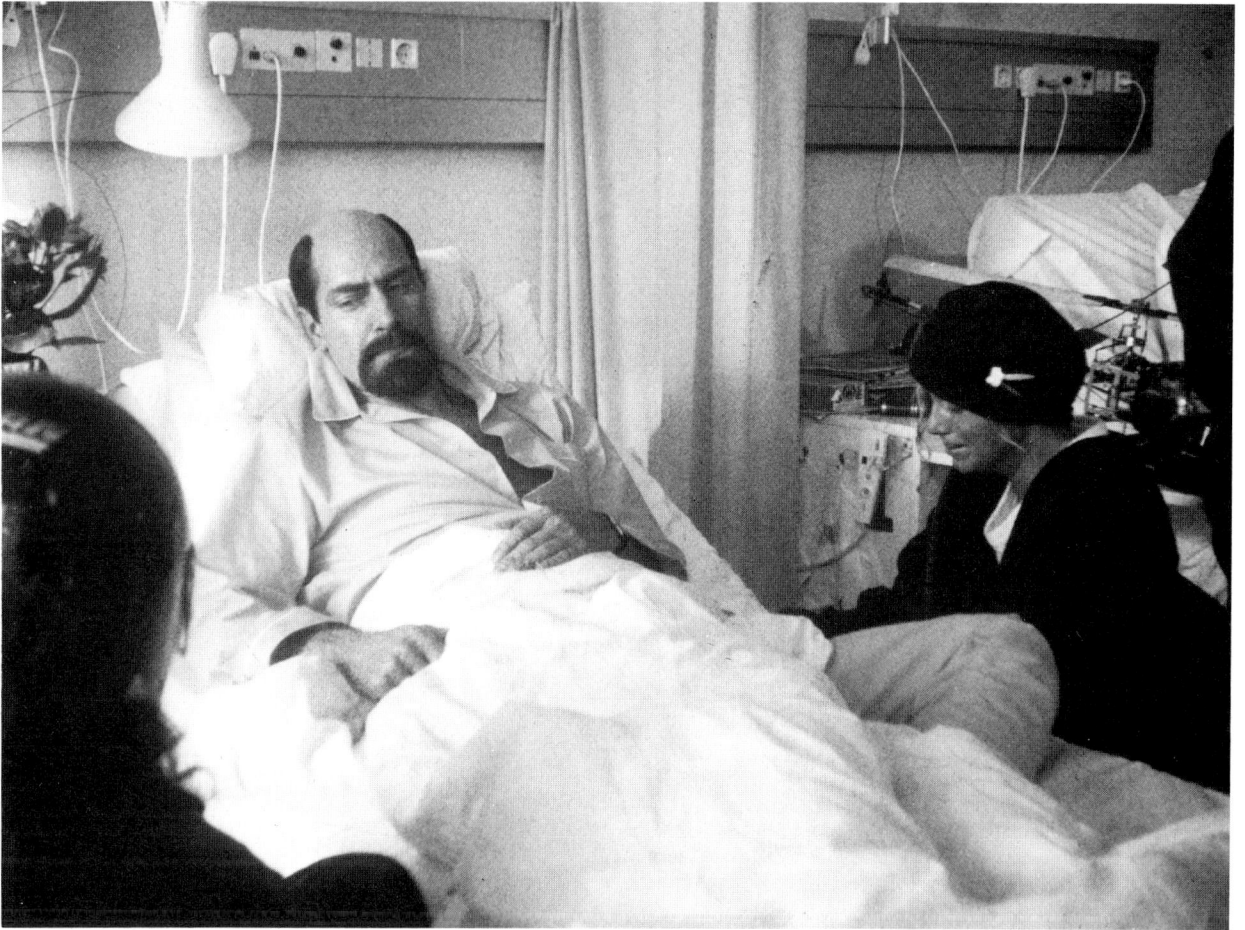

Egill Olafsson in *Magnús* (1989) by Thráinn Bertelsson

Pan (1922) by Harald Schwenzen

NORWAY

Anne, the Gypsy-Girl
(Fante-Anne)

Year of production: 1919

Production: Rasmus Breistein; 93 mins

Release: September 11, 1920 in Oslo

Screenplay and Direction: Rasmus Breistein, from the novel by Kristofer Janson

Photography: Gunnar Nilsen-Vig

Players: Johanne Bruhn, Lars Tvinde, Aasta Nielsen, Einar Tveito

Anne has been abandoned by her real mother on a farm, and grows up with the son of the estate, Halldor. She falls in love with him, but his mother forces him to marry a wealthy neighbour's daughter. Anne sets fire to Halldor's new home, but he is blamed and sent to prison . . .

Pan

Year of production: 1922

Production: Rasmus Breistein; 96 mins

Release: October 16, 1922 in Oslo

Screenplay and Direction: Harald Schwenzen, from the novel by Knut Hamsun

Photography: Johan Ankerstjerne

Players: Hjalmar Fries Schwenzen, Gerd Egede-Nissen, Lillebil Ibsen

During his furlough, Lieutenant Glahn becomes infatuated with Edvarda, but she soon breaks off their relationship. He meets another girl, Eva, but she dies in an accident. The Lieutenant cannot forget his first love . . .

The Magic Elk
(Troll-elgen)

Year of production: 1927

Production: Fürst-Film; 82 mins

Direction: Walter Fürst

Screenplay: Alf Rød, from the novel by Mikkjel Fønhus

Photography: Ragnar Westfelt

Players: Tove Tellback, Bengt Djurberg, Tryggve Larsen

People say that the magic elk is a dead man who returns to life in the guise of an animal. A rich farmer tells Hans that he must kill the magic elk if he wants to marry his daughter, but Hans finds himself caught in a tragic quandary . . .

Fant

Year of production: 1937

Production: Norsk Film A/S; 95 mins

Release: December 26, 1937 in Oslo

Screenplay and Direction: Tancred Ibsen, from the novel by Gabriel Scott

Photography: Adrian Bjurman

Players: Lars Tvinde, Alfred Maurstad, Guri Stormoen, Sonja Wigert

Josefa escapes from her uncle's care and hides in the boat of a gypsy, Fenrik. He forces her to sleep with him and to steal on their behalf. She longs for the return of her fiancé, Oskar, who is at sea, while Fenrik chafes at the absence of his beloved sister, Matilde. When the four of them do encounter one another, there is a tragic dénouement . . .

Gjest Baardsen

Year of production: 1939

Production: Norsk Film A/S; 99 mins

Release: December 26, 1939 in Oslo

Screenplay and Direction: Tancred Ibsen

Photography: Per Gunnar Jonson and Ulf Greber

Players: Alfred Maurstad, Vibeke Falk, Joachim Holst-Jensen

After the war between Sweden and Britain, Norway suffers from heavy state taxes. Gjest escapes from prison and begins to steal on behalf of the poor. He becomes a national hero, and even frees his beloved Anna when she is wrongfully jailed. Eventually he gives himself up to the law . . .

The Defenceless
(De vergeløse)

Year of production: 1939

Production: Merkur Produksjon A/S; 73 mins

Release: September 28, 1939

Screenplay and Direction: Leif Sinding, from the novel by Gabriel Scott

Photography: Per Gunnar Jonson and Ulf Greber

Players: Eva Lunde, Georg Richter, Tryggve Larssen

Albert is one of several children sent to a farm to be brought up, because his mother is a prostitute. He is maltreated by the farmer and his wife; he escapes, but is not punished. Eventually a sailor, father of one of the children, comes to the farm and takes the boys and girls away with him to Oslo to complain to the authorities . . .

Aïtanga, Woman of the Eagles
(Bastard)

Year of production: 1939

Production: Lunde-Film; 87 mins

Release: February 8, 1940

Screenplay and Direction: Helge Lund, from the novel by F.W. Remmler

Photography: Per Gunnar Jonson, Rudolf Frederiksen, Reidar Lund, Adrilan Bjurman, Ulf Greber

Players: Georg Løkkeberg, Signe Hasso, Alfred Maurstad

The Defenceless (1939) by Leif Sinding

Gjest Baardsen (1939) by Tancred Ibsen

Fant (1937) by Tancred Ibsen

We Leave for England (1946) by Toralf Sandø

Aïtanga, Woman of the Eagles (1939) by Helge Lunde

Burtaj is regarded as a bastard because his father married a woman outside his clan. He meets the beautiful Aïtanga, who is pledged to marry the son of a man who, Burtaj does not realise, has murdered his father . . . When Burtaj kills this man in the forest, after he himself has been attacked, he is accused of murder, but Aïtanga frees him and together they escape . . .

We Leave for England
(Englandsfarere)

Year of production: 1946

Production: Snorre Film A/S; 96 mins/117 mins

Release: April 22, 1946

Direction: Toralf Sandø

Screenplay: Victor Borg, Toralf Sandø, from the novel by Sigurd Evensmo

Photography: Per Gunnar Jonson

Players: Knut Wigert, Jørn Ording, Lauritz Falk, Ola Isene, Sigurd Magnussøn, Johannes Eckhoff, Elisabeth Bang, Ingeborg Cook, Lydia Opøien, Elsa Sandø

During the Occupation, seventeen men and a woman are pursued by the Gestapo to the coast. The woman, who is meant to be their guide, cannot locate the boat in which they have planned to cross the North Sea. They are obliged to return to Ålesund, and the Gestapo track them down . . .

The Battle for Heavy Water
(Kampen om tungtvannet)

Year of production: 1947

Production: Hero Film (Oslo)/Le Trident (Paris); 98 mins

Release: February 5, 1948 in Oslo

Direction: Titus Vibe-Müller and Jean Dréville

Screenplay: Jean Marin, Arild Feldborg, and Diana Robertson, based on real events

Photography: Hilding Bladh, Marcel Weiss

Players: Jens Anton Poulsson, Johannes Eckhoff, Arne Kjelstrup, Claus Helberg, Henki Kolstad, Claus Wiese, Knut Kaukelid, Andreas Aabel, Fredrik Kayser, Hans Storhaug, Einar Vaage

This film is a reconstruction of the wartime raid on Norsk Hydro's heavy water plant at Vemork. After an English operation fails to succeed, the Norwegians are brought in to prevent Hitler securing control of the heavy water (and thereby the atom bomb). The action (February 28, 1943) is a triumph . . .

Death is a Caress
(Døden er et kjærtegn)

Year of production: 1949

Production: Carlmar Film A/S; 92 mins

Release: August 29, 1949

Direction: Edith Carlmar, Kåre Bergstrøm (technical adviser)

Screenplay: Otto Carlmar, from the novel by Arve Moen

Photography: Kåre Bergstrøm, Ragnar Sørensen

Players: Claus Wiese, Bjørg Riiser-Larsen, Ingolf Rogde, Einar Vaage

Two young people, Erik and Sonja, meet. She is a wealthy middleclass girl and he a garage mechanic. One evening she brings her car in for repair, and a relationship begins . . . Soon Erik is working less and less and enjoying a more relaxed lifestyle. Sonja gets a divorce and she and Erik live together. But there are increasingly violent rows . . .

Street Urchins
(Gategutter)

Year of production: 1949

Production: Norsk Film A/S; 77 mins

Release: December 26, 1949 in Oslo

Direction: Arne Skouen and Ulf Greber

Screenplay: Arne Skouen, from his own novel

Photography: Ragnar Sørensen

Players: Tom Tellesfen, Ivar Thorkildsen, Pål Bang-Hansen, Svein Byhring, Per Arne Knobelauch

A gang of boys steal some cocoanut from a lorry. One of them is injured, and another is arrested by the police, but refuses to squeal on his friends. The gang gets into further scrapes, and eventually all the boys are dragged off to the police station . . .

Krane's Tea-Shop
(Kranes konditori)

Year of production: 1950

Production: Norsk Film A/S; 103 mins

Release: February 15, 1951 in Oslo

Screenplay and Direction: Astrid Henning-Jensen, from the novel by Cora Sandel

Photography: Arthur J. Ornitz, Per Gunnar Jonson

Players: Rønnaug Alten, Erik Hell, Wenche Foss, Harald Heide Steen, Kolbjørn Buøen, Lydia Opøien, Randi Kolstad, Toralv Maurstad

Katinka lives in a small Norwegian coastal village, and earns a living by making clothes. Her husband is vulgar and condescending, and her children make demands on her. One day Katinka meets a Swedish man at the small café where she sometimes drinks a glass of port to cheer herself up. She wants to run away with him, but the village gossip puts paid to her plans . . .

Nine Lives
(Ni liv)

Year of production: 1957

Production: A/S Nordsjøfilm; 99 mins

Release: October 3, 1957 in Oslo

Screenplay and Direction: Arne Skouen, from the novel by David Howarth

Photography: Ragnar Sørensen

Players: Jack Fjeldstad, Henny Moan, Alf Malland, Joachim Holst-Jensen

In March 1943, eleven Norwegian soldiers make a clandestine landing on the coast of their occupied country. But they have been betrayed and are all killed save one, who makes his way across the snow-covered country towards the Swedish border . . .

A Year with the Lapps
(Same Jakki)

Year of production: 1956

Production: Per Høst Film A/S; 100 mins

Release: March 21, 1957

Screenplay and Direction: Per Høst

Photography: Mattis Mathiesen

Players: Karen Anna Logje, Klemet Veimel, Matti Mikkel Sara, Jon Luoso

The Same people (or Lapps) were without doubt the first inhabitants of Norway. Discoveries made in Troms and Finnmark show these regions to have been inhabited already during the ice age, 12,000 years ago. Per Høst records the daily life of the Lapps over a period of one year.

About Tilla
(Om Tilla)

Year of production: 1963

Production: ARA-Film A/S; 77 mins

Release: September 12, 1953 in Oslo

Screenplay and Direction: Arne Skouen

Photography: Ragnar Sørensen

Players: Eva Henning, Toralv Maurstad, Synne Skouen, Wenche Foss

Tilla has retreated into silence for a year and a half, and her mother, Maria, is becoming as repressed as Tilla. A child psychologist gradually reconstructs the past trauma that has led to their condition . . .

Liv

Year of production: 1966

Production: Ed. Epstein – P.V.L. Produksjon; 88 mins

Release: March 27, 1967 in Oslo

Direction: Pal Løkkeberg

Screenplay: Pal Løkkeberg, Vibeke Løkkeberg, and Sverre Udnæs

Photography: Odd Geir Sæther, Halvor Næss

Players: Vibeke Løkkeberg, Per Theodor Haugen, Bente Børsum

During the course of a day between winter and spring, a beautiful young model undergoes an erotic experience which will change her life . . .

One Day in the Life of Ivan Denisovich
(En dag i Ivan Denisovitsj' liv)

Year of production: 1970

Production: Norsk Film A/S, Group W Films Inc., and Leontes Films Ltd; 105 mins

Release: November 26, 1970

Screenplay and Direction: Casper Wrede, from the novel by Alexander Solzhenitsyn

Photography: Sven Nykvist

Players: Tom Courtenay, Espen Skjønberg, Alf Malland, Frimann Falck Clausen

Condemned to ten years' hard labour for speaking his mind, Ivan is sent to Siberia. Deprived of everything, he manages to retain his self-respect and learns sufficient about men and their ways to survive the terrible conditions . . .

Wives
(Hustruer)

Year of production: 1975

Production: Norsk Film A/S; 84 mins

Release: September 4, 1975 in Oslo (premiered during a week of Norwegian films in London, in June 1975)

Screenplay and Direction: Anja Breien

Photography: Halvor Næss and Nils Raknerud

Players: Anne-Marie Ottersen, Katja Medbøe, Frøydis Armand

Three women get together to celebrate the tenth anniversary of their passing their final exams at school. The celebration lasts three days. After an escapade in Copenhagen, they decide to return to Oslo and their respective husbands.

Next of Kin
(Arven)

Year of production: 1978

Production: Norsk Film A/S; 95 mins

Release: August 13, 1979

Direction: Anja Breien

Screenplay: Anja Breien, Oddvar Bull Tuhus, Lasse Glomm

Photography: Erling Thurmann-Andersen

Players: Espen Skjønberg, Anita Björk, Hæge Juve, Jan Hårstad, Eva Opaker, Jannie Bonnevie, Svein Sturla Hungnes, Jack Fjeldstad, Ada Kramm

A wealthy shipowner dies, leaving his relatives an ostensibly impeccable will, according to the terms of which his vast empire must be administered by a united family. But envy and ambition gradually assert themselves . . .

Death Is a Caress (1949) by Edith Carlmar

One Day in the Life of Ivan Denisovich (1970) by Casper Wrede

Krane's Tea-Shop (1951) by Astrid Henning-Jensen

The Betrayal (1981) by Vibeke Løkkeberg

Northern Lights (1985) by Lasse Glomm

208

The Ice-Palace (1987) by Per Blom

The Women
(Kvinnene)

Year of production: 1979

Production: Marcusfilm A/S; 79 mins

Release: March 8, 1979

Screenplay and Direction: Per Blom

Photography: Odd Geir Saether

Players: Bente Børsum, Anna Godenius, Ivar Nørve, Kaare Kroppen

In the gynaecological section of a hospital, two women share the same room. One has just experienced a still-birth, the other has had her womb removed. Lying in bed, they learn to confront their loneliness and their memories . . .

Growing Up/Little Ida
(Liten Ida)

Year of production: 1980

Production: Norsk Film A/S, Svenska Filminstitutet; 80 mins

Release: March 5, 1981

Screenplay and Direction: Laila Mikkelsen, from the novel by Marit Paulsen (co-screenwriter: Marit Paulsen)

Photography: Hans Welin

Players: Sunniva Lindekleiv, Lise Fjeldstad, Rønnaug Alten, Gunnar Olram

In a small coastal village in the occupied Norway of 1944-45, Ida lives with her brother and her impoverished mother, who has become the mistress of a German officer. When the country is liberated, Ida's mother has her hair shaved, and Ida herself is rejected callously by the local people . . .

The Witch Hunt
(Forfølgelsen)

Year of production: 1981

Production: Norsk Film A/S, Svenska Filminstitutet; 93 mins

Release: August 24, 1981

Screenplay and Direction: Anja Breien

Photography: Erling Thurmann-Andersen

Players: Lil Terselius, Bjørn Skagestad, Anita Björk

Around the year 1625, a stranger comes to look for work in an isolated and mountainous district of western Norway. She soon proves capable of earning her own living and excites the jealousy of the local inhabitants, who accuse her of having supernatural powers. The political and religious authorities in the region mount a case against her, and pursue ''the witch'' . . .

The Betrayal/Kamilla
(Løperjenten)

Year of production: 1981

Production: As Film A/S; 110 mins

Release: August 25, 1981

Screenplay and Direction: Vibeke Løkkeberg

Photography: Paul René Roestad

Players: Nina Knapskog, Kenneth Johansen, Helge Jordal, Vibeke Løkkeberg, Karin Zetlitz Hærem, Renie Torleifsson Kleivdal

A seven-year-old girl, Kamilla, lives with her parents in Bergen just after the end of the Second World War. The father and mother run a shoe shop combined with a laundry, but the father has been involved in some shady dealings with the occupying Germans. One day, an attractive blonde turns up and becomes the father's mistress. Kamilla observes these goings-on and nourishes a budding love for her little cousin, Svein.

Blackout

Year of production: 1985

Production: Norsk Film A/S; 87 mins

Release: February 27, 1986

Direction: Erik Gustavson

Screenplay: Erik Gustavson, Eirik Ildahl

Photography: Kjell Vassdal

Players: Henri Scheele, Elisabeth Sand, Juni Dahr

Werner, a disenchanted private detective, is about to leave for Argentina to start a new life. Then a mysterious woman hires him to find her sister . . .

Orion's Belt
(Orions belte)

Year of production: 1984

Production: Filmeffekt A/S; 103 mins

Release: February 8, 1985 in Oslo

Direction: Ola Solum

Screenplay: Richard Harris, from the novel by Jon Michelet

Photography: Harald Paalgard

Players: Sverre Anker Ousdal, Helge Jordal, Hans Ola Sørlie, Kjersti Holmen

Three Norwegians earn a living by performing dangerous work with their old tug. One day, they discover a Soviet listening post in a remote cavern. They are pursued by a Soviet helicopter gunship. The discovery of the post means a great deal to the Norwegian authorities, but for diplomatic reasons they want to keep the fact secret at all costs . . .

Northern Lights
(Havlandet)

Year of production: 1985

Production: Marcusfilm A/S, Norsk Film A/S, Svensk Filmindustri; 90 mins

Release: September 26, 1985

Direction: Lasse Glomm

Screenplay: Andrew Szepessy, Lasse Glomm, from the novel by Idar Kristiansen

Photography: Erling Thurmann-Andersen

Players: Stein Bjørn, Arja Saijonmaa, Bjørn Sundquist, Sven Wollter, Anitta Suikkari

During the 1860's, Heikki lives with his parents and his sister on a small farm in northern Norway. One day, his uncle Matti arrives, full of stories of the great landscapes of the far north, and the luminous beauty of the night skies. Heikki now has but one goal — to reach this fabled land. He does so, but only after the death of his father and sister. Finally, when he comes to the Arctic Ocean, he meets Anne-Kreeta and a blind old man.

X

Year of production: 1986

Production: A/S Filmgruppe 84, Elinor Film, Christiania Film Companie; 94 mins

Release: August 21, 1986 in Oslo

Screenplay and Direction: Oddvar Einarson

Photography: Svein Krøvel

Players: Jørn Christensen, Bettina Banoun

Jon Gabriel is a young photographer who is successful in work but less so in human relationships. Flora is fourteen, and lives literally on the streets. She has a maturity and strength of character beyond her years. One day, she asks if she can stay with the photographer . . .

Pathfinder
(Ofelaš/Veiviseren)

Year of production: 1987

Production: Filmkameraten A/S, Mayco A/S, Norsk Film A/S, NorWay Film Development Co. A/S; 86 mins

Release: September 30, 1987 in Oslo

Screenplay and Direction: Nils Gaup

Photography: Erling Thurmann-Andersen

Players: Mikkel Gaup, Nils Utsi Jr., Helgi Skúlason

Based on a 12th Century legend, the film begins with a small boy seeing his parents and his sister massacred by marauding tribesmen. He is captured by the intruders, and forced to guide them through the mountains. But he manages to trick them and they plunge to their deaths from a precipitous path . . .

The Ice Palace
(Is-slottet)

Year of production: 1987

Production: Norsk Film A/S; 78 mins

Release: December 26, 1987 in Oslo

Screenplay and Direction: Per Blom, from the novel by Tarjei Vesaas

Photography: Halvor Næss

Players: Line Storesund, Hilde Byeggen Martinsen, Merete Moen, Sigrid Huun, Vidar Sandem, Knut Ørvig, Urda Bratterud Larsen, Charlotte Lundstad

Two eleven-year-old girls are neighbours and close friends. One evening they experience a moment of intense feeling for each other. The next day, Unn is unable to look Siss in the eye and vanishes into a huge house of ice that has formed near the girls' home. Siss cannot find her friend, and takes the entire winter to recover from the experience.

A Handful of Time
(En håndfull tid)

Year of production: 1989

Production: Norsk Film A/S, Svenska Filminstitutet; 97 mins

Release: October 12, 1989 in Oslo

Direction: Martin Asphaug

Screenplay: Erik Borge

Photography: Philip Øgaard

Players: Espen Skjønberg, Camilla Strøm Henriksen, Nicolay Lange-Nielsen, Susannah York, Nigel Hawthorne

The elderly Martin lives in a home for old folk. He has long conversations with his wife Anna, who died while giving birth to their son, Anker, some fifty years earlier. The film follows Martin during some weeks. He escapes from the old folks' home and tries to retrace his past. Gradually the intensity of his love for Anna becomes clearer . . .

Herman
(Herman)

Year of production: 1990

Production: Filmeffekt A/S; 100 mins

Release: September 13, 1990 in Oslo

Direction: Erik Gustavson

Screenplay: Lars Saabye Christensen

Photography: Kjell Vassdal

Players: Anders Danielsen Lie, Elisabeth Sand, Bjørn Floberg, Jarl Kulle, Harald Heide-Steen Jr., Linn Aronsen

The year is 1961, Herman is eleven years old, and suddenly begins to lose his hair. At first he is teased badly in class, but gradually his own laconic humour and gathering maturity enables him to survive this ''cosmetic'' crisis. He comes to terms with the loss of his hair and wins the respect and affection of everyone around him . . .

Hilda Borgström in *Ingeborg Holm* (1913) by Victor Sjöström

SWEDEN

Ingeborg Holm

Year of production: 1913

Production: Svenska Biografteatern; 70 mins

Release: November 3, 1913 in Stockholm

Direction: Victor Sjöström

Screenplay: Nils Krook, from his stage play

Photography: Henrik Jaenzon

Players: Hilda Borgström, Aron Lindgren, Erik Lindholm, Georg Grönroos, William Larson, Richard Lund, Hugo Björne, Bertil Malmstedt

Sven Holm and his wife lead a happy life until one day he becomes ill and dies. Ingeborg tries to keep the family grocery running but does not know the business and is forced to sell her children to pay the debts. Shut up in the poor house, she craves for her children, and eventually escapes in order to see them. Her daughter dies, and Ingeborg Holm is overwhelmed with shock and loss . . .

The Wings
(Vingarne)

Year of production: 1916

Production: Svenska Biografteafern; 40 mins

Release: September 4, 1916

Direction: Mauritz Stiller

Screenplay: Mauritz Stiller, Axel Esbensen, from the novel *Mikaël* by Herman Bang

Photography: J. Julius (pseudonym for Julius Jaenzon)

Players: Egil Eide, Lars Hanson, Lili Bech, Albin Lavén, Bertil Junggren, Julius Häisig, Nils Asther, Mauritz Stiller, Julius Jaenzon

The sculptor Claude Zoret adopts a handsome young model and painter, Mikaël, but when the latter falls in love with his adopted father's companion, the wealthy princess Lucia, tensions emerge. Zoret falls gravely ill.

The Prisoner of Karlsten's Fortress
(Fängen pä Karlstens fängelse)

Year of production: 1916

Production: Hasselbladfilm; 57 mins

Release: November 14, 1916 in Stockholm

Direction: Georg af Klercker

Screenplay: Willy Grebst, Georg af Klercker

Photography: Gösta Stäring

Players: Nils Chrisander, Maja Cassel, Manne Göthson, Arvik Hammarlund

Somewhere in Europe, Count Faber is working on a new kind of explosive. A Swedish professor offers to support him, and Faber leaves for Sweden. On the way he meets the professor's daughter, Mary. The professor tries every means in his skill to pry the secret of the invention from Faber, and then shuts him up in Karsten castle.

Terje Vigen/A Man There Was
(Terje Vigen)

Year of production: 1916

Production: Svenska Biografteatern; 60 mins

Release: January 29, 1917 in Stockholm

Direction: Victor Sjöström

Screenplay: Gustaf Molander, Victor Sjöström, from the poem by Henrik Ibsen

Photography: Julius Jaenzon

Players: Victor Sjöström, Bergliot Husberg, August Falck, Edith Erastoff

During the Napoleonic wars, a Norwegian fisherman runs the blockade of Danish waters to fetch provisions for his ailing family. Betrayed, he is caught and flung into prison. After the war he returns to his village to find that his wife and child have died from hunger. Then, years later, he rescues an English captain from a storm; the man is the one who arrested him so long ago. . . .

Thomas Graal's Best Film
(Thomas Graals bästa film)

Year of production: 1917

Production: Svenska Biografteatern; 60 mins

Release: August 13, 1917

Direction: Mauritz Stiller

Screenplay: Harald B. Harald (pseudonym for Gustaf Molander)

Photography: Henrik Jaenzon

Players: Victor Sjöström, Karin Molander, Albin Lavén, Jenny Tschernichin-Larsson, Axel Nilsson, Adolf Blomstedt, William Larsson, Gucken Cederborg, Emil Fjellström

A young writer is at work on a screenplay, but finds that the ideas are slow in coming. When he hires a new secretary, he tries to kiss her and she runs off in a huff. Inspired by the incident, he writes an excellent screenplay . . .

The Outlaw and His Wife
(Berg-Ejvind och hans hustru)

Year of production: 1917

Production: Svenska Biografteatern; 73 mins

Release: January 1, 1918 in Stockholm

Victor Sjöström in his own *The Outlaw and His Wife* (1918)

Victor Sjöström in his own *Terje Vigen* (1916)

Direction: Victor Sjöström, Sam Ask from the novel by Johan Sigurjónsson

Photography: Julius Jaenzon

Players: Victor Sjöström, Edith Erastoff, John Ekman, Nils Arehn, Artur Rolén, Jenny Tschernichin-Larsson, William Larsson

During the 19th century, a widowed farmer runs her domain with an iron hand. One day a stranger named Kari arrives at the farm. The two fall in love, and it transpires that Kari is on the run for stealing a sheep. Pursued by the authorities, the lovers quit the farm and make their way higher and higher into the mountains, resolved to preserve their love against the disapproval of society.

The Sons of Ingmar
(Ingmarssönerna)

Year of production: 1918

Production: Svenska Biografteatern; 80 mins

Release: January 1, 1919 in Stockholm

Screenplay and Direction: Victor Sjöström, from the first part of *Jerusalem*, by Selma Lagerlöf

Photography: Julius Jaenzon

Players: Victor Sjöström, Harriet Bosse, Tore Svennberg, Hildur Carlberg, Hjalmar Peters, Gustaf Ranft, William Iwarson, William Högstedt, Jenny Tschernichin-Larsson, Axel Nilsson, Emil Bergendorff, Margit Sjöblom, Elsa Christiernson, Sigurd Wallén, Edith Wallén

A peasant farmer decides one day to consult his ancestors about life, and erects an enormous ladder so that he can clamber up to Heaven. But his adventure leads to his reliving his checkered youth, with marital problems that eventually persuade him to start afresh.

The Song of the Scarlet Flower
(Sången om den eldröda blomman)

Year of production: 1919

Production: Svenska Biografteatern; 100 mins

Release: April 14, 1919 in Stockholm

Direction: Mauritz Stiller

Screenplay: Mauritz Stiller, Harald B. Harald (pseudonym for Gustaf Molander), from the novel by Johannes Linnankoski

Photography: Ragnar Westfelt and Henrik Jaenzon

Players: Lars hanson, Axel Hultman, Louise Fahlman, Greta Almroth, Lillebil Christensen, Edith Erastoff, Doris Nelson, Hjalmar Peters

A farmer's son, Olof, leaves the family home in order to come to terms with himself. He takes different kinds of work, but especially log-rolling. He attracts young women with ease, but does not get involved with any of them. Finally he persuades Kyllikki, his real sweetheart, to accept the fact that he has mended his ways and can commit himself to love . . .

Sir Arne's Treasure
(Herr Arnes pengar)

Year of production: 1919

Production: Svenska Biografteatern; 109 mins

Release: September 22, 1919 in Stockholm

Direction: Mauritz Stiller

Screenplay: Mauritz Stiller, Gustaf Molander, from the novel by Selma Lagerlöf

Photography: J. Julius (pseudonym for Julius Jaenzon) and Gustaf Boge

Players: Richard Lund, Hjalmar Selander, Concordia Selander, Mary Johnson, Wanda Rothgardt, Axel Nilsson, Jenny Ohrström Ebbesen, Erik Stocklassa, Bror Berger, Gustav Aronson, Stina Berg, Gösta Gustafson

During the 16th century, three Scottish mercenaries try to flee from Sweden after their leaders have been rounded up. Ice around the tiny port of Marstrand forces the three men to delay their escape, and in a fury they burn down the mansion of Sir Arne. The only survivor of this raid is the young Elsalill, who has witnessed the murder of her sister. One of the mercenaries, Sir Archie, falls in love with her, but is obliged to use her as a human shield against Swedish troops when they attack.

Johan

Year of production: 1920

Production: Svenska Biografteatern; 84 mins

Release: February 28, 1921 in Stockholm

Direction: Mauritz Stiller

Screenplay: Mauritz Stiller, Arthur Nordén, from the novel by Juhani Aho

Photography: Henrik Jaenzon

Players: Mathias Taube, Jenny Hasselquist, Urho Somersalmi, Hildegard Harring, Lilly Berg

Johan lives in a remote farm and is dominated by his mother. Yet he succeeds in marrying Marit against her wishes. Their life seems idyllic when suddenly a stranger, Vallavan, arrives at the farm, and Marit falls under his spell. She flees with Vallavan down the river and through the rapids, pursued by Johan. After a struggle between the two men, Marit is overcome with remorse, and returns to the farm with her husband.

The Phantom Carriage/Thy Soul Shall Bear Witness
(Körkarlen)

Year of production: 1920

Production: Svensk Filmindustri; 93 mins

Release: January 1, 1921 in Stockholm

Screenplay and Direction: Victor Sjöström, from the novel by Selma Lagerlöf

Photography: Julius Jaenzon

Players: Victor Sjöström, Hilda Borgström, Tore Svennberg, Astrid Holm, Lisa Lundholm, Tor Weijden, Concordia Selander, Einar Axelsson, Nils Arehn, Simon Lindstrand, Nils Elffors, Olof Ås, Algot Gunnarsson, Hildur Lithman, John Ekman, Josua Bengtsson, Emmy Albiin, Mona Geijer Falkner, Anna Lisa Baude

David Holm is drunk on New Year's Eve. Set upon in a graveyard by other tramps, he is left for dead, but arises from his corpse to live out the legend of the man who dies on the stroke of midnight on December 31 and must roam the world gathering up the souls of sinners. Holm relives his checkered past, in particular his cruelty and insensitivity towards those he has loved, due in part to his dependence on liquor. At the last moment, just as his wife is about to commit suicide, Holm awakes from his nightmare and rushes home to save the situation. . . .

Erotikon/Just Like a Man
(Erotikon)

Year of production: 1920

Production: Svensk Filmindustri; 81 mins

Release: November 8, 1920 in Stockholm

Direction: Mauritz Stiller

Screenplay: Stiller & Co (pseudonym for Mauritz Stiller and Arthur Nordén), from the novel by Ferenc Herczeg

Photography: Henrik Jaenzon

Players: Anders de Wahl, Tora Teje, Karin Molander, Elin Lagergren, Lars Hanson, Vilhelm Bryde, Bell Hedqvist, Torsten Hammarén

Professor Charpentier, an entomologist, devotes more time to his studies than to his charming wife, Irene, who flirts with Baron Felix while at the same time nourishing a secret infatuation for a sculptor named Preben. Preben tries to provoke a duel between the baron and the professor, but desists when he realises that Irene has in fact been faithful to her husband. Irene promptly seeks a divorce so that she can marry Preben.

Wild Bird
(En vildfågel)

Year of production: 1921

Production: Svensk Filmindustri; 85 mins

Release: October 3, 1921

Direction: John W. Brunius

Screenplay: John W. Brunius, Sam Ask, from the novel by Samuel A. Duse

Photography: Hugo Edlund

Players: Paul Seelig, Pauline Brunius, Tore Svennberg, Renée Björling, Jenny Tschernichin-Larsson, Nils Lundell, Edwin Adolphson

The injured Paul Henning is cared for by an old lady, Hanna. She believes his name to be Holger Wall, and that he is the illegitimate son of Berta Brenner, since married to Consul Brenner, who knows nothing of this skeleton in his wife's past. Berta Brenner takes the sick man under her wing, he falls in love with her daughter, and things get complicated. . . .

Witchcraft through the Ages
(Häxan)

Year of production: 1922

Production: Svensk Filmindustri; 90 mins

Release: September 18, 1922 in Stockholm. November 7, 1922 in Copenhagen

Screenplay and Direction: Benjamin Christensen

Photography: Johan Ankerstjerne

Players: Benjamin Christensen, Elisabeth Christensen, Astrid Holm, Karen Winther, Maren Pedersen, Ella La Cour, Emmy Schenfeld, Kate Fabian, Oscar Striholt, Clara Pontoppidan, Elsa Vermehren, Alice O'Fredericks, Johannes Anderssen, Aage Hertel, Wilhemine Henriksen, Elith Pio, Ib Schenberg, Holst Jørgensen, Herre Westermann, Gerda Madsen, Carina Bell, Tora Teje, Poul Reumert, H.C. Bilssen, Albrecht Schmidt

Blending documentary and fiction, this film analyses the attitude of medieval man towards witches and the supernatural, spicing its observations with some contemporary references.

Gunnar Hede's Saga/The Blizzard
(Gunnar Hedes saga)

Year of production: 1922

Production: Svensk Filmindustri; 70 mins

Release: January 1, 1923

Direction: Mauritz Stiller

Screenplay: Mauritz Stiller, Alma Söderhjelm, from the novel by Selma Lagerlöf

Photography: J. Julius (pseudonym for Julius Jaenzon)

Players: Einar Hansson, Pauline Brunius, Hugo Björne, Mary Johnson, Adolf Olchansky, Stina Berg, Thecla Ahlander, Gösta Hillberg

Gunnar Hede is a young aristocrat dominated by his mother on their ancestral estate. He falls in love with Ingrid, the daughter of two travelling entertainers, and gets it into his head to go off to northern Sweden and bring back to the manor a herd of reindeer. But during the round up, Gunnar Hede attaches the reins of the head reindeer to his belt, and is dragged through the snow by the beast, and badly injured, losing his reason.

The Norrtull Gang
(Norrtullsligan)

Year of production: 1923

Production: Bonnierfilm; 90 mins

Release: December 26, 1923

Direction: Per Lindberg

Screenplay: Hjalmar bergman, from the play by Elin Wägner

Photography: Ragnar Westfelt

The Song of the Scarlet Flower (1919) by Mauritz Stiller

Johan (1920) by Mauritz Stiller

Erotikon (1920) by Mauritz Stiller

Mary Johnson and Richard Lund in *Sir Arne's Treasure* (1919) by Mauritz Stiller

The Norrtull Gang (1923) by Per Lindberg

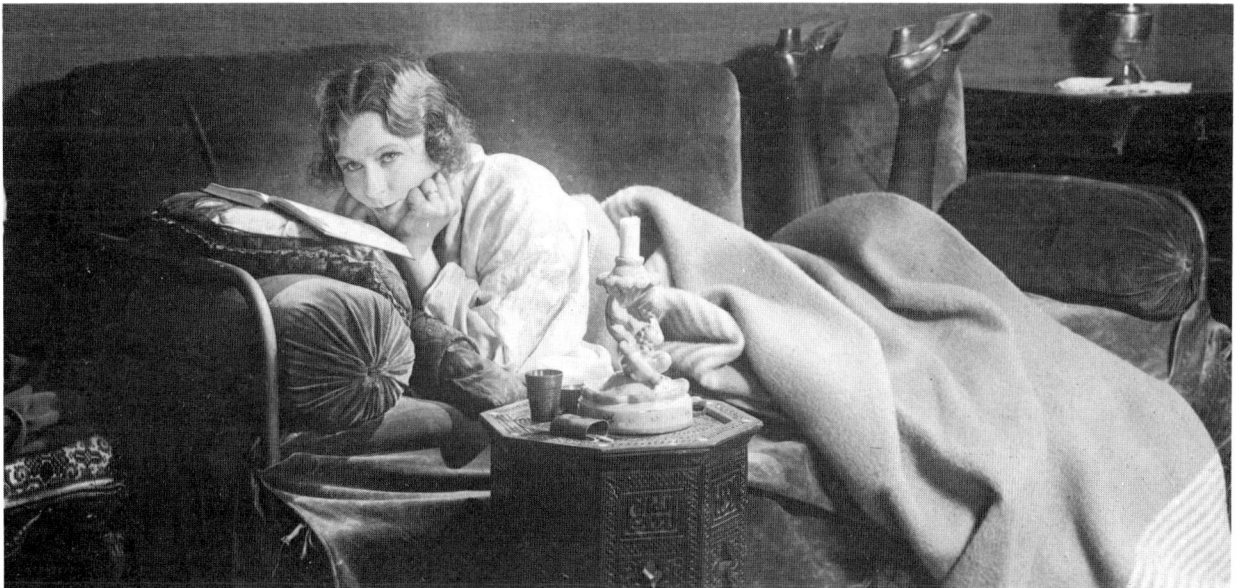

Mai Zetterling in *Frenzy* (1944) by Alf Sjöberg

Iris and the Lieutenant (1946) by Alf Sjöberg

Greta Garbo in *The Atonement of Gösta Berling* (1924) by Mauritz Stiller

Ingrid Bergman and Gösta Ekman in *Intermezzo* (1936) by Gustaf Molander

Players: Tora Teje, Inga Tidblad, Renée Björling, Linnéa Hillberg, Egil Eide, Tollie Zellman, Olav Riégo, Stina Berg, Lili Diedner, Lauritz Falk

Pegg comes to live and work in Stockholm. She shares an apartment with her little brother, Putte. She runs into the "Norrtull gang", composed of three irresponsible young women. Pegg's boss is infatuated with her, but are his intentions honourable?

The Atonement of Gösta Berling/
The Legend of Gösta Berling
(Gösta Berlings saga)

Year of production: 1923

Production: Svensk Filmindustri; 175 mins (both parts)

Release: March 9, 1924 (Part I), March 17, 1924 (Part II) in Stockholm

Direction: Mauritz Stiller

Screenplay: Mauritz Stiller, Ragnar Hyltén-Cavallius, from the novel by Selma Lagerlöf

Photography: J. Julius (pseudonym for Julius Jaenzon)

Players: Lars Hanson, Gerda Lundequist, Hilda Forsslund, Otto Elg-Lundberg, Sixten Malmerfelt, Karin Swanström, Jenny Hasselquist, Ellen Cederström, Torsten Hammarén, Mona Mårtenson, Greta Garbo

Gösta Berling, a defrocked priest, must look after the young Ebba Dohna. Her mother believes him to be a good man despite his past, and concocts a scheme, exploiting her daughter-in-law Elisabeth, whereby he will end up marrying Ebba. Gösta escapes to the neighbouring castle of Ekeby, but is soon involved in a new emotional imbroglio, which nearly turns to tragedy when one of the residents of Ekeby, Margaretha, sets fire to the castle.

His English Wife
(Hans engelska fru)

Year of production: 1926

Production: Isepa (Sweden)/Wengeroff (Germany); 90 mins

Release: January 17, 1927 in Stockholm

Direction: Gustaf Molander

Screenplay: Paul Merzbach

Photography: J. Julius (pseudonym for Julius Jaenzon), Åke Dahlqvist

Players: Lil Dagover, Urho Somersalmi, Gösta Ekman, Karin Swanström, Håkan Westergren, Brita Appelgren, Stina Berg

The young widow Cathleen Paget, daughter of wealthy English parents, wants to remarry with Ivor Willington, who is more interested in his inheritance than he is in her. Cathleen's brother has frittered away the family fortune, and urges her (with their mother's agreement) to marry their biggest creditor, the Swedish industrialist Birger Holm. But nobody knows what he looks like and so when Holm himself rescues Cathleen from some rapids during her first trip to Sweden, she falls for his charms in all innocence. They marry, but life in northern Sweden proves boring, and Cathleen hankers after the bright lights of London.

The Strongest
(Den starkaste)

Year of production: 1929

Production: Svensk Filmindustri; 95 mins

Release: October 28, 1929

Direction: Alf Sjöberg

Screenplay: Axel Lindblom

Photography: Axel Lindblom

Players: Bengt Djurberg, Anders Henrikson, Gösta Gustafsson, Gun Holmquist, Hjalmar Peters, Maria Röhr

Gustaf is a young unemployed sailor who takes some seasonal work at a farm. He is soon fascinated by the daughter of the house, but she is already engaged to Ole, the second son of the old sea-dog who owns the farm and other properties. Gustaf, however, proves himself a worthy suitor during a crisis in the icy seas when he goes north on a hunting expedition.

Intermezzo

Year of production: 1936

Production: Svensk Filmindustri

Release: November 16, 1936

Direction: Gustaf Molander

Screenplay: Gustaf Molander, Gösta Stevens

Photography: Åke Dahlqvist

Players: Gösta Ekman, Inga Tidblad, Ingrid Bergman, Hasse Ekman, Britt Hagman, Erik "Bullen" Berglund, Hugo Björne, Emma Meissner

After two years touring abroad, the violinist Holger Brandt comes home to his wife and children. The wife does not want to accompany him on his forthcoming tour of Russia, and prefers to stay with their son and daughter. The daughter's piano teacher, Anita Hoffman, catches the maestro's fancy, and soon they are infatuated with each other. They spend an idyllic holiday in the Austrian Tirol, but Anita learns that she has been offered a scholarship at the Swedish Music Academy. They both realise that Holger will return to his family.

Frenzy/Torment
(Hets)

Year of production: 1944

Production: Svensk Filmindustri;   mins

Release: October 2, 1944 in Stockholm

Direction: Alf Sjöberg

Screenplay: Ingmar Bergman

Photography: Martin Bodin

Players: Stig Järrel, Alf Kjellin, Mai Zetterling, Olof Winnerstrand, Gösta Cederlund, Stig Olin, Jan Molander, Olav Riégo

Jan-Erik is in his last year at high school in Stockholm. One of his teachers, nicknamed Caligula, likes to humiliate him in front of the class. Jan-Erik meets Berta in a tobacconist's, and later in the street, where she is drunk and depressed. She takes him home to her apartment, and they spend the night together. She tells him she is frightened of a sinister man who follows her regularly. One day, Jan-Erik finds Berta dead in her room, and comes upon Caligula lurking in the shadows of the staircase. Clearly he has killed Berta, but the autopsy shows her to have died from cardiac arrest, and Caligula is let free, enabling him to fail Jan-Erik in his exams.

Iris and the Lieutenant
(Iris och löjtnantshjärta)

Year of production: 1946

Production: Svensk Filmindustri; 86 mins

Release: December 16, 1946

Screenplay and Direction: Alf Sjöberg, from the novel by Olle Hedberg

Photography: Gösta Roosling

Players: Mai Zetterling, Alf Kjellin, Holger Löwenadler, Ingrid Borthen, Åke Claesson, Margaretha Fahlén, Einar Axelsson, Stig Järrel

A rich young officer, Robert, falls in love with a housemaid, Iris. He wants to marry her instead of the wealthy heiress handpicked by his father. There is a row, and Robert and Iris go off to live in a studio together. Just after Robert resigns from the army in order to marry, he is killed in an accident. Iris returns to her job and decides to raise the child she is expecting by Robert. . . .

Girl with Hyacinths
(Flicka och hyacinter)

Year of production: 1949

Production: Terraproduktion; 85 mins

Release: March 6, 1950 in Stockholm

Screenplay and Direction: Hasse Ekman

Photography: Göran Strindberg

Players: Eva Henning, Ulf Palme, Birgit Tengroth, Anders Ek, Marianne Löfgren, Gösta Cederlund, Karl-Arne Holmsten, Keve Hjelm, Anne-Marie Brunius

After a party, Dagmar Brink commits suicide. A writer, Anders Wikner, decides to find out the truth behind the tragedy. An enigmatic picture emerges. Dagmar had been married for four years, but had divorced because of her husband's jealousy of her affair with a certain "Alex". She lived for some time with a drunken artist, and posed for a portrait by him. She also had a relationship with a singer, who claims that he was the cause of her suicide. But finally it is the writer's wife who solves the mystery: Alex was not a man . . .

Miss Julie
(Fröken Julie)

Year of production: 1950

Production: Sandrewproduktion; 88 mins

Release: April 6, 1951 in Cannes; June 28, 1951 in Paris; July 30, 1951 in Stockholm

Screenplay and Direction: Alf Sjöberg

Photography: Göran Strindberg

Players: Anita Björk, Ulf Palme, Märta Doff, Anders Henrikson, Lissi Åland, Inger Nordberg, Jan Hagerman, Kurt-Olof Sundström, Max von Sydow

The young countess Julie has had an unstable childhood, torn between a weak, degenerate father and a mother from the lower classes who hovers on the verge of insanity. One Midsummer's Eve, Julie, who has just broken off her engagement, gives herself to the family valet, Jean (who has yearned for her since childhood). But as dawn breaks, they lack the courage to flee together, and Julie kills herself to escape the wrath of her father . . .

The Great Adventure
(Det stora äventyret)

Year of production: 1952

Production: Arne Sucksdorff; 73 mins

Release: August 19, 1953

Direction and Screenplay: Arne Sucksdorff

Photography: Arne Sucksdorff

Players: Anders Nohrberg, Kjell Sucksdorff, Sigvard Kihlgren, Holger Stockman, Arne Sucksdorff

Anders and Kjell are the sons of a farmer in central Sweden. Each new season brings a changing landscape. The wild animals fight for survival in the woods near the farm. One winter, the boys capture an otter, and keep her in a cage in the farm buildings. They tame her and feed her in secret. But when spring comes, and they let the otter swim in the lake, she eludes them, and they are miserable as the rest of the farm workers celebrate the onset of summer . . .

Raven's End
(Kvarteret korpen)

Year of production: 1963

Production: Europa Film; 100 mins

Release: December 26, 1963

Screenplay and Direction: Bo Widerberg

Photography: Jan Lindeström

Players: Thommy Berggren, Keve Hjelm, Emy Storm, Christina Främback

It is 1936, and the social democratic era is beginning in Sweden. Unemployment is rife among the working quarters, while Hitler rants over the radio. Anders is a young factory worker with aspirations as a novelist. His father, a failed underwear salesman, steeps himself in alcohol in an effort to sustain his dreams of better circumstances. His mother does scrubbing and washing to bolster the family income. Anders is encouraged by an invitation to meet a Stockholm publisher; but his first novel is rejected. He becomes involved with a local girl and she soon becomes pregnant. Spurred by the prospect of a horrible marriage, Anders makes up his mind to leave "Raven's End."

Loving Couples
(Älskande par)

Year of production: 1964

Production: Sandrews; 118 mins

Release: December 21, 1964

Direction: Mai Zetterling

Screenplay: Mai Zetterling, David Hughes, from the novels by Agnes von Krusenstjerna

Photography: Sven Nykvist

Players: Harriet Andersson, Gunnel Lindblom, Gio Petré, Anita Björk, Gunnar Björnstrand, Jan Malmsjö, Heinz Hopf, Eva Dahlbeck, Anja Boman, Frank Sundström, Hans Strååt, Inga Landgré

Stockholm, 1915. The Great War has just broken out. At a clinic where they are expecting their babies, three women recall the key events in their lives. For Angela, everything began with the burial of her mother and the family's deciding her future. For Adèle, it was the death of her father which forced her to start work at an early age. For Agda, it was her encounter with a man who offered her cakes if she would come to his room . . .

Love 65
(Kärlek 65)

Year of production: 1964

Production: Europa Film; 96 mins

Release: March 17, 1965 in Stockholm

Screenplay and Direction: Bo Widerberg

Photography: Jan Lindeström

Players: Keve Hjelm, Inger Taube, Björn Gustafson, Evabritt Strandberg, Ann-Marie Gyllenspetz, Kent Andersson, Nina Widerberg, Ben Carruthers, Thommy Berggren, Agneta Ekmanner

Keve is a film director, and tries to replicate his private life in his films − a life full of ups and downs, love and despair, humour and bitterness. Frustrated, he is briefly stimulated by an affair with Evabritt, the wife of a conference organiser. Keve and his wife Ann-Marie have a small daughter, Nina, and she alone offers some optimism and assurance for the future . . .

Here Is Your Life
(Här har du ditt liv)

Year of production: 1966

Production: Svensk Filmindustri; 150 mins

Release: December 26, 1966

Direction: Jan Troell

Screenplay: Bengt Forslund, Jan Troell, from the novels by Eyvind Johnson

Photography: Jan Troell

Players: Eddie Axberg, Gudrun Brost, Bo Wahlström, Ulla Akselson, Holger Löwenadler, Allan Edwall, Anna Maria Blind, Max von Sydow, Ulf Palme, Jan-Erik Lindqvist, Gunnar Björnstrand, Åke Fridell, Ulla Sjöblom, Friedrich Ochsner, Per Oscarsson, Bengt Ekerot

It is 1914, in Norrbotten, in northern Sweden. Olof is fourteen and leaves his foster mother in order to learn a trade. He gets his first job as a log floater. Later he is taken on at a brickworks and then a sawmill. In the spring of 1916, he is given a post as a bill sticker and sweet seller at a cinema in Boden. Soon he is promoted to be projectionist, and travels round the country from one summer fair to another. He becomes attracted to socialist ideals, and also to a lusty, older woman, Olivia, "Queen of the Rifle Range". A rolling stone, he gets a job next on the railways, is involved in the staging of a strike which fails, and sets off towards the south, dillusioned but unbowed . . .

Who Saw Him Die?
(Ole dole doff)

Year of production: 1967

Production: Svensk Filmindustri; 110 mins

Release: March 18, 1968 in Malmö

Direction: Jan Troell

Screenplay: Bengt Forslund, Jan Troell, and Clas Engström, from the novel by Engström

Photography: Jan Troell

Players: Per Oscarsson, Ann-Marie Gyllenspetz, Kerstin Tidelius, Bengt Ekerot, Harriet Forsell, Per Sjöstrand, Georg Oddner

Mårtensson is a schoolteacher in Malmö, and tries in vain to control the children in his class. He cannot communicate with them, and is teased unmercifully. At home, he sits listening to music over his headphones, and enjoys no real intimacy with his wife. One day, during a school outing in the woods, he strikes up an unexpected friendship with a bright and open colleague, Anne-Marie . . .

The Girls
(Flickorna)

Year of production: 1968

Production: Sandrews; 95 mins

Release: September 16, 1968

Direction: Mai Zetterling

Screenplay: Mai Zetterling, David Hughes

Photography: Rune Ericson

Players: Bibi Andersson, Harriet Andersson, Gunnel Lindblom, Gunnar Björnstrand, Erland Josephson, Frank Sundström, Åke Lindström, Stig Engström

A theatre company is touring the Swedish provinces with a production of Aristophanes's *Lysistrata*. There are three actresses in the play, and three in the film, different and yet complementary to one another on stage and in private life. The rebellious tone and feminist undercurrent of the play stir the three actresses to react against their circumstances, each in a different manner . . .

Ådalen 31/The Ådalen Riots
(Ådalen 31)

Year of production: 1968

Production: Svensk Filmindustri; 105 mins

Release: May 1, 1969

Screenplay and Direction: Bo Widerberg

Photography: Jörgen Persson

Players: Peter Schildt, Kerstin Tidelius, Roland Hedlund, Marie de Geer, Anita Björk, Olof Bergström, Jonas Bergström, Tommy Holmström

In the course of a countrywide strike in 1931, the northern area of Sweden around Ådalen was paralysed. The factory-owners tried to get black labour to keep the machines running, but this resulted in demonstrations, confrontations, and finally bloodshed . . . Widerberg's film is a docudrama inspired by these events.

The Assault
(Misshandlingen)

Year of production: 1969

Production: Lasse Forsberg Produktion

Release: November 6, 1969

Screenplay and Direction: Lasse Forsberg

Photography: Lasse Forsberg

Players: Knut Petersen, Björn Granath, Berit Persson, Stig Billberg, Dr. Tom Fahlén, Barbro Printz-Bräcklund

Knut is a young worker with radical views. After a scuffle in the street with the owner of a luxury car, he comes up against Swedish justice. Knut is not really violent, but cannot compromise with the "system" under which he is supposed to live. Finally, when all attempts at remedial care have failed, he is forced into a strait-jacket . . .

Like Night and Day
(Som natt och dag)

Year of production: 1968

Production: Sandrews; 103 mins

Release: February 13, 1969 in Stockholm

Screenplay and Direction: Jonas Cornell

Photography: Lars Swanberg

Players: Agneta Ekmanner, Gösta Ekman, Keve Hjelm, Claire Wikholm

Four well-off characters in the Sweden of the late 1960's find their paths interweaving . . . One is a chic TV announcer, another a distinguished surgeon. But envy and emotional jealousy conspire to undermine the decorative surface of their lives. . . .

Harry Munter
(Harry Munter)

Year of production: 1969

Production: Sandrews; 101 mins

Release: December 20, 1969 in Stockholm

Screenplay and Direction: Kjell Grede

Photography: Lars Björne

Players: Jan Nielsen, Carl-Gustaf Lindstedt, Gun Jönsson, Elina Salo, Georg Adelly, Gerda Calander, Märta Allan-Johnson

A poetic young man whose gifts as an inventor win him a trip to the United States finds it hard to come to terms with the adult world. He refuses the holiday, believing that he should serve those in need of him, and he surrounds himself with offbeat and pathetic characters . . .

The Father
(Fadern)

Year of production: 1969

Production: Svenska Filminstitutet, Sveriges Radio; 98 mins

Release: October 6, 1969

Screenplay and Direction: Alf Sjöberg, from the play by Strindberg

Photography: Lasse Björne

Players: Georg Rydeberg, Gunnel Lindblom, Lena Nyman, Sif Ruud, Jan-Olof Strandberg, Tord Stål, Axel Düberg, Aino Taube

Like the play, the film of Strindberg's *The Father* tells the story of a couple whose only daughter is used like a weapon in the battle between them. The husband is a soldier and scientist, and represents the patriarchal society found in Sweden at the turn of the century. But the wife, although weaker, gradually exerts control over her husband by implying that he is not the father of her child. The "father" drifts inexorably into madness . . .

You're Lying
(Ni ljuger)

Year of production: 1969

Production: Sandrews; 106 mins

Release: October 27, 1969 in Stockholm

Screenplay and Direction: Vilgot Sjöman

Photography: Olle Ohlsson

Players: Stig Engström, Börje Ahlstedt, Sif Ruud, Anita Ekström

Although the last execution in Sweden took place in 1910, and although the prison conditions are regarded as almost ideal in Sweden, this docudrama claims that the penal system still has grave flaws in it, and traces the fate of one particular prisoner both in confinement and on the outside . . .

A Swedish Love Story
(En kärlekshistoria)

Year of production: 1969

Production: Europa Film; 126 mins

Release: April 24, 1970

Screenplay and Direction: Roy Andersson

Photography: Jörgen Persson

Players: Rolf Sohlman, Anne-Sofie Kylin, Bertil Norström, Margreth Weivers, Lennart Tellfeldt, Gunnar Ossiander, Anita Lindblom

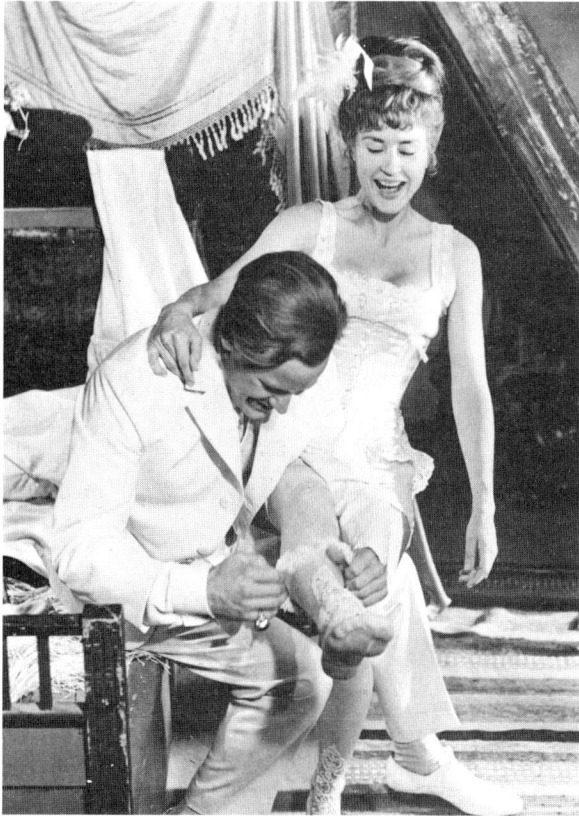

Loving Couples (1964) by Mai Zetterling

Harry Munter (1969) by Kjell Grede

Love 65 (1965) by Bo Widerberg

A Swedish Love Story (1970) by Roy Andersson

Giliap (1975) by Roy Andersson

Our Life is Now (1982) by Suzanne Osten

Two youngsters, Annika (aged 13), and Per (15), meet one day and fall in love, each for the first time. During a long summer, they get to know each other and themselves, and discover the meaning of sensitivity and tenderness . . .

Giliap
(Giliap)

Year of production: 1975

Production: Sandrews; 137 mins

Release: November 16, 1975 in Stockholm

Screenplay and Direction: Roy Andersson

Photography: John Olsson

Players: Thommy Berggren, Mona Seilitz, Willie Andréason, Lars-Levi Læstadius

In a small Swedish town, at the Hotel Busarewski, works a man known as ''The Count'', who dreams of founding a gangster organisation. Anna, the pretty waitress, works in the same hotel but is eager to leave and pursue her life elsewhere. Then a new waiter arrives, a stranger in the town and someone who also wants to get away from it all . . .

Hallo Baby
(Hallo Baby)

Year of production: 1975

Production: Svenska Filminstitutet, Sandrews; 105 mins

Release: January 28, 1976 in Stockholm

Direction: Johan Bergenstråhle

Screenplay: Marie-Louise de Geer Bergenstråhle, Johan Bergenstråhle

Photography: Staffan Lamm

Players: Marie-Louise de Geer Bergenstråhle, Toivo Pawlo, Siv Ericks, Håkan Serner, Keve Hjelm

A violently authentic and humourous description of the life of a woman painter. She is a young woman in search of her own identity, working among the actors and artists of Stockholm during the 1960s.

Near and Far Away
(Långt borta och nära)

Year of production: 1976

Production: Svensk Filminstitutet; 98 mins

Release: November 8, 1976 in Stockholm

Direction: Marianne Ahrne

Screenplay: Marianne Ahrne, Bertrand Hurault

Photography: Hans Welin

Players: Lilga Kovanko, Robert Farrant, Annicka Kronberg, Helge Skoog, Jan-Erik Lidqvist, Bodil Mårtensson, Bengt C.W. Carlsson, Tom Deutgen, Jan Nielsen, Mimi Pollak, Owe Stefanson, Rolf Skoglund

A young woman begins working at a psychiatric institution. Soon she is taking a keen interest in one of the patients, a man suffering from mutism. She also finds herself confronted with two kinds of doctor, one who believes that all patients are simply medical cases, the other for whom the understanding of each personality is vital.

Paradise Place
(Paradistorg)

Year of production: 1976

Production: Cinematograph AB, Svenska Filminstitutet, Svensk Filmindustri; 113 mins

Release: February 18, 1977 in Stockholm

Direction: Gunnel Lindblom

Screenplay: Ulla Isaksson, Gunnel Lindblom, from the story by Isaksson

Photography: Tony Forsberg

Players: Birgitta Valberg, Sif Ruud, Margaretha Byström, Agneta Ekmanner, Inga Landgré, Solveig Ternström, Dagny Lind, Holger Löwenadler, Per Myrberg, Göran Stangertz, Maria Blomkvist, Pontus Gustafsson

''Paradise Place'' is the name of the house in the Stockholm archipelago where a large family (four generations in fact) spend their summer holidays. But this year, things are different. Two outsiders, much less well-off than the others, join the party. . . .

Sven Klang's Quintet
(Sven Klangs kvintett)

Year of production: 1976

Production: Svenska Filminstitutet, Europa Film, Stockholm Film, Sveriges Radio, FHR, Musikteatergruppen Oktober; 100 mins

Release: September 22, 1976 in Helsingborg

Direction: Stellan Olsson

Screenplay: Henric Holmberg, Ninne Olsson, based on a play staged by the Musikteatergruppen Oktober

Photography: Kent Person

Players: Anders Granström, Henric Holmberg, Eva Remæus, Jan Lindell, Christer Boustedt

In 1958, a dance ensemble is starting its rehearsals in a small mid-Swedish town. Sven Klang is head of the group, and is also a dab hand at selling cars. Sven employs a new saxophonist, Lasse, from Stockholm and this provokes arguments and dissension among the members of the band . . .

Linus
(Linus)

Year of production: 1979

Production: Svenska Filminstitutet, Trevklövern H.B.; 97 mins

Release: August 20, 1979 in Stockholm

Screenplay and Direction: Vilgot Sjöman

Photography: Tony Forsberg

Players: Harald Hamrell, Viveca Lindfors, Ernst Günther, Harriet Andersson, Sven Wollter, Hans Ernback, Christina Schollin, Birgit Carlstën, Monica Dominique, Pernilla Wahlgren, Lasse Pöysti, Carl-Axel Elfving

During the 1920's a sixteen-year-old boy from the working classes finds himself witnessing a crime in a Stockholm backyard. There is a brothel at the top of the building, and Linus's father was called there just before the crime to "do a job". Linus realises that his father might be accused . . .

Children's Island
(Barnens ö)

Year of production: 1980

Production: Svenska Filminstitutet, Treklövern H.B.; 108 mins

Release: November 25, 1980 in Stockholm

Direction: Kay Pollak

Screenplay: Kay Pollak, Ola Olsson and Carl-Johan Seth, from the novel by P.C. Jersild

Photography: Roland Sterner

Players: Tomas Fryk, Anita Ekström, Ingvar Hirdwall, Lars-Erik Berenett, Hjördis Pettersson, Sif Ruud, Lena Granhagen, Malin Ek

Reine, aged eleven, is meant to spend the summer in a children's camp. But he decides to drop out, and instead he stays alone in Stockholm, where he finds food, work, money, and a number of strange new friends. Gradually he begins to assess his own identity, and recognises that he is an offbeat character . . .

Our Life Is Now
(Mamma)

Year of production: 1982

Production: Moviemakers Sweden, Svenska Filminstitutet; 92 mins

Release: September 22, 1982 in Stockholm

Direction: Suzanne Osten

Screenplay: Suzanne Osten, Tove Ellefsen

Photography: Hans Welin

Players: Malin Ek, Etienne Glaser, Serge Giambernardini, Philip Zandën, Hans V. Engström, Annelise Gabold, Iwa Boman, Helge Skoog

Gerd, a film critic, and her husband David, a painter, are forced to interrupt their stay in France when war breaks out in 1939. In the train, Gerd has a brief liaison with a Frenchman who has been called up for army service. This provokes a breakup with her husband, and Gerd embarks on a new life as a single mother. Torn between the child and her work, she tries to finish directing a film . . .

The Second Dance
(Andra dansen)

Year of production: 1982

Production: Svenska Filminstitutet, Sandrews, Zip Zap Produktion, Kim Anderzon, Lars Lundholm; 92 mins

Release: February 9, 1983 in stockholm

Direction: Lárus Ýmir Óskarsson

Screenplay: Lars Lundholm

Photography: Göran Nilsson

Players: Kim Anderzon, Lisa Hugoson, Hans Bredefeldt, Tommy Johnson, Sigurdur Sigurjónson, Göte Fyhring, Thore Segelström, Thomas Norström

Two women meet by chance in a café. Anna is around forty, aggressive and experienced, eager to seek her roots in the north of Sweden. Jo is twenty, and takes notes about everything and everyone, and also snaps her Polaroid at all and sundry. They decide to go north together in Jo's battered car, and their voyage of discovery begins . . .

The Flight of the Eagle
(Ingenjör Andrées Luftfärd)

Year of production: 1981

Production: Bold Productions, Svenska Filminstitutet, Sveriges Television TV2, Svensk Filmindustri, Norsk Film A/S (Oslo), Polyphon (Hamburg); 140 mins

Release: August 27, 1982

Direction: Jan Troell

Screenplay: Georg Oddner, Ian Rakoff, Klaus Rifbjerg, Jan Troell, from the book by Per Olof Sundman

Photography: Jan Troell

Players: Max von Sydow, Goran Stangertz, Sverre Anker Ousdal, Lotta Larsson, Eva von Hanno, Jan-Olof Strandberg, Henric Holmberg, Lasse Pöysti, Knut Husebö

In 1897, a middle aged engineer, Andrée, sets off by balloon from Spitsbergen in an attempt to reach the North Pole. With him are two younger assistants. But their balloon comes down on the ice, and after a harrowing journey they lose their way and are attacked by bears. Their corpses are discovered thirty-three years later, preserved by the cold . . . .

A Hill on the Backside of the Moon
(Berget på månens baksida)

Year of production: 1983

Production: Moviemakers, Svenska Filminstitutet, Sveriges Television TV1, Sandrews; 101 mins

Release: 1983

Direction: Lennart Hjulström

Screenplay: Agneta Pleijel

Max von Sydow in *The Flight of the Eagle* (1982) by Jan Troell

Stellan Skarsgård in *Hip, Hip, Hurrah!* (1987) by Kjell Grede

Photography: Stan Holmberg

Players: Gunilla Nyroos, Thommy Berggren, Lina Pleijel, Bibi Andersson, Ingvar Hirdwall

Sweden in the 1880's – a period when debates about morality and women's rights were in full flow. Sonya Kovalevsky arrives in Stockholm, she is the first woman in the world to be a university professor in mathematics. She meets a man, a radical, who sees her as the ideal strong, liberated woman. But she becomes possessed by her love for him . . .

Amorosa

Year of production: 1985

Production: Sandrews, Svenska Filminstitutet, Sveriges Television TV1; 118 mins

Release: March 7, 1986

Screenplay and Direction: Mai Zetterling

Photography: Rune Ericson

Players: Stina Ekblad, Erland Josephson, Philip Zandén, Peter Schildt, Olof Thunberg, Cathérine de Seynes, Lauritz Falk, Gunnel Broström

The story of Agnes von Krusenstjerna, the most prolific but also the most attacked of all Swedish female authors, the most admired and the most hated. Each of her books, appearing early in the 20th century, focused on taboos in Swedish society, and unleashed some form of scandal. Born to an aristocratic family, she fought to escape from stifling family love and found "liberation" in a strange, perverse relationship with an older man who would serve as her agent, publisher, and nurse. The artistic creativity that unites the couple declines gradually into madness . . .

The Serpent's Way
(Ormens väg på hälleberget)

Year of production: 1986

Production: Crescendo Film, Svensk Filmindustri, Svenska Filminstitutet, Sveriges Television TV1; 112 mins

Release: October, 1986

Screenplay and Direction: Bo Widerberg, from the novel by Torgny Lindgren

Photography: Jörgen Persson

Players: Stina Ekblad, Stellan Skarsgård, Ernst Günther, Reine Brynolfsson, Tomas von Brömssen

In the north of Sweden, in the 19th century, an impoverished mother, in order to keep her children under one roof in a rented farm, gives herself to the ruthless landowner; later, her daughter will have to follow suit . . .

Demons
(Demoner)

Year of production: 1986

Production: Viking Film, Svenska Filminstitutet; 127 mins

Release: September 5, 1986

Screenplay and Direction: Carsten Brandt, from the play by Lars Norén

Photography: Güran Nilsson

Players: Ewa Fröling, Lars Green, Björn Gränath, Pia Oscarsson

Katarina and Franck make up a modern couple, free of children and illusions. After ten years of living together, their relationship has descended to the level of a macabre and demoniac ritual . . .

The Mozart Brothers
(Bröderna Mozart)

Year of production: 1985

Production: Crescendo Film, Svenska Filminstitutet, Sveriges Television TV2; 110 mins

Release: February 21, 1986 in Stockholm

Direction: Suzanne Osten

Screenplay: Suzanne Osten, Niklas Rådström, Étienne Glaser

Photography: Hans Welin

Players: Étienne Glaser, Philip Zandén, Henry Bronett, Loa Falkman, Agneta Ekmanner, Lena T. Hansson, Helge Skoog, Grith Fjeldmose

What really goes on behind the scenes at a theatre, and who controls things? The director? His wife? The theatre manager? This comedy satirises the various machinations that go into the creation of a new production – in this case, Mozart's *Don Giovanni*.

Hip, Hip, Hurrah!
(Hip, hip, hurra!)

Year of production: 1986

Production: Svenska Filminstitutet, Palla Fogtdal A/S, Danish Film Institute, Norsk Film A/S, Sandrews; 110 mins

Release: September 4, 1987

Screenplay and Direction: Kjell Grede

Photography: Sten Holmberg

Players: Stellan Skarsgård, Lene Brøndum, Pia Vieth, Helge Jordal, Morten Grunwald, Ulla Henningsen, Karen Lise Mynster, Jesper Christensen, Stefan Sauk, Lene Tiemroth, Ghita Nørby, Ove Sprogøe, Johan H:son Kjellgren

Towards the end of the 19th century, a group of Scandinavian painters gathered in Skagen, on the northern tip of Jutland. They were inspired by the extraordinary light that marked this particular stretch of the Danish coast. The most famous and talented of them, Søren Krøyer, is fuelled by an intense desire for happiness, which he tries to find in his relations with different women . . .

The Women on the Roof
(Kvinnorna på taket)

Year of production: 1988

Production: Svenska Filminstitutet, Svensk Filmindustri, Sveriges Television TV1; 90 mins

Release: May, 1989 in Cannes

Direction: Carl-Gustaf Nykvist

Screenplay: Carl-Gustaf Nykvist, Lasse Summanen

Photography: Ulf Brantås, Jörgen Persson

Players: Amanda Ooms, Helena Bergström, Stellan Skarsgård, Percy Brandt, Lars Ori Backström, Katarina Olsson, Leif Andrée

During the summer of 1914 a young woman, Linnéa, arrives in Stockholm to work as a salesgirl. She lives in a studio apartment next to an empty photographer's studio. One day, Anna, the photographer, pops up. She is the same age as Linnéa and declares that she is at a turning point in her life . . .

The Guardian Angel
(Skyddsängeln)

Year of production: 1989

Production: Mekano Pictures, Svenska Filminstitutet, Sandrews, Sveriges Television TV2; 104 mins

Release: February, 1990 in Stockholm

Direction: Suzanne Osten

Screenplay: Suzanne Osten, Madeleine Gustafsson, Étienne Glaser, from the novel *Der letzte Sommer* by Ricarda Huch

Photography: Göran Nilsson

Players: Philip Zandén, Étienne Glaser, Malin Ek, Björn Kjellman, Gunilla Röör, Lena Nylén

A country in Europe at the beginning of the 20th century. Tumultuous student uprisings have obliged the hated Minister of the Interior, Joel Birkman, to close the universities. One student has been condemned to death. Birkman, his wife, and their three grown-up children withdraw to the countryside. But the young man whom they hire as their secretary cum bodyguard is not all that he seems . . .

The Ox
(Oxen)

Year of production: 1990

Production: Sweetland (New York), Sandrews, Svenska Filminstitutet, Nordisk Film (Denmark)

Release: November, 1991 in Stockholm

Direction: Sven Nykvist

Screenplay: Sven Nykvist, Lasse Summanen

Photography: Sven Nykvist

Players: Stellan Skarsgård, Ewa Fröling, Liv Ullmann, Max von Sydow, Björn Granath, Helge Jordal, Lennart Hjulström, Erland Josephson

For two years in a row, at the end of the 1860's, the harvest has failed in Sweden. People migrate to America in the tens of thousands. One man decides to take a desperate measure to preserve his family in the bitter winter of Smaland — and pays dearly for his action . . .

Stellan Skarsgård and Amanda Ooms in *The Women on the Roof* (1989) by Carl-Gustaf Nykvist

Hasse Ekman and Harriet Andersson in *Sawdust and Tinsel* (1953)

234

INGMAR BERGMAN

Note: This filmography does not include TV films made by Bergman except for those that received a theatrical release outside Sweden.

Crisis
(Kris)

Year of production: 1946

Production: Svensk Filmindustri; 93 mins.

Release: February 25, 1946 in Stockholm

Screenplay: Ingmar Bergman, from the play by Leck Fischer

Photography: Gösta Roosling

Players: Dagny Lind, Inga Landgré, Marianne Löfgren, Stig Olin, Alla Bohlin, Ernst Eklund, Signe Wirff, Svea Holst, Arne Lindblad, Julia Caesar

Nelly lives with her foster-mother. Jenny, her real mother, arrives and wants to get back her daughter. Nelly abandons her foster-mother and comes to work in Stockholm. One evening she is seduced by Jack. Jenny surprises them together and, after a row, Jack kills himself.

It Rains on Our Love/The Man with an Umbrella
(Det regnar på vår kärlek)

Year of production: 1946

Production: Sveriges Folkbiografer; 95 mins

Release: November 9, 1946 in Stockholm

Screenplay: Ingmar Bergman and Herbert Grevenius, from the play by Oskar Braaten

Photography: Göran Strindberg

Players: Barbro Kollberg, Birger Malmsten, Gösta Cederlund, Ludde Gentzel, Douglas Håge, Hjördis Pettersson, Julia Caesar, Sture Ericsson

Maggi and David meet in the rain outside Stockholm railway station. Both are unhappy: she is pregnant, and he has just been released from prison with a mere 5 crowns in his pocket. They decide to face the future together.

A Ship Bound for India/The Land of Desire
(Skepp till Indialand)

Year of production: 1947

Production: Sveriges Folkbiografer; 102 mins

Release: September 22, 1947 in Stockholm

Screenplay: Ingmar Bergman, from the play by Martin Söderhjelm

Players: Holger Löwenadler, Anna Lindahl, Birger Malmsten, Gertrud Fridh, Lasse Krantz, Jan Molander, Erik Hell, Naemi Briese, Hjördis Pettersson, Åke Fridell

The film is in the form of a long flashback in which Johannes, searching for his beloved Sally in the grim streets of a port town, remembers how their romance began . . .

Stig Olin in *Crisis* (1946)

Music in Darkness/Night Is My Future
(Musik i mörker)

Year of production: 1947

Production: Terraproduktion; 85 mins

Release: January 17, 1948 in Stockholm

Screenplay: Dagmar Edqvist, from her novel

Photography: Göran Strindberg

Players: Mai Zetterling, Birger Malmsten, Bibi Skoglund, Olof Winnerstrand, Naima Wifstrand, Åke Claesson, Hilda Borgström, Douglas Håge, Gunnar Björnstrand, Bengt Eklund

Bengt and Captain Blom are both physically handicapped, the one by blindness, the other losing his sight inexorably. This handicap produces an inferiority complex and a latent masochism. But while Blom is condemned, because he belongs to an older generation, Bengt has his youth before him.

Port of Call
(Hamnstad)

Year of production: 1948

Production: Svensk Filmindustri; 99 mins

Release: October 11, 1948 in Stockholm

Doris Svedlund in *Prison* (1949)

Screenplay: Olle Länsberg and Ingmar Bergman

Photography: Gunnar Fischer

Players: Nine-Christine Jönsson, Bengt Eklund, Erik Hell, Berta Hall, Mimi Nelson, Sture Ericson, Birgitta Valberg, Hans Strååt

Berit tries to drown herself in the harbour. Gösta, a sailor, saves her and becomes a catalyst for the young woman's sadness.

Prison/The Devil's Wanton
(Fängelse)

Year of production: 1949

Production: Terraproduktion; 78 mins

Release: March 19, 1949 in Stockholm

Screenplay: Ingmar Bergman

Photography: Göran Strindberg

Players: Doris Svedlund, Birger Malmsten, Eva Henning, Hasse Ekman, Stig Olin, Irma Christensson, Anders Henrikson, Marianne Löfgren

During the making of a film, the director Martin Grandé's old professor of mathematics visits him. He has just been released from a psychiatric clinic and suggests to Martin that he embark on a screenplay. . . .

Thirst/Three Strange Loves
(Törst)

Year of production: 1949

Production: Svensk Filmindustri; 84 mins

Stig Olin and Victor Sjöström in *To Joy* (1950)

Release: October 17, 1949 in Stockholm

Screenplay: Herbert Grevenius, from the short stories by Birgit Tengroth

Photography: Gunnar Fischer

Players: Eva Henning, Birger Malmsten, Birgit Tengroth, Mimi Nelson, Hasse Ekman, Bengt Eklund, Gaby Stenberg, Naima Wifstrand, Sven-Eric Gamble, Gunnar Nielsen, Astrid Hesse, Helge Hagerman

A marital crisis racks a young couple, at first in a sordid hotel room, and then in the cramped quarters of a train on its way through the ruins of postwar Germany. The wife, Rut, is aggressive and owes her bitterness towards men to a father who had abused her. The husband, Bertil, is more reasonable, but he too has suffered from an affair which ended in suicide for the woman. In the end, the lovers are reconciled. Hell together is better than Hell alone.

To Joy
(Till glädje)

Year of production: 1950

Production: Svensk Filmindustri; 98 mins

Release: February 20, 1950

Screenplay: Ingmar Bergman

Photography: Gunnar Fischer

Players: Maj-Britt Nilsson, Stig Olin, Victor Sjöström, Birger Malmsten, John Ekman, Margit Carlqvist, Sif Ruud, Erland Josephson, Ernst Brunman, Allan Ekelund, Maud Hyttenberg, Berit Holmström

Stig and Martha are musicians. Called out in the middle of an orchestra rehearsal, Stig learns that his wife has died in a fire at their home. Their young son has escaped, but Stig's life is shattered. Throughout a lengthy flashback he recalls the romance that had begun seven years earlier. . . .

237

Waiting Women (1952)

This Couldn't Happen Here/High Tension
(Sant händer inte här)

Year of production: 1950

Production: Svensk Filmindustri; 84 mins

Release: October 18, 1950 in Stockholm

Screenplay: Herbert Grevenius, from a novel by Waldemar Brøgger

Photography: Gunnar Fischer

Players: Ulf Palme, Signe Hasso, Alf Kjellin, Gösta Cederlund, Yngve Nordwall, Hannu Kompus, Rudolf Lipp

An agent from Eastern Europe is trying to sell his secrets to America. In Stockholm, he is pursued by agents from his own country. . . .

Summer Interlude
(Sommarlek)

Year of production: 1951

Production: Svensk Filmindustri; 96 mins

Release: October 1, 1951 in Stockholm

Screenplay: Ingmar Bergman and Herbert Grevenius from a story by Bergman

Photography: Gunnar Fischer

Players: Maj-Britt Nilsson, Birger Malmsten, Alf Kjellin, Georg Funkquist, Renée Björling, Mimi Pollak, Annalisa Ericson, Stig Olin

Marie, a ballet dancer, receives a diary about a love affair she had experienced some years earlier, and which was ended tragically by the accidental death of her friend. She recalls the development and high points of that first love. . . .

Waiting Women/Secrets of Women
(Kvinnors väntan)

Year of production: 1952

Production: Svensk Filmindustri; 107 mins

Release: November 3, 1952

Screenplay: Ingmar Bergman

Photography: Gunnar Fischer

Harriet Andersson and Lars Ekborg in *Summer with Monika* (1953)

Players: Anita Björk, Jarl Kulle, Karl-Arne Holmsten, Maj-Britt Nilsson, Birger Malmsten, Eva Dahlbeck, Gunnar Björnstrand, Gerd Andersson, Björn Bjelvenstam, Aino Taube, Håkon Westergren, Naima Wifstrand

In a lakeside villa, four women married to four brothers exchange memories while awaiting the men's return for the weekend.

Summer with Monika/Monika
(Sommaren med Monika)

Year of production: 1952

Production: Svensk Filmindustri; 96 mins

Release: February 9, 1953

Screenplay: Ingmar Bergman and P.A. Fogelström, from a novel by the latter

Photography: Gunnar Fischer

Players: Harriet Andersson, Lars Ekborg, John Harryson, Georg Skarstedt, Dagmar Ebbesen, Naemi Briese, Åke Fridell, Gösta Eriksson

Monika and Harry steal a boat and escape to the archipelago. There they spend the summer hiding out and living like savage innocents. But when autumn comes, the reality of daily life returns and their relationship sours. . . .

Sawdust and Tinsel/The Naked Night
(Gycklarnas afton)

Year of production: 1953

Production: Sandrews; 92 mins

Release: September 14, 1953 in Stockholm

Screenplay: Ingmar Bergman

Photography: Hilding Bladh (exteriors), Sven Nykvist, Göran Strindberg

Players: Åke Grönberg, Harriet Andersson, Hasse Ekman, Anders Ek, Gudrun Brost, Annika Tretow, Gunnar Björnstrand, Erik Strandmark

A circus stops in a small Swedish town. The director, Albert, dreams of leaving his young and pretty mistress, Anne, in order to return to his wife who lives in the town. He longs for middle-class security. Anne, for her part, lets herself be seduced by a local actor.

A Lesson in Love
(En lektion i kärlek)

Year of production: 1954

Production: Svensk Filmindustri; 95 mins

Release: October 4, 1954 in Stockholm

Screenplay: Ingmar Bergman

Photography: Martin Bodin

Players: Eva Dahlbeck, Gunnar Björnstrand, Yvonne Lombard, Harriet Andersson, Åke Grönberg, Olof Winnerstrand, Renée Björling, Brigitte Reimar

A gynaecologist deceives his wife, who plans to get her revenge by having a fling with an old flame, a Danish sculptor. She leaves for Copenhagen. Her husband, annoyed, joins her on the train. And a series of flashbacks ensues, describing the various episodes in their married life. . . .

Journey into Autumn/Dreams
(Kvinnodröm)

Year of production: 1955

Production: Sandrews; 86 mins

Release: August 22, 1955

Screenplay: Ingmar Bergman

Photography: Hilding Bladh

Players: Eva Dahlbeck, Harriet Andersson, Gunnar Björnstrand, Ulf Palme, Inga Landgré. Sven Lindberg, Naima Wifstrand, Benkt-Åke Benktsson

Two women from Stockholm, Doris and Susanne, visit Göteborg. Susanne tries to pry an old lover away from his shrewish wife, while Doris meets an elderly consul who flatters her with lavish gifts and compliments. . . .

Smiles of a Summer Night
(Sommarnattens leende)

Year of production: 1955

Production: Svensk Filmindustri; 108 mins

Release: December 26, 1955 in Stockholm

Screenplay: Ingmar Bergman

Photography: Gunnar Fischer

Eva Dahlbeck in *Journey into Autumn* (1955)

Wild Strawberries (1957)

Players: Eva Dahlbeck, Ulla Jacobsson, Gunnar Björnstrand, Harriet Andersson, Margit Carlqvist, Jarl Kulle, Åke Fridell, Björn Bjelvenstam, Naima Wifstrand, Jullan Kindahl, Gull Natorp, Birgitta Valberg, Bibi Andersson, Anders Wulff

In the course of a long summer's night party at a country manor, various couples and lovers intermingle and coalesce. . . .

The Seventh Seal
(Det sjunde inseglet)

Year of production: 1956

Production: Svensk Filmindustri; 95 mins

Release: February 16, 1957 in Stockholm

Screenplay: Ingmar Bergman

Photography: Gunnar Fischer

Players: Max von Sydow, Gunnar Björnstrand, Bibi Andersson, Bengt Ekerot, Nils Poppe, Åke Fridell, Inga Gill, Maud Hansson, Inga Landgré, Gunnel Lindblom, Bertil Anderberg, Anders Ek, Gunnar Olsson

A knight returns from the Crusades, disillusioned and seeking a reason for living. In his native Sweden he finds the plague taking its toll; Death stalks him; and only a young innocent couple, Jof and Mia, seem to offer some hope for the future. . . .

241

The Seventh Seal (1957)

Wild Strawberries
(Smultronstället)

Year of production: 1957

Production: Svensk Filmindustri; 90 mins

Release: December 26, 1957

Screenplay: Ingmar Bergman

Photography: Gunnar Fischer

Players: Victor Sjöström, Bibi Andersson, Ingrid Thulin, Gunnar Björnstand, Folke Sundquist, Björn Bjelvenstam, Naima Wifstrand, Jullan Kindahl, Gunnar Sjöberg, Gunnel Broström, Gertrud Fridh, Åke Fridell, Max von Sydow, Sif Ruud, Gunnel Lindblom

Professor Isak Borg travels south to Lund to receive an honorary doctorate. The journey becomes a voyage into the past, with flashbacks covering various parts of his unsatisfactory emotional life.

So Close to Life/Brink of Life
(Nära livet)

Year of production: 1957

Production: Nordisk Tonefilm; 84 mins

Release: March 31, 1958 in Stockholm

Screenplay: Ingmar Bergman and Ulla Isaksson, from the latter's story

Photography: Max Wilén

Players: Eva Dahlbeck, Ingrid Thulin, Bibi Andersson, Barbro Hiort af Ornäs, Erland Josephson, Inga Landgré, Max von Sydow, Gunnar Sjöberg, Anne-Marie Gyllenspetz, Sissi Kaiser, Margareta Krook, Lars Lind

Cecilia is recovering in a maternity clinic after a miscarriage. There she meets two other women, Stina who will lose her baby in labour and Hjördis who wants an abortion because her lover refuses to marry her.

Lars Ekborg, Ingrid Thulin and Max von Sydow in *The Face* (1958)

The Devil's Eye (1960)   Harriet Andersson in *Through a Glass Darkly* (1961)

Birgitta Valberg and Max von Sydow in *The Virgin Spring* (1960)

The Face/The Magician
(Ansiktet)

Year of production: 1958

Production: Svensk Filmindustri; 100 mins

Release: December 26, 1958 in Stockholm

Screenplay: Ingmar Bergman

Photography: Gunnar Fischer

Players: Max von Sydow, Ingrid Thulin, Gunnar Björnstrand, Bibi Andersson, Åke Fridell, Naima Wifstrand, Gertrud Fridh, Erland Josephson, Bengt Ekerot, Toivo Pawlo, Ulla Sjöblom

A small group of entertainers enters a town where they are subjected to interrogation and humiliation. The local chief of police believes in the supernatural; the doctor does not. A battle of wills and nerves develops. . . .

The Virgin Spring
(Jungfrukällan)

Year of production: 1959

Production: Svensk Filmindustri; 88 mins

Release: February 8, 1960 in Stockholm

Screenplay: Ulla Isaksson, based on a medieval legend

Photography: Gunnar Fischer

Players: Max von Sydow, Birgitta Valberg, Birgitta Pettersson, Gunnel Lindblom, Axel Düberg, Tor Isedal, Allan Edwall

A young girl is sent by her parents to take candles to a local church. On her way through the forest she is attacked, raped, and killed by three beggars, who seek shelter that very night at the home of her parents. . . .

Ingrid Thulin in *The Silence* (1963)

The Devil's Eye
(Djävulens öga)

Year of production: 1960

Production: Svensk Filmindustri; 86 mins

Release: October 17, 1960 in Stockholm

Screenplay: Ingmar Bergman, based on the radio play by Oluf Bang

Photography: Gunnar Fischer

Players: Jarl Kulle, Bibi Andersson, Stig Järrel, Nils Poppe, Gertrud Fridh, Sture Lagerwall, Georg Funkquist, Birger Sjöberg

Satan finds he is suffering from a stye in his eye. It can only be cured if a virtuous young girl, the daughter of a pastor, loses her virginity. . . .

Through a Glass Darkly
(Såsom i en spegel)

Year of production: 1961

Production: Svensk Filmindustri; 89 mins

Release: October 16, 1961 in Stockholm

Screenplay: Ingmar Bergman

Photography: Sven Nykvist

Players: Gunnar Björnstrand, Harriet Andersson, Max von Sydow, Lars Passgård

A young woman and her doctor husband, along with her adolescent brother and her father, are on holiday on a remote island. The young woman undergoes a psychological crisis, which may or may not be due in part to her father's egocentricity and her husband's lack of sensitivity. . . .

Liv Ullmann in *Shame* (1968)

Bibi Andersson and Liv Ullmann in *Persona* (1966)

<table>
<tr><td>

Winter Light
(Nattvardsgästerna)

Year of production: 1962

Production: Svensk Filmindustri; 80 mins

Release: February 11, 1963 in Stockholm

Screenplay: Ingmar Bergman

Photography: Sven Nykvist

Players: Gunnar Björnstrand, Ingrid Thulin, Gunnel Lindblom, Max von Sydow, Allan Edwall, Kolbjörn Knudsen, Olof Thunberg, Elsa Ebbesen-Thornblad

Tomas, a village pastor, finds his faith wavering in the aftermath of his wife's death and in the face of his relationship with another woman, Märta. She, an atheist, tries to rekindle Tomas's capacity for human love. . . .

</td><td>

The Silence
(Tystnaden)

Year of production: 1963

Production: Svensk Filmindustri; 95 mins

Release: September 23, 1963 in Stockholm

Screenplay: Ingmar Bergman

Photography: Sven Nykvist

Players: Ingrid Thulin, Gunnel Lindblom, Jörgen Lindström, Håkon Jahnberg, Birger Malmsten

Two sisters arrive in an alien town on their way back to their own country. Cooped up in a hotel room, one grows more and more bitter and introspective while the other tries to find sexual gratification with a local waiter. A small boy, son of one sister and nephew of another, watches these developments. . . .

</td></tr>
</table>

Now About These Women/All These Women
(För att inte tala om alla dessa kvinnor)

Year of production: 1964

Production: Svensk Filmindustri; 80 mins

Release: June 15, 1964 in Stockholm

Screenplay: Ingmar Bergman and Erland Josephson

Photography: Sven Nykvist

Players: Jarl Kulle, Bibi Andersson, Harriet Andersson, Barbro Hiort at Ornäs, Eva Dahlbeck, Karin Kavli, Gertrud Fridh, Mona Malm, Allan Edwall

A pompous music critic wishes to write a biography of a great 'cellist, and finds himself diverted by the ladies who inhabit the maestro's rococo villa. . . .

Persona
(Persona)

Year of production: 1965

Production: Svensk Filmindustri; 84 mins

Release: October 18, 1966 in Stockholm

Screenplay: Ingmar Bergman

Photography: Sven Nykvist

Players: Bibi Andersson, Liv Ullmann, Gunnar Björnstrand, Margareta Krook, Jörgen Lindström

A famous actress suddenly loses her voice during a performance. A nurse is charged with treating her in tranquillity on an island in the archipelago. Gradually, the two women's personalities intermingle and overlap. . . .

Hour of the Wolf
(Vargtimmen)

Year of production: 1967

Production: Svensk Filmindustri; 89 mins

Release: February 19, 1968 in Stockholm

Screenplay: Ingmar Bergman

Photography: Sven Nykvist

Players: Max von Sydow, Liv Ullmann, Ingrid Thulin, Georg Rydeberg, Erland Josephson, Gertrud Fridh, Naima Wifstrand, Bertil Anderberg

A painter, Johan Borg, uses a remote island for working. One day he and his wife are invited to dine with the Baron von Merkens. During the evening, Borg is humiliated before the assembled guests.

Shame/The Shame
(Skammen)

Year of production: 1968

Production: Svensk Filmindustri; 102 mins

Release: September 29, 1968 in Stockholm

Screenplay: Ingmar Bergman

Photography: Sven Nykvist

Players: Max von Sydow, Liv Ullmann, Gunnar Björnstrand, Birgitta Valberg, Sigge Fürst, Hans Alfredson, Ingvar Kjellson, Frank Sundström

Jan and Eva are retired musicians living on an island, when war suddenly engulfs them. As one side and then the other overrun their district, they are swept up in the chaos of the conflict, and are reduced to a desperate struggle for survival and escape. . . .

A Passion/The Passion of Anna
(En passion)

Year of production: 1969

Production: Svensk Filmindustri; 101 mins

Release: November 10, 1969 in Stockholm

Screenplay: Ingmar Bergman

Photography: Sven Nykvist

Players: Max von Sydow, Liv Ullmann, Bibi Andersson, Erland Josephson, Erik Hell, Sigge Fürst, Svea Holst, Annika Kronberg, Hjördis Pettersson

Andreas Winkelmann is separated from his wife and has exiled himself to an island in the Baltic. But his existence is shaken by the presence of a maniac on the island, and his encounter with a beautiful widow, Anna Fromm, whose husband was also called Andreas. . . .

The Touch
(Beröringen)

Year of production: 1970

Production: ABC Pictures (New York), Cinematograph; 113 minutes

Release: August 30, 1971 in Stockholm

Screenplay: Ingmar Bergman

Photography: Sven Nykvist

Players: Elliott Gould, Bibi Andersson, Max von Sydow, Sheila Reid, Barbro Hiort af Ornäs, Staffan Hallerstam, Maria Nolgard

A young archaeologist falls in love with the wife of his consultant doctor. . . .

Cries and Whispers
(Viskningar och rop)

Year of production: 1972

Production: Cinematograph, Swedish Film Institute; 91 mins

Release: March 5, 1973 in Stockholm

Screenplay: Ingmar Bergman

Photography: Sven Nykvist

Players: Harriet Andersson, Kari Sylwan, Ingrid Thulin, Liv Ullmann, Erland Josephson, Henning Moritzen, Georg Åhlin, Anders Ek, Inga Gill

Agnes lies dying in her family's country manor. Her sisters and the family maid try to relieve her suffering. . . .

The Magic Flute (1975)

Scenes from a Marriage
(Scener ur ett äktenskap)

Year of production: 1972

Production: Cinematograph; 168 mins [theatrical version]

Release: April 11 to May 16, 1973, on Swedish TV

Screenplay: Ingmar Bergman

Photography: Sven Nykvist

Players: Liv Ullmann, Erland Josephson, Bibi Anderson, Jan Malmsjö, Anita Wall, Gunnel Lindblom, Barbro Hiort af Ornäs, Bertil Norström

Johan and Marianne constitute the ideal Swedish bourgeois couple. But then Johan has an affair with Paula and leaves home; over the years they try to renew their relationship. . . .

The Magic Flute
(Trollflöjten)

Year of production: 1974

Production: Swedish Television/TV2; 135 mins

Release: January 1, 1975 on Swedish TV

Screenplay: Ingmar Bergman from the opera by Mozart, libretto by Schikaneder

Photography: Sven Nykvist

Players: Josef Köstlinger, Irma Urrila, Håkon Hagegård, Elisabeth Eriksson, Ulrik Cold, Birgit Nordin, Ragnar Ulfung, Erik Saeden, Britt-Marie Aruhn

Screen version of Mozart's opera.

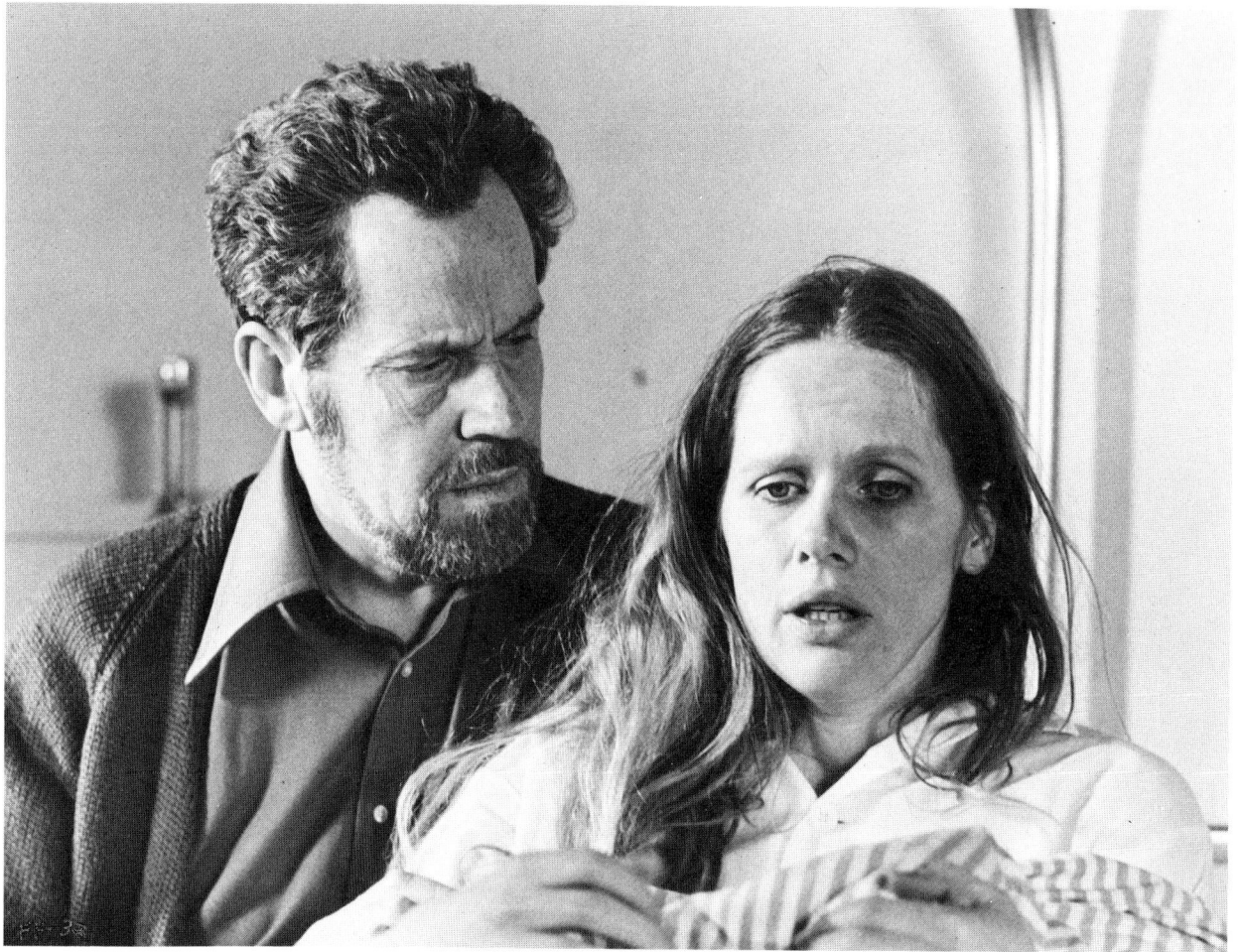

Erland Josephson and Liv Ullmann in *Face to Face* (1976)

Liv Ullmann and Ingrid Bergman in *Autumn Sonata* (1978)

Face to Face
(Ansikte mot ansikte)

Year of production: 1975

Production: Cinematograph; 136 mins [theatrical version]

Release: April 25 to May 19, 1976 on Swedish TV

Screenplay: Ingmar Bergman

Photography: Sven Nykvist

Players: Liv Ullmann, Erland Josephson, Gunnar Björnstrand, Aino Taube-Henrikson, Kari Sylwan, Sif Ruud, Sven Lindberg

The story of a psychiatrist, Jenny Isaksson, whose life is disrupted and sent off course after she is attacked by two men while visiting an empty apartment. . . .

From the Life of the Marionettes
(Aus dem Leben der Marionetten)

Year of production: 1979

Production: Personafilm (Munich) in collaboration with the Bavarian State Theatre; 104 mins

Release: 1980 in Germany

Screenplay: Ingmar Bergman

Photography: Sven Nykvist

Players: Robert Atzorn, Martin Benrath, Christine Buchegger, Rita Russek, Lota Müthel, Walter Schmidinger, Ruth Olafs, Karl-Heinz Pelser

A businessman, Peter Egermann, murders a prostitute in Munich. Her nickname is 'Ka', short for Katarina, the same name as Egermann's wife. . . .

The Serpent's Egg
(Das Schlangenei)

Year of production: 1976

Production: Rialto Film (West Berlin), Dino De Laurentiis Corporation (Los Angeles); 119 mins

Release: October 26, 1977 in West Germany

Screenplay: Ingmar Bergman

Photography: Sven Nykvist

Players: Liv Ullmann, David Carradine, Gert Froebe, Heinz Bennent, James Whitmore, Glynn Turman, Georg Hartmann, Edith Heerdegen, Kyra Mladeck, Fritz Strassner, Hans Quest, Wolfgang Weiser, Paula Braend

The film unfolds during a single week in November 1923 when inflation in the Weimar Republic was at its most catastrophic. The first manifestations of Nazi terror are emerging. . . .

Fanny and Alexander
(Fanny och Alexander)

Year of production: 1982

Production: Swedish Film Institute. Swedish Television/TV1, Personafilm (Munich), Gaumont (Paris); 188 minutes [theatrical version]

Release: December 1982 in Stockholm

Screenplay: Ingmar Bergman

Photography: Sven Nykvist

Players: Gunn Wållgren, Allan Edwall, Ewa Fröling, Bertil Guve, Pernilla Allwin, Börje Ahlstedt, Christina Schollin, Jarl Kulle, Mona Malm, Maria Granlund, Emelie Werkö, Kristian Almgren, Angelica Wallgren, Käbi Laretei, Erland Josephson, Stina Ekblad, Jan Malmsjö, Harriet Andersson, Gunnar Björnstrand

At the turn of the century, the Ekdahl family, owners of the local theatre, celebrate Christmas but must come to terms also with the death of the pater familias, Oscar. His daughter Helena continues his work, and marries the local Bishop. Meanwhile, her children Fanny and Alexander observe the adult world around them. . . .

Autumn Sonata
(Herbstsonat/Höstsonat)

Year of production: 1977

Production: Personafilm, for ITC; 92 mins

Release: October 8, 1978 in Stockholm and New York

Screenplay: Ingmar Bergman

Photography: Sven Nykvist

Players: Ingrid Bergman, Liv Ullmann, Lena Nyman, Halvar Björk, Arne Bang-Hansen, Gunnar Björnstrand, Erland Josephson, Georg Løkkeberg, Linn Ullmann

Charlotte is a famous concert pianist, who visits her daughters in a Norwegian vicarage. The reunion uncovers old family wounds. . . .

After the Rehearsal
(Efter repetitionen)

Year of production: 1984

Production: Cinematograph for Personafilm (Munich); 72 mins

Release: 1984 on Swedish TV

Screenplay: Ingmar Bergman

Photography: Sven Nykvist

Players: Erland Josephson, Lena Olin, Ingrid Thulin, Bertil Guve, Nadja Palmstierna-Weiss

An elderly stage director muses on his past and his romantic involvements. . . .

Fanny and Alexander (1982)

Carl Theodor Dreyer shooting *They Caught the Ferry* in 1948

CARL THEODOR DREYER

The President
(Præsidenten)

Year of production: 1918

Production: Nordisk Films Kompagni; 1,397 metres

Release: February 1919 in Sweden, and February 9, 1920 in Copenhagen

Screenplay: Carl Th. Dreyer from a novel by Karl Emil Franzos

Photography: Hans Vaagö

Players: Halvard Hoff, Elith Pio, Carl Meyer, Olga Raphael-Linden, Betty Kirkeby, Richard Christensen, Peter Nielsen, Jacoba Jessen

A magistrate must pass judgement on a young woman accused of killing her child. He recognises her as his daughter by a woman he had long ago abandoned. . . .

Leaves from Satan's Book
(Blade af Satans bog)

Year of production: 1919

Production: Nordisk Films Kompagni; 2,375 metres

Release: January 24, 1921 in Copenhagen

Screenplay: Edgar Høyer (officially from the novel by Marie Corelli); rewritten by Dreyer

Photography: George Schnéevoigt

Players: Helge Nissen, Halvard Hoff, Jacob Teixeire, Erling Hanson, Hallander Helleman, Ebon Strandin, Johannes Meyer, Tenna Kraft Frederiksen, Viggo Wiehe, Carlo Wieth, Clara Wieth Pontoppidan, Carl Hillebrandt

Inspired by Griffith's *Intolerance*, this film contains four episodes in which the Devil's influence can be discerned: the trial of Christ, the Spanish Inquisition, the French Revolution, and Bolshevism in Finland in 1918.

The Parson's Widow
(Prästänkan)

Year of production: 1920

Production: Svensk Filmindustri, Stockholm; 1,901 metres

Release: October 4, 1920 in Stockholm and April 26, 1921 in Copenhagen

Screenplay: Carl Th. Dreyer from a story by Kristofer Janson

Photography: George Schnéevoigt

Players: Hildur Carlberg, Einar Röd, Greta Almroth, Olav Aukrust, Kurt Welin

In a Norwegian village during the 17th century, Sofren, in order to become the pastor, marries Lady Margaret. But he tries to hasten her death in order to retrieve his former fiancée. . . .

Love One Another
(Die Gezeichneten)

Year of production: 1921

Production: Primusfilm, Berlin, 2,019 metres

Release: February 7, 1922 in Copenhagen and February 23, 1922 in Berlin

Screenplay: Carl Th. Dreyer, from the novel by Aage Madelung

Photography: Freidrich Weinmann

Players: Polinka Piekovska, Vladimir Gadjarov, Torleif Reiss, Richard Boleslawski

A complex narrative featuring a small Jewish girl reunited with her brother in St. Petersburg. But in the same city there is a young fascist who incites hatred against the Jews and even finds his way to the girl's native village. . . .

Once Upon a Time
(Der var engang)

Year of production: 1922

Production: Sophus Madsen, Copenhagen; 1,165 metres

Release: October 3, 1922 in Copenhagen

Screenplay: Carl Th. Dreyer and Palle Rosenkrantz, from the play by Holger Drachmann

Photography: George Schnéevoigt

Players: Clara Pontoppidan, Svend Methling, Peter Jerndorff, Håkan Ahnfeldt-Rønne, Torben Meyer, Valdemar Schiöler-Linck

A fairy tale in a 17th-century setting.

Michael
(Mikaël)

Year of production: 1924

Production: Erich Pommer, Decla-Bioscop (UFA), Berlin; 1,975 metres

Release: September 29, 1924 in Berlin and November 17, 1924 in Copenhagen

Screenplay: Carl Th. Dreyer, from the novel by Herman Bang

Photography: Karl Freund and Rudolf Maté

Players: Benjamin Christensen, Walter Slezak, Nora Gregor, Robert Garisson, Greta Mosheim, Alexander Murski, Max Auxinger, Didier Aslan

A young man is adopted by a rich and famous sculptor. Falling in love with a glamorous young woman, he abandons his mentor and 'father'. The sculptor dies in loneliness.

The Bride of Glomdal (1925)

Master of the House (1925)

The Passion of Joan of Arc (1928)

The Bride of Glomdal
(Glomdalsbruden)

Year of production: 1925

Production: Victoria-Film, Oslo; 1,393 metres

Release: January 1, 1926 in Oslo, and April 15, 1926 in Copenhagen

Screenplay: Carl Th. Dreyer, from two stories by Jacob B. Bull

Photography: Einar Olsen

Players: Stub Wiberg, Tove Tellback, Harald Stormoen, Alfhild Stormoen, Einar Sissener, Oscar Larsen, Einar Tveito, Rasmus Rasmussen

The tempestuous relationship, ending in marriage, of the idignant Tore and the wealthy Berit.

Master of the House
(Du skal ære din hustru)

Year of production: 1925

Production: Palladium, Copenhagen; 2,323 metres

Release: October 5, 1925 in Copenhagen

Screenplay: Carl Th. Dreyer and Svend Rindom from the latter's play

Photography: George Schnéevoigt

Players: Johannes Meyer, Astrid Holm, Karin Nellemose, Mathilde Nielsen, Clara Schønfed, Johannes Nielsen, Petrine Sonne

A man rules his wife and daughter with a rod of iron. But his childhood nurse, still a formidable personality, manages to take him in hand during his wife's absence and makes him a decent husband and father after all.

Vampyr (1932)

The Passion of Joan of Arc
(La Passion de Jeanne d'Arc)

Year of production: 1927

Production: Société générale de films, Paris; 2,400 metres

Release: April 21, 1928 in Copenhagen and October 25, 1928 in Paris

Screenplay: Carl Th. Dreyer, from the book by Joseph Delteil

Photography: Rudolf Maté

Players: Marie Falconetti, Eugène Silvain, André Berley, Maurice Schutz, Antonin Artaud, Michel Simon, Jean d'Yd, Ravet, André Lurville, Jacques Arma, Alexandre Mihalesco, Robert Narlay

An account of Joan's condemnation and torture, which unleash a popular revolt.

Vampyr
(Vampyr)

Year of production: 1931

Production: Carl Th. Dreyer Filmproduktion Paris-Berlin; 2,035 metres

Release: May 6, 1932 in Berlin and March 27, 1933 in Copenhagen

Screenplay: Carl Th. Dreyer and Christian Jul, loosely based on the stories by Sheridan Le Fanu

Photography: Rudolf Maté

Players: Julian West (alias Baron Nicolas de Gunzberg), Henriette Gérard, Jan Hieronimko, Maurice Schutz, Rena Mandel, Sibylle Schmitz

During a long night in a French village, David Gray arouses the wrath of a female vampire and a mad doctor. . . .

259

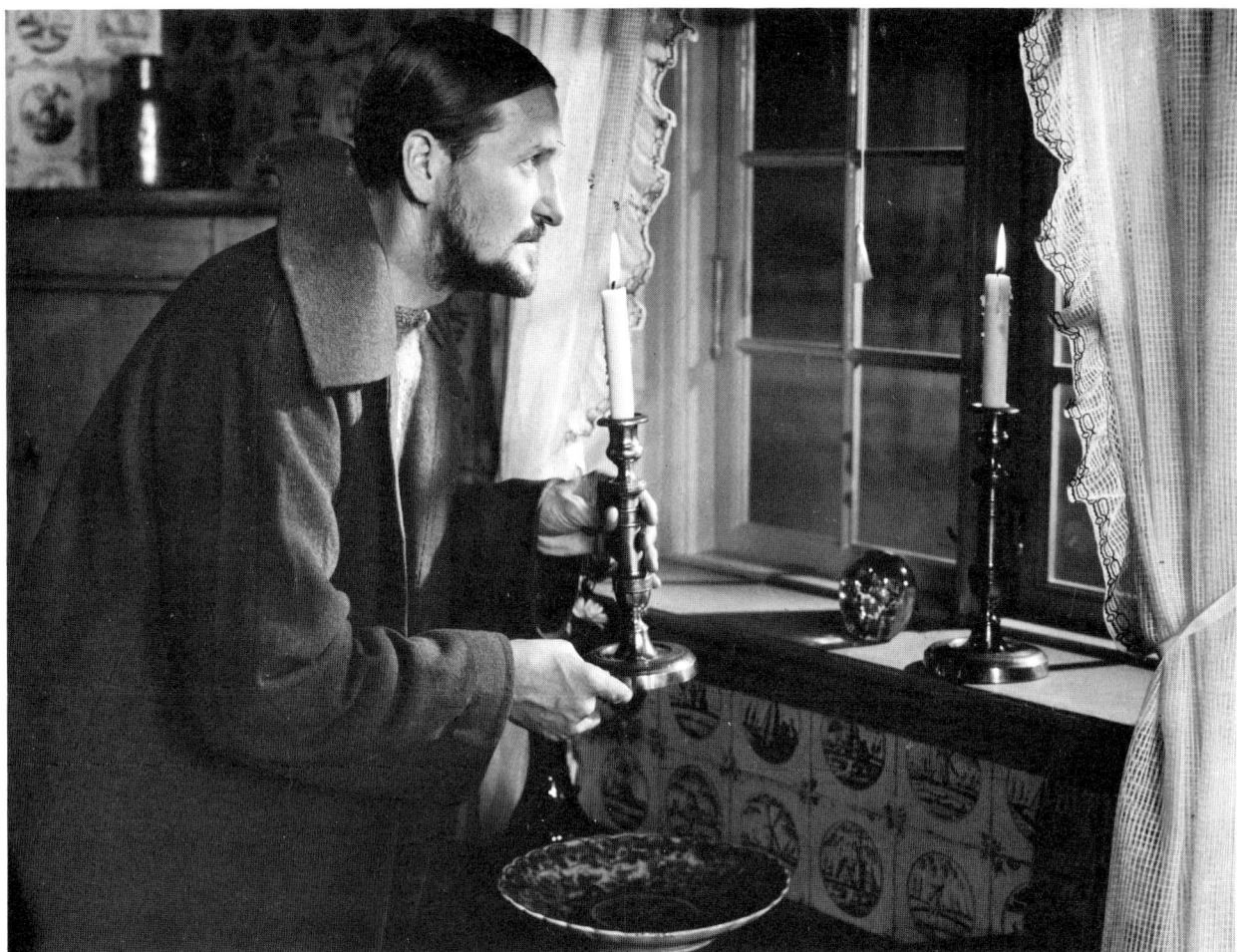

The Word (1955)

Day of Wrath
(Vredens dag)

Year of production: 1943

Production: Palladium, Copenhagen; 2,675 metres

Release: November 13, 1943 in Copenhagen

Screenplay: Carl Th. Dreyer and Mogens Skot-Hansen (and officially Poul Knudsen), based on the play by Hans Wiers-Jenssen

Photography: Karl Andersson

Players: Thorkild Roose, Lisbeth Movin, Sigrid Neiiendam, Preben Lerdorff Rye, Alberg Høberg, Olaf Ussing, Anna Svierkier

An elderly pastor has married a young woman. When the pastor's son by an earlier marriage returns to the village and falls in love with the wife, the latter is denounced as a witch by her vicious mother-in-law. . . .

Two People
(Två människor)

Year of production: 1944

Production: Svensk Filmindustri, Stockholm; 2,015 metres

Release: March 23, 1945 in Stockholm

Screenplay: Carl Th. Dreyer and Martin Glanner from a play by W.O. Somin

Photography: Gunnar Fischer

Players: Georg Rydeberg, Wanda Rothgardt, Gabriel Alw, Stig Olin

A scientist is accused of plagiarising a colleague's thesis; then he learns that his wife has been the lover of the colleague in question. . .

The Word
(Ordet)

Year of production: 1954

Production: Palladium, Copenhagen; 3,440 metres

Release: January 10, 1955 in Copenhagen

Screenplay: Carl Th. Dreyer, from the play by Kaj Munk

Photography: Henning Bendtsen

Players: Henrik Malberg, Emil Hass Christensen, Preben Lerdorff Rye, Cay Kristiansen, Birgitte Federspiel, Ann Elisabeth

In a Jutland village, two men argue fiercely about a forthcoming marriage, but are reconciled after Inger dies during childbirth. The fervently religious Johannes speaks the word which revives Inger from the dead. . . .

Gertrud

Year of production: 1964

Production: Palladium, Copenhagen; 3,240 metres

Release: December 18, 1964 in Paris and January 1, 1965 in Copenhagen

Screenplay: Carl Th. Dreyer, from the play by Hjalmar Söderberg

Photography: Henning Bendtsen

Players: Nina Pens Rode, Bendt Rothe, Ebbe Rode, Baard Owe, Axel Strøbye, Karl Gustav Ahlefeldt, Vera Gebuhr

Early in the century, Gertrud leaves her husband; she runs off not with Gabriel, a former lover, nor with the young Erland who disappoints her, but with Axel, a childhood friend. . . .

Gabriel Axel

Carl Theodor Dreyer

Bille August

Henning Carlsen

Dictionary of Directors

Françoise Buquet

DENMARK

Arnfred, Morten

Born August 2, 1945 in Copenhagen. He began his film career as an assistant at Petra Film in 1967. He worked on all aspects of film-making, behind the camera, as a sound recordist, and writing screenplays. Also a musician, Arnfred wrote scores for promotional films and shorts. He then worked independently as a director of photography with many film-makers, notably Anders Refn. Arnfred has received the Danish Critics' Prize ('Bodil') three times, and had his greatest success to date with *Johnny Larsen*, a film in which he shows once again his skills as a director of young people.

Filmography

1976: *Let's Do It (Måske ku'vi*, co-dir Lasse Nielsen and Morten Bruus); 1978: *Me and Charly (Mig og Charly*, co-dir Henning Kristiansen); 1979: *Johnny Larsen*; 1983: *Land of Plenty (Det er et yndigt land)* ; 1988: *Heaven and Hell (Himmel og helvede)* .

August, Bille

Born in 1948. After studying architecture, he moved to Stockholm in 1987, where he studied photography and learned the craft of documentary films. In 1971, he obtained his diploma as a director of photography at the Danish Film School. He then made several commercials, shorts, and TV programmes. In Sweden, he worked as a cinematographer with various directors including Jörn Donner (q.v.). In 1978, he made his first feature. A very popular director in Denmark. August is attracted above all to the world of children and adolescents (*Zappa, Twist and Shout, Buster's World*). His career took off internationally when *Pelle the Conqueror* won the Palme d'Or at Cannes in 1988 and then the Oscar for the Best Foreign Film in Hollywood.

Filmography

1978: *In My Life (Honningmåne)* ; 1983: *Zappa*; 1984: *Twist and Shout (Tro, håb og kærlighed), Buster's World (Busters verden)* ; 1987: *Pelle the Conqueror (Pelle erobreren)* ; 1991: *Best Intentions (Den goda viljan)*, in Sweden.

Axel, Gabriel

Real name Gabriel Morch, born April 18, 1918. After training at the Royal Theatre in Copenhagen, Axel moved to Paris and worked under Louis Jouvet at the Théâtre Athénée. He proceeded to direct several stage productions in Denmark, especially the French classics. In 1967, *The Red Mantle* won the Technical Prize at the Cannes Film Festival, and *Beloved Toy* and *Love* were screened in the Directors' Fortnight in 1968 and 1970. At the end of the 1940's and since 1977, Axel made many films for French television. He made a brilliant return to the cinema with *Babette's Feast*, which took the Oscar for Best Foreign Film in Hollywood in 1988.

Filmography (main films)

1955: *Always the Fight (Altid ballade)*; 1957: *A Woman Not Wanted (En kvinde er øverflodig)*; 1958: *Welcome, Mr. Dollar (Guld og grøne skove)*; 1959: *I Want Helen (Heller for Helene)*; 1960: *Flemming and Kvik (Flemming og Kvik)*; 1962: *Oskar*; 1967: *The Red Mantle (Den røde kappe)*; 1968: *The Goldcabbage Family (Familien Gyldenkål)*; 1976: *The Goldcabbage Family Breaks the Bank (Familien Gyldenkål sprænger banken)*; 1987: *Babette's Feast (Babettes gæstebud)*; 1989: *Christian*.

Bang Carlsen, Jon

Born September 28, 1950. During the 1970's, he directed several plays on stage and for television. In 1976 he received his diploma from the Danish Film School. Then he shot a number of shorts, mingling documentary and fiction, which marked him as one of the new talents in the Danish cinema. Carlsen has often returned to the subject of old age (e.g. *Jenny, Before the Guests Arrive, I Wanted to Find the Truth*).

Filmography

Main short features − 1977: *Jenny;* 1981: *Hotel of the Stars;* 1984: *Phoenix (Fugl fenix);* 1986: *Before the Guests Arrive (For gæsterne kommer);* 1987: *I Wanted to Find the Truth (Jeg ville først finde sandheden).*

Full-length features − 1977: *A Fisherman in Hanstholm (En fisker i Hanstholm);* 1980: *Next Stop Paradise (Næste stop Paradis);* 1985: *Hamlet − Ophelia Comes to Town (Hamlet − Ofelia kommer til byen);* 1988: *Time Out, Baby Doll.*

Blom, August

Born December 26, 1869 in Copenhagen, died January 10, 1947, *id.* He began as a singer at the Royal Opera in Copenhagen, before entering the cinema at the suggestion of his friend Ole Olsen. He wrote some scripts and played various small roles. In 1909 he joined Nordisk, succeeding Viggo Jensen as artistic director, head of production, and director. There he launched the career of Valdemar Psilander and gave Asta Nielsen her very first part in one of his own films (*The Temptations of a Great City*). His skills as an artist and as an entrepreneur made him one of the major pioneers of the Danish film. In 1913 he made the most ambitious film of the period, *Atlantis*, from the novel by Gerhardt Hauptmann, which marked the start of the 'literary' spell in Danish cinema. With his favourite cinematographer, Johan Ankerstjerne, he made significant advances in lighting technique. He regarded the décor as crucial for intensifying the dramatic content of a scene and for revealing the characters (e.g. his use of mirrors). A prolific director, Blom was also a businessman who remained loyal to Nordisk Films Kompagni well into its declining years.

Filmography

1910: *The Storms of Life (Livets storme), Robinson Crusoe, The White Slave Trade I (Den hvide slavehandel I), The Spy from Tokyo (Spionen fra Tokio), Dr. Jekyll and Mr. Hyde/The Fatal Invention (Den skæbnesvangre opfindelse), The Hunt for the Robber (Jakten paa Gentlemanrøveren), Singaree, Hamlet, A Ghost in the Vaults (Spøgelset i gravkælderen), The Necklace of the Dead (Den dødes halsbaand);* 1911: *The White Slave Trade II/The White Slave Trade's Last Victim (Den hvide slavehandel II), The Price of Beauty (Den farlige alder), The Temptations of a Great City/At the Prison's Gate (Ved fængslets port), Potiphar's Wife (Potifars hustru), The Superintendent (Politimesteren), The Fortuneteller's Daughter (Den blaa natviol), These Ladies' Newspaper (Damernes blad), The Ballet Dancer (Balletdanserinden), The Railway Girl (Jernbanens datter), Deceitful Love (Vildledt elskov), The Gracious Kiss (Den naadige frøken), A Lesson/The Aviator and the Journalist's Wife (En lektion/Aviatikeren og journalistens hustru), The Shopgirl (Ekspeditricens/Ungdom og letsind), Desdemona, The Aeroplane Inventor (En opfinders skæne), Father and Son (Fader og søn), Dream of Death (Dødsdrømmen), My First Monocle/Mr. Strom's First Monocle (Min første monocle/Herr Stroms første monocle), Mrs. Potiphar/A Fatal Lie (Fru Potifar/Den skæbnesvangre løgn), The Power of Love (Kælighedens styrke), The Mormon's Victim (Mormonens offer), Revenge (Haevnet), The Black Point (Den mørke punkt), The Escaped Convict (Eventyr paa fodrejsen/Den udbrudte slave), The Right of Youth (Ungdommens ret), Love under the Tropics (Tropisk kærlighed), The Vampire-Dancer (Vampyrdanserinden), The Old Grocery Shop/Midsummer (Det gamle købmandshus/ Midsommer), The Bride of Death (Dødens brud);* 1912: *The Shining Star (Brillantstjernen), The Governor's Daughter (Guvernørensn datter), Love is Blind (Kærlighed gør blind), Dearly Purchased Friendship (Dyrekøbt venskab), The Black Chancellor (Den sorte kansler), Heart of Gold (Hjertets guld/Et hjerte af guld), The Director's Daughter (Direktørens datter), The First Patient (Det første honorar), The Power of Love/The Ham Actor (Elskovs magt(Gøgleren), The Story of a Mother/A Mother's Love (Historien om en moder/En moders kærlighed), The Three Comrades (De tre kammerater), The Opera is Burning/Grandmother's Lullaby (Operabranden/Bedstemoders vuggevise), The First Love (Den Secret Treaty (Den tredie magt), The Birthday Present (En Hofintrigue), The Fugitives (Den sunde kærlighed?/Samvittighedsnag), The Gold from the Gutter (Alt paa et kort/Guldmønten); 1913: The Power of the Press/The Hold-Up (Pressens magt/Et bankrum), The Artists (Trols/Gøglerblod), A Dangerous Game (Højt spil/Et forfejlet spring), When Women Seek Adventure (Naar fruen gaar paa eventyr/Pompadourtasken), Lost Paradise (Bristet Lykke), Five Copies (Fem kopier), Atlantis, A Dangerous Murderer (En farlig forbryder/Knivstikkeren), Elskovsleg, By Love's Mercy (Af elskovs naade), The Chinese Vase (Den kinesiske vase/Vasens hemmelighed); 1914: The Son (Sønnen), The Big Dinner (Den store middag), The Prisoner/A Guest from Another World (Tugthusfange NP97/En gæst fra anden verden), The Ancestors' Sin (Fædrenes synd), The Adventures of Mr. King (Aegteskab og Piges/Mr. King faa eventyr), Exiled (Aeventyrersken), A Woman Alone/Who Is He? (En ensom kvinde/Hvem er han?), A Wedding under The Revolution (Revolutionsbryllup), One Year to Learn (Et læreaar), The Little Chauffeur (Den lille chauffør), A Mother's Love (Den største kærlighed/En moders kærlighed), Pro Patria, The Challenge of Love (Kærligheds bæddemaalet); 1915: Love Thy Neighbour (Du skal elske din næste), The Poisoned Arrow (Giftpilen), The Storms of Love (Hjertestorme), The Longing for Love/The Hunchback (Kærligheds længsel/Den pukkelryggede), Blind Destiny (Lotteriseddel No. 22152/Den blinde skæbne), The Wild Spider/The Red Widow (Rovedderkoppen/Den røde enke), The Daughter of Sin (Syndens datter), Guilty Love (Syndig kærlighed/Eremitten), The Crazy Genius (Truet lykke/Et skud i mørket), The End of the World (Verdens undergang/Flammesværdet), For His Country's Honour (For sit lands ære/Hendes ære); 1916: The Mysterious Lady's Companion (Den mystike selskabsdame), The Spider (Gillekop); 1918: The Honour of the Countess (Grevindens ære), The Maharajah's Favourite Wife II (Maharadjæns yndlinghustru II), Via Crucis; 1919: Prometheus I-II; 1920: His Good Genius (Hans gode genius/Mod stjernene), The Parson of Vejlby (Præsten i Veljby); 1924: The Great Heart (Det store hjerte), The Big Treaty (Den store magot); 1925: His Grace (Hendes naade), The Dragon (Dragonen).*

Carlsen, Henning

Born June 4, 1927, in Aalborg. Carlsen gave up a career in medicine in 1948 to become assistant to Theodor Christensen, the founder of the Danish documentary movement after the war. Between 1949 and 1965 he made some forty shorts and, during the 1950's, made publicity films and documentaries. Among his shorts, *Old People* (1961) revealed his gift for analysing individuals which one finds in such later features as *The Cats* or *Oh, To Be on the Bandwagon!*. In 1966, the actor Per Oscarsson won the Best Actor award at Cannes for *Hunger*, and in 1975 *A Happy Divorce* opened the same festival. During the 1970's, Carlsen managed the Dagmar Cinema in Copenhagen, succeeding Carl Dreyer there.

Filmography

Main shorts − *Old People (De gamle); 1964: Family Portrait (Familiebilleder); 1965: Being Young (Ung). Features − 1962: Dilemma; 1963: How About Us/Epilogue (Hvad med os?); 1964: The Cats (Kattorna); 1966: Hunger (Sult); 1967: People Meet and Sweet Music Fills the Heart (Mennesker mødes og sød musik opstår i hjertet); 1969: We are All Demons (Klabautermanden); 1971: Are You Afraid? Of What? (Er i bange? Hvad er i bange for?); 1972: Oh, To Be on the Bandwagon! (Man ska 'bære hoget ved musikken); 1975: A Happy Divorce (En lykkelig skibmisse), Svante's Disappearance (Da Svante vorsvandt); 1978: Did Somebody Laugh? (Var der ikke en, som lo?); 1982: Your Money or Your Life (Pengene eller livet); 1986: Oviri/The Wolf at the Door (Oviri).*

Christensen, Benjamin

Born September 28, 1879 in Viborg, died April 2, 1959 in Copenhagen.

After obtaining his diploma in medicine, he became an opera singer in 1902, then a stage actor, and, from 1906 onwards, appeared in Danish films. Although his early films as a director showed his talents, it was with *Witchcraft through the Ages* that Christensen earned a worldwide reputation. In 1923, he was hired by a German studio to shoot some feature films. After playing the part of the painter in Dreyer's *Mikaël* (1924), he went to Hollywood and made several horror and fantasy movies, often tinged with black humour. During the late 1930's, back in Denmark, he made various melodramas. In 1944, he became manager of a cinema in Copenhagen.

Filmography

1913: *The Mysterious X (Det hemmelighedsfulde X,* Denmark); 1915: *The Night of Revenge/Blind Justice (Haevnens nat,* Denmark); 1921: *Witchcraft through the Ages (Häxan,* Sweden); 1923: *Among Jews (Unter Juden,* Germany), *His Wife, the Unknown (Seine Frau, die Unbekannte,* Germany); 1925: *The Woman with the Bad Voice (Die Frau mit dem schlechten Ref,* Germany); 1926: *The Devil's Circus* (U.S.A.); 1927: *Mockery* (U.S.A.), *The Hawk's Nest* (U..S.A.), *The Haunted House* (U.S.A.); 1929: *Seven Footprints to Satan* (U.S.A.), *The House of Horror* (U.S.A.); 1939: *Children of Divorce (Skilsmissens børn,* Denmark); 1940: *The Child (Barnet,* Denmark); 1941: *Go Home with Me (Gaa med mig hjem,* Denmark); 1942: *The Lady with the Gloves (Damen med de lyse handsker,* Denmark).

Dreyer, Carl Theodor

Born February 3, 1889, in Copenhagen, died March 20, 1968 id. An adopted child, Dreyer knew nothing of his family background until the age of 17; he was the son of a Swedish governess who had abandoned him at birth. After appearing briefly as a pianist in a café-restaurant, Dreyer worked for the Northern Telegraph Company. Bored, he went freelance in 1909 and contributed articles on sport, aeronautics (his hobby), and subjects ripe for satire. In 1911, he married Ebbe Larsen, who would be his companion for life. In 1912, he joined Nordisk Films Kompagni where he edited inter-titles and helped out with writing and editing chores. Some of his screenplays were brought to the screen by August Blom and Holger-Madsen (qq.v.).

In 1918, Dreyer signed a contract as a director at Nordisk. He shot in Norway, Berlin, and also in Denmark. *The Master of the House* brought him international renown. In 1926, he was invited to Paris, and made *The Passion of Joan of Arc* there during a nine-month spell. At the start of the 1930's he shot his first sound film, *Vampyr*, and became acquainted with the English documentary movement, and especially John Grierson. But he suffered from nervous depression and after abandoning *The White Slave* on location in Somalia, he returned to journalism as a critic and legal commentator. He made a comeback during the war years with his masterpiece on intolerance, *Day of Wrath*. In 1946 he established, with government help, a documentary school for which he made several shorts. From 1952 until his death, Dreyer was manager of the Dagmar Cinema in Copenhagen. In his final years he nurtured two dreams projects, one a version of *Medea* and the other a film on the life of Christ.

Filmography

Features − 1918: *The President (Præsidenten,* Denmark); 1919: *Leaves from Satan's Book (Blade af Satans bog,* Denmark); 1920: *The Parson's Widow (Prästänkan,* Norway); 1922: *Love One Another (Die Gezeichneten,* Germany); *Once Upon a Time (Det var engang,* Denmark); 1924: *Mikaël* (Germany); 1925: *Master of the House (Du skal ære din hustru,* Denmark); *The Bride of Glomdal (Glomdalsbruden,* Norway); 1927: *The Passion of Joan of Arc (La passion de Jeanne d'Arc,* France); 1932: *Vampyr (L'Etrange aventure de David Gray/Vampyr,* France); 1943: *Day of Wrath (Vredens dag,* Denmark); 1944: *Two People (Två människor,* Sweden); 1954: *The Word (Ordet,* Denmark); 1964: *Gertrud* (Denmark).

Shorts − 1942: *Helping Young Mothers (Mødre hjælpen);* 1946: *Water in Our Country (Vandet på landet);* 1947: *Old Country Churches (Landsbykirken), The Fight Against Cancer (Kampen mod kræften);* 1948: *They Caught the Ferry (De naaede færgen);* 1949: *Thorvaldsen;* 1950: *Storstrøm Bridge (Storstrømsbroen);* 1954: *A Castle within a Castle (Et slot i slot).*

Fleming, Edward

Born July 25, 1924. Of Scottish origin, Fleming chose Denmark as his adopted country. He began in the theatre and then worked in various cities: New York, Rome, and Paris (he was at the Lido for ten years). From 1960 to 1963 he was Artistic Adviser at the Monte Carlo Opera. After assisting directors such as Fellini and Visconti, he attended the Danish Film School from 1966 to 1969. Alongside his activities as a film director, Fleming is also an actor and director of programmes for TV and the stage in Denmark. His films have often attracted large audiences at home.

Filmography
1970: *And There's Dancing Afterwards (Og så er det bal); 1976: Brief Summer (Den korte sommer); 1978: Mirror, Mirror (Lille spejl); 1979: Traditions, Up Yours! (Rend mig i traditionerne); 1983: The Indecent Ones (De vanstændige); 1985: Chronic Innocence (Der kroniske uskyld); 1987: Waiting in the Wings (Sidste akt); 1991: Hay Fever (Høfeber).*

Gad, Peter Urban

Born February 12, 1879 in Skaelsor, died December 26, 1947 in Copenhagen. A nephew of Paul Gauguin, he gave up his studies to be a painter and opted for the theatre instead. But the triumph of his first film, *The Abyss*, persuaded him to devote all his energy to the cinema. This success was in large measure due to the actress Asta Nielsen, whom Gad married in 1911. In 1912, the couple left Denmark for Germany and enjoyed several screen successes together before separating in 1916. Gad went on to make films under the influence of German expressionism during the 1920's. In 1922, he quit Berlin to become head of a cinema in Copenhagen, the Grand. Gad is also the author of the first Danish book on the theory of cinema.

Filmography
1910: *The Abyss (Afgrunden,* Denmark); 1911: *The Black Dream (Den sorte drøm,* Denmark), *Hulda Rasmussen* (Denmark), *An Aviator's Curiosity (Den store flyver,* Denmark), *Through Trials to Victory (Gennem kamp til sejr,* Denmark), *The White Slave Trade III (Den hvide slavehandel III,* Denmark); 1912: *The Dance of Death (Die Totentanz,* Germany), *When the Masks Fall (Wenn die Maske fällt,* Germany), *Nine* (Germany). 1913: *The Maiden without a Homeland (Das Mädchen ohne Vaterland,* Germany), *Death in Seville (Der Tod in Sevilla,* Germany), *The Little Angel (Engelein,* Germany), *White Roses (Weissen Rosen,* Germany), *The Suffragette (Die Suffragette,* Germany); 1914: *Zapata's Gang (Zapatas Bande,* Germany); 1916: *The Eternal Night (Die ewige Nacht,* Germany); 1919: *The Wide Way (Der breite Weg,* Germany), *The Game of Love and Death (Das Spiel von Liebe und Tod,* Germany); 1921: *Christian Wahnschaffe − The Island of the Vanishing (Christian Wahnschaffe − Die Insel der Verschollenen,* Germany); 1922: *Christian Wahnschaffe − Hennele Mattern's Assumption (Christian Wahnschaffe − Henneles Himmelfahrt,* Germany); 1926: *The Wheel of Fortune (Lykkehjulet,* Denmark [*The Long and Short* series].

Henning-Jensen, Astrid and Bjarne

Astrid, maiden name Smahl, born December 10, 1914 in Copenhagen; Bjarne, born October 6, 1908, in Copenhagen. Bjarne was a stage actor at first and a dramaturge in the provinces and in Copenhagen from 1931 to 1938. He made his first documentaries from 1941 onwards for Statens Filmcentral. Astrid began as an assistant director at Nordisk and, with Bjarne, made several films. The couple shot numerous documentaries on social subjects during the 1940's and 1950's. But they were appreciated above all for their studies of young people. From 1949, Astrid and Bjarne directed most of their films separately, although they continued to collaborate actively. Astrid has also worked for the theatre, radio, and TV. She has won several prizes including a Silver Bear at the Berlin Festival for *Winter Born.*

Filmography
(Main films) 1943: *While Still Young (Naar man kun er ung,* B & A); 1946: *Ditte, Child of Man (Ditte, menneskebarn,* B); 1947: *Those Damned Kids (De pokkers under,* B & A); 1948: *Kristinus Bergman* (B & A); 1949: *Palle, Alone in the World (Palle alene i verden,* A); 1950: *A Western Harbour/Boys of the Western Sea (Vesterhavs drenge,* B & A); 1951: *Krane's Tea-Shop (Kranes konditori,* A, in Norway); 1952: *The Unknown (Ukjent man,* A, in Norway); 1953: *Solstice (Solstik,* B & A); 1955: *Love on Credit (Kærlighed pa kredit,* A); 1959: *Paw, a Child between Two Worlds (Paw,* A); 1961: *One among Many (En blandt mange,* A); 1962: *Short is the Summer/Love under the Midnight Sun (Kort er sommaren,* B), in Sweden); 1966: *Unfaithful (Utro,* A); 1970: *Me and You (Mej och dej,* A, in Sweden); 1978: *Winter Born (Vinterbørn,* A); 1980: *The Moment (Øjeblikket,* A); 1986: *Early Spring (Barndommensgade,* A). [A = Astrid, B = Bjarne]

Holger-Madsen, Forest

Born April 11, 1878 in Copenhagen, died November 30, 1943, *id.* He began work in the theatre at the age of 18 before being employed as an actor by Nordisk Films Kompagni in 1909. In 1912, he directed his first film, produced by Biorama, then returned to Nordisk, this time as a director. Extremely inventive, he made important advances for the cinema, especially in composition, production design, and camera movements and lighting (with his cinematographer Marius Clausen). He showed himself equally at home in all genres, from light comedy to social films, or mysteries. In 1920, he left to work in Germany. At the start of the 1930's, he returned to Denmark where he soon abandoned directing and became head of a cinema in Copenhagen, the Bio Enhave.

Filmography
(Main films) 1912: *Just a Beggar (Kun en tigger);* 1913: *Game of Love (Ellskovleg,* co-dir August Blom), *Under the Yoke of Passion (Under kærlighedens aag), Daughter of the Ballet (Balletens datter), Under the Plague (Under pesten);* 1914: *Dream of Opium (Opiumsdrømmen), The Evangelist (Evangeliemandens liv), Down with Weapons/Lay Down Your Arms (Ned med vaabnene), A Pact with the Devil (Den mystike fremmede), Alone at Last (Endelig alene), Adventure in the Harem (Et haremseventyr);* 1916: *The Spiritualists (Spiritisten);* 1917: *Eternal Peace (Pax æterna);* 1918: *The Sky Ship (Himmelskibet);* 1919: *Towards the Light (Mod lyset);* 1921: *Am Webstuhle der Zeit* (Germany); 1922: *Pömperty's Struggle with the Snowshoe (Pömpertys Kampf mit dem Schneeshuh,* Germany), *Zaida, a Model's Tragedy (Zaida, die Tragödie eines Modells,* Germany); 1928: *Free Will (Freiwild,* Germany); 1936: *The Sun over Denmark (Sol over Danmark).*

Kjærulff-Schmidt, Palle

Born July 7, 1931 in Esbjerg. His parents were both stage actors. After studying French and English, he turned to directing for both theatre and television. He made his debut in the cinema as an assistant director at Asa and in 1962, in collaboration with the writer Klaus Rifbjerg, made his first feature, *Week-end.* This film, which launched the Danish new wave, was banned in several countries and appeared in France, for example, some eighteen months after its premiere in Denmark. During the 1970's Kjærulff-Schmidt directed many productions for TV stations in Denmark, Germany, and Norway.

Filmography
1957: *Dregs (Bundfald);* 1959: *Time of Innocence (De sjove är);* 1962: *Week-end;* 1964: *Two (To);* 1965: *Summer War (Sommerkrig),* part of the portmanteau production, *4 x 4);* 1966: *Once There Was a War (Der var engang en krig);* 1967: *The Story of Barbara (Historien om Barbara);* 1968: *In the Green Forest (I den grønne skov);* 1969: *Think of a Number (Tænk på ett tal);* 1984: *Tukuma;* 1987: *Peter von Scholten.*

Kragh-Jacobsen, Søren

Born March 2, 1947. He attended the film school (FAMU) in Prague from 1970 to 1971. In 1972, he joined Danish Radio and TV where he became head of children's programmes until 1973. He also directed several shorts and TV programmes for a young audience. When it came to directing his first film, he also wrote the music. He deals primarily with youngsters and their rites of passage from childhood to adult life. He has won several prizes in Denmark and abroad.

Filmography

1978: *Wanna See My Beautiful Navel? (Vil du se min smukke navle?)*; 1980: *Goodbye Lulow* (TV, Danish contribution to a Scandinavian series about children in the 1930's); 1981: *Rubber Tarzan (Gummi Tarzan)*; 1983: *Thunderbirds (Isfugle)*; 1988: *Emma's Shadow (Skyggen av Emma)*; *Shower of Gold (Guldregn)*; 1991: *The Boys from St. Petri (Drenge fra St. Petri)*.

Leth, Jørgen

Born in 1937 in Århus. After leaving university, he became a journalist, covering sport, theatre, jazz, and the movies. During his career, he has held the post of head of production at the Danish Short Film Council, and taught at the Danish Film School. He is also the author of various literary essays and collections of poetry. Regarded as the best Danish documentarist of his generation, Leth communicates a very personal vision of reality, tinged with a poetic instinct. He is a familiar figure at international film festivals, an inveterate traveller, and an expert on cycling.

Filmography

1963: *No Parking (Stopforbud*, short); 1965: *The Future Looks Bright (Se frem til en tryg tid*, short); 1967: *The Perfect Human Being (Det perfekte menneske*, short); 1968: *Ophelia's Flower (Ofelias blomster*, short); *Near Heaven, Near Earth (Nær himlen, nær jorden*, short); 1970: *Chinese Ping-Pong (Kinesisk bordtennis*, short); *The Search (Eftersøgningen*, short), *Motion Picture* (short), *Dyrehaven, the Romantic Forest (Dyrehaven, den romantiske skov*, short); 1971: *Life in Denmark (Livet i Danmark*, short); 1973: *Stars and Watercarriers (Stjernerne og bandbærerne)*; 1974: *Klaus Rifbjerg* (short); 1975: *The Impossible Hour (Den umulige time*, short); *Good and Evil (Det gode og det onde*, short); 1976: *A Sunday in Hell (En forårsdag i helvede)*; 1978: *Peter Martins, A Dancer (Peter Martins, en danser*, short); 1979: *Dancing Bournonville (Att danse Bournonville*, short); 1981: *66 Scenes from America (66 scener fra America*, short); 1982: *Step on Silence* short); 1983: *Haiti Express (Udenrigskorrespondenten)*; 1984: *Pelota* short); 1986: *Moments of Play (Det legende menneske)*; 1987: *Notebook from China (Notater fra Kina)*; 1989: *Notes about Love (Notater om kærligheden)*.

Malmros, Nils

Born in 1944. Studied medicine, then turned to film, where he taught himself as he went along and made his first two films with the support of the Danish Film Institute. *Lars Ole 5c, Boys*, and *The Tree of Knowledge* form a semi-autobiographical trilogy on childhood and adolescence. Malmros won the Danish Critics' Prize for the first two films, and *The Tree of Knowledge* was shown in the 'Certain regard' section at Cannes. Malmros lives in Århus, the scene of his latest feature.

Filmography

1973: *Lars Ole 5c*; 1976: *Boys (Drenge)*; 1981: *The Tree of Knowledge (Kundskabens træ)*; *Beauty and the Beast (Skønheden og udyret)*; 1989: *Århus by Night*.

Roos, Jørgen

Born August 14, 1922 in Gilleleje. He learnt cimematography alongside his brother, the director Karl Roos, and Theodor Christensen, the pioneer of documentary film in Denmark. From 1942 to 1947, he made several experimental films with the Danish painter, Albert Mertz. They founded an influential film society together in 1945. From then on, Roos directed, photographed and edited his own films. He was assistant to Dreyer (q.v.) on *They Caught the Ferry* and *Castle within a Castle*. His documentaries included studies of cities such as Copenhagen, Oslo and Hamburg. He also made film portraits of various leading figures in Denmark, such as Dreyer himself and also the Nobel prizewinner Johannes V. Jensen. But his abiding interest has been Greenland, where he has brought his skilled technique and discerning eye to bear on the customs and life of the islanders. Roos's shorts have won many awards, including a Silver Bear in Berlin for *Knud* (1966).

Morten Arnfred

Astrid Henning-Jensen

Nils Malmros

Filmography

Films co-directed with Albert Mertz — 1942: *The Escape (Flugten)*; 1943: *Love on Rollerskates (Kærlighed paa rulleskøjter)*, *The Thief of Hearts (Hjertetyven)*; 1944: *Story of a Man (Historien om en man,* incomplete); 1947: *A Visit to King Tingeling (Paa besøg hos kong Tingeling)*, *Hello Animal! (Goddag dyr!)*. Films made alone — 1944: *Richard Mortensen's Mobile Painting (Richard Mortensens bevægelige maleri)*; 1947: *Johannes V. Jensen, Opus I, Reflexfilm*; 1948: *Mikkel;*

1949: *Paris from Two Angles (Paris på to moder), Jean Cocteau, Tristan Tzara Father of Dadaism (Tristan Tzara, dadaismens fader), The Final Rejection of an Appeal for a Kiss (Det definitive afslag på anmodningen om et kys;* co-dir.); 1950: *Eroded Horizons (Spiste horisonter,* co-dir.); *Johannes Jørgensen in Assisi (Johannes Jørgensen i Assisi), Hamlet's Castle (Shakespeare og Kronborg);* 1951: *Story of a Castle, J. F. Willumsen (Historien om et slot, J. F. Willumsen);* 1952: *The Streamlined Pig (Den strømlinjede gris), Slum, Holiday Child (Feriebørn);* 1953: *The Light in the Dark (Lyset i natten), The Infant (Spædbarnet), The New-born (Goddag børn!), Guilty − Not Guilty (Skyldig − ikke skyldig);* 1954: *Frescoes (Kalkmalerier), Inge Becomes an Adult (Inge bliver voksen), The Newspaper (Avisen), Martin Andersen Nexø's Last Journey (Martin Andersen Nexø's sidste rejse), Johannes Jørgensen in Svendborg (Johannes Jørgensen i Svendborg);* 1955: *The Story of My Life (Mit livs eventyr);* 1956: *Money (Sølv);* 1957: *Ellehammer, Johannes Larsen;* 1958: *Magic of the Diamond, The Six-Day Bicycle Race (6-dagesløbet);* 1059: *Pure Air;* 1960: *A City Called Copenhagen (En by ved navn København), Danish Design, The Dangers of Staphylococcus (Staphylokok-faren);* 1961: *The Faroe Islands (Føroyar/Færøerne), Hamburg;* 1962: *We Are Hanging by a Thread (Vi hænger i en tråd);* 1963: *Oslo;* 1965: *Noise (Støj);* 1966: *Carl Th. Dreyer, Knud, Sisimiut;* 1967: *A Hunting Family in the District of Thule (En fangerfamilie i Thuledistriktet); 17 Minutes Greenland (17 minutter Grønland), Recordings of Dialects and Drum-dancing in the District of Thule (Grønlandske dialektoptagelser og trommedanse fra Thuledistriktet), A Year with Henry (Et år med Henry);* 1968: *Ultima Thule;* 1969: *Weakmindedness Is Allowed (Det er tilladt at være andssvag);* 1970: *Kaláliuvit/Are You a Greenlander? (Kaláliuvit/Er du Grønlænder?);* 1971: *Andersen's Secret (Andersens hemmelighed);* 1972: *The House of Man (Huset til mennesker), The Emigrants (Udflytterne, Two Men in the Desert (To mænd i ødemarken), Ulrik Tells a Story (Ulrik fortæller en historie);* 1974: *In the Big Pyramid (I den store pyramide), J. Th. Arnfred;* 1975: *Andersen at the Photographer's (Andersen hos fotografen);* 1977: *Fifteen Days during the Iron Age (15 dage i jernalderen), Monarchy and Democracy (Monarki og demokrati);* 1978: *Carl Nielsen 1865-1931;* 1979: *Nuuk at 250 (Nuuk − 250 år);* 1980: *The Sirius Patrol (Slædepatruljen Sirius), Greenland (Grønland);* 1982: *The Commemorative Expedition of Knud Rasmussen to Cape Seddon (Knud Rasmussens mindeekspedition til Kap Seddon).*

Trier, Lars von
Born in 1956. He studied film at the University of Copenhagen from 1976 to 1979. In 1982, he obtained his diploma in directing at the Danish Film School. His short films as a student earned him various awards and his diploma work, *Images of a Relief,* was sold to several European TV stations. *The Element of Crime* won a prize for technique at Cannes and *Epidemic* also appeared at Cannes, in the section 'Un Certain Regard'. Regarded as the enfant terrible of Danish cinema, von Trier works in a sombre and experimental idiom, heavily influenced by German expressionism. *Europa* won two major prizes at Cannes in 1991.
Filmography
1984: *The Element of Crime (Forbrydelsens element);* 1987: *Epidemic;* 1991: *Europa/Zentropa (Europa).*

FINLAND

Blomberg, Erik
Born September 18, 1913 in Helsinki. He began his career working in a film lab, then attended the Regent Polytechnic in London. From 1935 onwards, he worked with contemporaries like Nyrki Tapiovaara (q.v.) and Risto Orko as an assistant and production manager. He also photographed some twenty films himself. In 1952 he made his first feature film, *The White Reindeer,* a masterpiece which won a major prize at Cannes among other awards. After 1965, Blomberg turned to television and making documentaries for the small screen.
Filmography
1952: *The White Reindeer (Valkoinen peura);* 1954: *When There Are Feelings (Kun on tunteet);* 1955: *Hunting for Miss Europe (Miss Eurooppaa metsästämässä), The Betrothal/The Engagement (Kilhaus);* 1962: *The Wedding Night (Hääyö/Noc poslubna,* co-prod with Poland).

Donner, Jörn
Born February 5, 1933 in Helsinki. After making some shorts in Finland, Donner moved to neighbouring Sweden where he worked as a high-profile film critic and, between 1963 and 1967, made four features there. From 1968 onwards he settled back in Finland and directed and produced several films, many imbued with his particular brand of irony. Donner is also known as the co-founder of the Finnish Film Archive, as a producer who takes risks on young directors' work, and as an energetic Member of Parliament. From 1972 to 1975 he managed the archive at the Swedish Film Institute, and between 1978 and 1980 was President of the same body. From 1982 to 1984 and, between 1986 and 1989, Donner served as the influential Chairman of the Finnish Film Foundation. His novels have brought him additional fame in Finland, as well as the coveted Finlandia Prize.
Filmography
1963: *A Sunday in September (En söndag i september,* Sweden); *To Love (Att älska,* Sweden); 1965: *Adventure Starts Here (Här börjar äventyret,* Sweden); 1967: *He-She (Han-hon,* episode for *Stimulantia,* Sweden); *Rooftree (Tvärbalk,* Sweden); 1968: *Black on White (Mustaa valkoisella);* 1969: *Sixtynine (Sixtynine);* 1970: *Portraits of Women (Naisenkuvia);* 1971: *Anna* (Sweden), *Fuck Off! Images of Finland (Perkele! Kuvia suomesta,* documentary); 1972: *Tenderness (Hellyys);* 1975: *Hangover (Baksmälla/Krapula);* 1976: *Three Scenes with Ingmar Bergman* (documentary); 1978: *The Bergman File* (documentary), *Men Can't Be Raped (Miestä ei voi raiskata);* 1985: *Dirty Story (Likainen tarina).*

Honkasalo, Pirjo; Lehto, Pekka
Pirjo Honkasalo (born February 22, 1947 in Pori) attended the Faculty of Industrial Arts in Helsinki before studying at the Film department of the University of Philadelphia. On her return to Finland, she worked as a stills photographer, then as a cinematographer, before assisting Rauni Mollberg (q.v.) on *Earth Is Our Sinful Song* (1973). She then directed various shorts and TV films, before shooting her feature films in collaboration with Lehto. He had begun as a sound engineer, and the worked together with Honkasalo to make the highly-acclaimed short, *Their Age,* in 1976. In 1981, *Flame-Top* earned excellent reviews and was selected for competition at Cannes. During the 1980's, Lehto was head of production at the Finnish Film Foundation, and now works independently.
Filmography
1976: *Their Age/Age Class (Ikäluokka,* short), *Swastika* (short), *Two Forces (Kainuu 39);* 1980: *Flame Top (Tulipää);* 1983: *250 grammes −A Radioactive Testament (250 grammaa,* short); 1985: *Da Capo;* 1991: *The Well (Kaivo,* dir. Lehto alone), *Mysterion* (documentary, dir. Honkasalo alone).

Jarva, Risto
Born July 15, 1934 in Helsinki, died December 16, 1977 *id.* Jarva became interested in the cinema during his school years and, while

qualifying as a chemical engineer, he retained a lively interest in both sciences and the humanities. He produced his own films (with Kullervo Kukkasjärvi) and then often took his actors from the amateur ranks. His range extended from documentaries to fiction films and dramatic comedies. From 1970 to 1975 he served as Artistic Professor and was chairman of the state committee dealing with film issues. Killed in a car accident on the night of the premiere of *The Year of the Hare*, Jarva left behind him a suite of films that epitomised the Finnish new wave of the 1960's, admired by critics and audiences alike.

Filmography
1962: *Night or Day (Yö vai päivä,* co-dir Jaakko Pakkasvirta); 1964: *Baron X (X Paroni,* co-dir Jaakko Pakkasvirta and Spede Pasanen); 1965: *Game of Chance (Onnenpeli);* 1967: *A Worker's Diary (Työmiehen päiväkirja);* 1969: *Time of Roses (Ruusujen aika);* 1970: *Rally (Bensaa suonissa);* *When the Heavens Fall (Kun taivas putoaa);* 1973: *One Man's War (Yhden miehen sota);* 1975: *The Man Who Couldn't Say No (Mies joka e osannut sanoa ei);* 1976: *Holidays (Loma);* 1977: *The Year of the Hare (Jäniksen vuosi).*

Karu, Erkki

Born April 10, 1887 in Helsinki, died December 12, 1935 *id.* Founder of two very important, and rival, companies: Suomi-Filmi Oy (1919) and Suomen Filmiteollisuus (1933), Karu produced more than forty films and directed some twenty features which are among the most significant and pioneering of the period. He was as at home with making documentaries as he was with comedy and melodrama.

Filmography
1920: *War Profiteer/Kaiku's Disrupted Summer Vacation (Sotagulashi Kaiun häiritty kesäloma),* *Student Pöllövaara's Betrothal (Ylioppilas Pöllövaaran kilhaus);* 1922: *Finlandia* (documentary, co-dir Eero Leväluoma), *The Lumberjack's Bride(The Logroller's Bride (Koskenlaskijan morsian);* 1923: *The Village Shoemakers/The Heath Cobblers (Nummisuutarit),* *When Father Has Toothache (Kun isällä on hammassärky);* 1924: *The Fisherman of Storm Skerry (Myrskyluoden kalastaja);* 1925: *Summer Fairytale (Suivinen satu);* 1926: *Fugitives from Murmansk (Muurmannin pakolaiset);* 1927: *The Poet Moves (Runoilija muuttaa),* *The Young Pilot (Nuori luotsi);* 1929: *Our Boys (Meidän poikamme);* 1931: *The Logdriver's Bride (Tukkipojan morsian);* 1933: *Our Boys at Sea (Meidän poikamme merellä),* *The Mother-in-Law Cometh! (Voi meitä! anoppi tulee),* *Those 45,000 (Ne 45000);* 1934: *Our Boys in the Air, We on the Ground (Meidän poikamme ilmassa, me maassa);* 1935: *The Scapegoat (Syntipukki),* *On the Roinila Farm (Roinilan talossa).*

Kassila, Matti

Born January 12, 1924 in Keuruu. He began his career in 1943 as a stage actor, both in the provinces and in Helsinki. From 1946, he worked as an assistant film director and made several shorts. From 1955 to 1958, he also directed plays in Helsinki and Pori. Regarded during the 1950's as the best Finnish film director, particularly for *Blue Week* and *Harvest Month*, Kassila found it hard to adapt to the changes of the 1960's. From 1977 to 1979, he was head of production at the Finnish Film Foundation. In 1988, however, he recovered his form with *Glory and Misery of Human Life*, which won the Grand Prix at the Festival of Nordic Cinema in Rouen.

Filmography
1949: *Professor Masa (Professori Masa),* *The Head of the House Plays the Accordion (Isäntä soittaa hanuria);* 1950: *Maija finds the Right Tune (Maija löytää sävelen);* 1951: *It Happened in Ostrobothnia (Lakeuksien lukko),* *The Radio Commits a Burglary (Radio tekee murron);* 1952: *The Radio Goes Crazy (Radio tulee hulluksi),* *Song of Warsaw (Varsovan laulu),* *The Girl From the Moon Bridge (Tyttö kuunsillalta);* 1954: *Blue Week (Sininen viikko),* *Hilma's Name Day (Hilmanpäivät);* 1955: *Father's New and Ex (Isän vanha ja uusi),* *The Reverend Jussilainen (Pastori Jussilainen);* 1956: *Harvest Month (Elokuu);* 1957: *Wild Generation (Kuriton sukupolvi),* *Scapegoat (Syntipukki);* 1959: *The Red Line (Punainen viiva),* *Heart of Glass (Lasisydän);* 1960: *Inspector Palmu's Mistake (Komisario Palmun erehdys);* 1961: *The Blood-red Pigeon (Tulipunainen kyykhynen),* *Step*

on the Gas, Inspector Palmu! (Kaasua, komisario Palmu!); 1962: *The Stars Will Tell, Inspector Palmu (Tähdet kertovat, komisario Palmu),* *The Faces of Three Cities (Kolmen kaupungin kasvot);* 1968: *Let Not One Devil Cross the Bridge (Äl' yli päästä perhanaa);* 1969: *Vodka, Inspector Palmu (Vodkaa, komisario Palmu);* 1970: *The Headquarters (Päämaja);* 1971: *In Adam's Clothes and a Little Bit in Eve's Too (Aatamin puvussa ja vähän Eevankin);* 1972: *I Want to Love, Peter (Haluan rakastaa, Peter);* 1973: *It's Up to Us (Meiltähän tämä käy);* 1979: *Natalia;* 1984: *The Tug of Home (Niskavuori);* 1987: *Farewell to the President (Jäähyväiset presidentille);* 1988: *The Glory and Misery of Human Life (Ihmiselon ihanuus ja kurjuus).*

Kaurismäki, Aki

Born April 4, 1957 in Orimattila. He began his career as an actor and screenwriter on the mid-length film, *The Liar* (1980), and then co-wrote *The Worthless*, both films directed by his brother Mika (q.v.). In *Shadows in Paradise, Ariel,* and *The Girl from the Match Factory,* Kaurismäki brings a beady eye, tinged with black homour, to bear on characters dwelling in the margins of society. He has become a cult figure at festivals around the world.

Filmography
1981: *The Saimaa Gesture (Saimaa-ilmiö,* co-dir Mika Kaurismäki); 1983: *Crime and Punishment (Rikos ja rangaistus);* 1985: *Calamari Union;* 1986: *Shadows in Paradise (Varjola paratiisissa);* 1987: *Hamlet Goes Business (Hamlet liikemaailmassa);* 1988: *Ariel;* 1989: *Leningrad Cowboys Go America;* 1990: *The Match Factory Girl (Tulitikkutehtaan tyttö),* *I Hired a Contract Killer;* 1991: *Scenes from a Bohemian Life (Boheemielämää).*

Kaurismäki, Mika

Born September 21, 1955 in Orimattila. He studied at the Munich Film School. After depicting a young and rebellious generation in *The Worthless*, Kaurismäki turned to various genres, chief among them comedy and adventures, in the road movie idiom. The family unit, and relationships that stretch beyond his native Finland, are important to this director. *Zombie and the Ghost Train* won a major award at San Sebastian in 1991.

Filmography
1980: *The Liar (Valehtilija,* short); 1981: *The Saimaa Gesture (Saimaa-ilmiö,* co-dir Aki Kaurismäki); 1982: *The Worthless (Arvottomat),* *Jackpot 2* (short); 1984: *The Clan − Tale of the Frogs (Klaani − tarina sammakoitten suvusta);* 1985: *Rosso;* 1987: *Helsinki-Napoli All Night Long;* 1989: *Cha, Cha, Cha;* *Paper Star (Paperitähti);* 1990: *Amazon;* 1991: *Zombie and the Ghost Train (Zombie ja kummitusjuna).*

Kurkvaara, Maunu

Born July 18, 1926 in Vyborg. Began as assistant director in 1949. He made short films, established his own film laboratory, and worked as a producer. Between 1955 and 1971, Kurkvaara directed seventeen films. He then abandoned the cinema to become a boat designer and builder. He usually wrote his own screenplays, as well as photographing and editing his films.

Filmography
1955: *Island of Happiness (Onnen saari);* 1956: *No More Tomorrows (Ei enää elispäivää);* 1958: *Tweet Tweet (Tirlittan);* 1959: *The Queen of Spades (Patarouva);* 1960: *Car Girls (Autotytöt);* 1961: *Darling (Rakas . . .);* 1962: *Private Property (Yksityisalue);* 1963: *Festival at Sea (Meren juhlat),* *Saturday Games (Lauantaileikit);* 1964: *Women (Naiset),* *Report − or The Ballad of the Sailors' Girls (Raportti eli Balladi laivatytöistä);* 1965: *Why* (episode from the pan-Scandinavian production, *4 x 4*), *The Forbidden Book (Kielletty kirja);* 1966: *Today, You Are Here (Tänään olet täällä);* 1968: *The Rat War (Rottasota),* *The Million Dollar Gang (Miljoonaliiga),* *Redhead (Punatukka);* 1971: *The Gauntlet (Kujanjuoksu);* 1983: *A Taste of Success (Menestyksen maku);* 1986: *Butterfly's Dream (Perhosen uni).*

Laine, Edvin

Born July 14, 1905 in Isalmi, died November 18, 1989, in Helsinki. He was a stage actor and director in Turku from 1928 to 1935, then until 1943 at the theatre in Tampere. From 1943 to 1950 he was head of that establishment. He also worked at the People's Theatre in Helsinki for ten years, in tandem with his film activities. From 1931 onwards he was involved in the Finnish film industry as both actor and, from the wartime period, director also. His great moment came in 1955, with the release of the national epic, *The Unknown Soldier*. Laine ended his days attached to the National Theatre.

Filmography
1943: *The Sin of the Lady of Yrjänä (Yrjänñ emännän synti)*; 1945: *In the Shadow of the Prison Bars (Ristikon varjossa)*, *Crime and Gold (Nokea ja kultaa)*; 1946: *The Golden Candlestick (Kultainen kynttilänjalka)*, *The Glorious Melody (Kirkastuva sa: The Gold Medallist's Wife (Kultamitalivaimo)*, *Little Matti Out in the Wide World (Pikku Matti maailmalla)*; 1948: *The Song of the City Outskirts (Laitakaupungin laulu)*, *The Singing Heart (Laulava sydän)*, *Lucky Peter (Onnen-Pekka)*; 1949: *Ugly Elsa (Ruma Elsa)*, *Sleeping Beauty (Prinsessa ruusonen)*, *Aaltonen's Missus Takes Charge (Aaltoska organiseeraa)*; 1950: *The Old Man and the Youngster (Isäpappa ja keltanokka)*, *Love North of the Arctic Circle (Tapahtin kaukana)*; 1951: *Darling, I Hate You (Vihaan sinua — rakas)*; 1952: *The Price of One Night (Yhden yön hinta)*, *Heta from Niskavuori (Niskavuoren Heta)*; 1953: *After the Fall of Man (Jälkeen syntiinlankeemuksen)*; 1954: *With Respect (Kunnioittaen)*, *Arne of Niskavuori (Niskavuoren Aarne)*, *Opri*; 1955: *The Veteran's Victory (Veteraarin voitto)*, *The Unknown Soldier (Tuntematon sotilas)*; 1957: *Black Love (Musta rakkaus)*, *The Niskavuori Fights (Niskavuori taistelee)*; 1958: *Soldier Sven (Sven tuuva)*; 1960: *Scandal in the Girls' School (Skandaali tyttökoulussa)*, *The Delayed Wedding Night (Myöhästynyt hääyö)*; 1962: *Little Iris Klewe (Pikku suorassu)*, *The Baron of Pinsiö (Pinsiön parooni)*; 1968: *Here Beneath the Polar Star (Täällä pohjantähden alla)*; 1970: *Akseli and Elina (Akseli ja Elina)*; *The North Star (Pohjantähti)*; 1976: *Trust (luottamus*, co-dir Viktor Tregubovits)*; 1977: *The Last Lumbercamp (Viimeinen savotta)*; 1979: *Winter of Black Snow (Ruskan jälkeen)*; 1983: *How To Find a Wife for a Farmer (Akaton mies)*; 1986: *The Farmer Takes a Wife (Akallinen mies)*.

Lehmuskallio, Markku

Born December 31, 1938 in Rauma. He was a water engineer and qualified forester until 1969. From 1970 to 1972 he made industrial and advertising short films. From 1973 onwards, Lehmuskallio concentrated on directing full-length documentaries and assisting directors like Mikko Niskanen (q.v.) and Heikki Partanen (q.v.) on the photography of their films. Since 1980 he has made feature films combining his documentary skills with a profound love of nature.

Filmography
1973: *Echoes from the Nordic Forests (Pohjoisten metsien ääniä*, docu.)*; 1974: *Tapiola (docu.)*; 1976: *Dance of Life (Elämän tanssi*, docu.)*; 1980: *The Raven's Dance (Korpinpolska)*; 1982: *Skierri — Land of the Dwarf Birch (Skierri — vaivaiskoivujen maa)*; 1985: *Blue Mammy (Sininen imettäjä)*; 1988: *Inuksuk*; 1991: *I Am 1 and 2 (Minä olen 1 & 2*, docu.)*.

Mollberg, Rauni

Born April 15, 1929 in Hämmeenlinna. During the 1950's, he worked at the theatres of both Joensuu and Kuopio as actor, director and producer. From 1963 onwards, he made numerous films and series for the Finnish television. His first feature for the cinema, *Earth Is Our Sinful Song*, adapted from a novel by Timo K. Mukka, had a huge success at home and abroad, establishing Mollberg as the most incisive director of his generation. Each of his subsequent feature films has been long in gestation, but each has proved thoughtful in writing and magisterial in execution.

Filmography
1963: *Kuopio short)*; 1964: *The Ants of Our Lord (Meidän Heramme muurahaisia*, TV series)*; 1967: *My Childhood (Lapsuuteni*, TV series)*; 1969: *In the Shadow of the Factory (Tehtaan varjossa*, TV series)*; 1971: *The Shop Steward (Pääluottamusmies*, TV series)*; 1972: *The War Hermit (Sotaerakko*, TV film)*; 1973: *Earth Is Our Sinful Song*

(Maa on syntinen laulu); 1975: *The Merry Madness (Siunattu hulluus*, TV series)*; 1976: *Turo short)*; 1977: *Pretty Good for a Human Being (Aika hyvä ihmiseksi)*; 1978: *Kustaa Vilkuna (short)*; 1979: *Tampere 200 (short)*; 1980: *Milka, a Film about Taboos (Milka — elokuva tabuista)*; 1985: *The Unknown Soldier (Tuntematon sotilas)*; 1990: *Friends, Comrades (Ystävät, toverit)*.

Niskanen, Mikko

Born January 2, 1929 in Äänekoski, died November 25, 1990 in Helsinki. From 1947 to 1950 he studied at Finland's National School of Dramatic Art, and then began acting on stage in Kuopio and Jyväskylä. In 1955, he worked at Filmiteollisuus as a camera operator. Between 1958 and 1960 he attended the famed VGIK Film School in Moscow and took various small roles on screen. He enjoyed conspicuous success a director with *Skin, Skin* (1966) and *Eight Deadly Shots* (1972, first a TV mini-series, then re-edited for theatrical release). From 1964 onwards he worked also for television, although until the end of his life Niskanen remained loyal to the cinema and to his socially committed ideals.

Filmography
1962: *Boys (Pojat)*; 1963: *The Partisans (Sissit)*, *Silver from across the Border (Hopeaa rajan takaa)*; 1966: *Skin, Skin (Käpy selän alla)*; 1967: *Girl of Finland (Lapualaismorsian)*; 1968: *The Asphalt Lambs (Asfalttilampaat)*; 1971: *Song of the Scarlet Flower (Lauli tulipunaisesta kukasta)*; 1972: *Eight Deadly Shots (Kahdeksan surmanluotia)*; 1977: *The Horse Rebellion (Pulakapina)*; 1978: *In the Autumn, Everything Will Be Different (Syksyllä kaikki on toisin)*; 1982: *Gotta Run! (Ajolähtö)*; 1984: *Mona and the Time of Burning Love (Mona ja palavan rakkauden aika)*; 1986: *Life's Hardy Men (Elämän vonkamies)*; 1988: *Lumbercamp Tales (Nuoruuteni savotat)*.

Partanen, Heikki

Born January 29, 1942 in Helsinki; died November 26, 1990 *id.* He began by directing animation films for children. During the 1970's he created, in collaboration with Riitta Rautoma, a series of tales called *Power*, in which each episode dealt with a social phenomenon such as violence or racism. In 1976, he directed his first feature, *Antti Treebranch*, based on a famous fairy story, and then *Ramses and the Dreams*, a kind of docudrama about ancient Egypt. In 1984, he enjoyed his finest hour with *Pessi and Illusia*, inspired by Yrjö Kokko's book of fairy stories.

Filmography
1964: *Hinku and Vinku (Hinku ja Vinku*, animation)*; 1966: *Good Behaviour Flower (Käytöskukka*, animation)*. 1976: *Antti Treebranch (Antti Puuhaara*, co-dir Riitta Rautoma)*; 1982: *Ramses and the Dreams (Ramses ja unet)*; 1984: *Pessi and Illusia (Pessi ja Illusia)*. During the 1970's, Partanen made a series called 'Power' including *The Pencil, the Penny, and the Hammer*, *The Perfumed Pig*; *The Baker*; *Blue Man*; and *The Fox and the Bear*.

Salminen, Ville

Born October 2, 1908 in Maariahamina. He was a set decorator and stage actor from 1932 to 1938. Between 1941 and 1961, he directed thirty films, while continuing to be active in the theatre. His films aimed to please a broad public and were distinguished by their slick technique and fast pace. From 1961 to 1973, Salminen worked at the commercial TV station, MTV, in charge of the cinema section. (Kari Uusitalo).

Filmography
1941: *The Last Guest (Vimeinen vieras*, co-dir Arvi Tuomi)*; 1945: *What a Night (Mikä yö)*; 1946: *Shadow of the Past (Menneisydan varjo)*; 1948: *Leeni of Haavisto (Haaviston Leeni)*, *May Magic (Tuokokuun taika)*, *Irmeli — Sweet Seventeen (Irmeli seitsentoistavuotias)*, *The Virile Bomber Boys (Pontevat pommaripojat)*; 1949: *The Orphan's Waltz (Orpopojan valssi)*; 1950: *The Poor Singer (Köyhä laulaja)*, *Beautiful Vera/Ballad of Lake Saimaa (Kaunis Veera eli Ballaadi Saimaalta)*; 1951: *The General's Fiancée (Kenraalin morsian)*, *A Night in Rio (Rion yö)*, *The Scarf (Tytön huivi)*; 1952: *Just We Artists (Mitäs me taiteilijat)*, *The Sailor*

Quartet (Kipparikvartetti); 1953: *Esa Flies to Kuopio (Lentävä kelekukko)*, *Pete Blockhead (Pekka Puupää)*, *Snow White and the Seven Loggers (Lumikki ja 7 jätkkä)*, *The Nude on the Run (Alaston malli karkuteillä)*; 1954: *Naval Recruits on Shore Leave (Laivaston monnit maissa)*, *On Deck (Laivan kannella)*; 1955: *The Säkkijärvi Polka (Säkkijärven polkka)*; 1956: *Evacuated (Evakko)*, *Anu and Mikko (Anu ja Mikko)*; 1957: *Another Girl Lost (Taas tyttö kadoksissa)*; 1959: *Just an Ordinary Finn (Yks' tavallinen Virtanen)*; 1960: *Oho! Said Emil*

Erik Blomberg

Erkki Karu

Risto Jarva

Aki Kaurismäki

Rauni Mollberg

Valentin Vaala

270

(Oho, sanoi Eemeli), Two Ordinary Guys (Kaks' tavallista lahtista), Kerplunk, Said Emil (Molskis, sanoi Eemeli, molskis!); 1961: *Song after the Heart's Desire (Toivelauluja).*

Särkkä, Toivo J.

Born November 20, 1890 in Mikkeli, died February 9, 1975 in Helsinki. He only entered the cinema at the age of 44 and in 1935 became managing director of Suomen Filmiteollisuus, founded two years earlier by Erkki Karu (q.v.). During the next three decades, Särkkä produced no fewer than 233 films and directed 49 of them off his own bat. Although he left no works of great consequence, he displayed undoubted talent as a screenwriter. Along with Risto Orko of Suomi-Filmi Oy, Särkkä was an unquestioned leader of the Finnish cinema during the 1930's and 1940's.

Filmography

[YN=films directed with Yrjö Norta] 1936: *All Kinds of Visitors (Kaikenlaisia vieraita,* YN), *The Bothnians/The Northerners (Pohjalaisia,* YN); 1937: *The Assessor's Love Troubles (Asessorin naishuolet,* YN), *Like Dream and Shadow (Kuin uni ja varjo,* YN), *The Old Railroad Worker (Lapatossu,* YN); 1938: *Out to Borrow Matches (Tulitikkuja lainaamassa,* YN), *Have I Entered a Harem? (Leuko minä tullut haaremiin?,* YN), *The Black Sheep of the Regiment (Rykmentin murheenkryyni,* YN); 1939: *Forward – Towards Life (Eteenpäin – Elämään,* YN), *The February Manifesto (Helmikuun Manifesti,* YN). *God's Judgement (Jumalan tuomio,* YN), *The Little Fiddler (Pikku pelimanni), Serenade with a War Trumpet (Serenaadi sotatorvella);* 1940: *The Girl from Suotorppa/The Tenant Farmer's Girl (Suotorpan tyttö), The King of Poets and the Bird of Passage (Runon kuningas ja muuttolintu), The Department Store 'Lapatossu and Vinski' (Tavaratalo Lapatossu ja Vinski);* 1941: *The Vagabond's Waltz (Kulkurin valssi), The Suominen Family (Suomisen perhe), Beautiful Regina of Kaivopuisto (Kaivopuiston kaunis Regina), The Lucky Cabinet Officer/The Happy Minister (Onnelin ministeri);* 1942: *The Wheel of Chance (Onni pyörii), To a New Life (Uuteen elämään), August Will Fix Everything (August järjestää kaiken);* 1944: *The Wooden Pauper's Bride (Vaivaisukon morsian), Ballad (Ballaadi), Silvi (Silvi), Anja Come Back Home! (Anja tule kotiin), Olli Falls in Love (Suomisen Olli rakastuu);* 1946: *Youth in a Fog (Nuoruus sumussa);* 1947: *Finland Great Games of 1947 (Suomen Suurkisat 1947), Destinies of Women (Naiskohtaloita), The Wild Rosemary Blooms (Suopursu kukii);* 1948: *The Fourteenth Guest (Neljästoista vieras);* 1949: *From the Little Fiddler to the King of Violinists (Pikku pelimannista viulun kunikaaski), Behind the Street Scene/Behind the Street Mirror (Katupeilin takana);* 1950: *Dance over the Graves (Tanssi yli hautojen), Katarina, the Beautiful Widow (Katariina kaunis leski);* 1953: *Hilja, the Milkmaid (Hilja, maitotyttö);* 1955: *Beloved Rascal (Rakas lurjus);* 1956: *Five Jolly Rascals (Viisi vekkulia), Juha;* 1957: *1918 (1918 – mies ja hänen omatuntonsa);* 1958: *The Little Girl with the Broom (Pieni luutatyttö);* 1959: *Playing a Hard Game Up North (Kovaa peliä pohjolassa), The Suominen Family Is Here Again (Taas tapaame Suomisen perheen);* 1960: *At the Well (Kankkulan kaivola,* co-dir Aarne Tarkas); 1961: *Short by a Million (Miljoonavaillinki), The Moon Is Dangerous (Kuu on vaarallinen), Us (Me);* 1962: *The Beautiful Adventure (Ihana sakkailu).*

Tapiovaara, Nyrki

Born September 10, 1910 in Pitäjänmäki, died February 29, 1940 near Tohmajärvi. He began his career as a critic and as a stage director. In 1937, he made his first film, *Juha,* from the bestselling novel by Juhani Aho (already brought to the screen by Sweden's Mauritz Stiller under the title *Johan*). Missing presumed dead on the Karelian front during the Winter War with the Soviet Union, Tapiovaara was unable to complete *The Way of a Man,* which was edited after his death by Hugo Hytönen and Erik Blomberg (q.v.). He is widely regarded as the greatest talent the Finnish cinema has produced, and serves still as an inpiration to younger directors.

Filmography

1937: *Juha;* 1938: *Stolen Death (Varastettu kuolema);* 1939: *Two henpecked Husbands/The Two Victors (Kaksi vihtoria), Mr. Lahtinen Takes French Leave/Mr. Lahtinen Takes Off (Herra Lahtinen lähtee lipettiin);* 1940: *The Way of a Man (Miehen tie,* co-dir Hugo Hytönen).

Vaala, Valentin

Born October 11, 1909 in Helsinki, died November 22, 1976 *id.* He entered the cinema in 1927, and soon became known for his comedies. Later he became adept at presenting romantic melodrama on screen, and especially convincing when dealing with bucolic themes (e.g. *People in the Summer Night* and *Loviisa*). Prolific and self-effacing in style, Vaala proved to be one of the mainstays of Finnish cinema during its most active period.

Filmography

1929: *The Gypsy Charmer (Mustalaishurmaaja), Dark Eyes (Mustat silmät);* 1931: *The Wide Road (Laveata tietä);* 1933: *The Blue Shadow or The Midnight Murder (Sininen varjo eli keskiyön murha);* 1934: *The Most Famous Businessman in Helsinki (Helsingin kuuluisin liikemies(Koustu, Fransi ja liljepekin Kalle);* 1935: *When Father Wants to . . . (Kun isä tahtoo . . .), Everybody's in Love (Kaikki rakastavat);* 1936: *Surrogate Wife (Vaimoke), Surrogate Husband (Mieheke);* 1937: *The Logroller's Bride/Bride of the Rapids Shooter (Koskenlaskijan morsian), Hulda of Juurakko/Hulda from Juurakko (Juurakon Hulda);* 1938: *The Women of Niskavuori (Niskavuoren naiset), The Man from Sysmä (Sysmäläinen);* 1939: *The Rich Girl (Rikas tyttö), Green Gold (Vihreä kulta);* 1940: *The Wrath of God (Jurmalon myrsky);* 1941: *Andreas and Sinful Yolanda (Antreas ja syntinen Jolanda), A Surprising Bride (Morsian yllättää);* 1942: *Safety Valve (Varaventtiili), The Bride on the Swing (Keinumorsian);* 1943: *Miss Hothead (Neiti tuittupää), With Serious Intent (Tositarkoituksella);* 1944: *The Dynamite Girl (Dynamiititytttö);* 1945: *The Green Room at Linnainen Manor (Linnaisten vihreä kamari);* 1946: *Loviisa, Niskavuoren nuori emäntä);* 1947: *Maaret – Daughter of the Fells (Maaret – tunturien tyttö);* 1948: *People in the Summer Night (Ihmiset suviyössä);* 1949: *The Crevice (Jossain on railo), It's You I want (Sinut minä tahdon);* 1951: *Gabriel, Come Back (Gabriel, tule takaisin!);* 1952: *The Vagabond's Girl (Kulkurin tyttö), The Apple Falls (Omena putoaa);* 1953: *April Is Coming (Huhtikuu tulee), The Steward of Siltala (Siltalan pehtoori);* 1954: *Me, a Father! (Minäkö isä!);* 1955: *Me and My Husband's Fiancée (Minä ja mieheni morsian);* 1956: *Our Common Wife (Yhteinen vaimomme);* 1957: *The Village Shoemakers (Nummisuutarit);* 1958: *The Young Miller (Nuori mylläri), The Women from Niskavuori (Niskavuoren naiset);* 1960: *Roads to Battle (Taistelujen tie);* 1961: *Swinging Youth (Nuoruus vauhdissa);* 1963: *The Truth Is Merciless (Totuus on armoton).*

Witikka, Jack

Born December 20, 1916 in Helsinki. He worked with Michael Powell on the making of his first film, *Aila, Girl of the North.* An inventive director, Witikka has a rigorous style that enables him to present his themes and ideas in a very logical manner. He was also a stage director, and head of the Finnish National Theatre. From 1957 to 1967 he was President of the Finnish Film Archive.

Filmography

1951: *Aila, Daughter of the North (Aila, Pohjolan tytär);* 1954: *Pessi and Illusia (Pessi ja Illusia), Upon the Highest Bough (Mä oksalla ylimmällä);* 1955: *The Doll Merchant and Beautiful Lilith (Nukkekauppias ja kaunis Lilith);* 1956: *Silja – Fallen Asleep When Young (Silja – nuorena nukkunut);* 1958: *The Motherless Ones (Äidittömät), A Man from This Planet (Mies tältä tähdeltä);* 1959: *A Big Hit Parade (Suuri sävelparaati), The Virtanens and the Lahtinens (Virtaset ja Lahtiset);* 1960: *Fun at the Amusement Park (Illoinen Linnanmäki);* 1961: *Little Peter's Yard (Pikku Pietarin piha).*

ICELAND

Thráinn Bertelsson

Ágúst Gudmundsson

Bertelsson, Thráinn

Born November 30, 1944 in Reykjavík. Earned his diploma at the Swedish Film School in 1977. From 1978 to 1980, he was a producer at the Icelandic Television. He enjoyed great popular success with a trio of comedies dealing with two guys in a fishing village (New Life), on a farm (Pastoral Life), and in the police force (A Policeman's Lot). Bertelsson has also worked as a journalist, teacher, and writer. One of his books won a prize as best children's book for 1984. He has his own production company and publishing house, New Life Productions. Since 1986, he has been editor in chief of the newspaper, Pjódviljinn. Magnús was nominated for a Felix as Best European Film of 1990.
Filmography
1981: The Twins (Jón Oddur og Jón Bjarni); 1983: New Life (Nýtt lif); 1984: Pastoral Life (Dalalif); 1985: Deep Winter/Twilight (Skammdegi), A Policeman's Lot (Löggulif); 1989: Magnús.

Fridriksson, Fridrik Thór

Born May 12, 1954 in Reykjavík. Started making 16mm shorts while still at college, and was co-founder of the first film magazine in Iceland. He also served as director of the first Reykjavík Film Festival in 1978. His documentaries gave notice of a fresh talent emerging, and Children of Nature deservedly won a European Film Award in 1991.
Filmography
1980: The Saga of Burnt Njal (Brennunnjálssaga, short); 1981: The Blacksmith (Eldsmidurinn, docu); 1982: Rock in Reykjavík (Rokk í Reykjavík); 1984: Cowboys of the North (Kúrekar nordursins, docu); 1987: White Whales (Skytturnar); 1991: Children of Nature (Börn náttúrunnar).

Gudmundsson, Ágúst

Born June 29, 1947 in Reykjavík. He earned his diploma from the National Film School in London in 1977, and in the same year won a first prize at the Chicago Festival for his short film, Lifeline to Cathy. His first feature, Land and Sons, received an ecstatic reception in Iceland, marking as it did the birth of a fledgling national cinema on the island. Gudmundsson soon proved that he could turn his hand to various genres: historical epic (The Saga of Gisli), musical comedy (On Top), and political satire (Golden Sands won a gold medal at the Lübeck Film Days). Gudmundsson currently works for Icelandic television.
Filmography
Shorts — 1977: My Friend Jonathan, Lifeline to Cathy; 1989: End of Term Journey (Skólafero); 1979: A Little Swelling (Lítil búfa). Features — 1980: Land and Sons (Land og synir); 1981: The Outlaw/The Saga of Gísli (Utlaginn); 1982: On Top (Med allt á hreinu); 1984: Golden Sands (Gullsandur); 1987: Nonni and Nanni (6-part TV series); 1990: Sea Dragon (series for Thames TV, U.K.); 1991: The Colours of the Earth (Litbrigdi jardar, Icelandic TV).

Gunnlaugsson, Hrafn

Born June 17, 1948 in Reykjavík. Graduated from the University of Stockholm in theatre and cinema in 1973. For the next two years, he studied production at the Swedish Film School. He then devoted himself to a career as a writer, stage director, and film-maker. Gunnlaugsson is known for his poetry, plays, and novels. Between 1973 and 1979 he made several films for Icelandic TV. His third feature, When the Raven Flies, was the first Icelandic film (co-produced with Sweden) to be screened in competition with the Berlin Festival. Gunnlaugsson has been programme director at Icelandic TV, but continues to devote himself to evoking the saga period on screen.
Filmography
Shorts — 1976: Ceramics (Keramik); 1977: Lilja, Silvermoon (Silfurtunglid); 1978: Whiplash (Vandarhögg). Features — 1975: Crimson Sunset (Blódrautt sólarlag, Icelandic TV); 1980: Father's Estate (Ódal fedranna); 1982: Inter Nos (Okkar á milli); 1984: When

the Raven Flies (Hrafninn flygur); 1986: The Headsman and the Whore (Bödeln och skökan, Swedish TV); 1988: In the Shadow of the Raven (I skugga hrafnsins); 1991: The White Viking.

Jónsson, Thorsteinn

Born December 6, 1946 in Reykjavík. Graduated from the FAMU (School of Cinema) in Prague in 1971. He made numerous films for Icelandic TV and also worked as a critic. He produced advertising spots and films through his company Kvikmynd. In 1984, his feature film,

The Atomic Station, was screened in the Directors' Fortnight at the Cannes Festival. Jónsson is at present director of the Icelandic Film Fund, having also served previously as president of the Icelandic Directors' Guild.

Filmography
1966: *The Harbour (Höfnin*, short); *Jump (Hopp*, featurette); 1974: *The Fish beneath the Stone (Fiskur undir steini*, TV docu); 1978: *Farmer (Bóndi*, docu); 1981: *Dot, Dot, Comma, Dash (Punktur, punktur, komma, strik)*; 1984: *The Atomic Station (Atómstödin)*.

Óskarsson, Lárus Ýmir

Born March 1, 1949 in Reykjavík. He studied philosophy, psychology, and film history before attending the Swedish Film School between 1976 and 1978. From 1979 to 1982 he worked in Iceland primarily as a stage director, and made *Our Daily Bread* for television. In 1982, Oskarsson returned to Sweden where he made a startling debut with *The Second Dance*, confirming his offbeat Polanski-like view of places and people. He returned to Iceland at the end of the 1980's and shot *Rust*.

Filmography
1978: *Caged Bird (Barfågeln*, short); 1979: *Our Daily Bread (Drottinn blessi heimilid*, Icelandic TV); 1983: *The Second Dance (Andra dansen*, Sweden); 1984: *Stalin Is Not Here (Stalín er ekki hér*, Icelandic TV); 1985: *The Frozen Leopard (Den frusna leoparden*, Sweden), *Poet of Things (Skáld hlutanna*, Icelandic TV); 1986: *The Eye of the Horse (Hästens öga*, Swedish TV); 1990: *Rust (Ryd)*.

NORWAY

Bang-Hansen, Pål

Born July 29, 1937 in Oslo. Having studied at Centro Sperimentale in Rome, Bang-Hansen became a film critic. He began his career as a director in 1966 with *Written in the Snow*. But the cinema was already familiar to him, for Bang-Hansen had made an impact as a child actor in *Street Urchins*, directed by Arne Skouen (q.v.) and Ulf Greber. He made several shorts and TV series. Apart from one comedy, Bang-Hansen focussed on socio-political issues in his feature films, especially in *The Crown Prince*, which attacks corrupt practices during an election campaign. Since 1976, Bang-Hansen has been a producer-director at Norwegian television (NRK).

Filmography
1966: *Written in the Snow (Skrift i sne)*; 1970: *Douglas*; 1972: *The Construction of Buildings in Norway (Norske byggeklosser*, docu); 1973: *The Canary (Kanarifuglen)*; 1974: *Departed for Ever (Bortreist på ubestemt tid)*; 1979: *The Crown Prince (Kronprinsen)*.

Berg, Arnljot

Born October 22, 1931 in Oslo, died December 1982 *id*. Berg started his career as a director of short films. He was very active in Norway in promoting and distributing good films, and founded various film societies. In 1972, he directed a semi-autobiographical feature, *Closed Ward*, about psychiatric confinement. He committed suicide in 1982.

Filmography
1966: *Before the Frost (Før frostnetter)*; 1968: *Her Royal Highness (Hennes meget kongelige høyhet)*; 1970: *Death in the Streets (Døden i gatene)*; 1972: *Closed Ward (Lukket avdeling)*; 1974: *Bobby's War (Bobbys krig)*; 1979: *The Sun Trail (Solveien seksten*, for Norwegian TV).

Breien, Anja

Born July 12, 1940 in Oslo. She studied at IDHEC in Paris, and cut her teeth on short films. In 1966 and 1967 she was assistant to Henning Carlsen (q.v.) on *Hunger and People Meet and Sweet Music Fills the Heart*. In her first solo feature, Breien attacked the Norwegian penal system, confirming her social commitment and interest in contemporary issues. In 1975, with *Wives*, she gave a feminist riposte to Cassavetes's *Husbands*. Ten years later, she took the same characters and described their development with wry humour. She has received many prizes, including the Oecumenical Award at Cannes for *Next of Kin*, and a prize at Venice for *Witch Hunt*, which recalls Dreyer's *Day of Wrath*.

Filmography
1970: *Growing Up* (episode from portmanteau film, *Days from 1,000 Years)*; 1971: *Rape (Voldtekt)*; 1975: *Wives (Hustruer)*; 1977: *Games of Love and Loneliness (Den alvarsamma leken)*; 1979: *Next of Kin (Arven)*; 1981: *The Witch Hunt (Forfølgelsen)*; 1984: *Paper Bird (Papirfuglen)*; 1985: *Wives, Ten Years After (Hustruene — ti år etter)*; 1990: *Twice Upon a Time (Smykketyven)*; 1992: *Troll Vision (Trollsyn)*.

Blom, Per

Born May 5, 1946 in Hov i Land. He started making short films in 1965, and then worked in collaboration with contemporaries like Anja Breien (q.v.) on *Rape* and Oddvar Bull Tuhus (q.v.) on *Red-Blue Paradise*. His own films are extremely sensitive, and filled with a discreet but powerful sexual undercurrent.

Filmography
1973: *Anton*; 1974: *Mother's House (Mors hus)*; 1979: *The Woman (Kvinnene)*; 1981: *Silvermouth (Sølvmunn)*; 1987: *The Ice-Palace (Is-slottet)*.

Breistein, Rasmus

Born November 16, 1990 in Åsane, died October 16, 1976 in Hollywood. He was at first a stage actor and orchestra musician. His first film, *Anna the Gypsy-Girl*, was in effect the first feature made in Norway. It enjoyed a huge success, due in particular to the boldness of the script. Breistein subsequently concentrated on popular comedies and peasant dramas, deriving from national romanticism. Although his work became somewhat lightweight, Breistein must be recognised as the pioneer director of Norwegian cinema, and its first true professional.

Filmography
1920: *Anna, the Gypsy-Girl (Fante-Anne)*; 1921: *Miss Faithful (Jomfru trofast)*; 1926: *Honeymoon in Hardanger (Brudeferden i Hardanger)*; 1930: *Kristine, Daughter of Valdre (Kristine Valdresdatter)*; 1932: *Love in the Archipelago (Skjærgårdsflirt)*; 1934: *A Life (Liv)*; 1938: *The Baby (Ungen)*; 1941: *The Golden Mountain (Gullfjellet)*; 1942: *Knut from Trysil (Trysil Knut)*; 1943: *The New Doctor (Den nye laegen)*; 1949: *Around the World in Ten Hours (Jorden rundt på to timer*, docu. released in 1952); 1952: *Himalayan Expedition (Tiric mir til topps*, docu.).

Einarson, Oddvar

Born February 7, 1949 in Oslo. He studied painting, photography, and film. His shorts and documentaries earned him several prizes. He has become an experimental director, specialising in long-held shots and economic dialogue — notably in *X*, which won a Silver Lion in Venice for its neophyte director.

Filmography
1972: *The Mardøla Battle (Kampen om Mardøla*, docu.); 1981: *Prognosis Innerdalen (Prognose Innerdalen)*; 1986: *X*; 1988: *Karachi*; 1990: *Rising Tide (Havet stigen)*.

Gaup, Nils

Born April 12, 1955 in Kautokeino, a tiny Lapp community in the north of Norway. He decided to become an actor (unusual for a Lapp) and in 1974 was accepted as a student in the Norwegian Theatre School. Graduating in 1978, he appeared at several theatres. He has written a play, made a TV series for children, and worked as a screen actor. But his glory thus far has been *Pathfinder*, shot in the Lapps' own language, and an international success, even earning an Academy Award nomination in 1988. This led to a contract with Disney and the co-production, *Shipwrecked*.

Per Blom

Anja Breien

Oddvar Einarson

Vibeke Løkkeberg

Laila Mikkelsen

Ola Solum

Filmography
1987: *Pathfinder (Ofelaš/Velviseren)*; 1990: *Shipwrecked (Håkon Håkonsen)*.

Glomm, Lasse
Born September 5, 1944 in Oslo. He studied French and History at the University of Oslo, and then became a freelance journalist before writing film criticism for the magazine *Fant*. He entered the cinema in 1971 and the following year served as assistant director on Joseph Losey's *A Doll's House*. He was co-screenwriter of Anja Breien's *Next of Kin* and Oddvar Bull Tuhus's *Strike!* From 1984 to 1987 he was artistic director at Norsk Film A/S.
Filmography
1978: *The Second Shift (Det andra skiftet)*; 1980: *Stop It! (At dere tør!)*; 1981: *Zeppelin*; 1983: *Black Crows (Svarte fugler)*; 1985: *Northern Lights (Havlandet)*; 1988: *Sweetwater*.

Ibsen, Tancred
Born on July 11, 1893 in Glausdal, died December 4, 1978 in Oslo. Grandson of the writer Henrik Ibsen, he studied commerce and became an army officer. In 1923 he left for Hollywood as assistant to Sjöström (q.v.), and worked in the MGM screenplay department. In 1925 he sailed to Denmark and returned to Norway the following year. He shot his first film, the documentary *A Norwegian Film* in 1926. In 1931 Ibsen made the first Norwegian sound movie, *The Big Baptism*. Active as a producer, he helped to set up Norsk Film A/S. At the start of the 1930's he directed several films in Sweden, notably *Synnöve Solbakken* with, among other actors, Victor Sjöström.
Filmography
1926: *A Norwegian Film (Norgesfilmen*, docu); 1931: *The Big Baptism (Den store barnedåben,* co-dir Einar Sissener); 1932: *He Who Takes the Back Door (Vi som går kjøkkenveien* — Norwegian version of Gustaf Molander's film); 1933: *Hold Your Head High (Op med hodet,* co-dir Erling Bergendahl); 1934: *Synnöve Solbakken* (in Sweden); 1935: *You Promised Me a Wife (Du har lovet mig en kone,* co-dir Einar Sissener), *Perhaps a Gentleman (Kanske en gentleman,* co-dir Ragnar Arvedson, Sweden), *Poor Millionaires (Stackars miljonärer,* co-dir Ragnar Arvedson, Sweden); *The Ghost of Bragehus (Spöket på Bragehus,* co-dir Ragnar Arvedson, Sweden); 1937: *Two Living and One Dead (To levende og en død)*, *Fant/The Gypsy (Fant)*; 1939: *Gjest Baardsen*; *Whalers (Valfångare,* co-dir Anders Henrikson, Sweden); 1940: *Tørres Snørtevold*; 1942: *Dangerous Game (Den farlige leken)*; 1946: *The Ghost Falls in Love (Et spøkelse forelsker seg)*; 1948: *The Mysterious Apartment (Den himmellighetsfulle leiligheten)*; 1950: *Two Suspects (To mistenkelige personer)*; 1951: *Tall People and Short People (Storfolk og småfolk)*; 1952: *The Olympic Film — A Winter Adventure (Olympiafilmen — et vintereventyr,* docu); 1955: *Disappeared since Monday (Savnet siden mandag,* co-dir Sigval Maartmann-Moe); 1960: *Friends (Venner)*; 1963: *The Wild Duck (Vildanden)*.

Løkkeberg, Vibeke
Born January 22, 1945 in Bergen. She studied decorative arts and painting in Bergen and in Denmark before becoming a model in both France and Italy. From 1964 to 1965 she attended the School of Dramatic Art in Norway. In 1967 and 1970, she played the lead in films by her then-husband, Pål Løkkeberg, *Liv* and *Exit*. Between 1970 and 1975, she made several shorts and documentaries for television concerning unmarried mothers and paternity. In 1981, her feature film *Betrayal* proved very successful at home and abroad, and especially at Cannes in the Critics' Week. In 1987, *Hud* was screened in the 'Certain Regard' section at Cannes. Løkkeberg has made all her features to date in collaboration with Terje Kristiansen.
Filmography
1975: *Rain* (short); 1976: *The Revelation (Åpenbaringen)*; 1981: *The Betrayal (Løperjenten)*; 1983: *The Headman (Høvdingen,* dir Terje Kristiansen, Vibeke Løkkeberg co-scr and act); 1987; *Skin (Hud)*; 1990: *Seagulls (Måker)*.

Mikkelsen, Laila
Born August 20, 1940 in Vardø. After studying Art at the University of Oslo, she worked as a script-girl from 1968 on. She soon managed to make some short films, and in 1976 wrote the screenplay for *We Others* with the author, Knut Falbakken. She has also been very active on the production side. *Little Ida* has been her greatest success as a director, and Andrew Lloyd Webber, no less, has said he would like to make a musical from it!
Filmography
1976: *Us (Oss)*; 1981: *Little Ida/Growing Up (Liten Ida)*; 1983: *Children of the Earth (Søsken på Guds jord)*; 1984: *Sweet Seventeen (Snart 17)*.

Sinding, Leif
Born November 19, 1895 in Oslo, died May 13, 1985, *id*. Sinding is known above all for his prewar screen adaptations of literary works, and in particular *The Defenceless*, from the novel by Gabriel Scott. In 1932, he made the first Norwegian musical, *The Gypsy*. During the war, with production in the hands of the German occupying forces, Sinding accepted the post as head of the film industry and directed the only subjects permitted — comedies or films with a propagandist tinge. When the war ended, he was rejected for his collaboration with the Nazis, and returned to the cinema only in 1953.
Filmography
1926: *The New Superintendent (Den nya lensmannen)*; 1927: *Adventure in the Fells (Fjelleventyret)*, *Seven Days for Elizabeth (Syv dage for Elisabeth)*; 1932: *The Gypsy (Fantegutten)*; 1936: *The Murderer without a Face (Morderen uten ansikt)*; 1937: *Good People (Bra mennesker)*; 1938: *Eli Sjursdotter*; 1939: *The Defenceless (De vergeløse)*; 1940: *Tante Pose*; 1941: *Love and Friendship (Kjaerlighet og vennskap)*; 1943: *The Song of Life (Sangen til livet)*; 1944: *Josefa*; 1953: *The Night of the Witches (Heksenetten)*; 1956: *Gilded Youth (Gylne ungdom)*.

Skouen, Arne
Born October 18, 1913 in Oslo. He gave up his profession as a seaman to work in journalism. In 1937 he published his first novel, *Ruth Must See Me*. In 1943, the occupying Nazis banned the staging of one of his plays, *The Gilded Chair*. Skouen went into voluntary exile in Sweden, and then in Britain and the U.S.A. where he worked as a press attaché. Returning to his native country in 1946, he continued to write novels and literary criticism. In 1949, in collaboration with Ulf Greber, he directed his first film, *Street Urchins*, adapted from his own novel. In 1955, *The Flame* met with a warm reception in the competition at Cannes. Skouen often returned to the war period in films like *Forced Landing*, *Nine Lives* (nominated for an Oscar), and *Surrounded*. In 1969, he directed *An-Magritt*, starring Liv Ullmann who had made a reputation with Ingmar Bergman (q.v.). With this latter film, Skouen confirmed his place among Norway's finest directors.
Filmography
1949: *Street Urchins (Gategutter,* co-dir Ulf Greber); 1952: *Forced Landing (Nødlandig)*; 1954: *The Fandango Circus (Cirkus Fandango)*; 1955: *Children of the Sun (Barn av solen)*, *The Flame (Det brenner i natt!)*; 1957: *Nine Lives (Ni liv)*; 1958: *The Return of Pastor Jarmann (Pastor Jarmann kommer hjem)*; 1959: *The Master and His Servants (Herren og hans tjenere)*; 1960: *Surrounded (Omringet)*; 1961: *The Bus (Bussen)*; 1962: *Cold Trail (Kalde spor)*; 1963: *About Tilla (Om Tilla)*; 1964: *Gold Medal for Daddy (Pappa lar gull)*; 1965: *The Guards (Vakpostene)*; 1966: *Journey to the Sea (Reisen til havet)*; 1967: *The Musicians (Musikanten)*; 1969: *An-Magritt*.

Solum, Ola
Born July 17, 1943 in Oslo. Director and producer of box-office movies, he has tended towards adventure stories for kids, such as *Journey to the Christmas Star* and *Operation Cobra*. His breakthrough came with *Orion's Belt*, which sold to numerous countries and set altogether new standards for narrative verve in Norwegian cinema. He has been artistic director at Norsk Film A/S.

Filmography

1976: *Journey to the Christmas Star (Reisen til Julesthernen);* 1978: *Operation Cobra (Operasjon Cobra);* 1982: *Carl Gustav and His Gang (Carl Gustav, gjengen og parkeringsbandittere);* 1985: *Orion's Belt (Orions belte);* 1987: *Turnaround;* 1989: *The Wanderers (Landstrykere);* 1991: *The Polar Bear King (Kvitebørn Kong Valemon).*

Tuhus, Oddvar Bull

Born December 14, 1940 in Ostre Aker. After completing his higher education, Tuhus made films for television and also some independent shorts. Considered during the 1970's as one of the most important filmmakers working in Norway, he brought *Strike!* to the Directors' Fortnight in Cannes with great success. Apart from his interest in social and political issues, Tuhus has tackled psychological drama in *Maria Marusjka* and the problems of adolescence in *1958.*

Filmography

1971: *Red-Blue Paradise (Rødblått paradis);* 1973: *Maria Marusjka;* 1975: *Strike! (Streik!);* 1976: *Fear (Angst), A Man of Trust (Tillitsmannen,* docu); 1980: *1958;* 1982: *Fifty-fifty (50/50);* 1983: *Hockey Fever (Hockeyfeber);* 1986: *Shall We Dance? (Skal de vere ein dans?* for Norwegian TV); 1988: *Blücher.*

Vibe-Müller, Titus

Born October 17, 1912 in Oslo, died June 19, 1986 id. He went to business school, then took up journalism. From 1933 to 1936, he lived in Germany and, working on various films, familiarised himself with film technique. He soon became an editor and an assistant director. Soon he was a much sought-after technician, and worked with Tancred Ibsen, Leif Sinding, and Rasmus Breistein (qq.v.). In 1948, he directed a Franco-Norwegian co-production, in collaboration with Jean Dréville, entitled *The Battle for Heavy Water,* which remains without doubt his best work.

Filmography

1946: *Two Lives (To liv,* co-dir Finn Bø); 1948: *The Battle for Heavy Water (Kampen om tungtvannet,* co-dir Jean Dréville); 1950: *Marianne at the Hospital (Marianne på sykehus);* 1951: *Escape from Dakar (Flukten fra Dakar);* 1952: *Haakon VII, King of Norway in Peace and War* (co-dir Per Ratvik and Sigurd Maartmann-Moe, docu); 1961: *Between Us Nuclear Experts (Oss atomforskere i mellom);* 1971: *The Life of the Lapps/Lapp Memories (Same aellin,* docu).

Lasse Glomm

SWEDEN

Ahrne, Marianne

Born June 25, 1940 in Lund. She studied theatre and literature in the United States, then film at the University of Lund before going on to the Swedish Film School in Stockholm. From 1970 to 1974, she directed several documentaries (some for French television), including a feature profile of Simone de Beauvoir, *A Walk into the Lane of Old Age* (1974). Alongside her sporadic activity as a film director, Ahrne also writes novels.

Filmography

1975: *Five Days in Falköping (Fem dagar i Falköping);* 1976: *Near and Far Away (Långt borta och nära);* 1978: *The Roots of Grief (Frihetens murar);* 1986: *A Matter of Life and Death (På liv och död).*

Alfredson, Hans

Born June 23, 1931 in Malmö. Graduated from the University of Lund in the History of Art, Literature, and Philosophy. Alfredson began his career as a writer and journalist. In 1956, he met Tage Danielsson with whom he wrote plays for radio and theatre. Together they founded the company Svenska Ord, through which they produced comedies and TV series. Alfredson pursued a busy life of appearing on stage and screen, all the while supervising other productions and acting as a dramatic advisor. He is co-author of various screenplays, notably with Tage Danielsson for *The Apple War.* From 1958 onwards, he popped up in more serious screen parts, including Bergman's *Shame,* Troell's *The Emigrants,* and Breien's *Games of Love and Loneliness.*

Filmography

1967: *The Rewards of Virtue (Dygdens belöning,* co-dir Tage Danielsson, episode in portmanteau film, *Stimulantia);* 1975: *Egg! Egg! – A Hardboiled Story (Ägget är löst – en hårdkokt saga);* 1982: *The Simple-Minded Murderer (Den enfaldige mördaren);* 1983: *P & B;* 1985: *False as Water (Falsk som vatten);* 1987: *Jim and the Pirates (Jim och piraterna Blom);* 1988: *Time of the Wolf (Vargens tid).*

Andersson, Roy

Born March 31, 1943 in Göteborg. He made his debut as a cameraman on the collective film *The White Sport* in 1968, and the following year worked as assistant director to Bo Widerberg (q.v.) for *Ådalen 31.* Graduated from the Swedish Film School in 1969, he attracted attentijon with his student short, *Saturday 5/10.* Although his first feature delighted younger audiences in Sweden, Andersson's career never really caught fire and he could not really recover from the failure of *Giliap.* But he has been active in a production capacity in the intervening years.

Filmography

1970: *A Swedish Love Story (En kärlekshistoria);* 1975: *Giliap.*

Bergenstråhle, Johan

Born July 17, 1935 in Stockholm. Started as an actor and then began directing for television and the Municipal Theatre in Stockholm. Bergenstråhle is one of the most socially committed directors to have emerged during the 1960's. He used the cinema to level serious charges against government policy on immigration and arms selling, for example. During the 1980's, Bergenstråhle devoted his energies more and more to the theatre.

Filmography

1969: *Made in Sweden;* 1970: *A Baltic Tragedy (Baltutlämningen);* 1972: *Foreigners (Jag heter Stelios);* 1976: *Hallo Baby;* 1978: *For Your Pleasure (Slumrande toner fjärran ur tiden).*

Bergman, Ingmar

Born July 14, 1918. In 1939, he became an assistant at the Royal Opera in Stockholm, while writing plays and taking an active role in Stockholm's student theatre world. In 1942, he joined the script department at Svensk Filmindustri, and two years later Alf Sjöberg (q.v.) brought his screenplay, *Frenzy*, to the screen. At 26, Bergman was appointed head of the Helsingborg Theatre (making him the youngest theatre director in Scandinavia). Soon afterwards, he moved to the Municipal Theatre in Göteborg, and six years later went to the newly-formed Malmö Municipal Theatre, where he met many of his future film actors and staged some remarkable productions. It was only in 1956, when *Smiles of a Summer Night* won a prize in Cannes, that Bergman's reputation as a film-maker grew beyond Sweden. Over his long and distinguished career, Bergman has received Academy Awards in Hollywood and prizes at the leading international festivals (e.g. the Golden Bear in Berlin for *Wild Strawberries*). He wrote the screenplays for the vast majority of his films. In April 1976 he left Sweden in high dudgeon after a brush with the tax authorities, and was vindicated subsequently, enabling him to return to Sweden for his screen swansong, *Fanny and Alexander*. Bergman has never abandoned the theatre, however, and has more than a hundred productions to his credit, most recently at the Royal Dramatic Theatre, Stockholm. In 1987 he published a perceptive, allusive volume of autobiography, *The Magic Lantern*, which was translated into several languages.

Filmography
1946: *Crisis (Kris)*, *It Rains on Our Love/The Man with an Umbrella (Det regnar på vår kärlek)*; 1947: *A Ship Bound for India (Skepp till Indialand)*; 1948: *Music in Darkness/Night Is My Future (Musik i mörker)*, *Port of Call (Hamnstad)*; 1949: *Prison (Fängelse)*, *Thirst/Three Strange Loves (Törst)*; 1950: *To Joy (Till glädje)*, *This Can't Happen Here/High Tension (Sånt händer inte här)*; 1951: *Summer Interlude/Illicit Interlude (Sommarlek)*; 1952: *Waiting Women (Kvinnors väntan)*, *Summer with Monika/Monika (Sommaren med Monika)*; 1953: *Sawdust and Tinsel/The Naked Light (Gycklarnas afton)*; 1954: *A Lesson in Love (En lektion i kärlek)*; 1955: *Journey into Autumn/Dreams (Kvinnodröm)*, *Smiles of a Summer Night (Sommarnattens leende)*; 1957: *The Seventh Seal (Det sjunde inseglet)*, *Wild Strawberries (Smultronstället)*; 1958: *So Close to Life/Brink of Life (Nära livet)*, *The Face/The Magician (Ansiktet)*; 1960: *The Virgin Spring (Jungfrukällan)*, *The Devil's Eye (Djävulens öga)*; 1961: *Through a Glass Darkly (Såsom i en spegel)*; 1963: *Winter Light (Nattvardsgästerna)*, *The Silence (Tystnaden)*; 1964: *All These Women/Now about These Women (För att inte tala om alla dessa kvinnor)*; 1966: *Persona*; 1967: *Daniel* (episode in portmanteau production, *Stimulantia*); 1968: *Hour of the Wolf (Vargtimmen)*, *Shame/The Shame (Skammen)*; *The Rite/The Ritual (Riten, for Swedish TV)*, *A Passion/The Passion of Anna (En passion)*, *The Fårö Documentary (Fårö dokument*, docu for Swedish TV)*; 1971: *The Touch (Beröringen)*; 1973: *Cries and Whispers (Viskningar och rop)*, *Scenes from a Marriage (Scener ur ett äktenskap*, for Swedish TV)*; 1975: *The Magic Flute (Trollflöjten*, for Swedish TV)*; 1976: *Face to Face (Ansikte mot ansikte*, for Swedish TV)*; 1977: *The Serpent's Egg (Das Schlangenei*, in Germany)*; 1978: *Autumn Sonata (Herbstsonat*, in Germany)*; 1979: *Fårö 1979 (Fårödokument 1979)*; 1980: *From the Life of the Marionettes (Aus dem Leben der Marionetten*, in Germany)*; 1982: *Fanny and Alexander (Fanny och Alexander)*; 1983: *After the Rehearsal (Efter repetitionen*, for Swedish TV)*; 1984: *Karin's Face (Karins ansikte*, short)*; 1986: *The Blessed Ones (De två saliga*, for Swedish TV)*.

Björkman, Stig
Born October 2, 1938 in Stockholm. After studying architecture, Björkman took up film criticism and became editor of the film magazine Chaplin, from 1964 to 1972. During the 1970's he was author or co-author of various books on the cinema, including the widely-translated *Bergman on Bergman*. From 1964, he made several documentaries and shorts. From 1973 to 1974, he taught at the Swedish Film School. From 1975 to 1977 he was a production counsellor at the Danish Film Institute.

Filmography
Shorts and Documentaries − 1964: *Letizia*; 1967: *Anna Susanna's True Story (Sanningen om Anna Susanna)*; 1969: *To Australia with Love, No (Nej)*; 1970: *In Other Words (Med andra ord)*; 1971: *Ingmar Bergman*

(docu), *Our Home on Earth (Vårt hem på jorden)*; 1988: *Tomorrow and Tomorrow and Tomorrow (Imorron & imorron & imorron*, docu)*.
Features − 1968: *I Love, You Love (Jag älskar, du älskar)*; 1971: *Georgia, Georgia*; 1975: *The White Wall (Den vita väggen)*; 1979: *Walk on Water If You Can (Gå på vattnet om du kan)*; 1980: *Through the Mirror (Kvindesind)*; *Behind the Shutters (Bakom jalusin)*; 1985: *Piecework* (part of the series, *The Fate of the Cat in the Year of the Rat [Vad hände katten i råttans år?)*.

Brunius, John W.
Born December 26, 1884 in Stockholm, died December 16, 1937 *id*. From 1902, he served his apprenticeship as an actor at the Royal Dramatic Theatre in Stockholm. He played numerous roles there before becoming head of the Oscar's Theatre in Stockholm. Noted for his humorous characters, both as an actor and as a director, Brunius achieved some distinguished work on screen, including the historical epic, *Charles XII*. He also scripted virtually all his early films, and appeared as an actor in some of them.

Filmography
1918: *Puss in Boots (Mästerkatten i stövlar)*; 1919: *Synnöve Solbakken*, *Oh Tomorrow Evening (Ah, i morron kväll!)*; 1920: *Thora van Deken*, *The Gyurkovics Family (Gyurkovicsarna)*; 1921: *The Windmill (Kvarnen)*, *A Fortune-Hunter (En lyckoriddare)*, *A Wild Bird (En vildfågel)*; 1922: *A Scarlet Angel/The Eyes of Love (Kärlekens ögon)*; 1923: *Iron Wills (Hårda viljor)*, *Johan Ulfstjerna*; 1924: *A Housemaid among Housemaids (En piga bland pigor)*; 1925: *Karl VII*; 1926: *Stories of Lieutenant Stål I & II (Fänrik Ståls sägner)*; 1928: *Gustaf Wasa I & II*; 1930: *We Two (Vi tvåa)*, *The Doctor's Secret (Doktorns hemlighet)*; 1931: *Longing for the Sea (Längtan till havet*, co-dir Alexander Korda)*; 1934: *The Ocean's Melody (Havets melodi)*, *False Greta*, co-dir Pauline Brunius).

Carlsten, Rune
Born in 1890, died in 1970. A man of the theatre above everything else (often a director but also an actor) for most of his life, he worked for the Royal Dramatic Theatre in Stockholm. In the early 1920's he made six silent films, simple but charming comedies. *The Bomb* and *The Young Count Wins the Girl and the Prize*, both starring Gösta Ekman, are the best. At the start of the 1930's, he returned to the cinema and made four flops. Between 1942 and 1947 he directed his six final films, including adaptations of novels by Hjalmar Söderberg (*Doctor Glas* and *The Serious Game* being outstanding). In fact, Carlsten was married to the writer's daughter. In *Doctor Glas* he played one of the leading roles and from time to time he popped up as a screen actor. His final parts were in *Salka Valka*, an Icelandic story based on Laxness, and the thriller *Model in Red*, both directed by Arne Mattsson (q.v.).

Filmography
1919: *A Dangerous Courtship (Ett farligt frieri)*; 1920: *The Bomb (Bomben)*, *Robinson in the Archipelago (Robinson i skärgården)*, *Family Traditions (Familjens traditioner)*; 1921: *Higher Purposes/Let No Man Put Assunder (Högre ändamål)*; 1924: *The Young Count Wins the Girl and the Prize (Unga greven tar flickan och priset)*; 1930: *The Voice of the Heart (Hjärtats röst)*; 1931: *Dangerous Paradise (Farornas paradis)*; 1932: *Halfway to Heaven (Halvvägs till himlen*, co-dir Stellan Windrow)*; 1933: *House of Silence (Tystnadens hus*, co-dir Eric Malberg)*; 1942: *Doctor Glas (Doktor Glas)*; 1943: *Anna Lans*; 1944: *Count Only the Happy Moments (Räkna de lyckliga stunderna blott)*; 1945: *Black Roses (Svarta rosor)*, *The Serious Game (Den allvarsamma leken)*; 1947: *Eternal Links (Eviga länkar)*.

Cornell, Jonas
Born August 2, 1938 in Stockholm. He studied at university, then enrolled at the Swedish Film School. Although known primarily as a director, Cornell is also a novelist, critic, and screenwriter. During the 1980's he worked on the production side of Swedish cinema, and directed for Stockholm Municipal Theatre as well as for television. He has produced films too, notably Óskarsson's *The Second Dance*.

Filmography

1967: *Hugs and Kisses (Puss & kram)*; 1969: *Like Night and Day (Som natt och dag)*; 1970: *The Pig Hunt (Grisjakten)*; 1977: *Bluff Stop*; 1981: *Beware of the Jönsson Gang (Varning för Jönssonligan)*; 1991: *Operation Striptease*.

Faustman, Hampe

Born July 3, 1919 in Stockholm, died August 22, 1961 *id*. Erik Faustman, known as 'Hampe' joined the Acting Academy at the Royal Dramatic Theatre, Stockholm, in 1937. He appeared frequently there from 1940 to 1942. Sjöberg (q.v.) gave him his first film role in 1940 in *They Staked Their Lives*. He also appeared in films by Molander (q.v.) and Ekman. A great admirer of Soviet cinema, Faustman became the most socially committed of all Swedish directors in the postwar period. He returned time and again to the struggle between tyranny and liberty, treating this theme with passion and skilful technique.

Filmography

1943: *Night in the Harbour (Natt i hamn)*, *Sonja*; 1944: *We Need Each Other (Vi behöver varann)*, *The Girl and the Devil (Flickan och djävulen)*; 1945: *Crime and Punishment (Brott och straff)*; 1946: *When Meadows Bloom (När ängarna blommar)*; 1947: *Harald Handfaste, A Soldier's Duties (Krigsmans erinran)*; 1948: *Lars Hård, Foreign Harbour (Främmande hamn)*; 1949: *Vagabond Blacksmiths (Smeder på luffen)*; 1950: *The Intimate Restaurant (Restaurant intim)*; 1951: *The Woman Behind Everything (Kvinnan bakom allt*, 2 episodes, shot 1950-51, released 1956); 1952: *Submarine 39 (U-båt 39)*, *She Came Like a Wind (Hon kom som en vind)*; 1953: *House of Women (Kvinnohuset)*; 1954: *God and the Gypsyman (Gud Fader och tattaren)*, *The 'Lunch-Break' Café (Café Lunchrasten)*; 1955: *Night Journey (Resan i natten)*, *No One Is Crazier than I Am (Kärlek på turné)*.

Grede, Kjell

Born August 12, 1936 in Stockholm. Journalist, writer, and teacher, Grede gained international attention for his first feature film, *Hugo and Josephine*. His television work has also been much appreciated in Sweden, in particular his version of Strindberg's *A Madman's Defence*, starring Bibi Andersson, his former wife. Grede's films are marked by a certain myticism and the sense of a dream of ideal happiness in conflict with everyday reality (e.g. *Claire Lust, A Simple Melody, My Beloved*).

Filmography

1967: *Hugo and Josephine (Hugo och Josefin)*; 1969: *Harry Munter*; 1972: *Claire Lust (Klara Lust)*; 1974: *A Simple Melody (En enkel melodi)*; 1979: *My Beloved (Min älskade)*; 1987: *Hip, Hip, Hurrah! (Hip, hip, hurra!)*; 1990: *Good Evening Mr. Wallenberg (God afton, herr Wallenberg)*.

Jarl, Stefan

Born March 18, 1941 in Skara. Graduating in Aesthetics, Jarl was among the first students to attend the Swedish Film School during the 1960's. He is also one of the founders of FilmCentrum, which is devoted to distribution of offbeat films, and of Folkets Bio, a network of independent cinemas. A committed director, Jarl has his own production company and has directed a series of documentaries that condemn man's devastation of the environment and of his own essential being, whether it be a nuclear accident or an overdose of heroin.

Filmography

1968: *They Call Us Mods (Dom kallar oss mods)*; 1979: *A Respectable Life (Ett anständigt liv)*; 1983: *Nature's Revenge (Naturens hämnd)*; 1985: *The Soul Is Greater than the World (Själen är större an världen)*; 1986: *Threat (Hotet)*; 1989: *Time Has No Name (Tiden har inget namn)*; 1990: *Good People (Goda människor)*; 1991: *Reindeer Herdsman in the Year 2000 (Jåvna rensköttare år 2000*, short).

Klercker, Georg af

Born December 15, 1877 in Kristianstad, died November 13, 1951 in Malmö. A former officer in the Swedish Royal Guards, he began his career as a stage actor in 1907. From 1909, he studied drama in Germany and Finland. In 1911, he was placed under contract at the Royal Dramatic Theatre, Stockholm. In 1912, he headed Svenska Bio's film studios out at Lidingö. From 1915 to 1918, he ran the Hasselblad Studios in Göteborg, where he directed most of his feature films, his favourite actress being Mary Johnson. Klercker also scripted, and acted in, many of his films. In 1931-32 he went to Paris where he worked on Swedish versions of American movies.

Filmography

1912: *Two Brothers (Två bruder)*, *The Death Ride under the Big Top (Dödsritten under cirkuskupolen)*, *The Power of Music (Musikens makt)*; 1913: *With Weapon in Hand (Med vapen i hand)*, *The Scandal (Skandalen)*, *Ringvall in Search of Adventure (Ringvall på äventyr)*; 1914: *For the Fatherland (För fäderneslandet)*; 1915: *The Rose on Thistle Island (Rosen på Tistelön)*, *In the King's Uniform (I kronans kläder)*; 1916: *In Memories' Trammels (I minnenas band)*, *The Top Prize (Högsta vinsten)*, *Calle's New Clothes (Calles nya kläder)*, *The Minister President (Ministerpresidenten)*, *Mother-in-Law on the Spree (Svärmor på vift)*, *The Victory of Love (Kärleken segrar)*, *Perseverance Does It or Calle as an Actor (Trägen vinner eller Calle som skådespelare)*, *Children of the Night (Nattens barn)*, *Calle as a Millionaire (Calle som miljonär)*, *The Prisoner of Karlsten's Fortress (Fången på Karlstens Fästning)*, *From the Diary of a Fox-Terrier (Ur en foxterriers dagbok)*, *The Gift of Health Ltd's Present (Aktiebolaget Hälsans gåva)*, *Bengt's New Love or Where Is the Child? (Bengt's nya kärlek eller Var är barnet?)*, *The Way Down (Vägen utför)*, *Those Servant Girls! Those Servant Girls! (De pigorna, de pigorna!)*; 1917: *The Mystery of the Night before the 25th (Mysteriet natten till den 25:e)*, *Between Life and Death (Mellan liv och död)*, *In the Fetters of Darkness (I mörkrets bojor)*, *The Suburban Vicar (Förstadsprästen)*, *Lieutenant Galenpenna (Löjtnant Galenpenna)*, *The Judge (Brottmålsdomaren)*, *For Hearth and Home (För hem och härd)*, *There Are No Gods on Earth (Det finns inga gudan på jorden)*, *Reveille (Revelj)*; 1918: *Night Music (Nattliga toner)*, *The Nobel Prizewinner (Nobelpristagaren)*, *The Lighthouse Keeper's Daughter (Fyrvaktarens dotter)*; 1926: *The Girls of Solvik (Flickorna på Solvik)*.

Lindberg, Per

Born March 5, 1890 in Stockholm, died February 7, 1944 *id*. Lindberg studied stagecraft with Max Reinhardt and mounted various important productions at the Lorensberg Theatre in Göteberg as well as the Royal Dramatic Theatre in Stockholm. He worked for the radio, and also wrote books on the arts. With his rigorous style, Lindberg seized the mood of his times in psychological dramas like *The Old Man's Coming* and social films such as *Steel*.

Filmography

1923: *Anna-Klara and Her Brothers (Anna-Klara och hennes bröder)*, *The Norrtull Gang (Norrtullsligan)*; 1939: *The Old Man's Coming (Gubben kommer)*, *Rejoice While You Are Young (Gläd dig i din ungdom)*; 1940: *Steel (Stål)*, *The June Night (Juninatten)*, *His Grace's Will (Hans nåds testamente)*; 1941: *Talk of the Town (Det sägs på stan)*, *In Paradise . . . (I paradis . . .)*.

Mattsson, Arne

Born December 2, 1919 in Uppsala. Mattsson started writing for the cinema while still a civil engineer, and his first screenplay, a comedy, appeared in 1940. In 1942 he made two documentaries and became assistant to Per Lindberg (q.v.) until 1944, the year in which he made his debut as a feature-film director. In 1951, he won notoriety in Sweden and abroad with *One Summer of Happiness*. But he owes his place in the annals of Swedish cinema to the three films that followed: *The Bread of Love, Salka Valka*, and *The People of Hemsö*. During the 1960's and 1970's, Mattsson concentrated on specious thrillers, the least bad of which were *The Doll* and *Woman of Darkness*.

Filmography

1942: *The Regiment of Halland (Hallands regemente*, short); 1944: *And All These Women (Och alla dessa kvinnor)*; 1945: *Marie in the*

Ingmar Bergman and his cinematographer Sven Nykvist

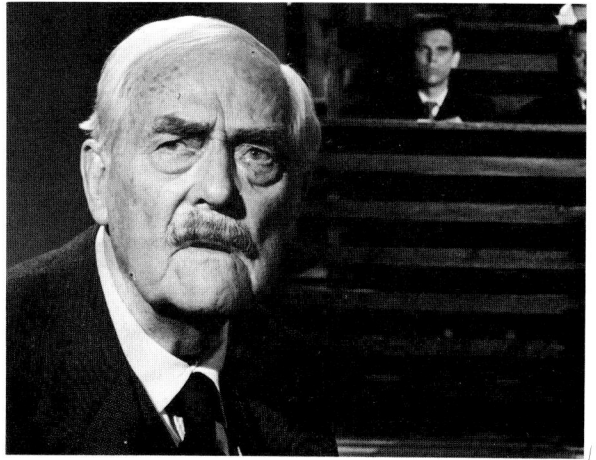

Victor Sjöström

Alf Sjöberg

Bo Widerberg

Jan Troell

Suzanne Osten

Windmill (Maria på kvarngården), Sussie, You Who Enter Here (I som här inträden); 1946: Peggy on a Spree (Peggy på vift), Bad Eggs (Röttägg); 1947: Father Wanted (Pappa sökes), A Guest Came (Det kom en gäst), Navvies (Rallare); 1948: Dangerous Springtime (Farlig vår); 1949: Woman in White (Kvinna i vitt); 1950: When Love Came to the Village (När kärleken kom till byn), The Kiss on the Cruise (Kyssen på kryssen), The Saucepan Journey (Kastrullresan); 1951: Rolling Sea (Bärande hav), One Summer of Happiness (Hon dansade en sommar); 1952: Dull Clang (Hård klang), Because of My Hot Youth (För min heta ungdoms skull); 1953: The Bread of Love (Kärlekens bröd), Storm over Tjurö (Storm över Tjurö), Enchanted Walk (Förtrollad vandring), Salka Valka, Nattens väv; 1955: A Little Place of One's Own (Litet bo), Men in Darkness (Männen i mörker), The People of Hemsö (Hemsöborna); 1956: Girl in a Dress-coat (Flickan i frack); 1957: Spring of Life (Livets vår, in Argentina), No Tomorrow (Ingen morgondag); 1958: Lady in Black (Damen i svart), There Came Two Men (in Spain), The Phantom Carriage (Körkarlen), Model in Red (Mannekäng i rött); 1959: May I Borrow Your Wife? (Får jag låna din fru!), Rider in Blue (Ryttare i blått); 1960: Summer and Sinners (Sommar och syndare), When Darkness Falls (När mörkret faller); 1961: The Summer Wind Is Sweet (Ljuvlig är sommarnatten); 1962: Ticket to Paradise (Biljett till paradiset), Lady in White (Vita frun), The Doll (Vaxdockan); 1963: Yes, He Has Been with Me (Det är hos mig han har varit), The Yellow Car (Den gula bilen); 1964: Blue Boys (Blåjackor); 1965: The Two Vikings (Här kommer bärsärkarna), Morianna (Morianerna), Nightmare (Nattmara); 1966: Woman of Darkness (Yngsjömordet); 1967: The Murderer – An Ordinary Person (Mördaren – en helt vanlig person), The Vicious Circle (Den onda cirkeln); 1968: Teddy Bear (Bamse); 1971: Ann and Eve (Ann och Eve – de erotiska); 1973: Dirty Fingers (Smutsiga fingrar); 1978: Man in the Shadows (Mannen i skuggan), The Lorry (Lastbilen, in Yugoslavia).

Molander, Gustaf

Born December 18, 1888 in Helskinki, died June 19, 1973 in Stockholm. He studied at the Royal Dramatic Theatre in Stockholm and then appeared on stage in both Helsinki (1909-1911) and Stockholm (1913-1926). He began his career in the cinema by scripting Sjöström's Terje Vigen, and then co-scripting Thomas Graal's Best Film, Thomas Graal's First Child, and Stiller's Gunnar Hede's Saga. Karin Molander, his first wife, was one of the greatest stars of the Swedish silent cinema. He was the brother of Olof Molander, head of the Royal Dramatic Theatre, Stockholm, from 1934 to 1938. Molander directed his first film in 1920, and forty-five years later he returned to make The Necklace with Ingrid Bergman, an episode in the portmanteau production, Stimulantia. His prolific output comprises many genres and excellent films, especially those made during the 1940's.

Filmography
1919: The King of Boda (Bodakungen); 1922: Thomas Graals myndling), The Amateur Film (Pärlorna); 1923: The Pirates of Lake Malar (Mälarpirater); 1924: 33.333; 1925: Constable Paulus's Easter Bomb (Polis Paulus'påskasmåll), The Ingmar Inheritance (Ingmarsarvet); 1926: To the Orient (Till Österland), She's the Only One (Hon, den enda); 1927: His English Wife (Hans engelska fru), Sealed Lips (Förseglade läppar); 1928: Women of Paris (Parisiskor), Sin (Synd); 1929: Triumph of the Heart (Hjärtats triumf); 1930: Frida's Songs (Fridas visor), Charlotte Löwensköld; 1931: One Night (En natt); 1932: Black Roses (Svarta rosor), Love and Deficit (Kärlek och kassabrist), We Go Through the Kitchen (Vi som går köksvägen); 1933: Dear Relatives (Kära släkten); 1934: A Quiet Affair (En stilla flirt), My Aunt's Millions (Fasters millioner); 1935: Bachelor Father (Ungkarlspappan), Swedenhielms, Under False Colours (Under falsk flagg); 1936: On the Sunny Side (På solsidan), The Honeymoon Trip (Brollopsresan), Intermezzo, The Family Secret (Familjens hemlighet); 1937: Sarah Learns Manners (Sara lär sig folkvett); 1938: Dollar, A Woman's Face (En kvinnas ansikte); 1939: Just One Night (En enda natt), It's Fun To Change (Ombyte förnöjer), Emilie Högqvist; 1940:

One, But a Lion (En, men ett lejon); 1941: Bright Prospects (Den ljusnande framtid), Tonight or Never (I natt eller aldrig), The Fight Goes On (Striden går vidare); 1942: Jacob's Ladder (Jacobs stege), Ride Tonight! (Rid i natt!); 1943: There Burned a Flame (Det brinner en eld), Darling, I Surrender (Älskling, jag get mig), The Word (Ordet); 1944: The Invisible Wall (Den osynliga muren), The Emperor of Portugal (Kejsaren av Portugallien); 1945: The Executioner (Galgmannen); 1946: It's My Model (Det är min modell); 1947: Woman without a Face (Kvinna utan ansikte); 1948: Life Begins Now (Nu börjar livet), Eva; 1949: Love Will Conquer (Kärleken segrar); 1950: The Quartet That Broke Up (Kvartetten som sprängdes); 1951: Fiancé for Hire (Fastmö uthyres), Divorced (Frånskild); 1952: Defiance (Trots), Love (Kärlek); 1953: The Glass Mountain (Glasberget); 1954: Sir Arne's Treasure (Herr Arnes penningar); 1955: The Unicorn (Enhörningen); 1956: The Song of the Scarlet Flower (Sången om den eldröda blomman); 1967: The Necklace (episode, co-dir Erland Josephson, in portmanteau film, Stimulantia).

Osten, Suzanne

Born June 20, 1944 in Stockholm. She came from a theatrical background (while her mother was a pioneering film critic) and has spent much of her career involved with the stage. During the 1960's, after studying Literature and the History of Art, she established the 'Pocket Theatre' with some friends, performing in schools and open areas. In 1975, she created, within the Municipal Theatre of Stockholm, a children's theatre, the 'Young Clara', which she still heads today. She has directed more than thirty plays, and her films have created a stir in Swedish circles.

Filmography
1982: Our Life is Now (Mamma); 1986: The Mozart Brothers (Bröderna Mozart); 1988: Lethal Film (Livsfarlig film); 1990: The Guardian Angel (Skyddsängeln).

Pollak, Kay

Born May 21, 1930 in Göteborg. Graduating in Science, Pollak trained as an actor and director before joining Swedish television (TV2). He made several programmes for the small screen, as well as TV-movies and series, between 1968 and 1978. Pollak is interested in children and young people; sometimes he selects his actors from the non-professional ranks.

Filmography
1977: Elvis! Elvis!; 1980: Children's Island (Barnens ö); 1986: Love Me! (Älska mej!).

Sjöberg, Alf

Born June 21, 1903 in Stockholm, died in 1980 id. Throughout his life, Sjöberg remained loyal to the theatre. Between 1923 and 1925 he studied at the Royal Dramatic Theatre in Stockholm where he served as an actor during the three following seasons. In 1930 he was named director of the same theatre at the remarkable age of 27. His film career began with a courageous effort, The Strongest, which marked the close of the silent period in Sweden. But he found himself out of tune with the lightweight cinema of the 1930's and only returned to the studios in 1939. His expressionist vision, somewhat theatrical in tone, reached its peak in Frenzy, with a screenplay written by the young Ingmar Bergman (q.v.).

Filmography
1929: The Strongest (Den starkaste); 1940: They Staked Their Lives (Med livet som insats), This Blossom Time (Den blomstertid); 1941: Home from Babylon (Hem från Babylon); 1942: The Road to Heaven (Himlaspelet); 1944: The Royal Hunt (Kungajakt), Frenzy/Torment (Hets); 1945: Journey Out (Resan bort); 1946: Iris and the Lieutenant (Iris och löjtnantshjärta); 1949: Only a Mother (Bara en mor); 1951: Miss Julie (Fröken Julie); 1953: Barabbas; 1954: Karin Månsdotter; 1955: Wild Birds (Vildfåglar); 1956: Last Couple Out (Sista paret ut); 1960: The Judge (Domaren); 1966: The Island (Ön); 1969: The Father (Fadern).

Sjöman, Vilgot

Born December 2, 1924 in Stockholm. He wrote his first play at the age of 17, then proceeded to publish novels, essays, and diaries (e.g. a day-by-day account of Bergman shooting *Winter Light*). After scripting films like Molander's *Defiance*, he visited Hollywood and served as intern on George Seaton's *The Proud and the Profane*. Sjöman directed his first feature in 1962, joining Jörn Donner and Bo Widerberg (qq.v.) in the vanguard of the Swedish new wave. A close friend of Bergman's, he appeared as an actor in *Shame*, and was an assistant on *Winter Light*. Sjöman is admired for his courage in tackling taboo topics, whether sexual, moral, or political.

Filmography

1962: *The Mistress (Älskarinnan)*; 1964: *491, The Dress (Klänningen)*; 1966: *My Sister My Love (Syskonbädd 1792)*; *The Negress in the Cupboard (Negressen i skåpet*, episode from portmanteau film, *Stimulantia), I Am Curious – Yellow (Jag är nyfiken – gul)*; 1968: *I Am Curious – Blue (Jag är nyfiken – blå)*; 1969: *You're Lying (Ni ljuger)*; 1970: *Blushing Charlie (Lyckliga skitar)*; 1971: *Troll*; 1974: *A Handful of Love (En handfull kärlek)*; 1975: *The Garage (Garaget)*; 1977: *Taboo (Tabu)*; 1979: *Linus*; 1981: *I Am Blushing (Jag rodnar)*; 1987: *Malacca*; 1989: *The Trap (Fallgropen)*.

Sjöström, Victor

Born September 20, 1879 in Silbodal, died January 3, 1960 in Stockholm. Brought up as a child in New York, Sjöström made his debut as a stage actor in 1896, and in 1898 became director of the Swedish Theatre in Helsinki. He was headhunted as a film director in 1912 by Svenska Bio, and also appeared as a screen actor in Stiller's *The Black Masks*. After an extraordinarily prolific and influential career in Swedish cinema, he left for Hollywood at the invitation of Louis B. Meyer, where during the 1920's he worked under the name 'Seastrom'. Some of his American films, such as *He Who Gets Slapped* and *The Wind*, achieved classic status. Sjöström's passion for natural landscapes and themes, and his skill at adapting literary material, gave his work a unique texture. In 1930 he returned to Sweden, and from 1943 to 1949 held the post of Artistic Director at Svensk Filmindustri, where he encouraged, among others, the young Ingmar Bergman (q.v.). His swansong came in 1957, when he took the lead in Bergman's masterpiece, *Wild Strawberries*.

Filmography

1912: *The Gardener/The Broken Spring Rose/The Cruelty of the World (Trädgårdsmästaren), Marriage Bureau (Äktenskapsbyrån), Laughter and Tears (Löjen och tårar), Lady Marion's Summer Flirtation (Lady Marions sommarflirt)*; 1913: *The Voice of Passion (Blodets röst), The Conflicts of Life (Livets konflikter*, co-dir Mauritz Stiller), *Ingeborg Holm/Margaret Day (Ingeborg Holm), The Miracle (Miraklet), Love Stronger than Hate/The Poacher/Secret of the Daughter of the Forest (Kärlek starkare än hat), Half Breed (Halvblod), The Parson/The Clergyman (Prästen), The Strike (Strejken)*; 1914: *Daughter of the Peaks (Högfjällets dotter), Judge Not (Dömen icke), A Good Girl Keeps Herself in Order (Bra flicka reder sig själv), Children of the Streets (Gatans barn), Hearts That Meet (Hjärtan som mötas), One of the Many (En av de många), Guilt Redeemed (Sonad skuld), It Was in May (Det var i maj)*; 1915: *The Governor's Daughters (Landshövdingens döttrar), Stick to Your Last, Shoemaker (Skomakare bliv vid din läst), The Price of Betrayal (Judaspengar), In the Hour of Trial (I prövningens stund), Ships That Meet (Skepp som mötas), Predators of the Sea/The Sea Vultures (Havsgamar), The Triumphs (Hon segrade)*; 1916: *Thérèse, Kiss of Death (Dödskyssen), A Man There Was/Terje Vigen (Terje Vigen)*; 1917: *The Girl from the Marsh Croft/The Girl from Stormycroft (Tösen från Stormyrtorpet), The Outlaw and His Wife (Berg-Ejvind och hans hustru)*; 1918: *The Sons of Ingmar/Dawn of Love (Ingmarssönerna I & II)*; 1919: *His Grace's Will (Hans nåds testamente), The Monastery of Sendomir (Klostret i Sendomir), Karin Daughter of Ingmar (Karin Ingmarsdotter)*; 1920: *Master Man (Mästerman), Thy Soul Shall Bear Witness/The Phantom Carriage (Körkarlen)*; 1921: *Mortal Clay/Love's Crucible (Vem dömer)*; 1922: *The Surrounded House (Det omringade huset), Fire on Board (Eld*

ombord); 1923: *Name the Man* (in U.S.A.); 1924: *He Who Gets Slapped, Confessions of a Queen* (both in U.S.A.); 1925: *The Tower of Lies* (in U.S.A.); 1926: *The Scarlet Letter* (in U.S.A.); 1927: *The Wind, The Divine Woman* (in U.S.A.); 1928: *The Masks of the Devil* (in U.S.A.); 1929: *A Lady in Love* (in U.S.A.); 1930: *The Markurells of Wadköping (Markurells i Wadköping)*; 1936: *Under the Red Robe* (in U.K.).

Stiller, Mauritz

Real name: Moshe Stiller, born July 17, 1883 in Helsinki, died November 8, 1928 in Stockholm. Born in Finland to a Russian Jewish family, Stiller emigrated to Sweden at the age of 27. In 1912 he joined Svenska Bio, and during the ensuing decade shared the spotlight with Victor Sjöström (q.v.), directing films of considerable skill and sophistication. His strength lay in comedy on the one hand and outdoor epics on the other. In 1925 he sailed for the United States with his protégée Greta Garbo, who had starred in his spectacular version of *The Atonemen of Gösta Berling*. But his Hollywood experience proved a disaster, and, disillusioned, he returned home in 1927, dying at 45 years of age.

Filmography

1912: *Mother and Daughter (Mor och dotter), The Black Masks (De svarta maskerna), The Tyrannical Fiancé (Den tyranniske fästmannen)*; 1913: *The Child (Barnet), The Vampire/A Woman's Slave (Vampyren/En kvinnas slav), When Love Kills (När kärleken dödar), The Unknown Woman (Den okända), When the Alarm Clock Rings (När larmklockan ljuder), The Smugglers (På livets ödesvägar), The Conflicts of Life (Livets konflikter*, co-dir Victor Sjöström), *The Suffragette (Den moderna suffragetten), Border Folk (Gränsfolken), The Struggle for Live (En pojke i livets strid), The Model (Mannekängen), The Gentleman of the Chamber (Kammarjunkaren)*; 1914: *The Brothers (Bröderna), When Mother-in-Law Reigns (När svärmor regerar), For His Love's Sake/The Stockbroker (För sin kärleks skull), Storm Bird (Stormfågeln), The Shot (Skottet), The Red Pine (Det röda tornet)*; 1915: *When Artists Are in Love (När konstnärer älska), Comrades at Play (Lekkamraterna), Madame de Thebes/The Son of Destiny, His Wife's Past (Hans hustrus förflutna), His Wedding Night (Hans bröllopsnatt), Ace of Thieves (Mästertjuven), The Avenger (Hämnaren), The Mine Pilot (Minlotsen), The Dagger (Dolken)*; 1916: *The Motor-car Apaches (Lyckonålen), Love and Journalism (Kärlek och Journalistik), The Struggle for His Love (Kampen om hans hjartat), The Wings (Vingarne), Anjuta, the Dancer (Ballettprimadonnan)*; 1917: *Thomas Graal's Best Film (Thomas Graals bästa film), Alexander the Great (Alexander den store)*; 1918: *Thomas Graal's First Child (Thomas Graals bästa barn)*; 1919: *The Song of the Scarlet Flower (Sången om den eldröda blomman), Sir Arne's Treasure (Herr Arnes pengar)*; 1920: *The Vengeance of Jakob Vindas (Fiskebyn Erotikon)*; 1921: *The Exiles (De landsflyktiga), Johan*; 1923: *The Old Manor/Gunnar Hede's Saga (Gunnar Hedes saga)*; 1924: *The Atonement of Gösta Berling (Gösta Berlings saga*, 2 parts); 1926: *The Temptress* (in U.S.A. completed by Fred Niblo); 1927: *Hotel Imperial* (in U.S.A.), *The Woman on Trial* (in U.S.A.), *Barbed Wire* (in U.S.A., completed by Rowland Lee); 1928: *The Street of Sin* (in U.S.A., completed by Ludvig Berger).

Sucksdorff, Arne

Born February 3, 1917 in Stockholm. After studying biology, Sucksdorff left Sweden for Germany, and during the late 1930's studied with the actor Rudolf Klein-Rogge, and attended Reinmann's art academy. From 1939 onwards he began making short films in Sweden, most of them documentaries about the natural world, sometimes blending fiction and reality. Between 1951 and 1964 he visited India several times, where he made *The Flute and the Arrow*. In 1964 he became head of a UNESCO institute for documentary films in Brazil, and his study of Rio, *My Home Is Copacabana*, came from this period.

Filmography

Shorts – 1939: *An August Rhapsody (En Augustirapsodi)*; 1940: *This Land is Full of Life/Your Own Land (Din tillvaros land)*; 1941: *A*

Summer's Tale (En sommarsaga); 1942: *Wind from the West (Vinden från väster);* 1943: *Reindeer People (Sarvtid);* 1944: *Gull! (Trut!), Dawn (Gryning);* 1945: *Shadows on the Snow (Skuggor över snön);* 1947: *Symphony of a City (Människor i stad), The Dream Valley/Tale of the Fjords (Den drömda dalen);* 1948: *The Open Road (Uppbrott), A Divided World (En kluven värld);* 1950: *Going Ashore (Strandhugg), The Living Stream (Ett hörn i norr);* 1951: *Indian Village (Indisk by,* in India), *The Wind and the River (Vinden och floden,* in India).

Features – 1953: *The Great Adventure (Det stora äventyret);* 1957: *The Flute and the Arrow (En djungelsaga);* 1961: *The Boy in the Tree (Pojken i trädet);* 1965: *My Home Is Copacabana (Mitt hem är Copacabana,* in Brazil); 1971: Antarctic exteriors for *Forbush and the Penguins.*

Troell, Jan

Born July 23, 1931 in Limhamn, Scania. Son of amateur film-makers, Troell got his first assignment at the age of 13 as an assistant photographer in a hospital. From 1960 on, he made several short films for Swedish television, and assisted Bo Widerberg (q.v.), honing his skills as a cameraman. Encouraged by the producer Bengt Forslund, who collaborated with him on various screenplays, Troell became a key director in the Swedish cinema of the 1960's and 1970's, starting with his wry, modulated episode for *4 x 4* (1964). *The Flight of the Eagle* was nominated for an Academy Award as Best Foreign Film. Troell can be regarded as the true heir to Sjöström (q.v.) in his love of the Swedish countryside and the natural rhythms of life.

Filmography
Short films – 1960: *The Town (Stad);* 1961: *Summer Train (Sommertåg,* for Swedish TV), *New Year's Eve on the Plains of Skåne (Nyår i Skåne,* for Swedish TV), *The Boat (Båten,* for Swedish TV); *The Little Boy and the Kite (Pojken och draken,* co-dir Widerberg); 1962: *The Return (De kom tillbaka,* for Swedish TV); *The Old Mill (Den gamla kvarnen);* 1963: *Portrait of Åsa (Porträtt av Åsa);* 1964: *Johan Ekberg, Interlude in the Marshland (Uppehåll i myrlandet,* episode of portmanteau film, *4 x 4), The Organ Teacher (Orgeladjunkten).*

Features – 1966: *Here Is Your Life (Här har du ditt liv);* 1968: *Who Saw Him Die? (Ole dole doff);* 1971: *The Emigrants (Utvandrarna);* 1972: *The New Land (Nybyggarna);* 1974: *Zandy's Bride* (in United States); 1975: *Kockums* (docu.); 1977: *Bang!;* 1979: *Hurricane* (in United States); 1982: *The Flight of the Eagle (Ingenjör Andrées luftfärd);* 1988: *Land of Dreams (Sagolandet,* for Swedish TV); 1991: *Il Capitano (Il Capitano).*

Werner, Gösta

Born in 1908 in Östra Vemmenhög. After studying at the University of Lund, he took up journalism, and then turned to the cinema, where he soon carved a niche for himself as one of the best short-film makers of his time (e.g., *The Train, Midwinter Sacrifice*). He also made a compelling screen version of Stig Dagerman's short story, *To Kill a Child,* as well as an excellent documentary portrait of Victor Sjöström (q.v.). Between 1948 and 1952 he directed some feature films also, marked by a violent, pessimistic naturalism. Werner has spent his later years in scholarship, becoming the leading expert on the work of Mauritz Stiller (q.v.).

Filmography
Shorts – 1945: *Midwinter Sacrifice (Midvinterblot); Morning Call/Morgonväkt);* 1946: *The Train (Tåget), Springtime at Skansen (Skansenvår);* 1950: *The Story of Light (Sagan om ljuset);* 1951: *Twilight (Skymningsljus), Spring (Våren);* 1954: *The Butterfly and the Flame (Fjärilen och ljuslågen);* 1955: *Destinies beyond the Horizon (Öden bortom horisonten);* 1956: *Responsibility (Ansvar);* 1957: *The Vanished Melody (Den förlorade melodin);* 1964: *The Landscape of Man (Människan landskap), Still Waters (Väntande vatten), To Kill a Child (Att döda barn).*

Features – 1948: *Loffe the Tramp (Loffe på luffen), A Ray of Sunshine (Solkatten);* 1949: *The Street (Gatan);* 1950: *Two Stories Up (Två trappor över gården);* 1952: *Meeting Life (Möte med livet).*

Widerberg, Bo

Born June 8, 1930 in Malmö. Widerberg first came to prominence in Sweden as a polemical journalist and budding novelist. His feature film, *The Pram/The Baby Carriage* in 1962 set an altogether new standard for Swedish film and offered a contemporary alternative to the metaphysical work of Ingmar Bergman (q.v.). In 1967, *Elvira Madigan* won the Best Actress prize in Cannes for Pia Degermark, and Widerberg became the lyrical, politically committed standard-bearer of the Swedish new wave with films like *Ådalen 31* and *Joe Hill.* During the 1970's he worked for both theatre and television and turned his hand to the crime thriller genre. *The Serpent's Way* marked a return to form and received the top critics' rating at the Moscow festival of 1987.

Filmography
1961: *The Little Boy and the Kite (Pojken och draken,* short, co-dir Jan Troell); 1963: *The Pram/The Baby-Carriage (Barnvagnen);* 1964: *Raven's End (Kvarteret korpen);* 1965: *Love 65 (Kärlek 65);* 1966: *Hi Roland! (Heja Roland!);* 1967: *Elvira Madigan;* 1968: *The White Sport (Den vita sporten,* docu in collab. with many others); 1969: *The Ådalen Riots (Ådalen 31);* 1971: *Joe Hill;* 1974: *Stubby (Fimpen);* 1976: *The Man on the Roof (Mannen på taket);* 1979: *Victoria;* 1984: *The Man from Majorca (Mannen från Mallorca);* 1986: *The Serpent's Way (Ormens väg på Hälleberget).*

Zetterling, Mai

Born May 24, 1925 in Västerås. At 16, she made her debut on the stage, and studied at the Academy of the Royal Dramatic Theatre, Stockholm, between 1942 and 1945. It was her performance in Sjöberg's *Frenzy* (1944) that marked her breakthrough, and soon afterwards she was put under contract in England by the Rank Organisation. She remained in Britain until 1964, having taken up documentary film-making in the early 1960's (*The War Game* won a major prize at Venice). Returning to Sweden, she made three features, starting with *Loving Couples,* which attracted attention not least for their outspoken views on sex and the role of women in society. She returned to these themes in 1986 with *Amorosa* based, like *Loving Couples,* on the work of the Swedish authoress Agnes von Krusenstjerna. Zetterling currently lives in France.

Filmography
1964: *Loving Couples (Älskande par);* 1965: *Night Games (Nattlek);* 1968: *The Girls (Flickorna);* 1969: *Doctor Glas (Doktor Glas,* in Denmark); 1972: *Vincent* (docu.); 1973: *Visions of Eight* (episode); 1977: *Stockholm* (co-dir.); 1979: *Of Seals and Men* (co-dir.), *Lady Policeman* (co-dir.); 1983: *Scrubbers;* 1986: *Amorosa.*

Bibliography

GENERAL

Autera, Leonardo. 'Prestigio e decadenza del cinema scandinavo'. *Bianco e Nero* (Rome, August – September, 1964).

Béranger, Jean. *Jeune cinéma scandinave* (Paris, Le Terrain Vague, 1969).

Dahlin, Tore. *Le Cinéma nordique* (Paris, Félix Alcan, 1931).

Delluc, Louis. *Cinéma et cie* (Paris, Bernard Grasset, 1919).

Gravier, Maurice. *Les Scandinaves* (Paris, Lidis-Brepols, 1984).

Hardy, H. Forsyth. *Scandinavian Film* (London, The Falcon Press, 1952).

Moussinac, Léon. *Naissance du cinéma* (Paris, J. Povolozky, 1925).

Usai, Paolo Cherchi. *Schiave bianche allo specchio – le origini del cinema in Scandinavia (1896-1918)* (Pordenone, Edizioni Studio Tesi, 1986).

DENMARK

Bordwell, David. *The Films of Carl Theodor Dreyer* (Berkeley/Los Angeles/London, University of California Press, 1981).

Brusendorff, Ove. *Filmen, Dens navne of historie, I-III* (Copenhagen, 1939-1941).

Delahaye, Michel. *Entre ciel et terre: entretien avec Carl Th. Dreyer* (Paris, *Cahiers du cinéma*, no. 170, September 1965).

Dreyer, Carl Th. 'Carl Dreyer nous dit: "Le principal intérêt d'un homme; les autres hommes" ' (Paris, *Les Lettres françaises*, no. 1060, 24 December 1964).

Dreyer, Carl Th. *(Oeuvres cinématographiques 1926-1934 (La Passion de Jeanne d'Arc, Vampyr, M. Lamberthier ou Satan, L'Homme ensablé,* (Paris, 1963).

Dreyer, Carl Th. *Jésus de Nazareth. Medée.* (Paris, 1986).

Dreyer, Carl Th. Special numbers of *L'Avant Scène Cinéma [Dies irae*, no. 100; *They Caught the Ferry*, no. 185; *Vampyr*, no. 228; *Gertrud*, no. 335; *La Passion de Jeanne d'Arc*, no. 367/368] (Paris).

Dreyer, Carl Th. *Réflexions sur mon métier* (Paris, Editions des Cahiers du cinéma, 1983).

Drouzy, Maurice. *Carl Th. Dreyer, né Nilsson* (Paris, Ed. du Cerf, 1982).

Dyssegaard, Søren and Uffe Stormgaard. *Danish Films* (Copenhagen, 1973).

Engberg, Marguerite. *Den danske stumfilm 1903-1930* (Copenhagen, Det Danske Filmmuseum, 1968).

Engberg, Marguerite. *Registrant over dansk film 1894-1914* (Copenhagen, Institut for Filmvedenskab, 1977).

Engberg, Marguerite. *Dansk Stumfilm*, 2 vols. (Copenhagen, Rhodos, 1977).

Hesselberg, Claus. *Film i 70 erne* (Copenhagen, Politikens Forlag, 1981).

Jensen, Bernhard. *Da Aarhus var Hollywood* (Aarhus, Universitetsforlaget, 1967).

Kau, Edvin. *Dreyers filmkunst* (Copenhagen, Akademisk Forlag, 1989).

Kau, Edvin. *Filmen i Danemark* (Copenhagen, Akademisk Forlag, 1983).

Ernst, John. *Benjamin Christensen* (Copenhagen, Det Danske Filmmuseum, 1967).

Gad, Urban. *Filmen: Dens midler og maal* (Copenhagen and Christiania, Gyldendal, 1919).

Gade, Svend. *Mit livs drejescene* (Copenhagen, 1941).

Lange-Fuchs, Hauke. *Pat und Patachon* (Lübeck, Nordische Filmtage, 1979).

Milne, Tom. *The Cinema of Carl Dreyer* (London/New York, The Tantivy Press/A.S. Barnes & Co., 1971).

Hending, Arnold. *Herman Bang paa film* (Copenhagen, Kaudrup & Wunschs Forlag, 1957).

Mottram, Ron. *The Danish Cinema Before Dreyer* (Metuchen, New Jersey, The Scarecrow Press, 1988).

Neergaard, Ebbe. *Historien om dansk film* (Copenhagen, Gyldendal, 1960; translated into English by Det Danske Selskab [Copenhagen] 1963).

Nielsen, Asta. *Den tiende muse* (Copenhagen, Gyldendal, 1945).

Passek, Jean-Loup. *Le Cinéma danois* (Paris, Editions du Centre Pompidou, 1979).

Olsen, Ole. *Filmens eventyr og mit eget* (Copenhagen, Jespersen og Pios Forlag, 1940).

Rasmussen Bjørn, *Filmens Hvem Hvad Hvor*, Vol: 1 (Copenhagen, Poltikens Forlag, 1968).

Sémolué, Jean, «Douleur, noibiesse unique on la passion chez Carl Dreyer» (Paris, *Etudes cinématographiques, no. 10–11, 1961).

Sémolué, Jean, *Carl Th. Dreyer* (Paris, L'Avant-Scène Cinéma Anthologie, 1970).

Skoller, Donald (ed.). *Dreyer in Double Relfection* (New York, E.P. Dutton & Co., 1973).

Monty, Ib. *Portrait de Carl, Th. Dreyer* (Copenhagen Fond Gouvern du Film, 1964).

FINLAND

Astala, Erkki (ed.). *Film in Finland* (Helsinki, Finnish Film Foundation, 1983, 1984, 1985, 1986).

Cowie, Peter, *Finnish Cinema* (London, New York, The Tantivy Press/A.S. Barnes & Co. 1976. Revised version 1991, Finnish Film Archive).

Cowie, Peter "Brothers in Revolt" [on the Kaurismäki brothers] (Helsinki, *Look at Finland*, no. 1, 1986).

Hillier, Jim (ed.) *Cinema in Finland* (London, British Film Institute 1975).

Toivianen Sakari, *Risto Jarva* (Helsinki, Finnish Film Archive, 1983).

Toivianen, Sakari, *Nyrki Tapiovaaran tie* (Helsinki, Finnish Film Archive, 1986).

Uusitalo, Kari, *Suomalaisen elokuvan vuosikymmenet 1896-1963* (Helsinki, Otava, 1965).

Uusitalo, Kari, *T.J. Särkkä, legenda jo elässüän* (Helsinki, WSOY, 1975).

Uusitalo, Kari (ed.) *Suomen kansallis filmografia, 1953-1956* (Helsinki Finnish Film Archive, 1989).

ICELAND

Icelandic Films 1980-1983 (Reykjavik: The Icelandic Film Fund, 1983) [brought up to date in 1984 and 1986].

Islantilaisia elokuvia/Islandska filmer/Islenskar kvikmyndir (Helsinki, Föreningen Islandia/Walhalla, 1985).

NORWAY

Bech, Leif-Erik (ed.), *Norsk Filmografi 1908-1979* (Oslo, Norsk Kino og Filmfond/Norsk Filminstitutt, 1980).

Björk, Bo-Christer, *Den nya norska filmen* (Helsinki, Walhalla, 1982).

Evensmo, Sigurd, *Det store tivoli, Film og Kino gjennom 70 dr* (Oslo, Gyldendal, 1967).

Holst, Jan-Erik, *Film in Norway* (Oslo, Norsk Filminstitutt, 1979).

Holst, Jan-Erik, Chapters on Norway in *International Film Guide* (London, The Tantivy Press, 1973-1988).

Heimbeck, Lingen, «Arn Skouens filmer» (Oslo, *Film og Kino, 6 A. 1979*).

Løchen, Kille. "The Lonely Child" [on Vibeke Løkkeborg] (Göteborg, Film Festival Catalogue, 1991).

Sinding, Leif. *En filmsaga* (Oslo, Universitetsforlaget, 1972).

Tørstad, Tor H. *Histoire du cinéma norvégien* (Paris, IDHEC, 1968).

Vibe, Nils, *Filmen i Norge etter den annen verdenskrig* (Stavanger, Rogalandsforskning/Filmforlaget, 1977).

SWEDEN

Béranger, Jean «Rencontre avec Ingmar Bergman» (Paris, *Cahiers du Cinéma*, October 1958).

Béranger, Jean, *Ingmar Bergman et ses films* (Paris, Le Terrain Vague, 1959).

Béranger, Jean, *La Grande Aventure du cinéma suédois* Paris, Le Terrain Vague, 1960).

Béranger, Jean, "Printemps suédois: Sjöman, Donner, Widerberg" (Paris, *Cahiers due Cinéma*, avril 1964).

Bérgman, Ingmar, *Œuvres (Jeux d'été, La Nuit des forains, Sourires d'une nuit d'été, Le Septième Sceau, Les Fraises sauvages, Le Visage)* (Paris, Robert Laffont, 1962).

Bergman, Ingmar, *Une trilogie (A travers le miroir, les Communiants, Le Silence)* (Paris, Robert Laffont, 1962).

Bergman, Ingmar. *The Magic Lantern* (London, Hamish Hamilton/New York, Viking Press, 1988).

Bergman, Ingmar. *Four Stories* (New York, Doubleday/Anchor Press, 1977).

Bergman, Ingmar. *Face to Face* (New York, Pantheon Books, 1976).

Bergman, Ingmar. *A Film Trilogy, Screenplays of Through a Glass Darkly, Winter Light, The Silence* (New York, Orion Press, 1967).

Bergman, Ingmar. *From the Life of the Marionettes* (New York, Pantheon Books, 1980).

Bergman, Ingmar. *Persona* and *Shame* (New York, Grossman, 1972).

Bergman, Ingmar. *Scenes from a Marriage* (New York, Pantheon Books, 1974).

Bergman, Ingmar. *The Serpent's Egg* (New York, Pantheon Books, 1978).

Bergman, Ingmar. *The Virgin Spring* (New York, Ballantine Books, 1960 [note: screenplay by Ulla Isaksson]).

Bergman, Ingmar. *Autumn Sonata* (New York, Pantheon Books, 1979).

Bergman, Ingmar. *Four Screenplays* (New York, Simon & Schuster/London, Secker & Warburg, 1960).

Bergman, Ingmar. *Fanny and Alexander* (New York, Pantheon Books, 1983).

Bergman, Ingmar. *Un souvenir d'enfance de Jack L'Eventreur* (Paris, *Cinéma 59*, no. 34, mars 1959).

Bergom-Larsson, Maria. *Ingmar Bergman and Society* (London, The Tantivy Press, 1978).

Beylie, Claude. "Sjöström et l'Amérique» (Paris, *Ecran*, no. 72, 1978).

Billard, Pierre. "Le Cinéma sans frontières" (Paris, *Cinéma 63*, fevrier1963).

Björkman, Stig. *Film in Sweden, The New Directors* (London, The Tantivy Press, 1977).

Björkman, Stig. Manns, Torsten, Sima, Jonas. *Bergman on Bergman.* (New York, Simon & Schuster, 1973).

Björnstrand, Tillie. *Inte bara applåder* (Stockholm, Tidens Forlag, 1975).

Burvenich, Jos. *Thèmes d'inspiration d'Ingmar Bergman* (Bruxelles, Club du du livre de cinéma, March 1960).

Chiaretti, Tommaso. *Ingmar Bergman* (Rome, Canesi, 1964).

Cowie, Peter. *Film in Sweden: Stars and Players* (London/New York, The Tantivy Press/A.S. Barnes & Co. 1977).

Cowie, Peter. *Swedish Cinema from Ingeborg Holm to Fanny and Alexander* (Stockholm, Swedish Institute, 1985).

Cowie, Peter. *Ingmar Bergman, A Critical Biography* (New York, Scribners/London, Secker and Warburg, 1983).

Cowie, Peter. *Max von Sydow from The Seventh Seal to Pelle the Conqueror* (Stockholm, Swedish Film Institute, 1989).

Donner, Jörn (et Braucourt, Guy). *Ingmar Bergman* (Paris, Cinéma d'aujourd'hui, Seghers, 1970).

Edström, Mauritz, *Sucksdorff – främlingen i hemmaskogen* (Stockholm, PAN/Norstedts, 1968).

Esnault, Philippe «Booz endormi» (Paris, *Cinéma 60*, no. 45, 1960).

Forslund, Bengt. *Från Gösta Ekman till Gösta Ekman. En bok om Hasse, far och son* (Stockholm, 1979).

Forslund, Bengt. *Victor Sjöström, hans liv och verk* (Stockholm, Bonniers, 1980 [published in English by New York Zoetrope, New York in 1988]).

Furhammar, Leif. *Filmen i Sverige – en historia i tio kapitel* (Stockholm, Wiken, 1991).

Gauteur, Claude. 'Ingmar Bergman' (Paris, *Cinéma 58,* July-August 1958).

Godard, Jean-Luc. 'Bergmanorama' (Paris, *Cahiers du cinéma*, July 1958).

Guyon, F.D. et Béranger, Jean. *Ingmar Bergman* (Lyon, Premier Plan/SERDOC, 1964).

Hervé, Alain. 'L'Univers d'Ingmar Bergman' (Paris, *Réalités*, February 1964).

Höök, Marianne. *Ingmar Bergman* (Stockholm, Wahlström & Widstrand, 1962).

Hoveyda, Fereydoun. 'Le plus grand anneau de la spirale' (Paris, *Cahiers du cinéma*, May 1959).

Idestam-Almquist, Bengt. *Classics of the Swedish Cinema* (Stockholm, Swedish Institute/Svensk Filmindustri, 1952).

Idestam-Almquist, Bengt. *När filmen kom till Sverige. Charles Magnusson och Svenska Bio* (Stockholm, 1959).

Idestam-Almquist, Bengt. *Sjöström* (Paris, L'Avant-Scène Cinéma Anthologie, 1966).

Idestam-Almquist, Bengt. *Stiller* (Paris, L'Avant-Scène Cinéma Anthologie, 1967).

Idestam-Almquist, Bengt. *Svensk film före Gösta Berling* (Stockholm, Swedish Film Institute/Norstedts, 1978).

'Ingmar Bergman: la trilogie' (Paris, *Etudes cinématographiques,* no. 46-47, 1966).

Jeanne, René and Charles Ford. *Sjöström* (Paris, Editions universitaires, 1963).

Jungstedt, Torsten. *Kapten Grogg och hans vänner. Om Victor Bergdahl, Emil Åberg, M.R. Liljequist och Paul Myrén som alla var med om den tecknade svenska stumfilmen* (Stockholm, Sveriges Radios Forlag, 1973).

Kwiatkowski, Aleksander. *Swedish Film Classics* (New York, Dover Publications, 1983).

Lauritzen, Einar. *Swedish Films* (New York, Museum of Modern Art Film Library, 1962).

Lefèvre, Raymond. 'Ingmar Bergman' (Paris, *Image et son*, March 1969).

Lundin, Gunnar, *Filmregi Alf Sjöberg* (Lund, Wallin & Dallholm, 1979).

Lundin, Gunnar et Olsson, Jan. *Regissörens roller—Samtal med Alf Sjöberg* (Lund, Bo Cavefors Bokförlag, 1976).

Marion, Denis. *Ingmar Bergman* (Paris, Gallimard).

Marker, Lise-Lone (and Marker, Frederick, J.). *Ingmar Bergman: Four Decades in the Theatre* (Cambridge, Cambridge University Press, 1982).

McIlroy, Brian. *World Cinema: Sweden* (London: Flicks Books, 1986).

Michalczyk, John L., *Ingmar Bergman* (Paris, Beauchesne, 1977).

Mosley, Philip. *Ingmar Bergman: The Cinema as Mistress* (London, Marion Boyars, 1981).

Oldrini, Guido. *La Solitudine di Ingmar Bergman* (Parma, Guanda Editore, 1965).

Olsson, Jan. *Svensk spelfilm under andra världskriget* (Lund, Liber Läromedel, 1979).

Petrić, Vlada (ed.). *Film and Dreams: An Approach to Bergman* (South Salem, N.Y., Redgrave, 1981).

Ranieri, Tino. *Ingmar Bergman* (Florence, La Nuova Italia, 1974).

Siclier, Jacques. *Ingmar Bergman.* (Paris, Editions Universitaires, 1960).

Simon, John. *Ingmar Bergman Directs* (New York, Harcourt Brce Jovanovich, 1972).

Sjögren, Henrik. *Ingmar Bergman på teatern* (Stockholm, Almqvist & Wiksell, 1968).

Sjögren, Henrik. *Stage and Society in Sweden* (Stockholm, Swedish Institute, 1979).

Sjöman, Vilgot. *Dagbok med Ingmar Bergman* (Stockholm, Norstedts, 1963).

Steene, Birgitta. *A Reference Guide to Ingmar Bergman* (Boston, G.K. Hall, 1982).

Steene, Birgitta. *Ingmar Bergman* (New York, Twayne, 1968).

Svensk Filmografi, 7 vols. (Stockholm, Swedish Film Institute, 1977-1988).

Tornqvist, Egil. *Bergman och Strindberg* (Stockholm, Prisma, 1973).

Waldekranz, Rune, *Swedish Cinema* (Stockholm, Swedish Institute, 1959).

Wennerholm. *Pappa Sandrew* (Stockholm, 1964).

Werner, Gösta. *Mauritz Stiller och hans filmer 1912-1916* (Stockholm, Norstedts, 1969).

Werner, Gösta. *Den svenska filmens historia* (Stockholm, Norstedts, 1978).

Werner, Glosta. *Mauritz Stiller – Ett livsöde.* (Stockholm, Prisma, 1991).

Widerberg, Bo. *Visionen i svensk film* (Stockholm, Bonniers, 1962).

Winquist, Sven G. *Filmforfattarlexikon 1896-1971. Supplement till svenska långfilmer samt svensk TV-teater* (Stockholm, Swdish Film Institute), 1972).

Winquist, Sven G. *Författare till svenska filmer samt svensk TV-teater* (Stockholm, Swedish Film Institute), 1969).

Winquist, Sven G. *Svenska stumfilmer 1896-1931 och deras regissorer* (Stockholm, Swedish Film Institute, 1967).

Winquist, Sven G. et Junstedt, Torsten. *Svenskt filmskådespelarlexikon* (Stockholm, Forum 1973).

Wood, Robin. *Ingmar Bergman* (London, Studio Vista, 1969).

Young, Vernon. *Cinema Borealis: Ingmar Bergman and the Swedish Ethos* (New York, David Lewis, 1971, Updated edition New York, Avon, 1972).

Index to Films

*Note: the directors' filmographies have not been included
in this index*

Rainbow's End (1983) by Kristin Jóhannesdóttir

Photo Credits
The illustrations in this book have been provided by the Danish Film Institute, the Danish Film Museum, the Finnish Film Archive, the Finnish Film Foundation, the Icelandic Film Fund, the Norwegian Film Institute, the Swedish Film Institute, and the private collection of Jean-Loup Passek.